We dedicate this book to God Most High and our Lord and Savior Jesus Christ for calling us, guiding us, loving us, feeding us, enduring in His patience with us as He taught us how to properly love one another, and for showing us the only Way, the Truth and The Life.

THOMAS N. TABBACK
& Family

THE LIFE

THE KINGDOM OF HEAVEN IS NEAR...

PearlGate
Inspirations for the glory of God Most High and Jesus Christ

THE LIFE
A PearlGate Publishing Book, a division of PearlGate Ministries, Inc.
Austin, TX
www.PearlGate.org
info@pearlgate.org

Contact PearlGate for bulk purchase discounts on our titles.

LIBRARY OF CONGRESS CATALOGING-IN-PUBLICATION DATA on file with the publisher.

ISBN-10: 0-9769740-4-5
ISBN-13: 978-0-9769740-4-8

Published & Printed in the United States of America

PearlGate and colophon are trademarks of PearlGate Publishing, LLC
Jacket design and artwork copyright © 2013 by PearlGate Publishing, LLC

Tabback family photo provided by:
Photobak Studios, Robin Worline, photobak@tds.net (419) 594-2549

11 10 9 8 7 6 5 4 3 2

CONTENTS

"If my people, who are called by my name, will humble themselves and pray and seek my face and turn from their wicked ways, then I will hear from heaven and will forgive their sin and will heal their land." —2 Chronicles 7:14

PREFACE

Refinement

Disaster is about to befall the United States of America unlike anything it has experienced in its history because it has forgotten the Lord its God. We have become just like the Israel of old, a rebellious nation that embraced all the detestable practices of the other nations and refused to repent. Much about repentance is spoken in America, but hardly anyone is practicing it such as the Lord requires. Unless we truly turn from our wicked ways and begin to obey God and His Holy Word, soon our nation *will fall by the sword, famine and plague*:

> *"This is what the Sovereign LORD says: Strike your hands together and stamp your feet and cry out "Alas!" because of all the wicked and detestable practices of the house of Israel, for they will fall by the sword, famine and plague."*
>
> —*Ezekiel 6:11*

In the spring of 2009, God Most High and Jesus Christ called my family out from our posh neighborhood in Austin, Texas to go forth heralding this warning, and to provide you with this guide to restoration. Along with my wife Clara, our ten-year-old daughter Rielle, our nine-year-old son Austin, our three-year-old daughter Jazelle, and our two-year-old son Justin, still in diapers, we got rid of our worldly belongings, including our home, and drove away from our *American Dream.* We had no plan and no direction save the Lord's wind in our sails. We left behind the life we knew as a fading picture in our rearview mirror and embarked on a journey into what might be the most difficult missionary field in the world—the United States of America.

Into this den of wolves we traveled, apart from the star-studded, mammon-driven mold of the establishment church, so the Lord might prove to you how ably He provides for those who obey Him. Accordingly, for three and a half years we have had no home, no RV, no paycheck, no backing or funding from any worldly or religious establishment, and no welfare. We went from riches to rags, from cultivating an international media sensation to managing persona non grata, from John McCain's 2008 campaign tour bus to the belly of *The Whale,* and from our American Dream to homelessness for Jesus—all for the sake of bringing you this message of the only hope for our nation's restoration. We made these sacrifices because we truly love the Lord our God, and because His Holy Spirit personally convicted us to trust in His provision and to endure every trial that lay before us. Indeed, along the way we have been greatly humbled. Right here, on American soil, we have been scorned, beaten, abused, arrested and nearly killed for our testimony about the only Way, the Truth and the Life of Jesus Christ.

"Those whom I love I rebuke and discipline. So be earnest, and repent."

—Revelations 3:19

Through obedience and refinement, the Lord has shown my family His plan for our nation's restoration, which will penetrate the heart of this nation all the way to the front doorstep of the White House. But first, the church in America must return to the Lord its God, because these days are not like the days before. Time is getting shorter and though so many of us used to see a world of gray, we are having our eyes opened to a critical choice between the Light and the darkness; a decision either for eternal life in Jesus Christ or eternal torment with Satan and his demons. Through this book you will see that there is a real spiritual war being waged at this late hour for the heart of our nation, and the world. There is no middle ground. Your survival depends upon your awakening to the purpose the Lord has invested in you from the womb. This is why you and others you know are suffering from all kinds of difficult trials at this late hour. You may have lost your job, your business, your house, your health, your financial security, a loved one, even your faith. At the very least, if your heart is with Christ, you feel unsettled inside. You see the moral fabric of your nation disintegrating around you like the ravages of a dark, encroaching storm, soon to land on your doorstep. Everything you once believed in or thought you could count on, including the American Dream, has been disrupted, taken away, or has been exposed as a lie. All of this is for your *refinement,* and though you may not have realized it, the Lord is giving you an opportunity to gain blessings you could never before have imagined.

In this book, we will share with you how the Lord miraculously provided for our family's needs all throughout our journey. You will learn about the God-given role *We The Church* must play in public affairs. You will receive a full-proof *Truth Serum* by which you must test the hearts of your leadership, both in government and in the church establishment, in order to discern servants in Christ from liars in shepherd's clothing. You also will discover the revelation God gave my family concerning the real *mark of the beast,* which is not what you might expect and is already in our midst. We will share with you how to make yourself immune to it. You will also come to understand our nation's biblical identity, our direct link with the Israel of old, as well as the God-given calling we must soon fulfill. Most importantly, through my family's example, our trials and faithful endurance, you will discover the purpose for which God created you and your family, and He will convict your heart to embrace your own personal mission for the glory of His Name. This is at the heart of true repentance, because no one can please God without faith, and true faith is demonstrated through obedience:

> *"Why do you call me, 'Lord, Lord,' and do not do what I say? I will show you what he is like who comes to me and hears my words and puts them into practice. He is like a man building a house, who dug down deep and laid the foundation on rock. When a flood came, the torrent struck that house but could not shake it, because it was well built." —Luke 6:46-48*

After three and half years in the iron-smelting furnace, we present you with this book of real-life testimony, revelation, prophecy and truth. Whether you heed God's appointed messengers is up to you, but know this: The fate of the nation hangs in the balance. The foremost duty of all who are called by the Lord's Name is to be His witnesses throughout the earth, beginning with the members of our own households, churches and communities:

> *Then Jesus asked, "What is the kingdom of God like? What shall I compare it to? It is like a mustard seed, which a man took and planted in his garden. It grew and became a tree, and the birds of the air perched in its branches."*

Again he asked, "What shall I compare the kingdom of God to? It is like yeast that a woman took and mixed into a large amount of flour until it worked all through the dough." —Luke 13:18-21

Whether as planters of seed or mixers of dough, we beckon you to share this book with everyone you can before judgment befalls our nation. Take up this book as something more than entertainment or a tool for Bible study, but engage it as a personal faith challenge. After reading it, my family's prayer is that the Lord's Light will enter your life, your household, community, and perhaps the entire nation such as it has never before. The harvest is more plentiful now than ever. Therefore, who will go forth into the harvest field to labor for the Lord and His lost sheep, such as He and His servants have labored for you?

After this the Lord appointed seventy-two others and sent them two by two ahead of him to every town and place where he was about to go. He told them, "The harvest is plentiful, but the workers are few. Ask the Lord of the harvest, therefore, to send out workers into his harvest field. Go! I am sending you out like lambs among wolves." —Luke 10:1-3

Above all, you must understand that no prophecy of Scripture came about by the prophet's own interpretation. For prophecy never had its origin in the will of man, but men spoke from God as they were carried along by the Holy Spirit.

—2 Peter 1:20-21

1

Swallowing Pride

What to do with a people who have forgotten their identity and their God? An overwhelming majority in America has grown up with some form of Christianity and God's Word in the Holy Bible, but few are living according to their faith. It seems many don't even know what it means to be a member of Christ's Body anymore. Indeed, we have become like the Israel of old, a people who have forsaken the God of our fathers and embraced all the detestable practices of the other nations, and we ignore the Lord's warnings. Unless we repent of these ways, we shall soon suffer the same fate as ancient Israel, which was systematically divided, conquered and carried away as slaves to other nations.

> *"If my people, who are called by my name, will humble themselves and pray and seek my face and turn from their wicked ways, then I will hear from heaven and will forgive their sin and will heal their land." —2 Chronicles 7:14*

Even before we set out from Texas the Lord brought these words to our attention, which He once spoke to King Solomon after the dedication of the First Temple in Jerusalem. This call has now gone forth across the nation, but who has truly understood it? By the wisdom of the Holy Spirit, King Solomon knew that a day would come when Israel would forget the requirements of its God, so he prayed during the dedication of the Temple that God would forgive the sins of His people and relieve them from the heavy Hand of His judgment. Afterwards, God appeared to Solomon at night and gave him this essential instruction concerning the fulfillment of repentance. Since God is not one-dimensional, nor is He limited by the fabric of time, He gave this Commandment not only for the Israel of old, but for all the inhabitants of the earth whom He would one day call through His Son. Jonah discovered this—much to his dismay—when the people of Nineveh were spared after obeying this word. This was a foreshadowing of the revealing of God's grace:

> *As the crowds increased, Jesus said, "This is a wicked generation. It asks for a miraculous sign, but none will be given it except the sign of Jonah. For as Jonah was a sign to the Ninevites, so also will the Son of Man be to this generation."*
>
> *—Luke 11:29-30*

Thus, the foretold Messiah, Jesus of Nazareth, shed his blood upon the cross as an eternal atoning sacrifice for the sins of the world, and resurrected Himself on the third day, fulfilling His Word. But that *"sign of Jonah"* of which He spoke was not merely about rising from the dead; it was also a key witness warning the rebellious that restoration can only be found on the other side of repentance. If there is no repentance, there is no salvation. Israel and all the nations of the Gentiles were not merely called to recognize Christ's sacrifice upon the cross, they were first compelled to acknowledge and repent of their sins. Therefore, only through repentance can an individual, a people or an entire nation become a part of God's chosen bloodline—not a people descended of Jacob in terms of flesh, but sanctified in the Spirit by the blood of Christ.

> *From that time on Jesus began to preach, "Repent, for the Kingdom of Heaven is near." —Matthew 4:17*

Can a man or woman fulfill repentance by prayer alone? Does fasting satisfy humbling if one returns to his wickedness the moment the fast is over? What the Lord your God wants you to know is that His Church can only fulfill repentance if it will *"turn from their wicked ways."* Short of this, the Lord's subsequent warning to Solomon will become America's reality, for He can and will reduce our nation to sackcloth and ashes by force!

> *"But if you turn away and forsake the decrees and commands I have given you and go off to serve other gods and worship them, then I will uproot Israel from my land, which I have given them, and will reject this temple I have consecrated*

for my Name. I will make it a byword and an object of ridicule among all peoples." —2 Chronicles 7:19-20

Before my family could be called to embark on our journey to decry the pride of our nation, I first had to learn to swallow my own pride. It's a lesson about what the Lord, versus man, deems as *wicked ways.* If righteousness comes by faith, and faith is demonstrated through obedience, such as the Lord declares in His Word, then sin is the result of lacking faith and the disobedience it spawns. As you might understand, choosing to forfeit a happy and comfortable lifestyle in Austin, Texas to serve the Lord on the road with four children with no plan, no paycheck and no funding is not a decision any man and wife would make lightly. In order to prepare us for such a decision, the Lord first had to teach me that I was not in charge of my life. Truth be told, only by force was I convinced to swallow my pride and become obedient to God's will.

I know, O LORD, that a man's life is not his own; it is not for man to direct his steps. Correct me, LORD, but only with justice—not in your anger, lest you reduce me to nothing. —Jeremiah 10:23-24

In our former life in the world I was a successful pharmacy benefit consultant and Clara proudly homeschooled our children. We were living what many would call the *American Dream*, but we were not satisfied. This became especially acidic in my gut on September 11, 2001. As was typical during this chapter in my family's life, I awoke to that terrifying reality in a hotel room 1500 miles from my family. I was at a conference in L.A., while Clara and our two children at the time, Rielle and Austin, were at home in Texas. I can still remember flicking on the television and wondering why the same movie was playing on every channel. I soon realized I was watching live news coverage of those passenger jets slamming into the World Trade Center buildings. All I wanted to do was get back home to my family—ASAP! My company, however, decided it had spent too much money to let its employees get home to their loved ones, even though the nation was under attack and no one knew what might come next. So, my supposed leadership team insisted on commencing with the conference. It took them a few hours to realize it was futile. No one could focus on something so mundane as *pharmacy benefits management* while this nation's greatest financial icons came tumbling down. Isn't it ironic that for money's sake this corporation held its people hostage while our nation's monetary backbone was crumbling? I wonder how many more corporations operated under similar delusions that day.

With flights everywhere grounded I wound up driving a rental carload of my fellow Texan colleagues all the way home over the next two days. Somehow, I could not stop fuming over the inane judgment of my corporate leadership, and worse, our nation's. How could they so casually encourage everyone to go on with business as usual? Many highbrow economic justifications have been offered, but while American elitists scrambled to salvage their precious financial system, the Lord's warning went unheeded. How else did an outcast band of cave dwellers from Afghanistan humble the greatest superpower on the face of the earth? They even struck the Pentagon! Can that happen apart from the Lord's will? No it cannot, but few among our national leadership, then and now, have the courage to speak the truth. 9/11 was a sign that our nation's spiritual covering is being removed.

Like most people, my ire subsided over the course of the months that followed the 9/11 attacks. I therefore continued in my veracious pursuit to waste an inordinate proportion of my family's time and energy pursuing a bigger American Dream. Subconsciously, I was ignoring the Lord's Voice; such as He was calling me to the purpose for which I was born. Instead, my eyes were fixed on a vision of a castle I desired to make in the world, and there my heart was also:

> *"Do not store up for yourselves treasures on earth, where moth and rust destroy, and where thieves break in and steal. But store up for yourselves treasures in heaven, where moth and rust do not destroy, and where thieves do not break in and steal. For where your treasure is, there your heart will be also."*
>
> *—Matthew 6:19-21*

Fortunately for me and my family, the Lord rescued us from the fated fall of that castle built upon sand, but in the most unexpected manner—*God lost me my job!* Though I had been a rising star within that corporate healthcare giant, just before Thanksgiving 2002, I was suddenly RIF'd (reduction in force). At the time it felt like I had been RIP'd! They simply told me they didn't need my position anymore, which is corporate code for: *'We want you out, but can't find a legitimate reason to fire you.'* This is what happens to rabble-rousers and troublemakers who sacrifice of themselves and their families to speak the truth about sensitive internal issues crippling a corporation. But that's another story...

Despite my impeccable qualifications and experience, what proceeded was a painful, seven-month, nonstop fruitless job-hunt. Every door I attempted to open was soundly shut in my face, and for the strangest reasons. After overturning nearly every stone in the country for another paycheck, I came up with nothing. For the first time in my life I couldn't land a job—me! Never had I interviewed for a job and not won it. I had a wife and two children to provide for and we were quickly burning through our entire savings, desperately trying to keep up with bills.

What seemed like a curse at the time was in reality a blessing in disguise. I'll never forget how convicted Clara was when I initially lost that job. She told me, "All right! Now you can get to work on that book." She was referring to *Things Forgotten*, a novel I had been tinkering with for three years that recounts the Israelite Conquest of Canaan through the eyes of a silent witness. "Don't waste your time looking for a job," she told me assertively. "You've been given this time to write that book!"

I had long prayed that the Lord would let me live the life of an author, the purpose for which I knew I had been born. But how was I to do that, seeing how I had a family to feed? It wasn't until I had exhausted every possible job opportunity that I was finally humbled. I was forced to swallow my pride and admit that I was not in charge. Although I had been raised to believe that a man makes his own breaks in the world and that *"God does for those who do for themselves,"* I had done all I could and nothing had worked. So, at the peak of my distress I bowed down and pleaded with the Lord, "What am I doing wrong?"

'You told me you wanted to live the life for which you were born, now get to it before things get worse,' was the Lord's simple, yet penetrating, response.

'Worse?' I thought, quickly imagining just how difficult my family's situation could get if the paycheck door remained sealed much longer. I didn't hear an audible voice, but it was a voice, spoken straight through my heart. Though it made absolutely no logical sense, I accepted that it was indeed the Lord speaking to me and I wholeheartedly committed myself to write that book! If only I had listened to Clara from the beginning, but I had foolishly wasted seven precious months trying to jump back into a prison from which the Lord had sprung me.

This is what you call an *awakening*. It feels like extreme gravity at first, as all your worldly expectations are dashed to pieces, followed by a strange sense of weightlessness, while a new and surreal reality sets in. You come to realize that you have arrived at a crossroads where there is no turning back, only the path you decide to take forward. On one hand, you have the wide and inviting road, which everyone seems to think is the right way, but on the other hand, you find a narrow and less traveled highway, which scarcely anyone recommends. Everyone comes to this place of decision at some point in their lives, but few commit themselves to put aside their worries and trust in the Lord. As for me and my family, we were going the Lord's route, even if it meant disaster!

Incredible as it may seem, when I told Clara what I understood the Lord was telling me, she immediately agreed. Any normal woman would have by then reached her limit, but Clara had great faith. She had already received the Lord's will in her heart. I was the one struggling to let go of our money worries.

Without delay, I got to writing *Things Forgotten* and it felt like the weight of the whole world, formerly crushing us, was suddenly and miraculously lifted. No matter what our family, friends, neighbors or anyone else had to say about it, I was not going to even glance at another job opportunity until that book was done. As a result of our obedience, the Lord took care of our needs. Somehow manna from heaven appeared whenever we needed it and our faith was exponentially grown. When I finally looked up from my computer, having put the finishing touch to *Things Forgotten*, our bank account was bone dry. We had exactly $8.52 left to our name. That was it! Worse yet, we had only enough food in our refrigerator to feed our children for the next week. We never resorted to food stamps or any kind of welfare, so we direly needed the Lord's deliverance, and it came. Within a couple of days I received a call about a job. They had found my resume online, which I had posted months earlier. "Are you still on the market?" asked my future manager. Not only did he give me a job over the phone for a better salary than I had lost, but he also offered me an advance. For my kind of position in the healthcare industry this is unheard of! The following Monday I was at the plant of my new employer. At lunch, I ran out to deposit the check so Clara could buy groceries. How awesome is the Lord!

Over the course of the next four years the Lord increased my family in every way. Clara and I had two more children, Jazelle and Justin, and I received three promotions, increasing my salary by 300%! Praise be to God, for He surely rewards those who dare to trust in Him and obey His will.

Nevertheless, just as we were getting comfortable in the world again, the Lord's Voice came to me about Thanksgiving 2007. With all of our increase in recent years we were moving forward with plans to build our castle in the beautiful Hill Country of Texas, but the Lord had another plan. He challenged me to walk away from my big fat paycheck in the world and pursue His purpose yet again, only this time I was not sure I understood what it was He wanted me to do. Having learned my lesson before, I sought to explain to my very happy wife how I was going to elect to become jobless again, rather than wait for the Lord to take it away. Though she had serious reservations, she ultimately agreed to follow what I believed the Lord was calling me to do, which at the time, I could not articulate. Regardless, by Christmas I had resigned from my position, along with its paycheck. The rest was in the Lord's capable Hands.

Over the course of our journey, I have often wondered what was spoken privately between Abraham and Sarah that is unrecorded in the Bible. How many times did they question that place to which the Lord was leading them? Did they never have an argument about it? Did Sarah never question if Abraham was hearing the Lord correctly? Did Abraham never have doubts? Sometimes we forget that the men and women revealed to us in the pages of the Bible were, in fact, real men and women. They had the same emotions, desires, frailties and concerns for the flesh. Sometimes they overcame and sometimes they stumbled. A window into their humanity is demonstrated in Genesis, as the Lord confirms to Abraham that he would indeed be given an heir by Sarah, then 90 years of age:

> *Then the LORD said to Abraham, "Why did Sarah laugh and say, 'Will I really have a child, now that I am old?' Is anything too hard for the LORD? I will return to you at the appointed time next year and Sarah will have a son."*
>
> *—Genesis 18:13-14*

Do you suppose Abraham had some choice words for Sarah after the Lord had called out her laughter? Perhaps she reminded him how he had twice given her over to powerful men he feared, once to Pharaoh in Egypt and later to Abimelech of Gerar.

Clara and I endured many challenges as we sought the Lord's will over the course of the following year, and by the end of summer 2008 we were once again facing a financial collapse. Suffice it to say, man's ways do not measure up with the Lord's; neither do the plans we humans make compare with the Lord's. We have this terrible habit of adjoining ourselves with objects of our desire and affection, ignoring their propensity for rust and decay and giving them undo value in our hearts. We convince ourselves we have need of them, when only one thing is truly needed:

> *"Martha, Martha," the Lord answered, "you are worried and upset about many things, but only one thing is needed. Mary has chosen what is better, and it will not be taken away from her." —Luke 10:41-42*

When our Creator set the foundations of the earth, He ordained a purpose in each and every one of us, a custom-fitted design for every individual by his or her type, measured according to body and spirit. There is no *one size fits all,* although there is one Spirit who fits all. The Lord has fashioned within His elect a calling perfectly fitted to bring Him the utmost glory through our service. Yet, so long as we try to attach perishables to His imperishable purpose, we will remain seeing and hearing impaired. This is what causes us to stumble on unforeseen objects obstructing our path. Even if this happens to you with undo frequency, don't fret! When one who is imperfect attempts to follow Him who is perfect, error is inevitable. It is a process of trial and error, or for some, much trial and error, but perfection is not a prerequisite for following Christ. If it were, we would not need His grace, but since we do, He anticipates our stumblings and makes compensations in His plan to lift us back on our feet so that we might complete the race. If this were not so, no one would ever make it to heaven. This may sound strange, but take heart in knowing that if the Lord must reduce you to your very lowest, to a place where no excuse and no answer can be found in the world, where you have nowhere else to turn but to Him in total submission to His will, then that is what He will do in order that He will not lose a one of His lambs. Clara and I know this, because we have, at times, stubbornly tried to return to building a castle upon that same worldly bed of sand. Had we to do it all over, we certainly would have been less resistant and more submissive along the way, but that's hindsight. The truth is the Lord has used our stumblings to strengthen our faith. This He does for all who follow Him and it is an essential element of His graceful plan.

> *And we know that in all things God works for the good of those who love him, who have been called according to his purpose. —Romans 8:28*

The important thing is that in the midst of the race, Clara and I did not give up, tuck tail and turn back to the world. Every challenge, every question of faith and every decision we made to stay true to the Lord's path were a preparation and refinement for the work we were being called to do. Does a man march out to battle without first being put through the rigors of training? Similarly, the Lord does not send His workers into a battlefield for which they are unprepared. Rather, He trains us up to be effective soldiers, capable of following His Commands and achieving His goals.

Heading into the fall of 2008, friends and family alike became concerned for us again, but I told them repeatedly not to worry. Besides, we had been through dire financial hardship before and the Lord had delivered us. Why wouldn't He do so again? I felt something big was coming our way, and I told them so, though I didn't know what exactly. By late October, that *"something big"* struck, and it was far bigger than anything we had expected. It turned out to be bigger than the whole country expected and my family was swept up into the middle of it. This began a host of all new experiences through which we learned just how hard swallowing pride can be.

2

Give Us A King!

Like many Americans over the course of 2008, Clara and I closely watched the national elections, and like some we were grieved to have been given yet another choice between *the lesser of two evils*. However, something else nagged at me especially. For the first time as a voter, I realized that all anyone seemed to be talking about was *money*. The only difference between the candidates was to which group of people they promised it. Moreover, in watching carefully the audiences who streamed to these candidates speeches and cheered them on, I was stuck by how they paralleled the ancient voices of Israel—*the first nation under God,* which had complained to the prophet Samuel: *"Now appoint a king to lead us, such as all the other nations have."* This grieved Samuel, but it angered the Lord:

> *And the LORD told him: "Listen to all that the people are saying to you; it is not you they have rejected, but they have rejected me as their king."*
>
> *—1 Samuel 8:7*

I couldn't shake the words the Lord spoke to Samuel after Israel had asked for a king, because it directly applies to the present mindset of this*, the second nation under God.* Instead of asking God what He requires from our nation that we might again receive His blessings, we continue to look to politicians for deliverance, as though they have any more power in this world than their predecessors in ancient Israel. Like Israel, the United States keeps asking for a king, and more often than not we are given King Saul, a man regal in appearance, but weak and abusive in heart. The Lord our God has always given His people the leadership they deserve. This is no more evident today than in a republic whose elected government is *of the people, by the people and for the people.* Therefore, our nation's present ailments, and those yet to befall us, are not about one man or a political party, but are a God-given reflection of our nation as a whole. If we want to see that reflection change, then We The People must change.

In the spring of 2008, before then-Senator Barak Obama was expected to win the primary, Clara had a dream that confirmed that he would indeed be the next President of the United States. When we awoke the next morning, she told me her dream and I knew in my heart that it was true. Consequently, we were conflicted. On the surface, the first black President of the United States is an historic and meaningful event. However, this man's politics were as far from pleasing to the Lord as any who had preceded him.

Later that October, as the U.S. presidential race came to a climax, something happened to my family that can only be explained as the Lord's providence. One day, like most of the world, we were spectators of the most important presidential contest since the Civil War. Then suddenly, we were thrown smack-dab in the middle of it. It all happened as a result of a phenomenon called *Joe The Plumber*.

While stumping in a typically pro-Democrat neighborhood in Holland, Ohio, then-Senator Barack Obama was approached by formerly unknown Samuel J. "Joe" Wurzelbacher, a plumber. Their exchange about tax policy and the American Dream made Joe an instant media sensation. As a man now committed to living my God-given gift as an author, Clara suggested we reach out to *Joe The Plumber* to see if he would be interested in me helping him tell a story about the struggles and aspirations of an average working-class American. Despite all the odds, we were able to get through the media barrage to Joe and he agreed to let me write that story. Ultimately, we got a whole lot more than we had bargained for.

I immediately flew out to Ohio and spent the final three weeks of the 2008 Presidential Campaign on the trail with Joe. At one point, I found myself riding aboard John McCain's *Straight Talk Express* campaign bus along with his entourage on their tour across Ohio—a place to which my family would be called back repeatedly over the next three and a half years. To our family and friends, landing a book deal with *Joe The Plumber* was a stunning confirmation of our faith and trust in the Lord. I said something big was coming and in 2008 there was nothing bigger. Still, this blessing from the Lord was not about politics or book sales. Rather, the Lord was giving me a bird's-eye view from within the highest echelon of the political process. He wanted me to see firsthand how hopeless America's plight was if left in the hands of man. I remember sitting inside McCain's campaign bus, rolling through farm country Ohio and looking around at the different players, thinking, 'This is it? This is the best my nation could muster?' I wasn't considering their political talent, for surely the Democrats had the edge in that department. I was bearing witness to the motives within their hearts, which I was sure was equally reflected within Barack Obama's campaign bus. The greatest lesson I learned from that experience is that politics in this nation is merely an extension of collegiate sports. The goal is not to change the game, but to win at virtually any cost. It is therefore important you understand that politics cannot solve America's problems, because it is an institution designed not to unite and heal, but to divide and conquer.

> *These are the men who divide you, who follow mere natural instincts and do not have the Spirit. —Jude 1:19*

Despite what Joe, Sarah, John and many others may have hoped, as Clara's dream had predicted, come November 4, 2008 Senator Barack Obama made history by being elected the first black President of the United States of America. Along with him was elected yet another government with practically no interest in reuniting our society with our Creator and Savior.

Nonetheless, like the majority of the country, Clara and I felt an emotional connection to the election of the new First Family. It was a strange sensation that the Lord's providence was being realized, albeit with ominous clouds looming on the horizon. The American people had received the leadership we deserved—a perfect reflection of our nation as a whole. And what does our reflection look like when examined under the microscope of Truth? Like it or not, the truth is that this nation's primary concerns, regardless of ideology, has little to do with God and almost everything to do with *money*.

> *"No servant can serve two masters. Either he will hate the one and love the other, or he will be devoted to the one and despise the other. You cannot serve both God and Money." —Luke 16:13*

By the spring of 2009, my family was exhausted, physically, spiritually and financially. When all was said and done, God did not will success for the *Joe The Plumber* book. In three years time the Lord would reveal why, but for the time being our financial security blanket was exhausted. The enemy whispered 'look back' in our ears, trying to persuade me to return to a lucrative career in healthcare. It was there, waiting for me, if only I would call out for it. However, by the Lord's grace, I had learned that my first priority in life was to bring Him glory. A life primarily focused on a self-centered pursuit for wealth and luxury is not a living, but a lie.

So I ignored Satan and asked the Lord to reveal His will for my family. Almost immediately He spoke to my heart, 'Restoration to God Most High and Jesus Christ.' Beyond human explanation, I quickly understood that my family was being called to rid ourselves of our worldly possessions and to go forth on the American Road in our Savior's service to inspire a national 'restoration.' So that I would not incessantly question, the Lord reminded me of His Word, which He had laid upon my heart from my youth:

> *Jesus looked at him and loved him. "One thing you lack," he said. "Go, sell everything you have and give to the poor, and you will have treasure in heaven. Then come, follow me." —Mark 10:21*

Our Savior spoke these words to that rich young man who sought to inherit eternal life. Unfortunately, that young man so loved his wealth in the world he turned and walked away from the gift freely being offered him. I was determined not to be that man. I was going to be obedient to the Lord and trust in His provision. If my family were going to be blessed financially again, it would be by His will and not mine. He had done it once before, and I was certain He would do it for us again in His appointed time—and His timing is always perfect.

Though my family had little-to-no resources heading into our journey, I had been armed with a rare and keen understanding that no political process, no man or woman had the solution our nation so desperately needed. I also saw that We The People have so zealously sought to protect our wallets rather than sacrifice what is necessary to honor our Maker, we have become a nation in rebellion against the King. We may be a nation born out of a rebellion against a king, but a nation engaged in an insurrection against God has no future. It will be crushed.

> *"What do you see, Amos?" he asked.*

"A basket of ripe fruit," I answered.

Then the LORD said to me, "The time is ripe for my people Israel; I will spare them no longer." —Amos 8:2

Naturally, my first step was to seek the Lord's grace for Clara. It's one thing to ask your wife to accept walking away from a job or to exchange one home for another, but to ask her to leave the nest entirely, with no plan, no money, no RV, and no exit strategy with her four children in tow? Nevertheless, I told Clara what the Lord was placing on my heart to do. Once upon a time, it was she who had told me to throw away reason and write *Things Forgotten,* but now the table was turned. I was the one believing and she was in doubt. Although Clara had endured the former difficult trials with grace, the notion that we should plunge headlong into homelessness was borderline insane. Who could blame her? I couldn't, but after having come to know the Lord my God through those former trials I also could not pretend that I did not know His call when I heard it.

Rather than question my belief, Clara very reasonably asked me something I was not prepared to answer, "How are we going to get by with no washing machine?" She was absolutely serious. With four kids it was already a daily struggle to manage the laundry pile, so how exactly were we going to manage that on the road? All I knew is that we had been called to testify the truth whenever and wherever we might be welcomed to speak. The nation had to know that we had become just like the Israel of old and that lest we suffer her same fate we must seek the Lord's Healing Hand, which is the very definition of a *restoration*, for what is broken is fixed, what is lost is found, and what is dead is brought back to life.

Even for a woman as faithful as Clara, it was hard for her to reconcile certain expectations of life on the road with our four children. Nonetheless, the Lord heard my prayer and spoke to my wife as well. One day, as she tearfully prayed for clarity about her husband's adamant claim that we must forsake our so-called *life*, the Lord led her to His Word. Holding her Bible, she said, "Okay Lord, this is it, whatever you show me when I open your Holy Word, I will believe and trust in You." Wiping her tears, she closed her eyes, took a deep breath and opened the Bible, pointing to a random spot on the page. Opening her eyes, she looked to the passage marked by her finger:

"Come, follow me," Jesus said, "and I will make you fishers of men."

—Matthew 4:19

I'll never forget that day. She came to me in tears and shared these words, which the Lord had lifted off the page to confirm in her heart what He had confirmed in mine. It was a comfort I could not humanly give her. She had to hear from her Father in heaven, and who can resist His Word? Like me, in her spirit she knew this was no coincidence and no suggestion, but a Command from the Lord. Yes, as a homeless mother with four children she has had to endure many severe trials on this journey, but she has also fulfilled the Lord's Word given to her on that day time and again—even amidst the most excruciating afflictions. It may not come in pretty packaging with ribbons and curls, but this is what true faith is all about.

Thus, the decision to go and follow the Lord to a place He would reveal to us along the way was final and the process of offloading our home and belongings immediately began. It took two months at a breakneck pace to detach from the world. You never realize how many meaningless things you can acquire over the years until you are getting rid of them! Again, I reflected on Abraham's journey and how he must have felt when he loaded up all his family and departed from his father's house. How many trials had he faced and how difficult were those lessons before the day came when he hearkened to the Lord's call? Were he not trained to hear would he have known the Lord's Voice? Would he have believed that he, a nomad from nowhere with no heir would come to bless all the nations of the earth through his seed?

> *He took him outside and said, "Look up at the heavens and count the stars—if indeed you can count them." Then he said to him, "So shall your offspring be."*
>
> *Abram believed the LORD, and he credited it to him as righteousness.*
>
> —*Genesis 15:5-6*

Every man or woman of God has had doubts along the Lord's path, but it is obedience born through faith and trust that the Lord honors, because it brings Him glory. Leaning on His Word, which teaches that the Lord leads not His flock to perish, but to everlasting life, I fought back any worries and pushed ahead with His plans. After giving tons of stuff away and fire selling the rest of our home and belongings, including Clara's brand-new, top of the line washer and dryer, we finally rolled out of our comfortable Austin neighborhood with our four kids crammed into a 3-row Chevy Tahoe. Behind us creaked our twenty-foot cargo trailer, *The Whale*, loaded down with books and luggage, but no washer and dryer. We considered it our tent, and it was little more than that without a toilet, running water or power. It was blazing hot in the summer and freezing cold in the winter, but it kept the rain off our heads more than once.

That day, what we had once called *the life* became a memory. It was Sunday, May 31, 2009, the Day of Pentecost. It was also the day a man named Scott Roeder shot and killed late-term abortionist George Tiller "The Baby Killer" during church services at Reformation Lutheran Church in Wichita, Kansas, where Tiller was a respected member. We didn't plan it this way, nor did we realize the significance until more than three years later. One man went forth that day to take life from another man—both devoted to death, but at the same time the Lord sent forth a family from Texas for the Sanctity of Human Life. Truly, the Lord's timing is *perfect.*

We embarked on our journey with hardly any funds and no plan, for the Lord's instruction was: 'Soon as you put your feet forward, then I will show you where you are to go and I will open doors for you.' We didn't even know just how long our homelessness would be required. Such was the faith and trust we had placed in the King of kings, rather than any king of this world.

> *"I love those who love me, and those who seek me find me. With me are riches and honor, enduring wealth and prosperity. My fruit is better than fine gold; what I yield surpasses choice silver. I walk in the way of righteousness, along the paths of justice, bestowing wealth on those who love me and making their treasuries full." —Proverbs 8: 17-21*

3

Casting Lots

Many people we have met on this journey have found it hard to comprehend how my family has managed to cover our expenses for over three years without a paycheck in the world. When we set out from Texas, we did so by no worldly authority, with no support, no financial backing and no plan. We had nothing of what has become the traditional missionary security blanket. All we had was the Lord's wind in our sails; meaning food, fuel, shelter and other resources were to be provided by the Lord's chosen appointments along the way. I can't say we understood hardly anything about how the Lord was going to provide at the time we set out, only that He would provide. So, in order to ensure the Lord directed our path and I didn't make a wrong turn into a ditch with the lives of my wife and four children at stake, we resolved ourselves to casting lots.

To better understand the value of casting of lots, we must go back to Moses after he led the children of Israel out from Egypt. At the Lord's Command he appointed his brother Aaron as High Priest and placed something called the *Urim* and *Thummim* within his ceremonial breastplate next to his heart:

> *"Also put the* ***Urim and the Thummim*** *in the breastpiece, so they may be over Aaron's heart whenever he enters the presence of the* L*ORD. Thus Aaron will always bear the means of making decisions for the Israelites over his heart before the* L*ORD." —Exodus 28:30*

Whatever they were, we know that the *Urim* and *Thummim* represent a foreshadowing of the Holy Spirit, which the Lord would one day pour out onto the hearts of all His children that we may know and follow His will. We also know that other objects were used in the Bible as lots to enquire of the Lord, such as when Gideon used a *wool fleece:*

Gideon said to God, "If you will save Israel by my hand as you have promised—look, I will place a ***wool fleece*** *on the threshing floor. If there is dew only on the fleece and all the ground is dry, then I will know that you will save Israel by my hand, as you said." And that is what happened. Gideon rose early the next day; he squeezed the fleece and wrung out the dew—a bowlful of water.*
—Judges 6:36-38

We have at least one account that even the original apostles cast lots to discern God's will when seeking a replacement for Judas Iscariot from among the disciples:

So they proposed two men: Joseph called Barsabbas (also known as Justus) and Matthias. Then they prayed, "Lord, you know everyone's heart. Show us which of these two you have chosen to take over this apostolic ministry, which Judas left to go where he belongs." Then they cast lots, and the lot fell to Matthias; so he was added to the eleven apostles. —Acts 1:23-26

Various items can be used as lots, but each are designed to set a 'Yes' or 'No' condition for a question asked of the Lord. Some might argue that the apostles had a fifty-fifty chance of selecting either Barsabbas or Matthias. However, when you cast lots in faith—not frivolously, but for important matters—the Lord will honor that act of faith and reveal His will.

The lots my family cast at the outset of our journey were designed to discern where to direct our course and before whom we would share the message the Lord had given us. First, we prayed that the Lord would open the right doors for His message and close the wrong ones, for He alone knows where to find the most bountiful harvest fields. Then we vowed to go wherever we were invited, believing His Hand had appointed it. Having done this, it was a simple matter to formulate and send out open invitations to share the Lord's message with a variety of civic groups and church organizations that had come to our attention. I explained that we charged no fee, for freely we had received and freely we would give. Neither did we require accommodations or remuneration for travel expenses, for we did not wish to be a burden to anyone. All I desired was to share the message I had been given. From this very simple approach a slow trickle of groups began to accept me as a speaker, though not always from the sources we expected.

Contrary to our expectations, at the beginning of our journey the religious establishment doors were soundly shut. After all, who were we? We had nothing of the credentials institutions of religion commonly seek, degrees in theology, sponsorship, ordainment by some religious order, or a letter of recommendation by an accepted authority. When they asked what church we had come from, we told them just what the Lord had instructed us to say, "We are servants of God Most High and Jesus Christ." Incredibly, a great many ordained pastors remarked, "I've never heard of that church."

This Melchizedek was king of Salem and priest of God Most High. He met Abraham returning from the defeat of the kings and blessed him, and Abraham gave him a tenth of everything. First, his name means "king of righteousness"; then also, "king of Salem" means "king of peace." Without father or mother, without genealogy, without beginning of days or end of life, like the Son of God he remains a priest forever. —Hebrews 7:1-3

That our commission had come directly from God Most High and Jesus Christ seemed an entirely foreign concept to much of the disparate and denominated church. Pastors, priests, overseers and elders of all types immediately felt threatened by us. Yet, if they truly had the Holy Spirit in their hearts, they should have recognized us. Nonetheless, desiring to be obedient in all matters, we sought the Lord's Face to confirm whether we were to indeed seek some sort of religious endorsement. This lot was answered in His Word:

Not that we are competent in ourselves to claim anything for ourselves, but our competence comes from God. He has made us competent as ministers of a new covenant—not of the letter but of the Spirit; for the letter kills, but the Spirit gives life. —2 Corinthians 3:5-6

Having no *letter*, and now no desire to waste time acquiring one, we accepted those doors the Lord had chosen to open, as well as those He had closed. Given our *Joe The Plumber* experience, it wasn't entirely surprising that many of these opened doors led to the burgeoning patriot movement in America, dubbed the *Tea Party*.

It's hard to explain, but the Spirit confirms when the Lord is with you. I knew that once we had set out many doors would be opened. I also knew that if we sat around home trying to map out a full plan and strategy for the year, those doors would close. When the Lord called His fishermen to follow Him, He didn't say, "Tie up your nets, say goodbye to your family and friends, and conclude all your business affairs, then follow me." Instead, when Christ called Peter and Andrew to be made fishers of men, the Word says:

At once they left their nets and followed him. —Matthew 4:20

I can't say my family dropped our nets at once and took off on the road, but we did what Christ told that rich young man to do. I also can't say we set out in exactly the manner prescribed by Christ when He sent His workers to the lost sheep of Israel, but in consideration of our children's needs, we did what seemed prudent.

These were his instructions: "Take nothing for the journey except a staff—no bread, no bag, no money in your belts. Wear sandals but not an extra tunic."
—Mark 6:8-9

Whatever we lacked, the Lord made sure to take care of along the way. Actually, just so we would have no misgivings about the One who had our provision, many needless things were stripped from us. As we have declared to many from the beginning, the Word of Truth as given in the Holy Bible is real. If you follow it to the letter, it's the only roadmap you'll need. If you heed the Word that is given, then the Word that was planted in you from the womb will bud. If you continue to obey the Word then those buds will bring forth fruit. Everything else that is needed will be given along the way. This is counterintuitive to man's way, but the Lord's way is paved with faith and obedience.

For example, at one point in our journey my family was faced with a difficult choice between two different speaking engagements a thousand miles apart. The events were being held a week from each other, the first down in Florida and the other up in the Ohio. We were already in the North, so getting to Ohio was little problem, but if we went to the one in Florida we had only enough fuel money to get there and none to get back. We might have expected that the Lord would send someone or some people our way while in the South to refill our fuel tank so we could make the round-trip, but the

Holy Spirit was already warning me that we would indeed become stranded. It was wintertime, so the idea of becoming stranded in Florida for a while was not so bad, but what did the Lord want? We had already made a faith commitment to Him that we would go wherever He opened the door. Were we now to reject one in favor of the other? If so, which one? Rather than lean on our own understanding, we cast a lot before the Lord. In faith, I simply prayed that if the event in Florida was important to Him, He would make it known to me and we would go, trusting that He would somehow get us the thousand miles back into Ohio in time for the other engagement. Shortly thereafter, I spoke with the event coordinator in Florida, politely suggesting that I might have a conflict and inquiring how important my speech was to them. She responded, "Yours is the most important. You're the anchor!" That settled it, and so we made the trip South. However, just as I had been forewarned, my family became stranded with no shelter but our tin tent—*The Whale!*

Given this outcome, one who applies worldly reason might easily be convinced that we somehow acted presumptuously, rather than in faith, but this was far from the case. In accordance with the Lord's timing, His random appointments came across our path, received our testimony, then—without prompting or sharing with them our need—these individuals contributed precisely the resources we needed to make the thousand-mile trek back up North, just in time to make that other event. At the conclusion of that Ohio event, a woman with a notepad in hand and no knowledge of what we had just endured, approached Clara and asked her, "Excuse me, what do you do when you feel the Lord telling you to go somewhere, but you only have enough money to get there and none to get back?"

Praise be to Jesus! This is exactly how the Lord's plans work! We small-minded humans can hardly see the next step ahead, but the Lord knows just how that step, the one after and the next hundred, thousand or a million are going to fit perfectly together within His puzzling masterpiece. Had we not cast that lot and instead made a decision based upon our own limited understanding, we would have been disobedient to God's will. How then would Clara have known what to tell that woman, and would she have believed Clara were it not for our recent real-life testimony?

> *Trust in the LORD with all your heart and lean not on your own understanding; in all your ways acknowledge him, and he will make your paths straight.*
>
> *—Proverbs 3:5-6*

In this life we are faced with all kinds of difficult decisions, because we have no idea what the next day will bring. We can make predictions, based upon past experience and human reason, but if these were truly reliable, why do weathermen make so many mistakes? Instead, before making any important decision in your life; such as whether to marry someone, to buy or sell a business, buy or sell a home, take a job, quit a job, give or stop giving money to an individual or charity, send your kids to a public school or homeschool them, invest your money in the stock market or get it out, or whether to go serve the Lord on the road, seek the Lord's will with a heart resolved to be obedient. If you do, then He will most certainly *make your paths straight.*

Over the course of time, after handing over many such decisions to the Lord, I began to dispense with physical lots, though not entirely, and rely more and more on His Holy Spirit. I found that the physical often just confirmed what the Spirit was already speaking to my heart. Maturing this gift depends primarily upon your willingness to listen to and obey the instructions you are given. Sometimes the Spirit feels like waves of heat, other times like weightlessness, as though your spirit is soaring up to the heavens. At the very least, your senses will disconnect from the weight of the physical world around you and you will be filled with perfect peace. When this happens for the first time, you'll know it and you'll never look at this world in the same light again. After that, the more you hearken to the Spirit, the stronger He will grow within you. Amazing things will begin to happen in your life and you will know Him to whom you belong.

> *And you also were included in Christ when you heard the word of truth, the gospel of your salvation. Having believed, you were marked in him with a seal, the promised Holy Spirit. —Ephesians 1:13*

No matter the method by which you begin to enquire of the Lord, be specific with your question so that you will understand His response. Start by praying to the Lord about your question, seeking both His will and a means by which you may understand it. Then be patient, be still, and keep your eyes and ears open. If your prayers are frequently interrupted, make the time and effort to find a secluded place, perhaps your closet. No matter where you go, keep asking until you get your answer. Even the most faithful of the Lord's subjects described in the Bible did not always get their answer on the first try. Elijah, for instance, had so much faith and obedience in God that he could slap the Jordan River with the rolled up edge of his cloak and it would part for him to cross over. Nonetheless, when it came time for him to pray for Israel's drought to end, the Lord did not immediately send the rain.

"Go and look toward the sea," he told his servant. And he went up and looked.

"There is nothing there," he said.

Seven times Elijah said, "Go back."

The seventh time the servant reported, "A cloud as small as a man's hand is rising from the sea."

So Elijah said, "Go and tell Ahab, 'Hitch up your chariot and go down before the rain stops you.'" —1 Kings 18:43-44

You may have to wait awhile for your answer, but when it comes, be prepared to do what the Lord Commands. In doing so, you will be blessed, especially if you are not deterred by bumps in the road. If the path on which He sends you is harsh, know that your obedience is being tested and stay the course. More importantly, make sure you share the testimony of faith the Lord is building in you with whomever He sends your way.

Many in the world would have called us fools for abandoning our home on a leap of faith. But who is the fool, the one who trusts in the world or the one who trusts in the Lord, who created both you and the world in which we live? Knowing the Lord, we have always pressed forward, rebuking the discouraging tactics of the enemy and casting lots at every crucial juncture in order to discern the Lord's will. As we would learn, the Lord's way may be right, but it is not always smoothly paved. In fact, sometimes the earth moves.

4

Patriotism vs. Christ

Easy choices lead to easy decisions, such as the choice between vanilla or chocolate, apples or oranges, and life or death. Yet, when the choice presented is seemingly less clear and presents no immediate contrast, the decision can become very complicated, such as with Republican or Democrat. Both are American and both are political, and often it can be difficult to distinguish the differences between them. But what if someone was to ask you, "Are you a patriot or are you with Christ?" You might be tempted to say, "Both." However, when things of patriotism come into conflict with things of Christ, which do you choose? Some things really boil down to a matter of taste, but can that be said about our Savior? Is He to be reduced to a mere option on a menu? Matters not categorized by taste are often decided by an individual's sense of loyalty. In other words, the one who has done something for you is the one you typically wish to do something for. It's human nature, and it's a debt-mentality. So I ask you, to whom do you owe more than your Savior? Has any greater debt been paid in this nation than the debt Jesus Christ paid for you?

> *Then he turned toward the woman and said to Simon, "Do you see this woman? I came into your house. You did not give me any water for my feet, but she wet my feet with her tears and wiped them with her hair. You did not give me a kiss, but this woman, from the time I entered, has not stopped kissing my feet. You did not put oil on my head, but she has poured perfume on my feet.*

Therefore, I tell you, her many sins have been forgiven—for she loved much. But he who has been forgiven little loves little." —Luke 7:44-47

Somewhere over the course of this nation's history, people of this land began taking more pride in being American than they did in being Christian. Isn't that foolish? Anyone who puts his nation above his Savior is just like Simon. He must feel he has little for which to be forgiven, so he loves Christ very little. Ask yourself then, what is America? It is a land set aside by the Lord our God for the people whom He chose to bring here. Many might feel as though they came to these shores by their own will, the will of an ancestor or perhaps were forced here by the will of a slaver, but all such thinking is short-sighted. It attempts to reduce the Lord God from Creator to the rank of a manager; such as some of the deist so-called Founding Fathers viewed God, but they are all dead and gone now, so you ought not risk your life standing on quicksand they left behind. Since the system of government they handed down to you cannot give you eternal life, why elevate patriotism in your heart anywhere near to the level of your Savior?

John said to the crowds coming out to be baptized by him, "You brood of vipers! Who warned you to flee from the coming wrath? Produce fruit in keeping with repentance. And do not begin to say to yourselves, 'We have Abraham as our father.' For I tell you that out of these stones God can raise up children for Abraham." —Luke 3:7-8

If the Israel of old could not boast of Abraham, then why do We The People feel so comfortable boasting about Washington, Jefferson and Lincoln? Did any of these men remotely compare with Abraham, obedient servant of the Most High God? Since Americans cannot boast of having been fathered by a prophet of God, we ought not boast at all. Moreover, if you should think you have gained anything for yourself apart from your Creator, you need to look in the mirror and reconsider. Everything appreciable about you is a credit to Him who made you—not to you! Do you have strength in your bones? Thank God. Do you have a savvy mind? Thank God. Were you born in this Christian nation? Thank God!

The wicked foe pulls all of them up with hooks, he catches them in his net, he gathers them up in his dragnet; and so he rejoices and is glad. Therefore he sacrifices to his net and burns incense to his dragnet, for by his net he lives in luxury and enjoys the choicest food. —Habakkuk 1:15-16

I tell you the truth, We The People have sacrificed much to our dragnets in this nation, but we have made few sacrifices for Him who created the fish! If you consider yourself a patriot, I am not saying this is evil. I am saying patriotism does not preclude you from evil, nor does being a good *patriot* satisfy repentance in the sight of Almighty God. First and foremost, become a good servant of Jesus Christ. By doing so, your Christ-like behavior will then mold your patriotism after the model of your Savior. Then it will not be hard to throw out from your life the things of *American patriotism* the Lord considers detestable, things that are leading you and your fellow Americans unto death and destruction.

Over the course of our first months on the road, as promised, the Lord began opening doors with various patriot organizations from Texas across the Midwest and into the North; from Missouri to Michigan, Illinois to Indiana, Kentucky and Ohio. After delivering just a few speeches, my family could hardly keep up with all the invitations pouring in. In every place we encouraged our patriotic brethren to understand that with Jesus Christ they would be unified and blessed, but without God there would be no *Life, Liberty and the Pursuit of Happiness*, because it was the Lord who bestowed these blessings upon our nation in the first place. The Lord giveth and the Lord can and will taketh away.

> *"She has not acknowledged that I was the one who gave her the grain, the new wine and oil, who lavished on her the silver and gold—which they used for Baal." —Hosea 2:8*

Despite being moved by the words the Lord had given me, every group we encountered was primarily focused on one core principle: *individual liberties,* which is just another word for *human rights*. This is our nation's greatest idol and the fuel burnt on its altar is *money*. Coming from a high-stakes business background, I understood very well that money rarely solves any problem. When you throw money at a problem, it often makes matters worse! This is especially true with sin. Put more money into an idolater's pocket and he will carve a bigger and more detestable image. So while I could agree with Tea Partiers' grievances concerning government wasteful spending, the Lord was also showing me that this was not the reason He was bringing forth judgment. In fact, putting our leadership into a drunken, money-burning stupor was a part of His judgment. This is the bitter harvest of rebellion against God and His Word.

As it is written: "God gave them a spirit of stupor, eyes so that they could not see and ears so that they could not hear, to this very day." —Romans 11:8

To make His lesson clear, the Lord arranged several demonstrative appointments along the way. Early on, one of these came at a Flag Day event at a park just outside Cincinnati on the banks of the Ohio River. It was an exhausting day. We had driven 500 miles from Columbia, Missouri to get there, only to arrive in the midst of a torrential thunderstorm. The rain was so thick, we could hardly see through the windshield with the wipers on full-speed. At a gas station in Cincinnati, I debated about waiting for the storm to pass before attempting to fill our tank, but we didn't have the time. Not wanting to miss any opportunity to share the Lord's message, I braved the storm and was immediately drenched from head to toe. That gave Clara and the kids a good laugh.

When we arrived at the park beside the Ohio River, the sun peered through the clouds and cast a golden glow upon the mist hovering over the pavilion where I was slated to speak. After the long drive, the kids happily jumped out of the Tahoe to run and play in the park with other children who had come with their parents. Early on, the national patriot movement was largely an effort supported by average American families.

Despite my dripping wet appearance, the gathered crowd that had braved the storm lent their ears to the message I had been given. In part, I explained that the real conflict in America could not be won with an "us versus them" mentality. "It's not about Republican versus Democrat or even capitalism versus socialism," I told them, further explaining that these meaningless labels had been created to divide our nation. When you consider both extremes of the political spectrum, Communist on one hand and Libertarian on the other, both have the same sentiments concerning kings—they don't want one! What divides these two political philosophies is their concept for the alternative. However, no political ideology is predicated upon the moral precepts of Jesus Christ. They are born primarily on the basis of *money*. Each will seek to use moral arguments to reinforce their claims, but soon as Christ competes with their money, His Word is either twisted to accommodate man's ulterior motives or is cast out altogether. Therefore, where does one turn when the lies on both sides of the political aisle are exposed?

After speaking, one of the Tea Party organizers approached me and said, "I really appreciated your message. It spoke to me personally." He was a big burly man with a thick beard, but spoke with a heartfelt sincerity. "You see, I'm a Communist."

"Are you lost?" I asked.

"No, really I am," he said plainly. "I'm just sick and tired of an unaccountable government like everyone else."

I told him, "You have every right to be a Communist, and it's a beautiful thing when human beings willingly collaborate together for a common good, such as you find on kibbutzes in Israel." Then I added, "But when a government attempts to force communism or socialism, or whatever they may call it in the future, that's when evil sets in. It's a ruse put forth by those who seek unmitigated power and authority, so they may lord it over the people."

Jesus said to them, "The kings of the Gentiles lord it over them; and those who exercise authority over them call themselves Benefactors. But you are not to be like that. Instead, the greatest among you should be like the youngest, and the one who rules like the one who serves." —Luke 22:25-26

His eyes became pensive and I could tell he would be pondering that truth for some time to come. Clearly, I have not forgotten this encounter, because it was profound. I had just been telling Clara on the drive up, "Even Communists may receive the truth the Lord has sent us forth to speak." What are the odds that I would shortly encounter a Communist at a Tea Party of all things? Whatever your ideology, it is important for you to realize that the few often lure the many into perpetuating great evil in a false pursuit for justice.

"The hired hand is not the shepherd who owns the sheep. So when he sees the wolf coming, he abandons the sheep and runs away. Then the wolf attacks the flock and scatters it. The man runs away because he is a hired hand and cares nothing for the sheep." —John 10:12-13

Behind every physical principle of this world there is a spiritual principle superseding it. There are many *hired hands* in this world, some in politics and some among the religious establishments, and they all serve *the wolf.* While their rhetoric in the name of *liberty* and *prosperity* can be inspiring, we have to be wise enough to recognize the tactics of *the wolf,* whose hired hands invariably hand us over to slaughter. This is made evident in a corporation whose leadership abandons its employees to unemployment lines the moment their profit projections become endangered. They care nothing for the sheep, only their money.

"Son of man, I have made you a watchman for the house of Israel; so hear the word I speak and give them warning from me." —Ezekiel 3:17

Alternatively, the *watchman* serves the Good Shepherd faithfully by leading the sheep to the Truth, where there is safe pasture. The difference between his voice and that of the *hired hand* is that one rails about *social justice,* while the other speaks of the Lord's justice. This is made clear when the establishment church goes into an uprising when jobs are at stake, but sits silent concerning our national sin.

Some months later, I met a self-proclaimed Libertarian; a *hired hand* in training. "The root of the problem in America is the income tax!" He asserted, completely ignoring the Lord's call to repentance.

"Let's say the income tax is abolished and the IRS is dismantled tomorrow, would that make us a better people?" I questioned.

"Yes," he snapped, launching into various conspiracy theories.

"Do not call conspiracy everything that these people call conspiracy; do not fear what they fear, and do not dread it. The LORD Almighty is the one you are to regard as holy, he is the one you are to fear, he is the one you are to dread."

—Isaiah 8:12-13

After determining he was a "Christian" I asked him, "Is our nation better off or worse without Christ?"

"It doesn't matter," he retorted, "because the Constitution says the church is separated from the state."

"No it does not state that," I declared.

"Oh yes it does," he insisted, "and it should be!"

"Then you're lost," I told him pointblank.

He reacted with great offense, expressing a few choice words. Regardless, as the Lord's appointed watchman, I told him plainly that anyone who believes you can separate Almighty God from His footstool is, in fact, lost. Just because someone doesn't like the truth doesn't change the fact that it is the truth. The clay has no right telling the Potter His business:

"Woe to him who quarrels with his Maker, to him who is but a potsherd among the potsherds on the ground. Does the clay say to the potter, 'What are you making?' Does your work say, 'He has no hands'?" —Isaiah 45:9

That same day, I met a man running for the U.S. Senate. He received my testimony, because Jesus had personally rescued him. In his former life, he had been sentenced to life in prison for repeated drug-related offenses, and there he opened the door for Jesus to set him on a personal path to restoration. By the grace of God, after serving 10 years of his sentence, this man was paroled, he began a prison ministry, he received a full pardon from the Governor, he became a successful businessman, and now he was running for the U.S. Senate. This is what the restoration of our whole nation can be like, but it must begin with repentance.

As my family toured the country, the words the Lord gave me to speak resounded with a majority of the patriots that gathered to hear them. Yet, unlike many notable and nationally renowned speakers with whom I shared the stage at times, the words I spoke were not rhetoric designed to puff up, but truths inspiring humility. It wasn't a message of carelessly flung red meat or carefully directed blame, but a reality concerning We The People's responsibility for the state of our nation. Without question, the first step towards restoration is an acknowledgement of wrongdoing. But like an alcoholic or drug addict, how can one begin to turn his life around unless he first confesses his sin? Unfortunately, most people require extreme humbling before they will admit to their problem.

Time and again, people attending patriot gatherings would tell me, "Thank you for talking about God. You're the only speaker today who did." Nonetheless, the majority of the organizational leadership, and especially those attached to large conservative foundations and political institutions, took issue with the Lord's message. They found it impractical, believing like that Libertarian that God should be confined behind the walls of the church building, and that social and economic issues were best dealt with in the construct of conservative *Constitutional* ideals. They just couldn't understand how honoring the Lord was going to solve healthcare, the deficit, our porous borders, oil prices, the economy or the war on terror.

> *Now this is what the LORD Almighty says: "Give careful thought to your ways. You have planted much, but have harvested little. You eat, but never have enough. You drink, but never have your fill. You put on clothes, but are not warm. You earn wages, only to put them in a purse with holes in it."*
>
> *—Haggai 1:5-6*

Before the close of 2009, the self-appointed national patriot leadership—like the federal government they so vociferously attacked, ignored the will of the majority of its constituents and shunned uniting for *God Most High and*

Jesus Christ. They had initiated a national poll to determine the *people's* top priority issues, but buried those that called for a national return to our Savior, including those that called for the Sanctity of Human Life. Instead, they codified their mission under a banner of *"constitutional principles of fiscal responsibility, limited government and free markets,"* while placing special emphasis on *"individual liberties."* In short, they sold out for *money*. After all, most can agree that money is good, but few can agree God is good, much less who God is.

For example, having been inspired by the Lord's message, a former delegate to the largest national patriot coalition, the *Tea Party Patriots,* shared the following exchange she initiated during a November 2009 nationwide leadership conference call. She told the listeners: *"The problem with this Nation is that God has been removed out of the public square...the problems we are facing today are because our representatives do not fear Jesus Christ. The only true CHANGE in America is to bring Jesus back to the center of our lives. We need to be a Nation that would be on our hands and our knees in repentance for our sins."*

Among the thirty state delegates, NO ONE stood with her. All remained silent, until one delegate finally spoke up, stating that she also was a "Christian," but they had two people on their board who were Jews, and therefore did not want to *"offend any one religion"* by taking a stand for Christ.

Consequently, the Tea Party movement is now like a withering vine with no root. It died precisely on the evening of November 30, 2009 when a servant of Christ testified His Name and was rejected. What began as a movement broadly supported by average American families rooted in Christ is now a haunt for ideological zealots, Napoleonic egomaniacs, conspiracy theorists and political party devotees. Today the national Tea Party has become a political shill and a moot point. If you love the Lord, you will abandon this movement for *money* and seek to embrace your own personal mission in Christ, joining others who are also unwilling to compromise their devotion to their Savior. Christ will lead you to good pasture and good company, if you have a heart to seek Him.

> *That is why it was called Babel—because there the LORD confused the language of the whole world. From there the LORD scattered them over the face of the whole earth. —Genesis 11:9*

The biblical account of the Tower of Babel is the first recorded rebellion of a people against the Lord their God after the Great Flood. As promised, the

Lord did not utterly destroy His people again, but confounded their language and *scattered them over the face of the whole earth.* No longer able to communicate and organize their efforts, this rebellion was quelled. The object lesson of Babel is that any endeavor apart from Lord's will, shall fail, while every endeavor for His Glory shall be blessed. In keeping with this truth, as you seek to do more for the restoration of this nation, first aspire to be a proper servant of Jesus Christ, and He will guide you in how best to serve your nation.

> *But our citizenship is in heaven. And we eagerly await a Savior from there, the Lord Jesus Christ, who, by the power that enables him to bring everything under his control, will transform our lowly bodies so that they will be like his glorious body. —Philippians 3:20-21*

The best patriots are those who honor their citizenship in heaven above all else. Trust in the Lord your God, for He knows how to reward a nation that is faithful to Him. What better patriotism is there than that?

5

The New Ministers

Immediately upon setting out from Texas the Lord began revealing to us what it means to be His ministers. The very idea of having a "ministry" was foreign to us, even problematic, because so many have dishonored Jesus' Name by their scandalous behavior. Like so many these days, my family has struggled to find an establishment church or ministry that has not sold its soul for *mammon.*

> *Unlike so many, we do not peddle the word of God for profit. On the contrary, in Christ we speak before God with sincerity, like men sent from God.*
>
> *—2 Corinthians 2:17*

Thus, my family's personal walk of faith and obedience with Christ did not begin within the walls of a church, but with me, the husband, father and covering or our household, deciding to set aside a Sabbath Day each week for my family to dedicate to the Lord our God and His Holy Word. In essence, we brought church into our home, and by this very simple act of faith and obedience, the real Spirit of the Lord entered our lives and began to convict us to not merely call ourselves "Christians" or be content only to study His Word, but to love and worship Him by obeying His Commands. Over time, in the Lord's time, this led us out from our worldly façade and into His harvest field, where we follow as the Spirit of the Lord prepares the way:

"See, I am sending an angel ahead of you to guard you along the way and to bring you to the place I have prepared." —Exodus 23:20

All my family wanted was to be faithful servants of God Most High and Jesus Christ. What the Lord has called us to do, He may call you to do as well, and it would be good for every man and woman calling themselves by His Name to remember that Christ is not merely a title, but a duty. After all, the meaning of *minister* is both ambassador and caretaker. Therefore, a minister of Christ must handle His Gospel with deep reverence, care and respect. Moreover, the minister must be willing to suffer to protect the precious message he bears. Thus, while the national debate revolved around people's fears for their wallets, my family refused to make *money* a personal issue as we struggled to keep fuel in our tanks, food in our bellies, and cover the cost of lodging.

"As for you, my flock, this is what the Sovereign LORD says: I will judge between one sheep and another, and between rams and goats. Is it not enough for you to feed on the good pasture? Must you also trample the rest of your pasture with your feet? Is it not enough for you to drink clear water? Must you also muddy the rest with your feet?" —Ezekiel 34:17-18

The first time a group offered to take up a "love offering" for us, I think Clara nearly fainted. "Love offering? What's that?" After explaining they wanted to take up a collection for our "ministry," we nearly rejected it. Still, if you're going to serve the Lord, His Word must prevail—not your will, but His. Through a series of witnesses the Lord made clear to Clara and me that to reject an offering was to deny the giver the blessings the Lord wished to bestow upon them for their obedience. This really put us in a pickle, because who wants to begrudge someone blessings? We certainly didn't, but we had been good givers before. Why now must the Lord place us in the ranks of *receivers?*

"In everything I did, I showed you that by this kind of hard work we must help the weak, remembering the words the Lord Jesus himself said: 'It is more blessed to give than to receive.'" —Acts 20:35

Truly, it is more rewarding to give, but for everything you do in following the Lord's Commands there is a season, a reason and a specific testimony He is building in you. As for me and my family, through us the church—shepherds and sheep—must know that the Lord provides just as ably today as He did when He first sent His apostles and disciples throughout Judaea. For more than three years they were separated from the world, but they never lacked anything.

> *Then Jesus asked them, "When I sent you without purse, bag or sandals, did you lack anything?"*
>
> *"Nothing," they answered. —Luke 22:35*

In reality, our aversion to receiving boiled down to pride. In our hearts, we were saying, 'We're too good for that,' but the Lord has ways of forcing the most stubborn of His children to accept His will.

> *Now when a man works, his wages are not credited to him as a gift, but as an obligation. However, to the man who does not work but trusts God who justifies the wicked, his faith is credited as righteousness. —Romans 4:4-5*

I do testify that for me and my family, working for a wage in the world was infinitely easier than living on the "good will" of the church, because most people don't make a habit of obeying the Lord, even though *obedience* is the first fruit of *true faith*. It's also more difficult when you're sent forth not merely to preach to the choir, but to admonish them about their sin. While the Lord moved certain people, usually of humble means, to always provide enough to keep us going, we rarely received enough to ease our sufferings. This is why many shepherds who begin their service in Christ with a devout heart fall away in deference to the demands of their corrupt religious institutions, which are incidentally funding their paychecks. I remember meeting one pastor who was deeply grieved because his religious order had hired an unrepentant homosexual to be their chief financial officer. Think about what this means, because one who indulges in such sin has aligned himself with Satan, who is *a liar and a thief.* Therefore, a portion of every dime tithed to that church establishment is going to pass right through Judas' hands:

> *He did not say this because he cared about the poor but because he was a thief; as keeper of the money bag, he used to help himself to what was put into it.*
>
> *—John 12:6*

Consequently, this brother contemplated leaving ministry for a paycheck in the world. The idea that his congregation would support his needs apart from a religious conference or approve a split from it was not realistic. If you are a shepherd in similar circumstances, I warn you not to capitulate to Satan's demands. Your ordainment does not come from man, but from God. If you fall away from serving Him faithfully for flesh concerns, you will be judged more harshly than the flock that will not support your needs. Just as the Lord declares in His Word, He shall stretch out His Hand against:

"Those who turn back from following the LORD and neither seek the LORD nor inquire of him." —Zephaniah 1:6

If you are a church congregant, remember that just as sheep support the needs of the shepherd by virtue of their wool and milk, so you too must support your shepherd. He is not meant to toil in the world, but to dedicate his energies to the Word and the flock he oversees. If you cause him to divide his attention by pursuing a paycheck in the world, you are hurting yourself, because your shepherd is your guide and teacher. Worse, you will make yourself guilty of neglecting God's Word:

"Will a man rob God? Yet you rob me.

"But you ask, 'How do we rob you?'

"In tithes and offerings. You are under a curse—the whole nation of you—because you are robbing me." —Malachi 3:8-9

Tithing is not limited to sheep. In accordance with Abraham's example, the Levites were instructed to give a tenth of their portion back to the Lord in the form of offerings to the alien, poor, widow and fatherless:

"Speak to the Levites and say to them: 'When you receive from the Israelites the tithe I give you as your inheritance, you must present a tenth of that tithe as the LORD'S offering.'" —Numbers 18:26

Whether a shepherd or a sheep, do not place limits on your giving, but ask the Lord what you should give. A tenth is the minimum, but if the Lord moves you to give more, do so. Everything belongs to the Lord anyhow, so why covet what is not yours? You should set this aside from the rest of your harvest, or earnings, reserving it for the source to which He directs you. Do not think you are giving to an individual, a family, ministry or a charity, but you are giving to the Lord Himself. So if He tells you not to tithe to a religious establishment, because it is justifying sin, then find another worthy source for your giving. Ask the Lord to send you one and He will. Furthermore, accept no "thanks" from the receiver, but tell them, "Thank Jesus, because this came from Him." If you reserve all the glory for the Lord in this manner, obeying to give whatever He directs you to give then you will be blessed, for God knows how to reward those who love Him:

> *"Bring the whole tithe into the storehouse, that there may be food in my house. Test me in this," says the LORD Almighty, "and see if I will not throw open the floodgates of heaven and pour out so much blessing you will not have room enough for it." —Malachi 3:10*

Most importantly, do not forget to always give the gift of testimony about Jesus Christ with every material offering, for this is a minister's most important duty. If you neglect to share Christ, what good have you done?

> *"Woe to you, teachers of the law and Pharisees, you hypocrites! You give a tenth of your spices—mint, dill and cummin. But you have neglected the more important matters of the law—justice, mercy and faithfulness. You should have practiced the latter, without neglecting the former." —Matthew 23:23*

My family has faithfully followed these examples all throughout our journey, despite having a pittance of our former worldly wealth. In fact, when you feel impoverished, this is the most important time to give, because this is the time when your faith is truly being tested. On several occasions my family has risked shelter, food and clothing by giving away nearly our last dollar to a stranger in need. This is what the Lord led us to do, so we did it, but we also gave them the gift of Jesus at the most conspicuous moments in their lives.

One day, when my family was hopping hotels and barely scraping by, we went to a grocery store and stumbled into one of the Lord's appointments. "Help me please!" a woman cried out from one of those motorized scooters and suddenly grabbed hold of Clara as she was passing by. She was a homeless mother, desperate, malnourished and had been living under a bridge with her three boys. Her health and hygiene were so bad all her teeth were falling out. She quickly confessed that she had been sitting there, praying for God to help her, because in her desperation she was ready to steal. She had already been to prison once before for theft, but through a prison ministry she had found Christ. You can imagine just how aggressively Satan was trying to tempt her to backslide. Before Clara had uttered a word, in tears the woman said, "I don't know why I grabbed you. I think it was God."

Clara sent the kids to find me and I came over quickly. She explained her situation, including that a housing program had accepted her and her boys, but they could not move in for another day. Before Clara had crossed her path, she had been asking other shoppers in the store to help her, but they had snubbed her. Indeed, it was the Spirit that had caused her to boldly grab Clara, because the Lord knew we would obey Him. Before tending to her physical needs, we embraced her and prayed for her, beseeching the Lord's mercy for her spiritual needs. At that moment, she suddenly declared, "¡Yo tengo frio!" For the first time in her life, the Holy Ghost had come upon her. She told us that many people had prayed for her, but never in her life had she felt anything like this. It felt to her like hot flashes while at the same time her spirit was soaring to new heights. Praise be to Jesus! We knew practically nothing about this woman, but we knew the Lord's Spirit, and He said, 'Help her.' He also lay on my heart that I was to give her $100 in cash, as well as to buy her some milk and meat. We had all of $300 to our name—literally! We also had no worldly expectation of any income. Nonetheless, we believed the Lord would somehow provide, and with an obedient heart, I gave up a third of our net worth—a laughable figure concerning the affluence from which we had come. Still, it was what this woman and her boys needed for food and shelter.

From the start of our journey, the Lord had repeatedly demonstrated the presence of His Spirit to the people before whom we appeared. The words both Clara and I spoke were coming from a place and having an effect on people that was well beyond us. People weren't merely inspired; *they were cut to the heart:*

> *When the people heard this,* ***they were cut to the heart*** *and said to Peter and the other apostles, "Brothers, what shall we do?"*
>
> *Peter replied, "Repent and be baptized, every one of you, in the name of Jesus Christ for the forgiveness of your sins. And you will receive the gift of the Holy Spirit." —Acts 2:37-38*

Suffice it to say, like most Americans today, Clara and I were once skeptical about matters of the Holy Spirit. Still, have you never grabbed at a piece of wax fruit on display, thinking it was real? The fake doesn't trump the existence of the real thing; it's merely a replica that tastes awful! Similarly, just because some televangelist with a shock of white hair, a silk suit and a blingy watch might make a mockery of the healing power of the Holy Spirit does not negate the real thing. In reality, most acts of the Spirit aren't being televised, complete with mood lighting and music, but are happening every day, all around us, through simple servants of Jesus Christ.

Whether you have been raised to believe in matters of the Holy Spirit or have witnessed them yourself, my family can tell you unequivocally that the Spirit is just as real as the Father and the Son. Not only does He come with truth, but with a power that can instantly pierce hearts and move the most stubborn of mountains.

For example, one evening in another grocery store, this one in Indiana, Clara saw a woman speaking harshly to her elderly mother as she pushed her through an aisle in a wheel chair. A few aisles later, Clara spotted them again, so she began asking the Lord, 'Am I supposed to say something to them?' Nothing specific had come, so she finished shopping. While checking out, these women appeared beside her again and that's when the Spirit gave Clara an understanding. She asked me to take care of loading the kids and groceries while she waited for an opportunity to engage her appointment. After they finished their checkout, the daughter left her mother to go to the return counter. Seeing her *in,* Clara came over to the mother and asked, "Hello, do you need help?"

The old woman began complaining about how poorly her daughter was treating her, but Clara patiently waited for the daughter to return. Meanwhile, I was struggling to hold my ground against four hostile natives in the *Battle of Chevy Tahoe.* When the daughter finally came back to retrieve her mother, she was frazzled and pressed for time. She also had two full shopping carts to manage. Calmly, Clara stepped in and offered to help her. Though wary, the daughter sighed and said, "Thank you, I didn't know how I was going to get out with just two hands."

As they made their way out of the store and into the parking lot, Clara looked out at our Tahoe, wondering if I was surviving the battle. When they reached their car, Clara helped the daughter load up all her groceries and her mother. "Thank you," said the woman.

Clara grabbed her hand and said, "I have something to share with you." The daughter was suddenly guarded, but Clara continued, "I am a servant of our Lord Jesus Christ. Our family was called to leave our home and go on the road to serve Him. Wherever we go we listen and obey His will. Do you know Jesus?"

"Yes," she replied cautiously.

Clara nodded approvingly and said, "I am to tell you that you are a good daughter."

The daughter's face went beet-red and she looked almost like she wanted to punch Clara, but suddenly she broke down crying. Clara warmly embraced her, reaffirming God's message, "God moved me to tell you this. That's how much He loves you."

"You can't possibly know what this means to me," she cried. "You just don't even know!" She explained that she worked long hours each day and was torn between the needs of her mother and her 13-year-old daughter, who was often left at home alone, because she didn't have anyone to help her. Clara encouraged her and embraced her again, giving this sister in Christ a refreshed peace and strength. Now if Clara had not listened for the Spirit to guide her, or had been too timid to say what He had put on her heart, or had been deceived by the old woman's complaints, then the daughter might never have received the peace she desperately needed at this moment in her life. More than that, this woman also received a confirmation that the Spirit is the ultimate messenger of God's love. Perhaps she'll remember this and follow the Spirit's lead herself when He gives her a word of comfort for another.

At another event on the road in Missouri, the Spirit did His work again through Clara when she met *Tattoo Jimmy,* a military veteran in his mid-seventies who was anguished by the loss of his wife. He had also been suffering from severe pain after recently having back surgery. "You remind me of my wife," he told Clara. "She was a beautiful woman, and smart too. The Lord took her away from me," he began to cry. "I miss her."

Giving him some time to gather himself, Clara said, "Let me share with you something I've learned. When we cry for our loved ones down here, we are really crying for ourselves, because they're in Paradise. It may be hard down here, but we should be happy for them, right?"

Thoughtfully, he replied, "I didn't think of it that way."

Then the Spirit put a strong feeling into Clara that Jimmy had been having suicidal thoughts. Deeply convicted, she said, "Jimmy, no matter how hard it is down here or how badly you want to join your wife, you cannot rush it."

Deliberately ignoring her, he asked, "Hey, do you want to see a picture of her?"

"I would love to," she replied, recognizing his diversion.

Expecting he had a picture of her in his wallet, you can imagine Clara's surprise when he pulled up his shirtsleeve exposing a tattoo of a beautiful woman with long hair and as shapely body!

"Wow Jimmy, that's some picture. I can see why you cry!" After a good laugh, she continued, "The Lord must love you very much, because He made her very beautiful for you."

"We were married all our lives," he said with distant eyes, clearly reflecting on cherished memories.

"Jimmy, I want you to know something very important," Clara told him seriously, "no matter how many times you have pondered what it would be like to leave this place, you have to wait your turn and leave it to our Father to call you."

"I know what you're saying," he admitted. "I just miss her so much and my body is so broken."

"Listen, when Jesus was here, He suffered for all of us, including you," she reminded him. "Imagine what His pain was like. He endured every bit of it for you, Jimmy, so that you could one day go to heaven. You have been bought for a very expensive price, because you're that valuable. As a veteran, you know about following orders, right?" He nodded and Clara continued, "So you have an obligation, not a choice, to follow our Savior's orders not to take the life God gave you into your own hands. You do not have that right!"

He was speechless.

"Do you understand what I am saying to you?" she questioned as he stood there staring at her. "If you disobey, you will not get to be with your wife," Clara asserted in the Spirit.

Finally, the lie in him broke and he cried deeply. Right there he let go of death and again cleaved to life. Clara sighed with relief and hugged him tightly. Before they parted, Jimmy told her, "Thank you, I won't forget you."

Clearly, we have not forgotten him either, but all thanks and gratitude belongs to God, because He's the One who sent us forth and it was His Spirit that revealed what Jimmy needed to hear.

Over the course of our journey, my family has discovered that servants of God Most High and Jesus Christ need not worry about our qualifications for the work of the harvest field, for by our willingness to serve we shall be equipped with everything we need, including the Counselor for every situation we mere humans know not how to handle. Whatever we may not have seen or heard, the Holy Spirit, which the Lord will ignite within us at the very moment of need, has seen and heard it all. Not only does He know our capabilities and our measure of faith, but He also knows the hearts of those before whom we go to testify the truth. He will reveal their *secrets*, and by this wonder they will come to believe:

> *And the secrets of his heart will be laid bare. So he will fall down and worship God, exclaiming, "God is really among you!" —1 Corinthians 14:25*

Still, not everyone to whom the Lord sends you will receive, and turn from their destructive path. To illustrate this lesson, the Lord arranged an awkward appointment for me at a laundry mat in downtown Springfield, Illinois.

When sharing our journey with people, men often want to know more about how we managed transportation, food and shelter needs. Women, on the other hand, can't wait to ask Clara about THE LAUNDRY! Clara tells it to them straight, "Sisters, it ain't easy!"

We were two months into our journey by this time and our laundry was piling higher than speaking engagements. Clara and I were both longing for the good ole days of our laundry room back in Austin, TX. We had tried to keep up with laundry at hotels, but we discovered that not every place has guest laundry facilities. The ones that do often don't function so well and some just plain stink. Making matters worse, Justin, our not fully potty-trained two-year-old, seemed determined to break the all-time record for diaper blowouts!

While Clara was inside the laundry mat, struggling to find a washer whose spin cycle was in gear and a dryer that actually dried, I decided to organize the trailer with the kids. After repeatedly tripping over a certain box, I discovered it was a sewing machine Clara had smuggled onboard. To get it out of the way, I took it out and set it on the Tahoe's bumper. A moment later, while back inside the trailer, I heard a man's loud and obnoxious voice. Suddenly, an emaciated, middle-aged face popped inside and ogled our meager possessions—my appointment! High as a kite, and holding himself steady in the doorway, he asked, "What we got in here?"

"Dirty clothes," I told him straightaway. With my kids surrounding me, my demeanor was less than inviting. He immediately moved on, but spotted that sewing machine. With a quick look around—missing me entirely—he casually grabbed it and started running off!

"Stop!" I shouted as he desperately tried to wobble straight up the road. "Bring it back or you're going to jail today!" I yelled, and to my surprise, he actually stopped in his tracks and came back. He must have figured out he wasn't going to get away, or perhaps he realized he was about to get arrested over a sewing machine!

Handing me the box, he apologized, "I'm sorry."

"What were you thinking?" I asked him.

"I was gonna try to sell it to buy drugs," he promptly admitted.

"So watch yourselves. If your brother sins, rebuke him, and if he repents, forgive him. If he sins against you seven times in a day, and seven times comes back to you and says, 'I repent,' forgive him." —Luke 17:3-4

Seeing he was contrite, I sat him down on a nearby parking block to see what I might do to help him. It was difficult to carry on a discussion with him in his inebriated condition, but I learned his name was *John,* and he was a Christian. I forgave him, and asked, "Does God want you stealing and destroying your life with drugs?"

"No sir, no He doesn't," he answered shamefully.

"Do you want to turn your life around?"

"I do," he began, but dove into a flurry of excuses, describing his crack cocaine addiction. He had been to jail and rehab, but the world's answers had done nothing for him.

"God will help you," I told him, "but you have to decide that you're through with this life."

"Do not give dogs what is sacred; do not throw your pearls to pigs. If you do, they may trample them under their feet, and then turn and tear you to pieces."
—Matthew 7:6

You have to be careful with people in John's condition, because cash can kill them. His soul was broken, so his body craved destruction. No doctor can cure this problem. He needed *The Doctor:*

Jesus answered them, "It is not the healthy who need a doctor, but the sick."
—Luke 5:31

Learning a local pastor had once helped him, I told John sternly, "I want you to go to your pastor and tell him what happened here today. Tell him the Lord sent you a man who forgave you and offered you another chance. Will you do that?"

"Yeah, I can do that," he agreed.

After that, I let him go. I could not force him to go to his pastor, nor could I know if that church would embrace him, be patient with him and forgive him seventy-seven times, if needed. Still, John had to want to get clean. Such as my family has witnessed, John's example is repeated millions of times across this nation—in every city, all over suburbia, in wholesome farm country, even behind the gates of elite mansions. They represent a great mountain of dirty laundry, for which our procrastinating society repeatedly hires out the cleanup job. People don't want to get their own hands dirty, so they send these soiled garments to counselors, psychiatrists and *step* programs. Inside many of those whitewashed walls, illegal drug habits are replaced with equally or more potent *legal* medications. Consequently, every garment we send out to be cleaned returns more soiled than before, and more dangerous. By neglecting to lead them to the *Doctor,* we have been doing more harm than good, for only Christ can truly cleanse body and soul:

> *The angel said to those who were standing before him, "Take off his filthy clothes."*
>
> *Then he said to Joshua, "See, I have taken away your sin, and I will put rich garments on you." —Zechariah 3:4*

Ask any mother and she'll tell you that if you wait too long to wash some clothes you can never get them fully clean again. They'll mildew. Then they're good for nothing—worthy only for the burn pile. I pray by now the Lord has given John a new set of clothes along with a new heart to keep them clean. Perhaps if the Lord would grant this for John, He would also grant it for our nation as a whole, for as the left hand steals the right hand shall also be convicted. After all, they belong to the same body.

> *"Nevertheless, I will bring health and healing to it; I will heal my people and will let them enjoy abundant peace and security." —Jeremiah 33:6*

That evening we drove out from the laundry mat having conquered our laundry pile, though it would soon rise again—especially Justin's clothes. John made me realize how little we really know of the people struggling to survive in our midst. Our hotel, only five miles up the road, seemed a world away, but it wasn't. Though you rarely see them, there are Johns living within five miles of every community in America. Often we ignore them, because we have so many other *priorities,* but sooner or later that pile of dirty laundry will demand attention, and woe unto us when it has become so large that it overruns the cleaners.

Months later in Ohio, we would encounter another John who would serve as reminder of what the world is really like outside the window. Then we would meet Harley, and that man taught us a lesson on a whole new level, if indeed he was a man.

6

Into The Fire!

"Thomas, be careful!" Clara yelled out to me from the Tahoe.

"I am!" I shouted, inching my way around the back of our trailer to inspect the damage as cars and semis whizzed by, causing it to sway in their wakes. After months with almost no incidents on the road, in five days we had suffered two blowouts and now a whole wheel had flown off the trailer! Not that I could do anything about it now, but I just wanted to see if the axle had been destroyed. If *The Whale* was beached, we were done—or were we? 'Lord, do you want us to quit?' I asked the silent question, though I had already been given the answer days before.

Before losing that wheel, I had stood before a mass of 18,000 people at the Voices of America Park in West Chester, Ohio on September 5, 2009, proclaiming a message of repentance for our nation. Naturally, God was listening, and the first thing He is going to do for His workers is make sure we have a personal understanding of what we have been sent forth to testify. So, when I told that crowd that it's always darkest before the light comes, that things were going to get tougher for America before they got better, and that on the other side of hardships are the Lord's blessings for those who persevere in faith and obedience, I should have anticipated what came next.

After delivering that speech, a man approached me and said, "Is that your trailer?" He gestured to *The Whale*. "I think you have a flat," he added.

"Oh, those tires always look low," I replied.

He shrugged. "Well, it looks pretty flat to me."

I decided I had better investigate and, sure enough, one of the tires was flat as a pancake! Right away, I said to myself, 'Okay Lord, I get it. Overcoming hardships with faith starts with me.'

"You got a spare I can help you with?" the man asked.

"Well," I sighed, wanting to kick myself, "I should have one, but I don't." We had been trying to pick up a couple of spares from day one when we set out, but everywhere we went they didn't have the right size wheel. I should have made it a higher priority, but I didn't and now we had a situation. It was Saturday evening, all the tire centers were already closed and in just two day's time we had to cross 1300 miles so I could deliver the keynote address to a Labor Day gathering in Boerne, Texas. If we got that trailer roadworthy by Sunday morning, we might just barely make it!

I told Clara what was happening and she gracefully took the liberty of reminding me how many times she had told me to get a spare. As a man, this is the kind of incident that takes months to live down. In spite of that, we both felt that somehow this would prove to be a blessing in disguise. Who knows what might have happened had we put out on the road that evening, as planned.

A couple of guys appeared in short order to offer their assistance, and thank God they did. First, I broke our Tahoe's jack trying to lift *The Whale,* so someone loaned me another. Someone else provided a 12-volt air pump, which I was going to need. With the loaner jack I got the rig up to inspect the source of the leak, quickly discovering a four-inch split piece of tread. "Oh there it is," the guys that were helping me said in unison.

Something told me that wasn't it. Surely I would have felt or heard a blowout. "That's not the leak," I told them.

"It's gotta be," they said.

Suspecting what the Lord had done, I rotated the tire and found a piece of metal protruding from the opposite end. That was the source. Were it not for that leak we would never have noticed the torn tread, and surely we would have suffered a blowout late that night in the middle of who knows where on the highway to Texas. More than once on the road we had seen devastating accidents involving trailers on the highway. We could have easily become another statistic were it not for the Lord's blessing in disguise.

After nearly every other soul had packed up and gone home that night, my homeless family remained stranded in the dark. Just two brothers in

Christ of the 18,000 stayed to help us, which has been a sadly recurring theme during our more than three-year journey. One of these brothers made a valiant, though futile effort to find an open tire center. When that failed, the other brother took it upon himself to make an hour-long drive home to retrieve a spare he thought might fit our hub. Unfortunately, it did not, but he also brought a tire repair kit, and that did work. With a temporary plug in place, we were able to air up the tire and limp *The Whale* over to a nearby hotel. After profusely thanking Jesus for our brothers' help, we finally packed up our children under the dark of night and gently rolled out of the park. We made a quick stop for a fast food dinner then checked into a hotel and got everyone to bed by 1 AM. Just another typical day's work in the Lord for the Tabback family!

The following morning we replaced our tire at a local tire center, but again they didn't have a spare wheel that fit our trailer hubs. With no time to waste on a spare tire goose chase we set out for Texas around noon, praying we wouldn't have a blowout. Boerne was about 1300 miles and 21 hours away—nonstop, which was hardly an option with four children, including two toddlers. With an RV we could have driven straight through, but a three-row Tahoe just doesn't cut it. One way or another, kids need potty breaks, food and rest. Still, we had to arrive at the event in Boerne by 6 PM the following evening, which left us absolutely no room for error.

In answer to prayer, the Lord blessed us with clear roads, stable tires and minimal potty breaks. After a brief layover in Little Rock, Arkansas, we did arrive in Boerne at exactly 6 PM the following night. With almost no sleep in two days and hardly a moment to gather my wits, event handlers quickly escorted me from my drivers' seat to the park pavilion and handed me a microphone to give the message. My family was tired, hungry, cranky and going broke, but I was determined to tell the crowd the truth about the state of our nation. They responded enthusiastically, although I really started to question if sacrificing all we had was worth it.

The Lord had indeed opened many doors for us since first setting out, but our meager moneybag just wasn't keeping up with our expenses, especially given the cost of gas at a mere 9 miles per gallon, hauling *The Whale*. No one had paid for our trip down to Texas, and in just a few days we would be traveling another 1300 miles to an event in Aurora, Illinois on September 12th. No one was paying for that either. We were holding up our commitment to go where called without charging a fee or demanding remuneration for travel expenses, but adding up all the costs for gas, hotels, meals, and other needs, I calculated that by November we were going to be both homeless and penniless. Even so, I refused to make money an issue.

That night in Boerne a man who had volunteered to provide security for the event sought me out. He thanked me for the moving message and said the Lord had given him a message for me, adding, "It's just something the Holy Spirit put on my heart."

Studying his demeanor, I asked, "What's the message?"

He replied, "The Lord wants you to know that He is proud of you and that He wants you to keep going. No matter how tough it gets—and it will get tougher, don't stop."

For those who step out on a limb for the Lord, it is these kinds of messages from random people you meet along the way that really pierce your heart. They come at precisely the right time, when you need confirmation that you have not gone forth in vain. It feels like a warming blanket on a cold winter's night; a sense that the Lord is watching, He is in control, and you are on His path. This man could not have known how much I needed to hear this, for I had shared nothing of our troubles. Neither could he know how these words would carry us through what was yet to besiege us.

Thankful for his faithfulness to share the Lord's message, I embraced him as a brother in Christ. He told me again that he appreciated our obedience and shared with me how some time ago the Lord had also taken him from the world. All the money his former life-sapping profession had made him could not replace his new life as an ever-present husband to his wife and father to his children. Despite now having to make ends meet on "odds and ends" jobs, he told me, "God always provides for our needs." Amen to that!

Clara and I pondered these things late that night as we drove to a nearby fast food joint for a much-needed filling of our children's growling stomachs. We had a mixed sense of peace, understanding that God was watching over us, but also having some anxiety about how our journey might "get tougher."

Completely exhausted, we arrived late that night at our hotel in San Antonio for a much needed Sabbath. We had been dreaming of a soft bed and a long peaceful sleep for 1300 miles. Unfortunately, our little guy, Justin, had an ongoing bout with eczema, which caused him to itch uncontrollably all that night. Over the next two days, by the time we got through Bible reading, meals and entertaining all the kids' needs, sleep remained in high demand.

On Thursday morning we began our next 1300-mile, 21-hour trek up to Aurora, Illinois. We were on the hunt for a trailer tire shop, but just north of Austin I felt a sudden shimmy and saw a thick plume of smoke billowing from one of the wheels in the side-view mirror. TOO LATE! I grabbed the steering wheel with both hands and pulled off the highway onto the shoulder. With a long sigh I realized our leisurely drive to Illinois had just been pushed.

As quickly as we could, we unhitched the trailer, removed the blowout and found a trailer supply center about twenty miles ahead. When I walked in the store, sweaty, tired, cranky and with a shredded and melted trailer tire in my cart no one had any doubts about what had happened to me. After a brief search, I finally found a match for the lug nut holes for our hubs. Done with procrastination, I loaded up three spares, a 3-ton jack, road flares and reflectors. Next time we had a flat, I was going to be prepared!

When we got back to our trailer, I thoroughly enjoyed using that 3-ton jack. No more incessant cranking! I just rolled the jack into position, pumped it a few times and viola! One massive caboose was hoisted and ready to receive a new wheel.

"Honey, check out this jack!" I shouted back to Clara who was nervously watching traffic zoom by. That's when a couple of loud pops got our attention.

"Thomas!" Clara called out.

Quickly, I got up and trotted back to her. She gestured out to the open field beside the road and more pops cracked through the air. It was shotgun fire! For Clara, having been born and raised in Los Angeles, gunfire could mean only one thing. In the Texas Hill Country, however, it means hunters. We were standing adjacent to a large ranch and there just happened to be three guys hunting quail.

"It's just some hunters, don't worry," I assured her, chuckling.

"Umm, they're shooting!" She quietly exclaimed.

Just then, two hunters appeared by the fence with shotguns in hand. I waved to them politely.

"Y'all need any help?" the hunter asked in a thick Texan drawl.

"Thanks, but we got it covered," I replied. "Any success today?"

"Yeah, we killed a few," he said. Then he heard something in the tree above him. Without hesitation, he turned and blasted another quail off its perch. That's Texas for ya!

As a result of our blowout delay, we decided to settle in North Dallas that evening and try to get the kids to bed at a reasonable hour. With an early start in the morning we would still have plenty of time to get to Aurora, Illinois by midday Saturday for the event.

After the kids were tucked in bed and fast asleep, I lay awake contemplating the road ahead and our dwindling funds. Not wanting to be irresponsible with my entire family on the road, I silently asked God if I was permitted to return to a paycheck in healthcare. His response over and over was 'Trust in Me.' I tried to reason that I could pursue a buck in the world and have plenty of spare time to continue to spread the message He gave us, but I knew that was a lie. I would become a servant of *money* rather than God Most High and Jesus Christ. A man who sets forth in the Name of the Lord and turns back for the sake of money or prosperity is no better than an idol worshipper. He is salt that has lost its saltiness:

> *"Salt is good, but if it loses its saltiness, how can it be made salty again? It is fit neither for the soil nor for the manure pile; it is thrown out. He who has ears to hear, let him hear." —Luke 14:34-35*

We got an early start the next morning, and I was really looking forward to a day of smooth sailing. Even if we blew another tire, I now had three spares, so what could possibly go wrong? As we made our way off highway 121 onto the 75-interchange ramp I thought I heard a rattling noise from *The Whale*. Despite the voice in my head loudly telling me, 'PULL OVER NOW,' I didn't listen. Coming off the ramp I felt a sudden violent shift in the trailer and I saw something I'll never forget. One of our trailer wheels rolled up alongside us, crossed traffic and slammed into the median! Incredibly, our trailer remained stable. I wouldn't have known we were missing anything were it not for the smoke and sparks shooting out from beneath it. All the same, we were grinding metal and I feared we might lose the axle, so I immediately pulled off the highway onto the narrow shoulder. We didn't have much clearance between our rig and the traffic blazing by, but I had to inspect the damage.

"Thomas, be careful!" Clara yelled out to me from the Tahoe.

"I am!" I shouted, inching my way around the back of our trailer as cars and semis whizzed by. 'Lord, do you want us to quit?' I questioned. Knowing little about the anatomy of an axle, I really couldn't fully assess the damage. The wheel was definitely missing!

Anyone who has experienced a similar event already knows what happened. Having traversed tens of thousands of miles and suffering a blowout the day before, the wheel's lug nuts had been shaken loose. Loose lug nuts equal a loose wheel and a loose wheel will soon become a lost wheel, if you don't pull over right away and retighten those lugs! However, it's important to understand that nothing happens apart from the Lord's will, especially when you're serving Him. This was a test. So rather than risk my life any further, I resolved in my heart to accept His will. What other choice did we have? This journey certainly wasn't about my will. If *The Whale* were through then we'd have to live without it. I was prepared to do that, though I wasn't sure what we were going to do with all our books and luggage. Whatever the outcome, the Lord would deliver us. I just needed to know if I had done something wrong so I could repent. 'Lord, do you want us to quit?' I asked the question again. Then I realized He had already given the answer four days prior.

"No matter how tough it gets—and it will get tougher, don't stop."

We managed to find a trailer repair shop just five miles up the road and called out a wrecker to pick up *The Whale.* This introduced another challenge, because the wrecker bed was only 8' by 20'. *The Whale,* also being 8' by 20', left no margin for error. As the wrecker began pulling our trailer onto his platform I cringed. The remaining three trailer tires were sitting half on, half off the edge of the platform. It was like taking a butter knife to a balloon and steadily applying pressure. At some point that balloon is going to pop!

Nothing popped during the loading process, but as we followed the wrecker out to the repair shop this guy drove like he was towing a Honda Civic, zipping in and out of traffic. Then he hit a large bump in the road that lifted *The Whale* off the platform and the wrecker off the asphalt with it! When gravity kicked in, the wrecker swerved, tilted onto two wheels and nearly toppled over. "What is he thinking?" Clara exclaimed.

Thankfully, we reached the repair shop without further incident. After offloading *The Whale* the wrecker guy handed me a bill and demanded prompt payment. A five-mile heart-stopping trip to the trailer repair shop can be yours for the cool sum of $250. Cha-ching!

Dismissing the stunt-wrecker, we turned our attention to the needed repairs. We were relieved to learn that the axle had sustained minor damage, so there were only a few expenses to repair the hub. By the time the repairs were complete it was a little after 6 PM, which left us 900 miles to cover in just 18 hours. Yet again, considering pit stops and whatever else the Lord might throw at us, I wasn't sure we were going to make the event in Aurora. Even if we did, I would again be required to deliver a heart-stirring speech with almost no sleep and probably no shower. Thank God for deodorant!

The rest of our drive to Illinois went off without a hitch, right? Nope. Late that night, on a dark stretch of highway in Missouri I felt a familiar shimmy from *The Whale* and could hardly believe the sparks I saw in the side view mirror. Another one? Clara and the kids were jostled awake and I think we were all ready to throw in the towel. Still, we couldn't forget that the Lord had warned us. He wanted us to keep going, so that is what we had to do.

Now a pro, I had a new spare on in about fifteen minutes flat—no pun intended. Having learned my lesson, I went around and tightened all the lugs and indeed found a couple needing extra torque. I also had a funny feeling and decided to check tire pressure. I asked the trailer guys to give our rig a complete exam, including adjusting tire pressure. They adjusted it all right—to 65psi! The maximum rating for those tires is 50psi. Had I not checked, we probably would have gone through all three spares. I let some air out, prayed the Lord would bar any further setbacks and gingerly drove back onto the highway. This is how my family spent our September 11th.

The next day, we arrived tired and beat at Kane County Cougar Stadium without a moment to spare. When it came time to speak, the Lord gave me the strength I needed, and His words. While I can't say everyone who heard the truth received it, a woman confined to her wheelchair in the front row did. Her light and faithful witness reinforced for my family that the greater the suffering one knows the greater we understand the One who suffered for us all.

That night, my family finally got some rest at a nearby hotel. As Clara and I lay in bed, looking upon our four children fast asleep in their rollaway beds, we actually felt blessed. We thanked the Lord that we had survived this particular stretch of our journey with our health, faith, and *The Whale* intact. Despite dwindling funds, we had full bellies and a warm roof for the night. What more can anyone ask for? Little did we know that these episodes with the trailer were among the least of trials we would soon come to face. I may make some light of our hardships, but truthfully they stretched us to the point of breaking. When you likewise pursue the Lord's path and find yourself suddenly thrown into the fire, remember that Jesus never said, "Take up your Cadillac and follow me," but a *cross:*

Then Jesus said to his disciples, "If anyone would come after me, he must deny himself and take up his cross and follow me." —Matthew 16:24

Denying yourself refers to the desires of your flesh, recognizing that you, a sinner, are an unworthy servant, so you must *take up your cross,* which is your burden of service for the Lord, and carry on in spite of many challenges. When you set out to serve the Lord and troubles spring up, the *tempter* asks, 'Can these things be happening to you if you are truly serving the Lord? Didn't Jesus promise rest for the weary and heavy ladened?' The answer is 'Yes,' but the Lord also made clear His meaning when He added:

"Take my yoke upon you and learn from me, for I am gentle and humble in heart, and you will find ***rest for your souls.*** *For my yoke is easy and my burden is light." —Matthew 11:29-30*

In *learning from Christ,* don't forget that this world hated Him, yet He still bore the cross to save us all. If the world maltreated our Savior in spite of His love and sacrifice, why do you, the mere servant, expect better? In Christ you will find *rest for your soul,* if you can remove your flesh and brain from the equation. This discipline does not come naturally, but the Lord will help you.

Dear friends, do not be surprised at the painful trial you are suffering, as though something strange were happening to you. But rejoice that you participate in the sufferings of Christ, so that you may be overjoyed when his glory is revealed.
—1 Peter 4:12-13

Peter spoke from experience, and he would ultimately suffer martyrdom for Christ. But he would never want us to mourn for him. Remember that Peter, along with all the apostles, abandoned Christ during the final hours before His crucifixion. This was to their shame, but after being restored, Peter and John boldly went into the Temple courts and preached that Jesus was the Christ. Despite the Sanhedrin's threats, they persevered. When subsequently jailed, an angel of the Lord sprung them that night and they went right back into the courts to preach the risen Christ again! For their boldness they were arrested and flogged. Nonetheless, they were honored:

The apostles left the Sanhedrin, rejoicing because they had been counted worthy of suffering disgrace for the Name. —Acts 5:41

If you truly love the Lord then you can imagine how healing it was to the apostles' souls to suffer just one ounce of what they witnessed our Savior suffer. So when your service in Christ gets hard for you, and it will, follow their example, and my family's, and press on toward the goal for which you were called, giving glory to the One who bore the weight of the cross for you.

7

Christ The Lord!

Towards the end of September, after speaking before a group in Elwood, Indiana, Clara and I decided to pull off the highway on the way to South Bend and cast an important lot before the Lord. It had become evident that our funds would not even get us into November, so we were going to be homeless and penniless with our four children right before the holidays. This was not what Clara and I had signed up for! Or so we thought. 'Trust in Me,' the Lord kept speaking to my heart, so I would have to decide whether to return to the world for a wage or press on in accordance with the rules of the race, which haven't changed since the Lord set them into being:

> *Endure hardship with us like a good soldier of Christ Jesus. No one serving as a soldier gets involved in civilian affairs—he wants to please his commanding officer. Similarly, if anyone competes as an athlete, he does not receive the victor's crown unless he competes according to the rules. The hardworking farmer should be the first to receive a share of the crops. Reflect on what I am saying, for the Lord will give you insight into all this. —2 Timothy 2:3-7*

Those *rules* require that you ignore what the world calls 'wisdom' and obey the Lord's Commands in faith, trusting that sooner or later you will reap your just reward. As I had spoken to that massive crowd in Ohio, *hardship* must come first, and who has any chance of *receiving the victor's crown* if he or she bows out of the race? Contemplating all this, my family sat in our

Tahoe and said a family prayer, seeking the Lord's will in His Word. Then Clara took our Bible, closed her eyes and randomly opened it to Isaiah 51:

> *"Awake, awake! Clothe yourself with strength, O arm of the LORD; awake, as in days gone by, as in generations of old. Was it not you who cut Rahab to pieces, who pierced that monster through? Was it not you who dried up the sea, the waters of the great deep, who made a road in the depths of the sea so that the redeemed might cross over?" —Isaiah 51:9-10*

As she read the entire chapter we both were moved to the point of tears. It is hard to describe just how penetrating the Lord's Word was to us at that moment. It was so personal, and the conviction of the Holy Spirit was upon us. He was telling us that we had an important mission to accomplish, and that if we fully trusted Him, He would not lead us to ruin. You might think we had already displayed that trust, but the Lord sees your heart, so He knows exactly where faith needs to be grown. As for Clara and me, we fought back our worries concerning the holidays and cleared our minds and hearts of any worldly pursuits, resolving ourselves yet again to serve our Maker and to firmly place our trust in His provision alone. We knew we had made the right decision, because a peace and contentment beyond reason immediately swept over us.

About ten minutes later, back on the highway, the Spirit hit me with a profound revelation, an answer to a question I had been continually asking of the Lord since before leaving Texas. I had asked, "What do We The People do when given no choice but *the lesser of two evils* on a ballot?" Indeed, this predicament has become a sad cliché in America. It was at this conspicuous moment, after my family had faithfully recommitted ourselves to His path, that the Lord decided to give me His answer. He said, 'Christ The Lord' and He opened a door in my heart to a convicting succession of truths that present a powerful challenge to we who are called by His Name: The truth is that unlike the days when Christ walked the earth We The People vote our Caesar's into office. The truth is that We The Voters shall therefore be held accountable for the evil committed by those whom we empower through our votes. The truth is that in consistently voting for *the lesser of two evils* we have progressively made evil our nation. The truth is that only by accepting Jesus Christ as Lord and Savior can our nation be restored, for the clay belongs not to the earth, but to the Maker's Hands. Therefore, when given no other choice apart from the lesser of two evils, where neither candidate will proclaim their allegiance to Christ, the truth is that We The Church in this nation must take a stand and write upon those ballots *'Christ The Lord.'*

The standard that must rise above the Star-Spangled Banner and every American creed is the Gospel of Jesus Christ, for in Him alone is our hope. I had a vision of the people of ancient Judaea in the days of Joseph and Mary, a land in Roman bondage. I visualized Joseph and Mary, coming to Jerusalem for the census to pay their taxes to Caesar. To whom did they complain about taxes and abuse of power in their day? Caesar was not accountable to them, for he had been appointed by means beyond their control. While the Judaeans were oppressed, they were also untainted by the evil Caesar committed in exercising his authority. In this way, the burden of the average Judaean was lighter than ours, but such is the price of maintaining a society of *Life, Liberty and the Pursuit of Happiness.*

When the firestorm of the Lord's judgment comes upon our nation, its people will cry out for the Lord's deliverance, saying, "Save us O Lord, we were powerless to oppose the evils our government committed." Yet our society has declared unto itself certain *'inalienable rights,'* and these now testify against us. A people who enact *'freedom of speech, or of the press; or the right of the people peaceably to assemble, and to petition the Government for a redress of grievances,'* but will not speak, write or stand for what is right are guilty of complacency and cowardice in the sight of the Lord. Worse, a church that stands behind *'freedom of religion,'* yet sits on its hands while Christ is made unwelcome in our public squares has committed apostasy in the sight of the Lord. Altogether, *'a government of the people, by the people and for the people'* cannot wash their hands of the evil its appointed leadership pursues on its behalf. From the greatest to the least, such a nation as this will be held to account before the Judge.

> *"Go up and down the streets of Jerusalem, look around and consider, search through her squares. If you can find but one person who deals honestly and seeks the truth, I will forgive this city. Although they say, 'As surely as the LORD lives,' still they are swearing falsely." —Jeremiah 5:1-2*

As we continued up the highway to South Bend, I understood that we who know the truth must never again endorse evil. I began to see more clearly how these days are truly not like the days gone by, where the Lord was enduring in His patience. The iniquity of the United States of America is nearly full, which means our nation's woes are about to eclipse mere politics and economics. Unless we get right with God Most High and Jesus Christ soon, we are going to suffer disaster on a biblical scale.

"My people are fools; they do not know me. They are senseless children; they have no understanding. They are skilled in doing evil; they know not how to do good." —Jeremiah 4:22

Recognizing the lies of the enemy is both powerful and necessary to obtain true freedom. The first lie the enemy will tell you is that by supporting a lesser evil you will be sparing your country from a greater evil. The truth, however, is that any servant of Christ has an enduring obligation to oppose all evil, lesser or greater, for we know that nothing evil can bring about any good. Those who neglect this truth succumb to a purely selfish desire to preserve their personal wallets. This is why politicians always wave some form of *money* in our faces in an attempt to damper our moral convictions. Therefore, anyone who endorses evil becomes guilty of neglecting his *first love:*

"Yet I hold this against you: You have forsaken your first love. Remember the height from which you have fallen! Repent and do the things you did at first. If you do not repent, I will come to you and remove your lampstand from its place." —Revelations 2:4-5

America was not founded by man for the sake of liberty, but by Almighty God for the purpose of spreading His Light to all nations. The moment we decide to take our shining city from atop the hill and place its light under a bowl, or snuff it out altogether, is the day the Sovereign Lord *removes our lampstand from its place.* Remember that our Savior could easily have made any number of concessions with the Sanhedrin and Pontius Pilate, but he refused to compromise with the enemy. Instead, He stood firmly upon the truth and sacrificed much more than His purse—He gave His Life.

Despite the lies people tell themselves, voting for the lesser of two evils has never benefited our nation. It has only worsened its condition; such as an unclean wound festers. American Slavery is the perfect example of such a wound. Despite declaring, *"all men are created equal"* in 1776, eleven years later, during the Constitutional Convention in 1787, anti-slavery Founders made what they deemed *lesser of two evils* compromises to preserve slavery in order to garner Southern delegate support for the establishment of the United States. Yet never in history has man's hand trumped the Lord's. So in 1861, the United States, bound together in sin, was ripped apart by a Civil War and the issue of human slavery was decided with finality, and at a terrible cost to all a party to its evil. You can be sure the Almighty spared our nation not one ounce of gold profited at the expense of all the blood, flesh and unrequited toil wrested from the backs of men, women and children who, for the sake of *money*, were reduced to beasts of burden. What seemed wise to the Founders in 1787 was proved foolish just 75 years later by the blood of their fallen children. As President Abraham Lincoln concluded in his second inaugural address, *"The Almighty has His own purposes."*

> *"Therefore once more I will astound these people with wonder upon wonder; the wisdom of the wise will perish, the intelligence of the intelligent will vanish."*
> *—Isaiah 29:14*

When given no other choice but the lesser of two evils, We The Church have to take a stand with Christ The Lord, knowing that He Lives and will hearken to our call if we appoint Him as Head of every post in the management of our affairs of state. Since a true "Christian" is supposed to embody Christ, we are to seek Him in every elected official; senators, congressmen, governors, and presidents, knowing that if we demand candidates who are obedient to Christ, refusing to settle for any other, then the Lord, by His sovereign authority, will both raise up candidates who are worthy of our votes and change the hearts of many presently in office. He has done it before to the most stubborn of His earthly subjects and He will do it again, if His people turn back to Him.

> *"I the LORD search the heart and examine the mind, to reward a man according to his conduct, according to what his deeds deserve." —Jeremiah 17:10*

Our Creator sees and hears all, so we cannot hide from Him the true reasons why we tolerate the evils we do. Even when we fool ourselves, God is not fooled. Likewise, He will witness those who stand with Christ The Lord, writing such upon future ballots where no servant of Jesus is offered. Then, should the Lord's judgment fall upon our nation, He will distinguish those stained with *money* as opposed to those covered by the blood of the Lamb. Therefore, ignore the voice of the mocker, because taking a stand with Christ The Lord is to your eternal credit, and life on this earth is not nearly as long as an eternity of Life in Christ.

Jesus Christ is the Answer, has been and always will be. At the core of what is broken in the United States of America is, indeed, that we have forsaken the God of our fathers, but the Name by which our fathers knew God was Christ Jesus:

> *"If you really knew me, you would know my Father as well. From now on, you do know him and have seen him." —John 14:7*

Plenty of people today will hail *"God,"* but few are willing to confess who God is, and that means everything! God will never bless a nation that refuses to honor His Son. Consequently, a nation that denies Christ denies the Father who sent His only begotten Son into the world. *Such a nation as* this is doomed to destruction:

> *"Like cages full of birds, their houses are full of deceit; they have become rich and powerful and have grown fat and sleek. Their evil deeds have no limit; they do not plead the case of the fatherless to win it, they do not defend the rights of the poor. Should I not punish them for this?" declares the LORD. "Should I not avenge myself on such a nation as this?" —Jeremiah 5:27-29*

The next evening, Clara, the kids and I traveled to a church in Elkhart, Indiana where a patriot group had invited me to speak. I knew little about this group, least of all their beliefs. Just because they were gathering in a Christian church meant nothing, such as my family had unfortunately discovered along the way. Regardless, I spoke boldly to them about our mutual responsibility to one another as servants of Christ. I further told them that our nation's foundation was not held together by liberty, but upon the precepts of Christ. Liberty without Christ is a foundation of quicksand. Freedom works well for a good people blessed by God, but it does not preclude evil people from doing evil.

> *But the man who looks intently into the perfect law that gives freedom, and continues to do this, not forgetting what he has heard, but doing it—he will be blessed in what he does. —James 1:25*

Finally, I told them that We The People were responsible for the state of our nation, because every voter alive today has invariably accepted the lesser of two evils for some form of public office, and in doing so has offended the Lord our God. I encouraged them to trust in the Lord, reminding them that Almighty God can and will part the waters of the deep for His people, if only we will return to Him in faith and obedience. At last, I told them that we must demand a restoration to God Most High and Jesus Christ from any who would seek our votes by forsaking the lesser of two evils on future ballots and writing in *'Christ The Lord.'*

When I concluded, the group was silent and I braced myself for flying chairs. Yet, to my surprise, they erupted in ovation and applause. "Amen!" some in the group lauded. "Praise Jesus!" I heard another say. "This is it!" yet another proclaimed. I can hardly describe the moment. It was so unexpected and beautiful. At the time, it filled me with hope for my children's future in this nation. How could I have expected that these people, my brothers and sisters, had actually been yearning to hear this message?

Driving back to our hotel in Mishawaka, my family could not contain our excitement, although Clara would have been happier if I had delivered the message quicker. As usual, while I spoke she was left to quell two toddlers that popped like popcorn every other moment. In spite of that, and our ever-diminishing purse, we knew we had crossed a major milestone in the Lord's service. Not only did playing by the Lord's rules feel good, it was right. At the time, I did not expect a message more significant than *"Vote 'Christ The Lord,'"* would be given, but I was oh so wrong. Truly, only Jesus Christ can restore our nation, but when my family learned of His plan to accomplish it, that's when the real engagement began.

8

Love One Another

The next day, my family could feel something different happening to us. In spite of the challenges, we had a new outlook on our purpose and a peace and resolve swept over us. God was with us, and we were excited to be working for His Great Name. Thus, the Lord continued to present us with His appointments, beginning with lunch. We took the kids to a local burger joint, and as we sat in a round booth, looking over the menu and trying to ignore prices, we quickly discovered the Lord had placed a *magnet* upon us. Some call it an anointing, but we like the concept of a *magnet,* because that's what it feels like. Basically, for no apparent reason, people become drawn to you. This had happened to us before, but on this particular day we felt it even stronger.

For example, nearly every server in the restaurant came over to compete for our table to wait on us. We told each new arrival that we were already being served, but each politely told us, "Oh I know, I just wanted to see if I could get you anything." Their faces also beheld a certain look we had come to recognize, an expression that said, 'Don't I know you?' Even the cooks were waving to us from their window.

Realizing the Lord's appointment was coming, my family exchanged grins and patiently watched, listened and waited for the Lord's timing. We were hardly able to contain that giddy feeling of knowing something was coming. Sure enough, after ordering, a young woman came to our table, identifying herself as the assistant manager. Like the others, she seemed intrigued by us and bluntly asked, "So who are you, where are you from?"

My family looked at one another and chuckled. Did she really know what she was asking? "We're a family who left our home in Texas to serve the Lord on the road," Clara explained.

"That's really interesting," she replied and decided to sit down with us in our booth.

Clara went on to describe our life on the road serving Christ, and as the young woman listened, her eyes progressively became wider. Dumbfounded, she said, "What you're telling me sounds crazy, but I'm looking at your kids and they look happy and balanced. I'm also looking at the two of you and you seem normal."

"We are normal," Clara laughed. "We just love the Lord."

The young woman then shared her beliefs in what has become the standard in our nation, which some call spiritualism, others call universalism, but we know is a dangerous lie. It sounds warm and romantic to suggest that all faiths have a singular belief in a supernatural Creator of all the heavens and the earth, and that everyone will be saved if we just live moral lives. Of course, unless you accept the Author of morality, you cannot know what it means to be moral. Can mankind be trusted to define what is moral?

Clara shared with her a truth that God is not a religion, but the One True God is sovereign over all, and He requires that we honor His Son, Jesus Christ. "Do you have a Bible?" Clara asked.

"I do," she replied, "but I haven't read it in a couple of years."

"I know because the Lord brought you here to sit with us that you are at a crossroads," Clara told her assertively, "and He wants you to know Him. If you start reading that Bible, you're going to find out who He is and what your purpose is in this life."

Feeling nudged by the Holy Spirit, I added, "And when you open that Bible, the Lord is going to give you something just for you."

This young woman's face flushed with emotion and her eyes began to tear. It was though her unspoken prayer was being answered through us. This is how the Hand of the Lord moves mountains by measure of your faith, that faith you demonstrate when you boldly testify the truth which can only be found in Jesus Christ.

After this, the young woman shared with us a story about one of their servers who had recently given birth to a baby girl with only a brainstem, a rare condition known as *anencephaly*. Usually this is fatal within the first few days of life, but this baby girl was struggling to live. Recognizing the immense spiritual and financial strain on this family, the staff of the restaurant came together and collected $200 for them. In telling this testimony, the young woman's face glowed with genuine love.

Now I knew why the Lord had brought us here. I told her that I was speaking before a group that evening and I was certain they would join my family in prayer for her employee and their family. I told her this blessing came through her, because she sat with us to share that family's need.

We finished lunch, said our farewells, and when we stepped outside Clara told me, "We have to do something."

"We will," I told her, knowing what she was going to propose.

In the privacy of our car, Clara spoke exactly what was weighing on my heart, "I know we need an offering tonight, but we are to give every penny to that family. They need it more."

I agreed, knowing the Lord was plainly showing my family what it means to be serving Him in faith. The kids may have had need of shoes and clothing, as did we, but our first desire was to obey the Lord and *love one another* as He has loved us:

> *"A new command I give you: Love one another. As I have loved you, so you must love one another. By this all men will know that you are my disciples, if you love one another." —John 13:34-35*

That evening at the Mishawaka Public Library, a sizeable group of people crammed into a meeting room, leaving standing room only, to hear the Lord's message. Many from the previous night in Elkhart had come to hear it again, bringing family and friends. Again I proclaimed that the collective church in America must reject the lesser of two evils on future ballots and boldly write in *'Christ The Lord,'* and again it was resoundingly received. I then shared the story of this family in their community whose baby daughter was struggling to live. I told them that while the rest of the nation incessantly debated about the morality of healthcare, we were going to demonstrate what it means to be true servants of Jesus Christ, because a people in Christ don't ignore their brothers and sisters in need. Before I could make the suggestion, a man blurted out, "We're going to pray for them, right?"

"Yes," I confirmed.

"Will you lead us in that prayer?" another asked.

"Yes, I will," I agreed.

"Don't forget to pray for the doctors," a woman suggested.

"And pray for the hospital staff and the nurses too," another woman behind her added.

We were so blessed and humbled to be a part of this beautiful display of the church in Christ—*in action.* That family was formerly strangers to these people, but they embraced them just as the Lord Commands. As I began the prayer my emotions surged and I could feel the same throughout the room. I don't think there was a dry eye amongst the group. When I concluded, everyone opened their eyes and looked around at one another with a deep sigh. The presence of the Lord was felt, for where two or more gather in His Name, whether under the roof of some religious establishment, in a living room, out under the open sky or inside the conference room of a public library, there He is with us:

> *"For where two or three come together in my name, there am I with them."*
>
> *—Matthew 18:20*

That night, my family deferred any *love offering* for ourselves and instead took up a collection for that family. Quickly as possible, this congregation in Christ, many in tears, lined up and dropped their offerings in a box on their way out. One particular woman approached me and shared that many years ago she had given birth to a daughter with anencephaly. She had lived just three days. I knew the Lord had appointed this evening for this woman, witnessing something to her that no manmade plan ever could.

Afterwards, my family gathered in our Tahoe and said a prayer, thanking the Lord for using us for something so special, and asking that He especially bless that young assistant manager who had initiated it. Then we counted the donation box. To the penny, that group gave $701. Without question, that extra dollar was a sign from the Lord that their baby girl was in His good keep.

The next day we sealed the money in an envelope with an encouraging note signed by *"servants of Jesus"* and took it into the restaurant. The young woman had the day off, so I handed it to her manager, asking him to have her take it to their employee. "This blessing came through her," I told him.

He didn't even know what was in the envelope, but he was so taken by the gesture he scrambled around for something he could give us in return. I told him nothing was necessary, but he hastily grabbed a couple of seasoning saltshakers and pressed them in my hand. “Here, you have to take these,” he insisted and I graciously accepted them. “Who do I tell her you are?” he asked.

“Just tell her we’re the family with the trailer,” I said, gesturing to *The Whale* sitting in their parking lot. “She’ll remember.”

Joining the rest of the family in the Tahoe, I handed the seasoning saltshakers back to the kids and we all had a good laugh. Where were we going to get an opportunity to use those with no home? What a wonderful feeling we had the rest of that day, knowing we had done our part in God’s masterful plan for that family.

Sometime later, a regional director for that restaurant tracked us down so he could express their thanks again. He reported that their corporate heads were so inspired by our gift they had decided to pitch in with their own *“substantial help”* for their employee’s medical expenses. This is just one example of the kind of *‘Jesus-reaction’* you too can inspire through your obedience. Anyhow, I reminded him that it was servants of Christ in their own community who had selflessly given that day, and he didn’t hesitate to proclaim his own faith in Jesus. We wound up having a long discussion about the need for a national restoration in “Christ The Lord.” It can happen, if only We The Church will faithfully follow the Lord’s Commands:

> *“The most important one,” answered Jesus, “is this: ‘Hear, O Israel, the Lord our God, the Lord is one. Love the Lord your God with all your heart and with all your soul and with all your mind and with all your strength.’ The second is this: ‘Love your neighbor as yourself.’ There is no commandment greater than these.” —Mark 12:29-31*

9

The Illusion of Freedom

On October 10, 2009, I spoke to more than a thousand patriots gathered in North Kentucky at the Boone County Fairgrounds. This speech signified yet another turning point in our journey, because I did not merely speak of repentance, but led this gathered crowd in a united prayer of repentance, appealing to God Most High and Jesus Christ to bring about our nation's restoration. This was not planned and would seem odd, given that this event was not supposed to be a church revival, but it was the church in America that had gathered.

When the invite to the North Kentucky event came in, I made a critical error as I contemplated our travel arrangements. The problem stemmed from my stubborn desire to 'budget,' even though we had no 'budget.' By this time, the Lord was sustaining my family's living needs from one appointment to the next, exhausting nearly every last dime in between. Consequently, as I considered lodging arrangements for Kentucky, I ignored the Lord's Voice, when He said, 'Do not arrange accommodations, because I will send someone to welcome your family into their home. Receive the blessing when it comes and trust that you and your family will be safe.' When I heard it, I stopped what I was doing and quickly made my first mistake—I doubted:

> *If any of you lacks wisdom, he should ask God, who gives generously to all without finding fault, and it will be given to him. But when he asks, he must*

believe and not doubt, because he who doubts is like a wave of the sea, blown and tossed by the wind. —James 1:5-6

Who in the world was going to welcome in a family of six? Moreover, how was I supposed to suggest to Clara that our children were going to be safe under the roof of perfect strangers? No matter the reason, logic or excuse, you must trust in the Lord and obey His every Command. Unfortunately, I did not, but made a 'logical' and 'sound budgeting' choice to rebook the room we had in Mishawaka. It would make a VERY LONG day trip down to Kentucky and back, but given the Indiana events I had coming up on the calendar it seemed the wisest thing to do.

In spite of my doubts, in the midst of that Kentucky event a couple did indeed approach Clara and offer our whole family shelter in their home for that night. With a note in hand, bearing their address and phone number, the woman handed it to Clara and said, "I am to give you this. We want to welcome you to stay with us tonight."

Clara was baffled, especially because I had never told her what the Lord had spoken to me.

"We make great pancakes for breakfast," the woman added.

When I was done speaking I rejoined Clara and our children and she shared this encounter with me. I felt an instant jolt. 'Oh no,' I said to myself, 'it was real.'

"She said they make great pancakes," Clara added.

But what was I to do with the hotel I had now reserved? We had left some luggage in that room, so we couldn't cancel. That's when I made another grave error, deciding to decline this couple's offer, despite the Lord having told me to accept it.

Later, as we were loading up to return to Northern Indiana, one of the event organizers came to find us, having been urged to pray for our journey. Before we knew it, others gathered with us as well and together they prayed God would safely deliver us to our next destination. This sort of thing didn't happen everywhere, but usually before a trial was about to ensue.

On the LONG DRIVE back through Indiana late that night we stopped off at a gas station in a small town south of Indianapolis to refuel. Tired and lamenting the four hours we had yet to go, I was strongly questioning my decision to pass on that couple's offer. Still, the inspiration of that crowd, all joining in a prayer of repentance for our nation's restoration filled us with joy. We were so excited to see what might be next on the road ahead. I swiped my credit card, waited for the pump to enable, then set the filling handle to autopilot while I helped Clara tend to our children's potty breaks. By the time I got back to the pump it had already reset itself. Not wanting to delay those beds in Mishawaka one moment longer than I had to, I gave up on the receipt, saddled up the family and slowly rolled our rig back out onto the two-lane highway.

About a mile up the dark road, Clara and I spotted two vehicles speeding up on our rear. Either these were impatient locals, wild teens or something worse. Keeping a watchful eye on our tailgaters, we looked for an opportunity ahead to pull over and let them pass, but none presented itself. After a short while, the second car following us made an abrupt U-turn and went back. Moments later, the remaining white car found an opportunity to pass, and with an obnoxious honk it surged by us using the oncoming traffic lane. At first, we were relieved, but that soon turned to horror as that car cut back into our lane and slammed on its breaks to a dead stop! I immediately slammed on my brakes, but it was too late. Even without the trailer, I couldn't have stopped in time. We hit that car hard, spinning it off into a ditch on the left side of the road. The impact sent us veering into oncoming traffic with a pair of headlights dead ahead! I sharply pulled our Tahoe right, and we narrowly evaded a head-on collision, slamming into the ditch on the other side of the road. The Lord miraculously delivered us, because our steering tie rod had broken and our airbags never deployed, otherwise we would have been struck by oncoming traffic.

"Is everyone okay?" I called out.

"Kids?" Clara turned to examine the children.

"We're okay," Rielle, Austin, Jazelle and Justin replied together.

No one had been seriously injured—thank you Jesus. Despite the shock, we knew we needed to stay vigilant, because someone had clearly attempted to kill us!

"Why did they do that?" Clara asked, charged with adrenaline.

"I don't know," I answered, looking back to see if anyone was approaching our rig from where that car went off the road. I handed Clara the cell phone and told her, "Call 9-1-1."

Taking the phone, she plaintively asked, "Who is in that car?"

"Stay here," I told her, forcing my door open and jumping out.

"Thomas, be careful!" Clara warned.

"I will," I replied and ran around to the back of the trailer. Up across the road in the ditch I could see the flashing hazard lights of the white car that had attacked us. It looked pretty banged up and I couldn't see any movement in or around it. I was tempted to go and see if anyone was hurt, but it was too dangerous to cross the road while other cars on the highway were evading wreckage and debris.

By the time Clara had gotten through to a 911 operator, others in nearby homes and cars had already reported the incident and sheriff's deputies were on the way. When authorities arrived on the scene, we immediately advised the supervising lieutenant that this had not been an *"accident,"* but an *"attack."* We tried to caution him that this was a hostile scene, but he said, "My first priority is to clean up this roadway for safe passage. Right now, you can get me your license and registration."

That was frustrating, but I complied. We were far from home, family and friends and I didn't want to irritate local law enforcement. With deputies on the scene, a further attack on my family seemed unlikely. So as the deputy tended to traffic, I decided to inspect the damage to our Tahoe and trailer. As I feared, the Tahoe was cooked. The front end was smashed in through the radiator, the wheels were pointing in opposite directions and the frame was clearly bent. It had to be the Hand of God that had steered us away from that near head-on collision. I went back to our trailer and when I opened the side door, I sighed ruefully. What a mess. Shelves, books, luggage, everything had been thrown into one big broken heap. It looked like the scene of a house hit by a tornado. Still, greater offenses were yet to come.

Sometime later, the lieutenant returned to take our statements. He first approached Clara, but when she asked who had attacked us and requested I be included in the discussion, he rudely snapped, "You had your chance, now I will not speak to you!" He then ordered her inside the Tahoe and slammed the door on her!

Hearing the commotion, I came over from the trailer and met the lieutenant as he approached, "Sir, you need to control your wife!"

"Control my wife?" I questioned, and Clara repeated it, having come back out from the Tahoe.

Almost immediately he caught his chauvinistic statement. "I shouldn't have said that. I know better than to say something like that." It wasn't exactly an apology. After reminding him that we had been "attacked" and questioning his demeanor, he relented and told us, "Well, it looks like the other driver is the owner of a gas station back up the road. She's insisting that you didn't pay for your gas."

"Are you kidding me?" I questioned.

He shook his head, "No sir, this is wrong, very wrong. Whether you stole gas or not doesn't matter. What she did is not right. Actually, it's criminal and will most likely be prosecuted."

"I used my credit card at the pump," I told him. "If my card didn't go through, how did their pump enable for me to fill up?"

Again, he shook his head, "I don't know." He explained that one of his deputies had gone to the gas station with the owner to investigate, so I asked if I could go as well to settle the matter. He agreed and sent me down with another deputy, leaving Clara and the kids with the Tahoe and *The Whale.*

When we arrived, I finally met the woman who had nearly killed my family, a Hindu by appearance. Despite the state of her car, she did not appear injured. When she saw me, she gave me the evil eye. Somehow I wasn't angry with her, though in my natural self I should have been. I just wanted to resolve this issue and get my family back on the road as soon as possible. Exactly how we were going to do that, I had no idea.

The deputies ordered me to remain in the store, while they accompanied the woman to a backroom to review camera footage. Nearly an hour later, a young man, who said he was a relative, came into the store and also went into the backroom to help them. Not long after his arrival they all emerged, confirming I had indeed swiped my card. It was suggested she had manually cancelled my transaction in error, though it was hard to trust anything they said at that moment. Regardless, she insisted my card had not been charged and that I still owed her for gas. Wanting to settle the matter, I asked the deputies to bear witness to me paying her in cash, promising to dispute any added charge to my credit card. With that done, my escort received a call and walked outside, leaving me alone with the store owners and the other deputy, who rather anxiously suggested we leave. However, I asked for a moment and proceeded to address the woman about her attack, expressing the difficult predicament she had created for my family. I also disclosed that we were missionaries serving Christ on the road. The mere mention of Christ and my plea that we handle the situation *"in a good Christian manner"* really roiled both the woman and the deputy. When I explained that we had no other mode of transportation and no home to hold up in until our Tahoe was fixed, the deputy snapped at me, "You are not allowed to discuss the accident! I'm warning you!"

Taken aback, I turned to him calmly and said, "I'm not angry. I just want to see that we resolve this the right way. Is that okay?"

The deputy shrugged and looked away, giving me leave to continue. After uttering hardly a few more words, none remotely threatening, the deputy snapped again, "That's it! You are not permitted to talk to her anymore! Let's go!"

"What's wrong?" I asked.

"I'm directing you not to speak!" he shouted. "One more word and I'm going to arrest you!"

"Arrest me, for what? I don't understand," I told him.

"Shut your mouth!" he yelled, exploding into a sudden cursing fit. "I gave you a direct order not to speak; now you're under arrest!" As he said these words, he seized me by the arm, twisted it behind my back and forcefully removed me from the store. All I could think of was Clara and the kids being left stranded on that cold dark road in the middle of nowhere. This just couldn't be happening. I could not go to jail tonight! When we got through the door, he let go of me and I backed up, saying, "I don't understand. They don't even know how to contact me. Why don't you give them my number?"

"Shut your mouth!" he shouted. "I told you not to speak! You will not say one more word or I will take you to jail!"

"Jail? For what? My family was attacked and now they're waiting for me in the cold." This entire ordeal was outrageous, but I kept hearing a voice in my head saying, 'Don't show aggression and don't say any unkind word.' I realized how precarious my situation was, being an out-of-towner subject to small town justice. It doesn't really matter what the law says, only how the law is enforced.

Furious and cursing, the deputy charged me again, but my escort suddenly appeared between us, totally confused. "What's going on?"

"I gave him a direct order to shut his mouth!" the other deputy railed in a cursing fit. It was like he had become possessed.

"Please take me back to my family," I told my escort, retreating to his car.

At this point, these two deputies began a sidebar, discussing how they were going to "report" this incident. Because issuing a "direct order" to shut my *"[expletive] mouth"* wasn't exactly enforceable under law, they agreed that I had disobeyed a "lawful order."

"I can hear you," I called out to them, hardly believing it all.

Deputy *Blown-A-Gasket* stormed over to the car and leaned in over the drivers' seat, pointing his finger right in my face, swearing at the top of his lungs. He had absolutely lost it!

Very calmly I told him, "You don't know what you're doing. Stop now before you do something you'll regret."

Appalled, he hustled around the front of the car, cursing up a storm, promising to drag me out and take me to jail. The other deputy, however, must have realized this was wrong, because he called his partner off and got in the driver's seat. "I'm taking him back to his family." Without wasting time, he started the car and put us out onto the road. I was both relieved and frustrated. How much injustice can a man suffer before he fights back? Of course, that's a question every servant of Christ ought to ask his Master:

> *"Remember the words I spoke to you: 'No servant is greater than his master.' If they persecuted me, they will persecute you also. If they obeyed my teaching, they will obey yours also. They will treat you this way because of my name, for they do not know the One who sent me." —John 15:20-21*

Upon returning to Clara and the kids, I immediately reported the deputy's tirade to his lieutenant, who had naturally been forewarned over the radio. Predictably, he did nothing, except to suggest that I file a complaint with the county sheriff. At the same time, a wrecker arrived to cart off our Tahoe and *The Whale*, which they towed rather than carry—thank God. Homeless and without any mode of transportation, my family was forced to receive a lift to a nearby hotel from the deputy who had delivered me from his partner's wrath, though he was no brother in Christ himself.

My family appeared at the hotel front desk tired and somewhat in shock from the whole ordeal. It was about 2 AM. As the lady behind the counter found us a room, I asked her, "Where are we anyhow?"

"You're in Batesville, the casket-making capital of the world," she mirthfully replied, having no idea what we had just endured.

Clara and I felt suddenly numb. 'Did she just say what we thought she said?' It was like we were in the midst of a nightmare and we desperately wanted to wake up. "You're serious?" I asked.

"Oh yes, there's a great big factory just up the road," she replied. She was a sister in Christ, and she blessed our children with a late night breakfast of cereal and cocoa as we recounted the events of the day. When we shared how a couple had unexpectedly invited us to stay with them, but we had turned down their offer for pancakes only to suffer this attack, our sister sighed and confirmed something that had been nagging at me since the split-second before we hit that woman's car. She held up her hand, palm down and said, "You walked out from the Lord's covering, and so the enemy got to you."

> *"I have put my words in your mouth and covered you with the shadow of my hand—I who set the heavens in place, who laid the foundations of the earth, and who say to Zion, 'You are my people.'" —Isaiah 51:16*

Once in our room and settled into bed, Clara and I thanked the Lord again that none of us had been seriously hurt. Still, Clara was shaken, for how could the Lord let Satan get to us like that? Sin, that's how. When the Lord tells you to do something and you disobey, that is sin in its most basic form, and I had sinned. Yes, even the Lord's emissaries make mistakes, and there are consequences, but the Lord has enough grace to carry you through, so long as you don't give up. Thus, I repented for having ignored His will and vowed to press on with greater obedience. I also had to apologize to my wife and children.

Ultimately, we received no apologies from either of the offending parties, the gas station owners or the sheriff's department. After receiving my complaint concerning the conduct of his deputy, the country sheriff sent me a contemptuous reply: *"You were treated, and will be treated, like any other citizen in the United States Of America."* He then noted Romans 13, claiming to be a "Christian" himself.

> *Everyone must submit himself to the governing authorities, for there is no authority except that which God has established. The authorities that exist have been established by God. Consequently, he who rebels against the authority is rebelling against what God has instituted, and those who do so will bring judgment on themselves. —Romans 13:1-2*

Perhaps that sheriff will reflect upon this Scripture himself when the Lord's judgment befalls this nation, including his county and his household, because God is the ultimate authority. Even so, I have taken him at his word, knowing that any servant of Christ who stands firmly with his Savior will be treated as I was in the days to come. As proof, Clara suffered arrest under similar circumstances two years later, in Texas of all places.

My family had gone into a model home and testified to a saleswoman. She opened the door when she asked about what we did for a living, hoping to sell us a house. Instead, she got a testimony about how Jesus is the "Only Way." Vehemently rejecting Christ, she hatefully ordered us out. When we questioned if her boss would approve, she promptly called the police, falsely claiming we were threatening her, although we were already leaving.

As we drove out of that neighborhood, two police cars arrived and pulled us over. Unfortunately, the senior officer was another of Satan's deputies, Deputy *Blown-A-Gasket II*. After exiting the Tahoe and walking over to explain the situation to his partner, *Blown-A-Gasket II* went right over and accosted Clara, because she had cracked open her door. She asked if she could come out, but ignoring her request, he went into a fit about her not "obeying" his "lawful order" to shut her door. Before she could react, he lurched forward, flung her door open and slapped handcuffs on her, then forcefully yanked her out onto the grass and dragged her to the back of his squad car. "This is not right. I did nothing wrong," Clara asserted. Our children were mortified, Justin was crying, and I was beside myself. I could not rescue my wife, because *Blown-A-Gasket II* had decided to use his *legal authority* to abuse her. Worse, he proceeded to accost our children. He ordered them out of the Tahoe and threatened to arrest me if they did not stop video recording him and comply. He also threatened me, "I will arrest you and have children's services take your children away."

Helpless, I told my children to obey the orders of a man they had just seen arresting their mother. So in the midst of the blazing sun he sat them down on the grass with fire ants crawling on them, displaying them to people driving by as if they were criminals. I told him, "You didn't have to do this. We did nothing wrong."

"Your wife was posing a threat to me and my partner and refused to obey a lawful order," he insisted, plainly exaggerating.

"We're missionaries, serving Jesus Christ," I replied.

"And God bless you for that," he said disingenuously, himself a "Christian."

Thanks be to God, because at that point He removed *Deputy Blown A Gasket II* from the scene. He decided to leave his subordinate partner alone to deal with our *threatening* family and drove off. The other officer, a brother in Christ, released Clara and expressed his shock at his partner's behavior. "This has been a day of days. I want you to know that what happened here should not have happened, and I am very sorry," he apologized. He also noted that his squad car camera had recorded everything.

That was just one of many severe attacks Satan was launching upon our family at that time, but we remained steady and vigilant in Jesus. Although Clara was bruised and deeply afflicted, as was I, we forgave the offender, commending restitution to the Lord, who knows how to repay and how to save. We also prayed for our brother, asking the Lord to protect him against the real criminals out on the streets, and to give him wisdom to deal kindly with the Lord's people. We still pray for him and his family, as well as other brothers and sisters in law enforcement today.

> *But Paul said to the officers: "They beat us publicly without a trial, even though we are Roman citizens, and threw us into prison. And now do they want to get rid of us quietly? No! Let them come themselves and escort us out."*
>
> *—Acts 16:37*

Satan has been inspiring such conduct in his officers long since before Paul first brought the gospel to the Gentiles in the Roman provinces. As a servant of Jesus Christ, be shrewd with the law, as Paul was shrewd. While you must submit to their authority, never deny your Savior, and always obey the Spirit. On our journey, my family has been taught an invaluable lesson about the illusion of freedom in this nation. We The People believe that we have been given certain inalienable rights endowed by our Creator. They have been etched in our Constitution, the highest law of this land, and yet the moment one walks out from beneath the Lord's protective shield those rights are stripped away in a flash. Even if your shield is intact, We The Church have been asleep so long, laws have been implemented that permit gross injustices, labeled as *'keeping the peace'* and *'maintaining order.'* Sadly, "Christian" law enforcement will abuse you just as quickly as pagans. *They are a law unto themselves:*

> *"I am raising up the Babylonians, that ruthless and impetuous people, who sweep across the whole earth to seize dwelling places not their own. They are a feared and dreaded people;* ***they are a law to themselves and promote their own honor."*** *—Habakkuk 1:6-7*

True servants of Christ in law enforcement are going to have an especially hard time in years to come, because like the military they are required to follow orders from their chain of command. Consequently, many may fall away from their faith and violate your rights with the authority you, ironically, have given them by your votes. My advice to law enforcers who fear God is that you remember your Judge and do not abuse your brothers or sisters, for He will not look kindly on anyone who does just because a law of man says he can.

> *"Listen to me, my people; hear me, my nation: The law will go out from me; my justice will become a light to the nations. My righteousness draws near speedily, my salvation is on the way, and my arm will bring justice to the nations. The islands will look to me and wait in hope for my arm."*
>
> *—Isaiah 51:4-5*

10

Shaking Off The Dust

For two solid weeks we were marooned in *Casketville,* paying not just for one hotel room, but also for the one I had foolishly extended in Mishawaka, which still had our luggage in it. We might have retrieved those items and cancelled the remaining reservation, but the rental car we'd been given by the nearest Chevy dealership would not have made it there and back!

The day after the attack, I had gone down to visit with the dealer owner and expressed to him our predicament, seeking his help. While they were repairing our Tahoe, I asked for a rental that had enough space for our children and luggage, but he was less than sympathetic. "I've heard it all before," he snickered. "We'll fix your Tahoe, but you'll get whatever rental we have on hand."

That "on hand" rental turned out to be a *cash-for-clunkers* trade-in they had been unable to pawn off on anyone. Not only did this vehicle not have enough seatbelts, it hardly seemed safe to drive to and from the hotel. The engine sounded like a hollowed-out eggbeater, likely to drop onto the asphalt with the next bump in the road, and the interior smelled like old musty socks. Worse yet, that dealer charged us the full rental rate as for a new vehicle!

Those days in *Casketville,* stuck in a hotel room that smelled little better than our rental car and watching every last dime bleed from our wilting wallet without a means of replenishment were just awful. To make matters worse, our family all caught the flu. Then we discovered that the Hindu woman's insurance company had voided her policy due to her criminal misconduct. That meant they weren't going to pay out one dime for damages or expenses, including our *cash-for-clunkers* rental car. Thankfully, we had full coverage insurance, but we had to cover the hotel and rental car expenses ourselves, which completely sapped our moneybag. We had absolutely nothing left to pay the deductible on our Tahoe to get it released from the shop when its repairs were completed; neither did we have any money to get *The Whale* back into the sea!

> *"But I tell you who hear me: Love your enemies, do good to those who hate you, bless those who curse you, pray for those who mistreat you."*
>
> *—Luke 6:27-28*

It seemed like the worst possible time, but we were being taught a lesson about overcoming personal affliction to forgive our enemies, whether they were repentant. This sparked a constant spiritual battle within Clara and me, hampering our ability to trust that the Lord would restore us. No matter how many times I calculated and recalculated what it would take to get our Tahoe and *The Whale* out of hock, we came up short. Surely the Lord wasn't going to require that we continue our journey on foot, was He? It was though the Lord had placed His Thumb on us and said, 'Here you will sit and ponder your mistake.' We had no choice but to sit, listen and learn.

There were several points where Clara and I could have exploded, but we forced ourselves to remain grounded in the Lord and His Word. I'm not saying we didn't have friction and didn't let certain anxieties escape our lips. I'm saying we persevered in spite of the challenges. Yes, we felt broken, dejected and we were suffering, but Christ is graceful, and He lifted us back on our feet.

Finally, after two weeks of soul-searching refinement, the Lord released us from *Casketville*. The Tahoe still wasn't ready; neither did we have the money for the deductible, but a local rental car company agreed to cut us a break on a tiny late-model SUV that would at least make it to Mishawaka. Clara and I will never forget how good it felt to escape that town. It was truly like seeing the bars of a prison draw apart and hear a voice say, "You are free to go." When again we stepped out into the sun, we just barely had enough gas money to get back up to Mishawaka to retrieve our belongings from that hotel room I had so foolishly reserved. Then the Lord swiftly and gracefully put us back to work. While in Northern Indiana, I began receiving invitations to speak again. Not only did these serve as a means for me to continue delivering the *'Christ The Lord'* message, but it also kept gas in our tank, food in our children's bellies, a roof over our heads, and beyond rhyme or reason we accumulated the funds necessary to bail out the Tahoe and *The Whale.* I marveled at how the Lord delivered, because we did not express our needs to those before whom we appeared, but the Lord inspired the right people to deliver exactly what we needed.

When our Tahoe was finally ready to be picked up from the shop, the service director reluctantly informed me that the owner was demanding cash for all the expenses not covered by insurance, totaling more than $1300. They wouldn't even accept payment by credit card! This was about the last straw, and for the first time on our journey, Clara and I seriously considered putting a particular set of the Lord's instructions into action:

> *"If anyone will not welcome you or listen to your words, shake the dust off your feet when you leave that home or town. I tell you the truth, it will be more bearable for Sodom and Gomorrah on the day of judgment than for that town."*
>
> —*Matthew 10:14-15*

As irritated as we were with this dealership, did we really want them to suffer an outcome worse than *Sodom and Gomorrah?* No, but when you've been put through the refinery, your fleshly concerns start to diminish in favor of your spiritual awareness. What we humans want for any given situation doesn't much matter. All that matters is that we obey the Lord's Commands, trusting that He will do what is just and right. By this time, we understood that the Lord's Word was far more than symbolic. It was real. If we testified against this establishment, it was going to be bad for them—the owners for sure, but also for anyone who worked there. At the very least, that dealership would soon be put out of business and those employees would be out of work. Of course, that didn't mean they couldn't get jobs elsewhere, perhaps better ones, but these were the considerations burdening our hearts as we drove back into *Casketville*, contemplating *shaking off the dust.*

I remember like it was yesterday, pulling into the dealership that afternoon. We had counted out twenties, tens, fives and slew of singles—whatever people had contributed to the *love offerings* at different events—and combined it into one large bundle in a paper bag. Then, to be sure we followed the Lord's will and not ours, Clara, the kids and I said a heartfelt prayer, asking the Lord what was proper. If this place was to be spared for the sake of the many employees working there, we asked the Lord to reveal to us just one individual who was with Him. For that one's sake, we would not testify against the place.

After our prayer, I grabbed our bag of cash and stepped out of our rental to go and buy back our Tahoe. I walked in the service entrance and quickly met the bright face of the service director, a man who tried to do better for us, but the owner had tied his hands. Standing alone behind the checkout counter, he greeted me warmly.

"Where's the owner?" I asked him.

"Soon as he heard you all were coming today he left early," he answered regretfully in his oddly southern accent for a Hoosier.

After reviewing my invoice, I opened the paper bag and began counting out that massive pile of cash. He looked on with sadness in his eyes, shaking his head. It really was ridiculous that we had to pay in cash, but I wonder how he would have felt if he knew the whole story, since we hadn't shared our challenges with him either. "That's all of it," I finally said, pushing the large pile of money in front of him.

"Thomas," he said, still shaking his head, "I feel terrible about how you've been treated here. I've never seen my boss act like this."

"I understand," I told him. "We work for the Lord. Those who don't love Him won't love us."

"Well, it ain't right," he stated plainly, "but I understand what you're saying. Say, you got a minute for me to share something with you?" he asked politely.

"Sure," I told him.

"I wasn't always a Christian," he began and proceeded to tell me his testimony. As a young man in the army, he once got punished with 40 days confinement to his barracks, except for duty. Stewing in his anger, he returned from duty one morning and stumbled into a black woman he had never seen before. She explained that she was on guard duty and asked him why he looked so troubled. Though not his nature, he sat with her and explained his situation. She then told him that salvation was available through Jesus Christ and asked if he would be willing to follow her in a prayer. He agreed, and after the prayer she joyously proclaimed, "You're saved!"

"I know this might sound crazy to some," he told me, "but afterwards, when I got in my room, it was bright—I mean everything was really bright. I can't explain it." He paused and I saw the sincerity in his eyes, as he continued, "I saw the light that day and everything in my life changed for the better. I didn't immediately become a saint, but when I did something wrong, I felt guilty about it. The Lord has always been there for me." He took a moment, then said, "Anyhow, for how you've been treated and what you've had to go through, for what it's worth, I'm sorry."

"Please forgive your servant's offense, for the LORD will certainly make a lasting dynasty for my master, because he fights the LORD's battles. Let no wrongdoing be found in you as long as you live." —1 Samuel 25:28

In a way, this man acted like Abigail who came before King David to atone for her husband's stinginess. He was the precise answer to the prayer my family had just lifted up to the Lord. As a result, we would not shake off the dust from our feet, relieving us from this burden. In the end, the Lord will correct every injustice and repay every man for the wrong he has done, just as He did Abigail's stingy husband Nabal.

As for Clara, the kids and me, we left the dealership that night with our Tahoe and a wallet $1300 lighter. What few dollars we had left would seem a joke to most ministries today, but as for me and my family, we were just happy to have some wheels again that didn't smell like dirty socks!

My family thought, or hoped, this might be the last time we visited *Casketville,* but when a vehicle sustains more than $10,000 in damage, inevitably there are going to be a few latent issues. Some weeks after getting the Tahoe back we had to return to address alignment problems. While our brother in Christ had his service team troubleshoot the issue, a young man came out to greet me warmly. He introduced himself as the new owner of the dealership and expressed deep regret over our ordeal, saying, "I've heard about all you've been through and I want to let you know that if you need anything, if there's anything I can do to help you, just let me know." I was quite taken aback by his graciousness, but when I found out that he was the son of the dealer owner, I was flabbergasted! How was the son so different from his father, and why wasn't he appointed the new owner during that period of our dire need? Everything was as the Lord appointed.

Seeing the Lord was teaching me a rare lesson in grace, I asked the son to go for a walk with me. We made a couple laps around his dealership as I explained my family's calling, the plight of the nation, as well as its God-given purpose. I also related Christ's expectations of him a business owner, likening him to a biblical landowner, in whose care are the lives of his workers and their families. Like many Americans, this businessman professed himself to be a "Christian," but he had many reservations about religion. As Clara and I have told many, "Jesus is well above religion."

We left the dealership that day struck by the complexity of God's plans. Long before my family was born, even going back all the way to the outset of His creation, the Lord knew I was going to error by turning down a night's stay with that couple in North Kentucky. He knew we were going to be attacked, that our Tahoe would wind up at that dealership, and that the dealer would mistreat us. He knew the service director's testimony about coming to Christ would soften our hearts and keep us from *shaking off the dust*, and He knew the heir of the dealership would have a different heart. That's how perfect the Lord's plans are, and that's not even taking into account everything that had to happen from Adam and Eve on so that everything would come together at precisely the right time. Wow, how awesome is the Lord!

In the end, Clara and I forgave all those who had hurt us—even tried to kill us—in *Casketville*. Though tempted, we overcame Satan's legal recourse trap, which ensnares so many in a futile attempt to *get even.* Instead, we moved on in our service to the King, leaving justice to the One who is perfectly *just,* and this set us free from the immense burden of bitterness. Take warning, because the Lord has taught my family that failing to forgive puts your soul into a life-sapping spiritual prison, manifesting itself with real physical ailments, and carrying with it the potential for an eternal sentence. So forgive all that wrong you, whether they are contrite.

"Blessed are the merciful, for they will be shown mercy." —Matthew 5:7

What greater *mercy* is there than to forgive your enemies? Consider that we were all enemies of God on account of our sin, but we have salvation through Christ's atoning sacrifice, by which God *forgave* our sins. Everyone will be sorted between heaven and hell on the basis of blood and fire. Either you will be *forgiven* by the blood of the Lamb and sanctified for heaven by His Holy Spirit fire, or all the blood that has ever been shed upon this earth will fall upon your head and your blood will be shed and your soul will be condemned to eternal torment in the lake of burning sulfur. This is why Jesus placed so much emphasis on forgiveness in His teachings, because when you withhold forgiveness from someone who afflicts you, you are spurning God's merciful pardon on your soul. You may not have intended to, but in your heart you are saying, 'They should go to hell,' and by doing so you become a murderer at heart. By this subconscious act, you give Satan legal authority to chastise you, for murder is his domain. This is how Jesus correlates murder to unforgiveness:

"You have heard that it was said to the people long ago, 'Do not murder, and anyone who murders will be subject to judgment.' But I tell you that anyone who is ***angry with his brother*** *will be subject to judgment. Again, anyone who says to his brother, 'Raca,' is answerable to the Sanhedrin. But anyone who says, 'You fool!' will be in danger of the fire of hell." —Matthew 5:21-22*

Notice how Jesus does not specify a 'repentant brother,' but only a *"brother,"* meaning a fellow human being. People have been misled into believing that the Lord's standard for *forgiveness* is conditional, when it is not, so they remain imprisoned beneath the invisible crushing weight of their unrelenting anger. Anger is a both a product and reproducer of sin. One who is afflicted by the sin of another becomes angry and in turns afflicts others, who in turn afflict still others, causing an endless chain-reaction of evil. Such is Satan's scheme, for he uses anger as a catalyst, turning injured people in *injurers.* The only way to counter this vicious cycle is to become an obedient servant of Jesus Christ by turning away from anger and affliction by expressing forgiveness and love for your enemies, which will open the way for peace to enter your heart and life. This is not an easy thing to do, but it is not complicated. All you have to do is put the importance of your afflicted flesh aside by reminding yourself that your soul belongs to heaven and the King, and He gives no one the authority to damage your soul! Don't let Satan trick into to believing otherwise, because when your duty on this earth is finished, you will not remember any of its afflictions. On the contrary, you will be eternally basking in the Lord's Glory without a single care in the world, as will many—we hope and pray—of the souls of those who afflicted you before they came to personal repentance and restoration in Christ. There are no vendettas in heaven, only eternal peace, love and unsurpassed joy.

It might help if you realize that every injustice you have suffered has been suffered a hundred times more by your Savior, because you are His child. If someone does evil to your child, are you not afflicted? So too is your Father in heaven, but His capacity for pain and sorrow goes far beyond yours, because He sees everything, including how that evil deed will breed so many more like it. Therefore, when you are wronged in this world, make every effort to avoid taking it personally, but understand that this world is rejecting your Heavenly Father. They may abuse you, but they sin against God, and He will surely repay them for their wickedness. But do not desire their death and destruction. Instead, pray for their salvation. No matter how vile the crime, isn't the best possible outcome for you and the Kingdom of Heaven to have that sinner come to repentance and salvation in Christ? What if the ancient Church had been empowered to *judge* Saul of Tarsus before he had the opportunity of becoming Paul the apostle?

> *"Do not judge, and you will not be judged. Do not condemn, and you will not be condemned. Forgive, and you will be forgiven." —Luke 6:37*

Do not let the world confuse you, because playing *'Judge'* is not the same as making proper *judgments* about sin. Condemn the sin, not the sinner. Only God is qualified to be Judge, although He calls upon testifiers to witness against unrighteous conduct both within and outside the Body of the Church. To find the proper balance, take for example that Samaritan village that rejected Jesus' coming, because he was a Jew *heading for Jerusalem:*

> *When the disciples James and John saw this, they asked, "Lord, do you want us to call fire down from heaven to destroy them?" But Jesus turned and rebuked them, and they went to another village. —Luke 9:54-56*

By Jesus' former instructions, I'm certain His disciples had already *shaken off the dust* of that village in formal protest and as a testimony to God in heaven. However, Jesus rebuked them because the time of *judgment* had not yet arrived. He was teaching His disciples, then and today, not to invest ourselves in offenses and judgment, but to obediently perform our duties as His witnesses and leave the rest to God. In His time, after every possible fruit has been harvested for His Kingdom, retribution and judgment WILL descend upon every wicked, unrepentant soul.

> *"I have given you authority to trample on snakes and scorpions and to overcome all the power of the enemy; nothing will harm you. However, do not rejoice that the spirits submit to you, but rejoice that your names are written in heaven." —Luke 10:19-20*

In all things, understand that Satan's power is sin, but he and his demons are *crushed* when you chasten yourself to God's Commands. Understanding this, separate yourself from those who afflict you by forgiving their offenses and letting go of anger. You were not put on this earth to *settle scores,* but to live a life that glorifies your Savior. So let God *get even* and your peace will be restored. You will never before have felt so light!

> *"Then the master called the servant in. 'You wicked servant,' he said, 'I canceled all that debt of yours because you begged me to. Shouldn't you have had mercy on your fellow servant just as I had on you?' In anger his master turned him over to the jailers to be tortured, until he should pay back all he owed.*
>
> *"This is how my heavenly Father will treat each of you* ***unless you forgive your brother from your heart.****" —Matthew 18:32-35*

Be sure that you have truly forgiven anyone who has wronged you *from your heart.* Sometimes the mind says one thing, but the truth residing in your heart says another. If you find that you are still afflicted, this denotes unforgiveness, and you must deal with it. This is not to suggest that one who is in the midst of abuse should not seek deliverance from evil. Forgiveness does not require that you continue to expose yourself to harm, or neglect the needs of the defenseless. But when you have been delivered, if you are having trouble forgiving anyone, ask the Lord to teach your heart how to forgive and He will set you free from the anger that is binding you.

> *"And when you stand praying, if you hold anything against anyone, forgive him, so that your father in heaven may forgive you your sins. But if you do not forgive, neither will your Father who is in heaven forgive your sins."*
>
> *—Mark 11:25-26*

My family's nightmare in *Casketville,* which the Lord turned into a blessing, is just one example of why it is good to hand over afflicting matters to His perfect judgment. I also know that my testimony had a profound impact on that dealership heir, because he has since taken his walk with Christ to heart. He endeavors to use his position of authority to help those in need, being mindful that everything he gives is an offering to the Lord. To think we almost *shook off the dust* from this brother in Christ. I thank God for him, and I might even buy a car from him someday—just not a *cash-for-clunkers* trade-in…

11

Spiritual Warfare

Leading into November, the Lord sent my family on a tour through Missouri, where He continued to expose the spiritual nature of the war we had been sent forth to wage, a war fought with faith:

> *For our struggle is not against flesh and blood, but against the rulers, against the authorities, against the powers of this dark world and against the spiritual forces of evil in the heavenly realms. —Ephesians 6:12*

One of our first encounters was with a very tall and rancorous woman, whom we called the *Windex Woman.* After hearing me deliver the *'Christ The Lord'* testimony before a statewide gathering of patriot organization leadership, *Windex Woman* stood abruptly and admonished the group for applauding it. Wagging her finger at them like schoolchildren, she grated, "Don't listen to this man!" She went on to highlight her ten-year volunteerism for the Republican Party, insisting that their political platform was the best hope for the nation, even when faced with *"the lesser of two evils."*

I let her vent, then politely asked, "After all that precious time you have sacrificed in their service, what have you accomplished?"

Flabbergasted, she began an *us versus them* rant, but I didn't have to respond, because a quiet and reserved librarian-like woman sitting in the middle row of the group suddenly stood and spoke out, "I don't care what she says, he's right. We've been wasting our votes all these years and nothing good has changed." The audience was stunned. You could tell this was not the kind of woman who normally speaks out, but I could see the fire of the Spirit on her face. "I'm never voting for the lesser of two evils again," she proclaimed. "I'm going to vote for Christ The Lord!"

The entire group erupted in cheers and applause. It was a powerful moment that forced Windex Woman to take her seat in bitter silence, planning her revenge.

At the close of the evening, while Clara and I gathered up our children and gear, Windex Woman went about the place earning her namesake. Evidently she was the steward of the meeting place, so cleanup was her responsibility. That's when the enemy in her showed his colors again, this time *blue*. Wielding a bottle of Windex in one hand and a washrag in the other, she ran around that room specifically spraying only what my family had touched. She even sprayed Windex in midair, forcing people who were talking with us to retreat from the blue mist. It was bizarre! When asked if she was going to spray down all the tables, she gestured to my family and said, "No, just what they were using." She even made a point to spray down the sofas and coffee table out in the waiting area where our two toddlers had been sitting, though they hadn't made the slightest mess. Recognizing what was happening, we maintained our composure. The other organizers, however, were appalled.

As we exited the building through a pair of glass doors, we said our farewells and even thanked Windex Woman for her hospitality. She wouldn't look at us, but closed the doors and promptly squeezed off several spray bursts onto the glass where our faces shown through, just to avoid further sight of us.

> *If your enemy is hungry, give him food to eat; if he is thirsty, give him water to drink. In doing this, you will heap burning coals on his head, and the LORD will reward you. —Proverbs 25:21-22*

We could have called her out and scorned her, but what would that prove? By treating her with kindness, we allowed her to expose herself through those *burning coals*. The enemy cannot stand Christ, especially when people reject his lies in favor of the truth. Oh yes, Windex Woman was also a professed "Christian," but her actions demonstrated that she was really a servant of Satan. In the world, doctors call her behavior *OCD (obsessive-compulsive disorder)*. As my family later discussed, we agreed that she was a clear-cut case of *WOW (Windex-obsessed-woman).* Either way, we know that in reality she was demonically enslaved.

Off to another remote part of Missouri, having been invited before a living room group hosted by a Messianic Jew, we were about to witness yet another example of the spiritual reality that envelopes this world. It was a special evening, the kind of intimate setting that's difficult to replicate in a stadium. After sharing the Lord's message, a man in the group testified about how the Lord had provided his family a home after losing his job and going bankrupt. When their mortgager repossessed their house and evicted his family they had no money and no place to go. Despite the difficult circumstances, he prayed to the Lord and trusted in His deliverance. Before long, he had a random encounter with a man who just happened to have a home on hand he didn't need. Not only did that man give him his home, but this house was better than the home they had lost. That's the measure of the Lord's deliverance. When you ask for something in faith, not selfishly or frivolously, but truly in need, the Lord our God will answer, and sometimes you will get more than you dared hope for.

> *"Until now you have not asked for anything in my name. Ask and you will receive, and your joy will be complete." —John 16:24*

The Spirit spoke to my heart at that moment, for I had been fervently praying to the Lord that my family would have a home for the holidays, though we had no means to acquire one. Through this man's testimony, given at this most conspicuous time, I understood that somewhere, somehow, the Lord was going to deliver.

On my way out that night, the host's wife embraced me to thank me for coming, promising to pray for the Lord's blessings for our continued journey. I thanked her and at that moment something spiritual shook loose. Her demeanor became discomfited and she asked me what I thought about antidepressants and other mood-altering medications. Having spent all those years in pharmacy benefits, I told her they were dangerous. With a sudden tearful outburst, she told me that she had been fed these pills and institutionalized because of severe side effects. "I haven't been the same since!" she cried out in distress. The world might label her *bipolar*, but in the spiritual realm, she was a woman besieged.

It would be another two and a half years before I would fully understand what the Lord was witnessing to me, at which time my family encountered another woman beset by prescription drugs. This woman had been taking powerful pain meds, antidepressants, sleep meds and high doses of various other drugs for nearly thirty years. She had a *celebrity tote bag* filled with them! By the time the Lord placed her in our path, she was already lacing her drugs with alcohol to increase their potency. She was on death's doorstep. Per her request, we put her through *"Holy Spirit detox,"* a combination of intensive prayer and physical care. In just seven days the demons attacking this woman were driven out and this woman's flesh and spirit were delivered from her drug dependency. Then the Lord spoke to me, 'Do you see why I would not let you return to pharmacy benefits?' Indeed, to the learned and wise there are no benefits in pharmaceuticals, only side effects that sooner or later will lead unto death. It would be good for anyone who deals in these demonic devices to abandon them for another profession. No paycheck of any size is worth it.

Prior to being sent back into Ohio, the Lord gave Clara a dream to reemphasize the nature of the spiritual battle we wage for the soul of our nation. She found herself in the dark of night, standing upon a dirt road that stretched out a short way to the left and a long distance to the right. As she looked up this road to the right, she saw something approaching her. It wore a gray hooded robe bound at its waist and a small pet walked beside it. It moved slowly, like it roamed aimlessly, and when it reached Clara, she saw within the hood that it had no face. Despite being aware of her presence, it did not come near her as it passed by. Her eyes were then drawn across the road to a small glass-enclosed atrium. Inside, she saw three people trapped. She immediately ran to free them, because she knew that atrium was about to be destroyed. When she reached the door and opened it, she asked two questions of those inside. After each had answered, she knew that only one was to be released, while the other two had to remain locked inside. Clara's spirit was saddened, but she knew she had to be obedient.

The following day we went to give an interview at a Christian radio station. The radio interview went fine, but then we met *Vinci* and his wife, who had come to us under the guise of offering support for our mission. It's difficult to explain, but Clara and I could feel a tangible presence of evil in Vinci, though not his wife. Not willing to accept false pretenses, I demanded that Vinci speak his true purpose, praying internally to the Lord that the truth be revealed. That's when Vinci dropped the ruse and began to tell us a dark story about his former career with the United Nations, where he and others had been trained to get in touch with their *"spirit guides."*

Immediately, his wife began to cry, for the Spirit had forced her husband to reveal himself, and he was not with Christ. Clara and I felt that she was, but having been so embattled by the enemy in her husband, she was worn and broken. She appealed to us for help, but healing was no more up to us than it had been up to her. Vinci had to want it, and in spite of the contemptuous words he used in recounting the evil things he had learned from his "spirit guide," his demeanor expressed a certain longing.

"What did its face look like?" Clara questioned.

"This thing didn't have a face. It always wore a gray hooded robe bound at its waist," Vinci replied. "So I'm telling you, you don't know what you're up against."

'Be afraid,' Clara and I both heard the enemy threaten. However, the Lord had prepared us for this encounter, and in Him we heard, 'You have nothing to fear.' Even so, we concluded that meeting with deep sadness of heart for Vinci and his wife.

People don't understand that we are surrounded by an unseen spiritual reality. In this realm there are angels and demons doing battle for our souls. The angels gain the upper hand when we obey God's Word, but Satan's demons gain ground when we fall into sin. Adults are constantly under fire through deceptions and temptation, but it is our children who are the most at risk. Satan targets children, because a tender shoot that is damaged while it is young will affect the rest of its growth. Though they are children, sin is still the culprit, and especially sexual immorality. It's like gum on a sidewalk on a hot summer day. Indiscriminant of shoe size, it sticks to the one who steps in it, and it takes a lot of work to clean it off. Even then, it leaves a residue. The only solvent that can expunge it completely is the Sword of Jesus Christ, which is His Holy Word.

This lesson was brought before my family one night as we spoke to a church congregation in Northern Ohio. While answering questions, a grieved woman plaintively asked what the church should do when a judge will not remove a child from an abusive household. She was referring to her grandchild. Firmly led by the Spirit, Clara admonished the congregation, saying, "The way we treat our children in this nation is among our worst offenses before the Lord. Because they're young, no one respects them, but respect is paid to the family members who abuse them!" She then told them, "Children suffer two kinds of abuses; the first is physical at the hands of the predator, while the second breaks their spirit, when those who are supposed to protect them repeatedly question, 'Are you sure? Tell me again what happened.' Because children are smart, they really hear, 'You're not valuable enough for me to believe.'"

By the time she had concluded, nearly the entire congregation was weeping and wailing bitterly. Being led away by relatives, one young woman in the last row cried out fiercely, "She's right!" Clara went after this woman and learned that as a toddler she had witnessed her father murder her younger sister, and he also nearly strangled her to death. The prolonged lack of oxygen to her brain had caused permanent memory loss and had trapped her within the mind of a child, or so the doctors said. Yet, after hearing the words inspired in Clara by the Holy Spirit, she had a breakthrough. Not only did she remember her sister's death, but also what had happened to her. "If someone had just listened," she wept, "my sister would be alive and I wouldn't be this way." After two decades of living with her disability, her family could not believe her cognitive ability. Simply speaking the truth had brought about a miracle; a beautiful blessing for the pastor of that church, who turned out to be that young woman's grandfather.

The lesson given that night is urgent for every guardian to whom the Lord has given little lambs for proper care and rearing. Whether you live in a city slum or an affluent suburban neighborhood, evil is lurking around every corner, so be on guard always! The enemy prowls around shopping malls, movie theaters, parks, public schools, daycare and other places children frequent. Still, the wily predator rarely looks like a predator. Instead, he or she comes in an innocent disguise. Moreover, the most dangerous place for a child is often in his or her own home, which becomes a prison the moment a parent welcomes evil right through the front door in the form of a family friend, relative, babysitter, or perhaps when you introduce your own sinful habits into your child's proximity.

Today, our children are being constantly bombarded with a steady media-driven diet of godlessness and depravity that no medicine on earth can fix. Yet, when they act out in strange and sudden outbursts, together with emotionally charged antics, the world quickly moves to brand them with *depression, attention deficit disorder, hyperactivity disorder, bipolar disorder,* or some other big word out of their psychobabble dictionary so they can make your child's damage permanent by drugging them. DON'T LET THEM DO IT! Your child's problems are not chemical—they are spiritual, and the only effective medicine against Satan's poison is the Holy Word of God:

> *"**You are already clean because of the word I have spoken to you.** Remain in me, and I will remain in you. No branch can bear fruit by itself; it must remain in the vine. Neither can you bear fruit unless you remain in me."*
>
> *—John 15:3-4*

Through Jesus—the Living Word—the disciples were cleansed of the worldly evil that had tainted them. He will surely do the same for your family if you read His Word faithfully, not forgetting to do what the Word says. At the very least, read your family the Scriptures each night before you go to bed. It really doesn't matter what book, chapter or verse you read, so long as you are reading God's Word. Science can't explain it, because science doesn't believe, but when we invest ourselves in reading, searching and studying God's Word, we systematically become immune to the evil of this world. Even a little dose of the Lord's Truth heals the deepest wounds.

You should also teach your children to read the Word for themselves, and make sure it's the adult version of the Gospel you read. Feed them God's whole grain and they'll grow up stronger. Whenever we attend church services, Clara and I don't send our children off to finger paint just before the real meat of God's message is to be delivered. We can testify that something supernatural and powerful occurs when they receive the full measure of God's Word. It may not be visible to the human eye, but it is real.

> *But Jesus called the children to him and said, "Let the little children come to me, and do not hinder them, for the kingdom of God belongs to such as these."*
>
> *—Luke 18:16*

Understand that through the Word, God is feeding your child's spirit, even if their mind does not yet comprehend what they are hearing. A day will come when their young minds will catch up with the spirit. Yet if you feed your children something synthetic or watered down, a day may come when they will be confused, because they have read something the real Word never said. Confusion is a powerful weapon if left in the enemy's hands, and it can be deadly. Therefore, don't give your children play armor; give them the real *spiritual* armor of God that is capable of standing against any of the enemy's schemes. You have made time for much less; now make time for what is more.

Finally, be strong in the Lord and in his mighty power. ***Put on the full armor of God*** *so that you can take your stand against the devil's schemes.*

—Ephesians 6:10-11

If you the parent have been the source through which evil has entered your home, you must take immediate action to purge it. Like you, your children will not respect a hypocrite. How will you train them to fear God and obey His Commandments when you don't? How can you mete out discipline, if you accept none for yourself? So get rid of any explicit or profane media from your home, smash them, burn them, throw them away, and block them from your Internet service. These things can only hurt your family. If you have a drug or alcohol habit, a propensity for anger, cursing, strife, selfishness or neglect, then get yourself straight so that your loved ones will not be damaged by your weaknesses. If the source of evil is a person, get rid of or get away from that person as well. No relationship is worth spoiling the seed God has given you. If you have any true love in your heart for your family, drive away the worries of this world, which are destroying you, so that you can demonstrate your love for them without any spiritual hindrance. In overcoming every obstacle, turn to Jesus and continually ask Him for help, because He loves you.

Children, obey your parents in the Lord, for this is right. "Honor your father and mother"—which is the first commandment with a promise—"that it may go well with you and that you may enjoy long life on the earth."

Fathers, do not exasperate your children; instead, bring them up in the training and instruction of the Lord. —Ephesians 6:1-4

After you have separated yourself from all evil then go to your child, whom you wrongfully exposed to sin, and ask for his or her forgiveness. You can teach them nothing if you don't first establish this respect. Remember that your children are on loan from God, and His anger will burn against you if you unrepentantly pollute His treasures. When your child has forgiven you, next take your repentance before the Lord, seeking His forgiveness. If your repentance is true, demonstrated by your newfound commitment to His Holy Word, then you will have won the spiritual battle. Both you and your child will be cleansed of the sin that has stained you, and a peace that transcends the flesh will enter your home.

12

The Lukewarm Church

Leading into November 2009, the Lord delivered us an opportunity to enjoy a brief respite from the dropping temperatures in the North with an invite to speak before a group in San Angelo, Texas. Having been given the provision to get there—though not enough to get back—we hit the southern road, again passing through Arkansas before we entered our home State of Texas. That first day passing through Dallas felt like summer again and we thanked God profusely for restoring us from *Casketville*, otherwise we could not have afforded to make this trip.

We arrived in San Angelo on the eve of Veteran's Day for a powerful evening before a room full of Texans. As I testified *'Christ The Lord,'* a tall, distinguished looking gentleman was transfixed. Either he embraced the message or he was appalled. No one is indifferent. At the conclusion of the evening, this tall man was the first to approach me. He shook my hand firmly, saying with exuberance, "This is the message I've been waiting for. I am going to preach this everywhere!" He was absolutely serious and it gratified me to know that one more servant of Christ was going to proclaim His message.

Not long after, a couple approached me, thanking my family for our obedience to God. They asked me if I knew who that tall man was and I shook my head. "That's the pastor of our church," they said. "We just saw him in the restaurant lobby, telling everyone about your message. He is so excited about this, he's on fire!"

The enthusiasm of this group was as good as anywhere we had been. It demonstrated to Clara and me that God's people could be found all throughout our country. All they needed was a catalyst, inspiring them to get out and actually do what the Lord Commands. In spite of that, the offering we received from this group barely measured up to what we needed to make a speaking engagement I had accepted in Wabash, Indiana. Thus, Clara and I had a decision to make; either we would use that money for fuel or for lodging, and if not for lodging then it was time to put *The Whale* to use. Two separate couples did inquire about our accommodations that night, but when we told them, "We don't have any yet," they did not follow through on their convictions. We also did not openly publicize our need. The Lord didn't Command His messengers to beg for shelter, but to *search for some worthy person:*

> *"Whatever town or village you enter, search for some worthy person there and stay at his house until you leave." —Matthew 10:11*

Consequently, my family spent the night in *The Whale* not anticipating the temperatures would dip into the low 40s. It was, after all, November in West Texas, but somehow we neglected to plan for blankets. No matter how many layers of summer clothes you put on they just don't replace a goose-down comforter, and we paid the price! In the morning, I looked at my babies' red, sniffling noses and puffy eyes and I could have just kicked myself. We really should have risked the money for a hotel, trusting the Lord would somehow provide, but for my lack of faith we didn't. Thankfully, God is patient as we learn and suffer from our mistakes.

The following night we began our journey north, planning to stay at a familiar hotel near Austin, and on a lonely stretch of highway we stumbled upon another of the Lord's appointments. In His perfect timing, we passed by a young woman, alone, stumbling along the dark, rugged roadside, shying away from our headlights.

Clara and I looked at each other. "Thomas?" she questioned.

"I know," I replied, already slowing down to make a BIG U-turn with *The Whale*. Though traffic is normally consistent on this stretch of highway, it was completely clear, which gave us all the time we needed to come about and drive back to where she was. Seeing our headlights again, she glanced back nervously as we slowed down beside her. Realizing what she had likely just suffered, Clara and I could only imagine her nerves at that moment. I put down my window and called out, "Do you need some help?"

She looked over and, seeing Clara and the kids, must have felt we were safe, so she nodded her head and answered, "Yes."

"Come on over and get in," I told her.

She crossed the highway, which was miraculously free from traffic in either direction. Clara jumped in the back with the kids and this young woman climbed aboard onto Clara's seat. She was in her early twenties, disheveled, very nervous, and tears of distress plainly shown upon her face. As we slowly drove on we all introduced ourselves and met *Shawna.* She asked us to take her to her brother's house just a few miles up the road and we naturally agreed. After this, a tense moment of silence ensued, for how does one break the ice in such a situation?

Finally, Clara asked her, "Did someone hurt you Shawna?"

Shawna bent over, falling into tears, exclaiming, "I did something so stupid!"

"What happened?" Clara asked.

After mustering her courage, she tearfully replied, "I went to a party with my brother's friend." She paused, shaking her head ruefully, "I really didn't know him. It was stupid. I shouldn't have been there, so I left."

"Can we take you to a hospital or the police?" I asked.

"No!" she snapped. Catching herself, she then said, "Thank you, really, I just want to go to my brother's house."

"Okay," I calmly replied, and Clara and I both were wondering if she would be safe there. It was her brother's friend that had apparently hurt her after all.

Clara began expressing to Shawna that we were servants of Jesus Christ, and that He had sent us to her precisely at that moment to help her. Learning that she had a home in North Texas, we offered to take her there in the morning, suggesting she share our hotel room, so long as she didn't mind dealing with "four squirmy kids."

"Yeah Shawna," our bright-eyed children chimed in from the back, "you can come with us!"

This lightened her up a bit, but she declined. Referring to her home, she said, "I can't go back there."

That struck Clara and me profoundly. You don't want to press a woman in this situation, but as servants of Christ we had to accomplish the purpose for which the Lord had sent us to her. "Why can't you go back?" I asked.

"I lived with my mom," she stammered, succumbing to tears again. Quietly, she concluded, "She just committed suicide."

Our hearts dropped to the floor. We were crushed for our sister, realizing the severity of her ordeal—first her mother and now her brother's friend? 'O Lord have mercy.' None of the trials we had recently endured even remotely compared. Clara placed her arm around her and spoke comfortingly, "Oh Shawna we're so sorry."

When we arrived at her brother's house, before letting her go, I asked Shawna, "Are you a believer in Jesus?"

Without hesitation she replied, "I am."

"I have a feeling you were crying out to God as you were walking along that path," I told her and her eyes filled with tears again. "He heard your prayer and He sent us to you so that you would know how much He loves you. No matter how dark these days seem the Lord wants you to live. Every day ahead of you from here on is going to get better and brighter."

"Thank you," she said with great emotion.

Clara and I embraced our sister and prayed with her. We gave her our phone number if she should need anything, then said our farewells and let her go.

Driving back up the highway we prayed the Lord would send both her and her brother other servants of Christ to help them through this challenging time. If we had lived there, we certainly would have made it a point to check in on them. That's when we passed through a town and the Spirit drew my attention to a large wooden cross, suspended over the main entrance of a church. Without hesitation, I turned into their parking lot and we went inside. Again, it was perfect timing, because the pastor and several of the church elders walked out to meet us, having just concluded their service. We exchanged greetings, simply introducing ourselves as "the Lord's workers," and I promptly shared Shawna's story. "The Lord drew us to your church to tell you that this family needs you," I concluded, giving them directions to the house.

They looked at my family with blank stares, standing frozen. "Maybe we should call the police," a woman finally suggested.

I had already explained Shawna's aversion to that, but how typical a response this was. "Let's call the pagans in so we can get back to feeding ourselves," says the sleeping church!

As they remained in spiritual paralysis, Clara and I made clear to them that this was their community, they were the church and it was their responsibility to take God's love to those in need. "The Lord brought us here to place this burden on you," Clara asserted.

They began making excuses to one another about it being late and how they had to get up early to "work" the next day. Do you suppose the Lord accepts one's job in the world as an excuse not to do His job? People will hardly think twice about staying up late for a party or some other engagement in revelry, but oh, how so many "Christians" have forgotten the supreme importance of making personal sacrifices for Christ's work.

> *"Who then is the faithful and wise servant, whom the master has put in charge of the servants in his household to give them their food at the proper time? It will be good for that servant whose master finds him doing so when he returns."*
> *—Matthew 24:45-46*

"Let's pray for them," the pastor offered.

'Pray?' God help them, these were the elders of that church! Why pray at a distance for those in need, when you can pray right with them? Clara and I always favor prayer, but we nearly declined. There are times to pray and times to act. This was a time to act! Yet for Shawna's sake we joined them, although we prayed God would convict this church to "Wake up!"

> *"To the angel of the church in Sardis, write: These are the words of Him who holds the seven spirits of God and the seven stars. I know your deeds; you have a reputation of being alive, but you are dead. Wake up! Strengthen what remains and is about to die, for I have not found your deeds complete in the sight of my God." —Revelations 3:1-2*

As for that pastor, does a true shepherd wait for his lost sheep to find themselves, or does he go out to find them? Moreover, when the Master of the household sends a messenger to one of His shepherds saying, *"This is where you may find my sheep,"* shall the shepherd pray the sheep find their own way home? A true shepherd would go to the lost sheep, speak the loving words of his Master, and they would recognize His Voice and be gathered into His pen:

"I have other sheep that are not of this sheep pen. I must bring them also. They too will listen to my voice, and there shall be one flock and one shepherd."
—John 10:16

There could be no mistaking that the Lord was showing us where stands the church in America today. It is the fissured foundation of our nation, pulling ever farther apart from the truth. How many churches in this country spend hours in *praise and worship,* dedicating themselves to Christ, only to falter when the call to action lands at their feet? We all have been guilty of this at one time or another, so let us not look down upon this or any other church, but rather ask ourselves, 'What would I do?' Would you spring into action or stand idle? If you pour oil in a cold frying pan it will sit in place. Pour that same oil into a lukewarm frying pan and it spreads little better. Now, if you were to remove the pan and pour oil directly onto the fire, flames would erupt with a great burst, setting fire to all in its path. This is what the Lord Commands of His people.

"So, because you are lukewarm—neither hot nor cold—I am about to spit you out of my mouth. You say, 'I am rich; I have acquired wealth and do not need a thing.' But you do not realize that you are wretched, pitiful, poor, blind and naked. I counsel you to buy from me gold refined in the fire, so you can become rich; and white clothes to wear, so you can cover your shameful nakedness; and salve to put on your eyes, so you can see." —Revelation 3:16-18

Nakedness is sin. This is why Adam and Eve hid in the Garden of Eden, and also why a young disciple had his *linen garment* stripped from him when Jesus was arrested in the Garden of Gethsemane:

A young man, wearing nothing but a linen garment, was following Jesus. When they seized him, he fled naked, leaving his garment behind.
—Mark 14:51-52

Whoever he was, when that disciple abandoned Christ, he was stripped of his linen garment, meaning he lost his *righteousness:*

"Fine linen, bright and clean, was given her to wear." (Fine linen stands for the righteous acts of the saints.) —Revelations 19:8

The *"her"* is the Bride of Christ—the Church, and the *"saints"* are her members, meaning you and every other true servant of Christ. Therefore a Christian who has his *"fine linen"* stripped from him is guilty of *disobedience* to

God, the most basic sin, for his righteousness is dependent upon *obedience.* It was disobedience that condemned Adam and Eve. It was disobedience that doomed the Israel of old. It will be disobedience that lays waste to the churches of this age that are content to *play* church but are unwilling to *act* as the church. The Scripture does not say 'righteous thoughts' or 'intentions' or even 'prayers'; it says: *"righteous acts."*

> *If one of you says to him, "Go, I wish you well; keep warm and well fed," but does nothing about his physical needs, what good is it? In the same way, faith by itself, if it is not accompanied by action, is dead. —James 2:16-17*

At another stage of our journey, my family bore witness of yet another 'play church,' this one in Arizona. Following the Spirit, we were led to a church service wherein the pastor dramatically called upon his congregation to tireless pursue "just one more" soul for the Kingdom of Heaven. Immediately after this sermon, the congregation bolted for the parking lot, got in their cars and sped off, many presumably to their air-conditioned living rooms to catch the ballgames on their big-screen televisions. On their way out, however, they could not avoid passing by two black children, a girl and her younger brother, who were stationed at the only exit, holding a sign that read, 'Need to help mom pay rent.'

> *"The King will reply, 'I tell you the truth, whatever you did for one of the least of these brothers of mine, you did for me.'" —Matthew 25:40*

This predominantly white affluent community paid them little notice. As cars impatiently exited the parking lot, one old pickup did stop to give the boy some money, but a Mercedes nearly ran him over! Had they not heard their pastor's sermon? I do testify that he had spoken Spirit-inspired words, but what good are they if left in the ears of the listeners, and do not extend to the hands and feet?

My family parked, got out of our Tahoe and engaged these children, testifying the love of Jesus, and gave them what we had, literally half of our net worth at the time—again a joke by former standards. Either way, we quickly learned that their single mother had moved with her six children down from New York for a job, only to be laid off. They had one more week before they were to be evicted. Gesturing tearfully to the church members breezing by, the sister said, "The Bible says the church is supposed to help those in need, so here we are. But it's difficult, because they don't do what God's Word says."

We understood, because we had by that time suffered much from the church's sense of giving. Clara comforted her and said, "Not everybody disobeys."

> *As he looked up, Jesus saw the rich putting their gifts into the temple treasury. He also saw a poor widow put in two very small copper coins. "I tell you the truth," he said, "this poor widow has put in more than all the others. All these people gave their gifts out of their wealth; but she out of her poverty put in all she had to live on." —Luke 21:1-4*

My family can testify that our needs have been sustained by a select number of faithful believers in Christ who, like that widow, have steadily given *out of their poverty* in the midst these challenging economic times. Some of these were formerly in the Mercedes class of drivers, but by the Lord's grace they have been forcefully taught to divest themselves of this world and its hollow façades. They now know the Lord Jesus better than they ever did, and they don't neglect to openly praise His Name.

Later we met the children's mother, and when she saw us with them, she was afraid. Shame is a powerful tool for the enemy, an acid that eats away at the heart. When you're desperately seeking help, it says you are 'begging,' and when your children are involved, it says you are guilty of 'neglect,' and when—despite your best efforts—you cannot deliver yourself or your family from hardship, it says you are 'worthless.' These lies are designed to separate you from your Savior, who can and will deliver you if you turn to Him. Thus, Clara diffused this anxiety by walking right over and giving her a long, warm embrace. The mother said in a tearful voice, "You hug me like my mother used to." Such was the Spirit of the Lord, loving her.

> *Through Jesus, therefore, let us continually offer to God a sacrifice of praise—the fruit of lips that confess his name. And do not forget to do good and to share with others, for with such sacrifices God is pleased. —Hebrews 13:15-16*

That afternoon, my family gathered with this woman's family to *praise God* and bring them His Word, which they had missed in pursuing the help of churchgoers. By this the Lord demonstrated to them that *church* is wherever the family gathers to honor His Name, not in meaningless praise and worship confined to a church auditorium, but by the surpassingly better offering of *obedience.*

Much of the church in America ignores *the fatherless, widow and alien* in their midst by choosing to instead chase after something called *the meaning of life.* It is an entirely *selfish* enterprise inspired by the enemy, a pursuit for the *inner-self*—replete with *self-indulgence, self-gratification*, *self-achievement,* and bearing with it the *self-awareness* goal toward which the religions of the other nations strive. If you call yourself a "Christian," do not fall prey to this seductive lie, because it can only separate you from Christ. It sound like this: 'As soon as I fill *myself,* heal *myself,* love *myself,* take care of *myself,* then I will help others.' Such people become *naked* in the sight of God. You, on the other hand, have been born to wear the *fine linen, bright and clean*, in which you are to serve Jesus Christ as you are—in spite of your imperfections—so that others, like you, might be redeemed.

> *Do nothing out of selfish ambition or vain conceit, but in humility consider others better than yourselves. Each of you should look not only to your own interests, but also to the interests of others. —Philippians 2:3-4*

13

Living with Strangers

On our way to Indiana, burning fuel we could not afford, Clara and I began to feel like we were insufficiently equipped to get the job done for which we had been sent forth. Just how was our one family to awaken the whole sleeping church in America?

And what was God's answer to him? "I have reserved for myself seven thousand who have not bowed the knee to Baal." —Romans 11:4

Without a doubt, we were not alone. There are others out there, hopefully many, boldly serving the Lord's Commands. Fortunately so, because as we drove back into the frigid North for my upcoming talk, we ran out of gas money somewhere outside of St. Louis. We weren't going to cover much ground on an empty tank!

On fumes, we pulled into a gas station and we all hopped out of the Tahoe to search *The Whale* for any spare change. We went through luggage, clothing, all kinds of gear, but finally we were forced to resort to our children's savings. It was terribly humbling to have to actually *borrow* money from our children. Aside from a car or house loan, we hadn't borrowed money from anyone since long before the kids were born.

"Hey Austin," Rielle nudged her brother, "maybe now we can be in charge, *he he...*"

When they started laughing, it restored Clara's and my joy and we laughed with them. Our children's spirits have uplifted the most difficult moments of this journey. The Lord's Light shines through them boundlessly, reminding us who is really in charge. When we promised to pay them back, they replied joyfully, "Oh come on guys, you can have it!" They were happy to be contributing to the Lord's work, vesting themselves in every way in our mission. If the world requires investments in order to have an expectation of a return then why is it so hard to understand how God requires the same? Either way, Clara and I can honestly and objectively say that our children have been exceptionally blessed by the Spirit. This is in part due to the sacrifices their parents have made, but more so as a result of their own personal sacrifices, and they have chosen to make many beyond counting.

Thanks to our children, we got to Wabash, Indiana on schedule. I entered the auditorium of a high school to deliver the Lord's message flat broke. In terms of *love*, if this event turned out to be a bust, we were going to have far greater problems than sleeping in a frigid trailer without blankets. Clara and I were cognizant of our situation, but we weren't stressed out about it, even with Thanksgiving and Christmas right around the corner. We had already been reduced to nothing in *Casketville*, so why doubt the Lord's ability to restore us now as He had then? Rather than lament our situation, we thanked the Lord for bringing us safely to our destination and trusted in His provision. Our faith had successfully been grown.

As I walked into the auditorium, I was pleased to see a good-sized group had turned out to hear the Lord's message. Like others, they responded enthusiastically to *'Christ The Lord,'* and despite not placing emphasis on my family's hardship, they filled our coffer more than the last three events combined! Praise be to Jesus, our faith was rewarded. Now we could afford to fuel up and get a heated hotel room for our sniffling children. Due to their colds, Clara and the kids had not come inside for this talk, but waited in the heated Tahoe in the parking lot. This did not, however, preclude people from seeking Clara out. When I walked out, I saw a line of folks standing outside Clara's window. No matter where we go, both men and women are determined to meet the woman crazy enough to embark on such a journey. Indeed, I thank the Lord that He gave me such a woman that does not neglect her duty to provide healing testimony to her brothers and sisters in need, regardless of her own personal trials and tribulations.

The last among these visitors to Clara's window was a woman who had nearly gone home, until the Lord convicted her to come back and offer us a room at her house for the week of Thanksgiving. She needed to clear it with her husband, but Clara and I instantly knew she was the *worthy person* we had been seeking.

One of those listening was a woman named Lydia, a dealer in purple cloth from the city of Thyatira, who was a worshiper of God. The Lord opened her heart to respond to Paul's message. When she and the members of her household were baptized, she invited us to her home. "If you consider me a believer in the Lord," she said, "come and stay at my house." And she persuaded us.

—Acts 16:14-15

We exchanged our contact information and agreed that if her husband were in agreement, we would come stay at her house. "I've never done anything like this before," she said, laughing at herself.

Late that night, we checked into a hotel and tucked our four sniffling children into their warm, makeshift beds in the hotel room. Like anyone, my family would have preferred a stable shelter; the comfort of knowing we didn't have to get up, check out, and search for another place to lay our heads the following evening, but we thanked God continually for His blessings. On a journey like ours, you have to live day by day, because you don't know what tomorrow may bring, and that is precisely what God is teaching us.

"Therefore do not worry about tomorrow, for tomorrow will worry about itself. Each day has enough trouble of its own." —Matthew 6:34

The next morning was Justin's third birthday. He was still sick, but his red nose and puffy eyes couldn't mask the light of joy upon his little face as his siblings and parents lavished him with attention. Clara has never let our children feel less than special on their birthdays, no matter what the circumstances.

Later that morning, I received a call from that woman's husband, approving of his wife's invitation. He also told me that his wife's parents had just bought a farmhouse, but wouldn't be moving in until the spring. He needed to confirm it, but he felt certain they would let us stay there through the winter. Clara and I were beside ourselves. This was exactly what we needed after so many months of bouncing from one hotel sardine can to another. Moreover, it was a realization of the testimony I had received at that Messianic Jew's house in Missouri, where the Lord had likewise provided a home for that man's family. We praised Jesus!

At checkout time, we packed up our runny-nose brood and made our way to our host's home in farm country Indiana, arriving that afternoon. Their children and ours immediately hit it off and went to play in the other room, while Clara and I sat with their parents in their living room to get better acquainted. It was a modest home, just big enough for their family, really, but for a time we would squeeze in with them. At least we wouldn't be cold. Their cast-iron wood-burning stove would see to that! In all, it was a warm and inviting place, but the master of the house was extremely tense. He seemed capable of only one expression—a glowering stare. He struck me like a piano string, over-tightened and ready to snap!

Finally, Clara pointedly asked him, "Are you okay with us staying in your house?"

He frowned and looked at his wife. "Well, frankly she's never done anything like this before, but I trust her judgment."

"Are you sure?" I asked, recognizing that his problem was fear.

"Sure, I guess. I mean none of this is mine. It belongs to the Lord. So, whatever we have, we'll share with you."

That was a proper response, but we could not ignore his disturbed spirit. It was like a vacuum sucking all the oxygen out of the room. His wife was aware of it, but seemed content that everything would work out. Of course, this was her husband and her home. Considering the safety of our four children, Clara and I could not ignore any negative sign. I decided to invite them to a speaking engagement in Lafayette that night, thinking it might help to alleviate the man's apprehension. Agreeing to come, they proceeded to show us our accommodations, a small room with two beds made ready for our arrival. It was formerly their baby room, and we were moved by their gracious gesture, displacing their youngest for us.

"So make yourselves at home," the woman told us. She then excused herself to go and milk their cow. That was something new. In our former life, we had seen plenty of cows grazing along the Texas countryside, but we had never spent any time with someone who actually owned a cow. We were definitely curious what it was like to have fresh cow's milk! With her departure, the husband's tension rose again. He kept staring out distantly, as if suddenly lost in thought.

Finally, Clara couldn't take the suspense any longer and pointedly asked him, "Are you going to hurt us?"

Somewhat taken aback, he replied, "No, I'm not gonna hurt you. If anyone should be worried, it's me. I just met you today and my children are going to be sleeping right across from you. I don't care what happens to me, but my kids are all I got." He then added, "You know, I got guns all around here."

"I understand," Clara said. "We're with the Lord, so you have nothing to fear from us." Indeed, Clara and I both understood that he was communicating his fear. One seeking to do us harm would not have disclosed anything about his weapons.

He nodded, and I asked him, "Would you like to pray with us?"

"Sure, we can pray," he agreed.

So we joined hands and prayed the Lord's blessings upon their family and home for welcoming us in. After saying "Amen" the husband opened his eyes and let out a long sigh of relief, "Phew..."

"Everything okay now?" Clara asked.

"Yeah, we're fine," he answered.

"I didn't want to offend you, but I needed to know the truth."

"No, I'm glad you asked," he assured her. "I respect that and it makes me feel better about you."

After that, Clara, the children and I went into our room to get ready for the event that night. Meanwhile, the husband sat in his living room, sapped for strength, staring at his floor in a daze. When his wife returned we prepared to leave and I followed the husband to his computer so he could print off a map to the venue. Standing in his doorway, I realized I had forgotten something:

> *"When you enter a house, first say, 'Peace to this house.' If a man of peace is there, your peace will rest on him; if not, it will return to you." —Luke 10:5-6*

Silently, I said a quick prayer to the Lord, 'Peace to this house, in Jesus' Name.' What happened next caught me by complete surprise. I can only describe it as a sensation that something went out from me then quickly came back and hit me right between the eyes. I became disoriented and lost my balance. Steadying myself, I looked at the man, but he hadn't noticed. I asked the Lord what had happened, and He said, 'Your peace came back to you.' He also reminded me that I had felt this sensation before. When I was about twelve, I once accompanied some friends from school over to their Mormon church. Soon as I walked inside I was hit with a sudden dizziness and disorientation. It was an awful feeling, and I immediately ran outside. At the time, I thought it was a gas leak, but my Mormon friends were unaffected. Little did I know—the Lord did—that a year later my family would move me to Mesa, Arizona, the Mormon's second settlement after Salt Lake City, Utah. During those subsequent adolescent years I would learn much about the demonic teachings of the Mormon faith, and most especially the one where they believe that they can become God—coequals with Christ! They may call themselves "Christians," but they are not following the true teachings of Christ. Nearly three decades later, this episode in an obscure farmhouse in Indiana taught me yet another level of truth concerning the spiritual warfare we wage against the enemy and his demonic forces. The only question now was what to do? Was it God's will that my family stay in this man's house?

Later, on the drive to Lafayette, I told Clara what had happened, concluding, "My peace came back to me."

"Are we not supposed to stay there?" she asked.

"I'm not sure," I replied.

"What about their Thanksgiving invitation, wouldn't declining after we've accepted be a negative witness?"

"I don't know. We'll see what happens this evening." After having the knowledge that my peace had come back to me, I honestly wasn't sure if their house was safe for my family.

That night, I spoke before a large group at the Ivy Tech Community College Auditorium, sitting on a panel with three experts in healthcare, economics and political science. While my fellow panelists engaged in a typical debate of worldly reason on issues ranging from healthcare to border security, I spoke about the moral imperatives taught by Christ. Two panelists seemed to sneer at my *'Christ The Lord'* testimony, but the audience received it exuberantly.

After the talk, the audience barraged my family, yet a blind woman named Pia most caught my family's attention. Her expressed devotion to Christ touched us deeply, reminding us yet again that trials and tribulations grow true faith. Though blind and single, she also invited us to stay at her home, saying, "I only have a small apartment, but my home is your home, because in Christ, we who are many form one body."

Just as each of us has one body with many members, and these members do not all have the same function, so in Christ we who are many form one body, and each member belongs to all the others. —Romans 12:4-5

Now we had a decision to make, for was our family to stay with a single blind woman with even less to give, or the man with no peace? After the crowd had gone, we finally got to reunite with that man and his wife. Sitting in the back row, they warmly greeted us and I saw an expression of relief on the husband's face. For the first time since we had met him, he was actually smiling. I realized we had underestimated the Lord's appointment. We had also doubted His Word, which already told us what we must do.

"Stay in that house, eating and drinking whatever they give you, for the worker deserves his wages. Do not move around from house to house." —Luke 10:7

Even if my *peace* did not rest upon the man, we were not to *move around from house to house.* The Lord had led us to that family, so we had to trust that He would protect us and manage any anxiety issues until our time in their household had completed His purpose.

"So are we staying there?" Clara asked me on the drive back.

"We just can't underestimate the Lord," I answered. "I thought for sure one night would be it, but you saw the difference in him."

"Yes, I did," she agreed. "I felt that whatever had a hold on him was released when we prayed in his kitchen."

"If the Lord says, 'Stay,' we stay. When He says, 'Go,' we'll go."

Often it's easier to say what is right then to do it, but in my family's case we have often had no choice but to follow through on our stated convictions. I thank God for this, because as we stayed in their home, celebrating Thanksgiving with their family, everything was surprisingly peaceful—just as the Lord had appointed. Their parents also followed through with providing us their farmhouse. It was dilapidated, with its old dusty carpets, leaning walls and red iron-tainted water. Truthfully, Clara and I would never have considered taking up residence in such a place before this journey, but after being so humbled—and giving it a thorough cleaning—we received it as a blessing and a comfort. We especially enjoyed the warmth of its wood-burning iron stove all through the ice-cold month of December. Still, none of that mattered to the kids, because they were delighted to find several abandoned bunnies on the property. They dubbed the place the *"Bunny Farm."* Chasing after these furry *"pets"* kept them busy on a daily basis. They actually managed to capture three, naming them *Gypo, Mit* and *Fuzzy*. Before Clara would let the kids play with them, she insisted on giving them a *"bath."* I'll never forget those wild bunnies' eyes bulging out of their tiny heads as Clara held them down in the kitchen sink, lathering them with lavender-scented soap. The kids had read something about calming bunnies by holding them upside down, so Clara held them up by their hind legs. Those poor bunnies were just sure the boiling pot was next! "No mom!" the children admonished her. "You're supposed to cradle the bunny like a baby."

Little did we know it when we originally set out from Texas, otherwise Clara might have collapsed right at the outset, but over the course of our three and a half year journey our family has been required live in some thirty different homes of perfect strangers in seven different states. Of course, none of them remained strangers after we met them, but you can be sure that it taught us quite a bit about people in general. Not only do you discover what they look like before they have a chance to groom and get that first cup of coffee in the morning, but you realize that none of us, even in Christ, are perfect. So, if the Lord should ever send you forth on His business before strangers, or send some strangers to you, be patient with one another. Some of us are further along in our walks with Christ than others, while some feel they are further along than they really are. Nonetheless, as Pia had told us, we are all a part of the same family in Christ. What a blessed gift the Lord bestowed upon my family to force us—and condition us—to spend time on this journey *living with strangers.*

> *"He who receives you receives me, and he who receives me receives the one who sent me. Anyone who receives a prophet because he is a prophet will receive a prophet's reward, and anyone who receives a righteous man because he is a righteous man will receive a righteous man's reward. And if anyone gives even a cup of cold water to one of these little ones because he is my disciple, I tell you the truth, he will certainly not lose his reward." —Matthew 10:40-42*

14

Master of the Harvest

Following the Lord's will can be challenging. One day you're told to go north, the next you're told south. Sometimes you're told to speak and other times to remain silent. Likewise, my family had been told to *'Go, go, go!'* for the last eight months, only to be told to suddenly *'Stand still!'* when came the month of December 2009.

> *"Be still, and know that I am God; I will be exalted among the nations, I will be exalted in the earth." —Psalm 46:10*

It's not the Lord who needs to speak clearer, but the servant who needs to listen better. For months, I had been speaking to politically minded groups, proclaiming *'Christ The Lord'* as the alternative to the lesser of two evils. The majority received this testimony when first delivered, but over time the enemy was able to steer many away from the truth, convincing them to foolishly reinvest their hope in the lies of this world. Not understanding the biblical truth unfolding before me, I began *"bucking the bull"* as we say down in Texas.

I felt like the Lord was trying to tell me to back off these groups and refocus my energy on the church in America, which was finally opening its doors. However, I rebuffed these notions, convincing myself that nothing significant is accomplished without hard work and perseverance, in which case I did not wish to let go of the fields I had sown. While this seems logical, it is not the way of the Spirit. Can a man command the rains to come and water his field or the pests to leave it alone? Of course not, and we forget that not even the fields belong to us.

"Who has a claim against me that I must pay? Everything under heaven belongs to me." —Job 41:11

As the Lord has often done, He sent Clara and me more than one witness to reveal how we were being received and where the masses were disconnecting from the truth He had sent us forth to proclaim. When the words you are sent forth to speak in the Lord's Name are rejected, this naturally lends the flesh to wonder just why you are bothering to sacrifice your life, and the lives of your wife and children, for the sake of ingrates. Frustrated one day, I began sharing with Clara, "The problem with this country is that it thinks everything has to be a *2+2=4* equation. But with the Lord, 2+2 can be a hundred or more! *2+2=4* never would have worked for Gideon and his 300 warriors going up against that Midianite army of 135,000!"

The LORD said to Gideon, "You have too many men for me to deliver Midian into their hands. In order that Israel may not boast against me that her own strength has saved her, announce now to the people, 'Anyone who trembles with fear may turn back and leave Mount Gilead.'" So twenty-two thousand men left, while ten thousand remained. —Judges 7:2-3

What the Lord was teaching Gideon then we must remember today. Because America has forgotten its God, we shall not be permitted to deliver ourselves from our troubles, for then we would only glorify ourselves. No righteousness would be restored and we would continue using *2+2=4* as an excuse to break every one of the Lord's Commandments. Thus, in His infinite wisdom and kindness, the Lord draws us kicking and screaming into repentance.

Or do you show contempt for the riches of his kindness, tolerance and patience, not realizing that God's kindness leads you toward repentance? —Romans 2:4

In her own gentle way, Clara reminded me that preaching to the choir never advances the playing field. Of course she was right, but the Lord served up a second witness a couple of days later when I was invited on a talk radio program in Chicago. The host who interviewed me was also the pastor of a local church. Although he was inspired by our journey, he just could not get past the fact that I had not formulated a plan for America's restoration.

"You've got to have a plan," he insisted, "a ten point plan, thirty point plan—something. Everybody has some sort of plan!"

"No manmade plan can do what needs to be done," I told him. "You are a minister, right? Turn to Acts of the Apostles in the Bible. That's the plan. If we follow it today, it will work."

After the program, we talked off-air and he said, "You see, I'm a *2+2=4* kind of guy..."

I was patient with my brother in Christ, but it was difficult. Did not even the shepherds of the church in America believe in the Power of the Almighty anymore? Was it Moses or the Lord who parted the waters of the deep for His people? Was it Joshua or the Lord who brought down the walls of Jericho? Unfortunately, ministers dislike being preached to even more than their congregations do. Somehow, because they have a theology degree, they believe only the elders of their religious institution have something to teach them. Yet, the Lord will use even our children to teach us, if we have ears to listen.

At that time Jesus said, "I praise you, Father, Lord of heaven and earth, because you have hidden these things from the wise and learned, and revealed them to little children." —Matthew 11:25

A third confirming witness was delivered in a snippet I caught in the news a couple of months later about Newt Gingrich's speech given at the CPAC 2010 convention. His theme was none other than *"2+2=4."* You just can't make this stuff up. The timing is incredible! It teaches you that not only does everything *under heaven* belong to God, but also everything *that happens* under it. It is His to approve, His to judge, and His to order so that through conspicuous circumstances He might teach His struggling disciples how to better understand, accept and fulfill His will.

Do not conform any longer to the pattern of this world, but be transformed by the renewing of your mind. Then you will be able to test and approve what God's will is—his good, pleasing and perfect will. —Romans 12:2

Yet again, if Shadrach, Meshach and Abednego had looked upon the flames of that furnace into which Nebuchadnezzar's soldiers were about to throw them from a *2+2=4* standpoint, then 2+2=BURNED TO A CRISP! Instead, they believed that *with God all things are possible*, and that was precisely what the Lord was trying to teach us at this particular stage of our journey. You see, by this time in our walk of faith I had come to a realization that only God could affect material changes for the betterment of America's future. Nonetheless, I still had to learn that only the Lord's Spirit could likewise affect spiritual changes in the hearts of His people. This happens not by measure of man's reason, nor the cunning of we who are the Lord's servants, but only in accordance with God's purpose and timing. Therefore, do you suppose that Shadrach, Meshach and Abednego walked into that fire knowing their lives would be spared, or did they do it willing to sacrifice their lives to honor the Lord their God?

"Do not be afraid of those who kill the body but cannot kill the soul. Rather, be afraid of the One who can destroy both soul and body in hell."

—Matthew 10:28

Still, at the time, Clara and I struggled to get past just how far the church in America has fallen. It bred a sense of hopelessness in our hearts. Time and again, we witnessed purported *believers* and their churches fall away from the truth given them and into the enemy's trap. They kept asking themselves, 'What's in it for me?' After witnessing so much of this, Clara and I began falling for the same temptation by asking ourselves, 'What are we suffering for?' Like it or not, the enemy is constantly seeking to convince those who serve the Lord that our work is either foolish, fruitless, or both.

I know that after I leave, savage wolves will come in among you and will not spare the flock. Even from your own number men will arise and distort the truth in order to draw away disciples after them. —Acts 20:29-30

History doesn't change. Nations may rise and fall, lands may be discovered and abandoned, but what has been done before will be done again. As it was for the apostle Paul, so we discovered. While it is sad to see an individual deny the Truth, it is sadder still when one who has accepted it falls away. In the world, a corporate CEO seeks a demonstrable return on his investment, but people who claim to serve Christ cannot operate this way. A corporation will make calculated adjustments to a poor-selling product or drop it altogether. A servant of Christ cannot, however, dispense with the truth, whether the recipient receives it. The truth is neither moldable by the hands of man, nor is it for sale, but it is free for all who are willing to accept it *as is.*

"This is the verdict: Light has come into the world, but men loved darkness instead of light because their deeds were evil." —John 3:19

What God Most High requires is that we seek His Face, meaning we have had it with the darkness and have regained our hunger for the Light. When we seek righteousness, not out of a desire for selfish gain, but in a true heartfelt repentance, then more than we desire shall be given. Unfortunately, the collective heart of America remains calloused and refuses to repent. For this reason, the Lord has determined to put away the carrots and pull out the sticks. When, through humbling, the calloused hearts of His people in America are pierced they will reflect on the truth His messengers proclaimed, embrace a heartfelt repentance, and at last realize a restoration. But how much must this nation suffer before it turns from its wickedness, and will it before it's too late?

Rather than letting the Lord's Word stand on its own and sprout in its due time, as I said, I kept *"bucking the bull."* Time and again, I readdressed the truth with groups and churches that had already refused to receive it. The harder I pushed, the further they strayed and the more time I realized I was wasting. So, the Lord's solution for my stubbornness was to render my whole family *still* with a terrible flu just before Christmas. It was fierce! We had never been so sick in our lives. It was so bad, our children turned down Christmas cookies! We had pink eye, strep throat, chest infections, ear infections, and who knows what else, because we could not afford to go to the doctor for a diagnosis. Either the *Doctor* was going to heal us or we were all going to the emergency room, and this was precisely His point. We knelt down and asked the Lord to spare us, and He did. First, He kept our little Jazelle and Justin from the worst of it, which could easily have jeopardized their lives. He also healed the rest of us, doing the work for which people of this world typical run to antibiotics. By the time we welcomed the 2010 New Year our *stillness* had taught me not to fight the *Lord's will!* We resolved ourselves to wait on the Lord, and so He sent us back into His harvest field to work the soil again, beginning with Ohio.

During this time I began asking the Lord, 'What is it about Ohio?' Our first introduction to the state had come during the last weeks of the 2008 elections when I was traveling aboard the presidential candidate's bus. Since putting out from Texas, Ohio had consistently opened her doors to us. Even as winter crept in and we desperately sent *lots* out to groups and churches in Florida, Texas, Arizona, California and any other warm climate, it was Ohio that continued to beckon. I knew the Lord was trying to tell us something, because there have been *no* coincidences on this journey. Thus, as we ventured into Ohio in the dead of winter, the Lord began to answer my question through His designated witnesses.

First, you must understand that Ohio is the *bellwether* state of our times, meaning its broad diversity in color, culture and class makes it a perfect pulse for the rest of the nation. This is why, during presidential elections, you hear, *"As Ohio goes, so goes the rest of the nation."* With only two exceptions, Ohio has decided the victor of every presidential contest since 1896. Secondly, Ohio's mottos are not without meaning, for she is called *"The Heart of It All,"* and more appropriately, her official motto is *"With God All Things Are Possible."*

Jesus looked at them and said, "With man this is impossible, but with God all things are possible." —Matthew 19:26

Finally, as my family toured various parts of the state, we met other servants of Christ who had likewise been called to Ohio from around the world. Each expressed a similar sentiment that Ohio was going to be the epicenter of something special, not only for America, but for the world.

The thought that struck me about Ohio, and I quickly realized it was the Holy Spirit, was 'What better place to begin a restoration than in the heart, for when the heart is pierced with the truth, the rest of the body soon follows.' Thus, it was in Ohio that the doors of the religious establishments really began to open. Many Ohioans who heard me speak took it upon themselves to spread the *'Christ The Lord'* testimony and the call to *repentance* throughout their communities and churches. Although not every religious establishment subsequently welcomed us in, many invitations sprouted throughout the entire state. By the spring, we felt as if the Lord was telling us to remain in Ohio, because He had many people in this state:

One night the Lord spoke to Paul in a vision: "Do not be afraid; keep on speaking, do not be silent. For I am with you, and no one is going to attack and harm you, because I have many people in this city." —Acts 18:9-10

Nonetheless, it wasn't all smooth sailing along the way. Although many first received the word the Lord had given us with joy, as had occurred in Indiana and elsewhere, a certain biblical truth kept cropping up time and again. It was the parable of the seed:

"The farmer sows the word. Some people are like seed along the path, where the word is sown. As soon as they hear it, Satan comes and takes away the word that was sown in them. Others, like seed sown on rocky places, hear the word

and at once receive it with joy. But since they have no root, they last only a short time. When trouble or persecution comes because of the word, they quickly fall away. Still others, like seed sown among thorns, hear the word; but the worries of this life, the deceitfulness of wealth and the desires for other things come in and choke the word, making it unfruitful. Others, like seed sown on good soil, hear the word, accept it, and produce a crop—thirty, sixty or even a hundred times what was sown." —*Mark 4:14-20*

Some of the pastors and priests, who at first welcomed us in with open arms, later turned their backs on our mission and attempted to discredit the truth the Lord had sent us forth to proclaim. One pastor, after I had spoken more than once in his church, later told me defiantly, "I thank God I have *the lesser of two evils* to vote for." These recurring betrayals were painful, heart-breaking and discouraging, but no more than Christ suffered for us all. After all, it was His chosen apostle who handed Him over to the Sanhedrin to be persecuted and His very own children who crucified Him later that day.

No matter the excuses given, the primary reason both shepherds and sheep reject the truth is that they love the world, their money and themselves more than they love their Savior. You can pry their eyes open for a moment to see the truth, but many just can't stand their reflection in the mirror, so they shut them again.

"Everyone who does evil hates the light, and will not come into the light for fear that his deeds will be exposed. But whoever lives by the truth comes into the light, so that it may be seen plainly that what he has done has been done through God." —*John 3:20-21*

One night, I was afforded an opportunity to briefly address a gathering of ministers, pastors and missionaries at a church in Central Ohio. The main event that night was a message given by a charismatic pastor, the founder of a large profitable ministry. At the end of that night, I came over to meet him along with another brother in Christ whose family we were staying with at the time. Soon as I walked up this pastor and held out my hand to shake his, he began backing away. The closer I inched towards him, the further he moved away. He could hardly look me in the eye and couldn't seem to stand still. I call him *Pastor Ants in the Pants.*

On the drive back to his house, I asked my brother in Christ, "Did you see him backing away?"

He chuckled, "Yes, I sure did."

"What's that all about?"

"It's your zeal, my brother. It's like you're a mirror, reminding them of their inequities."

My family has encountered this dynamic repeatedly over the course of our journey. While it's normal for those harboring the enemy to react to us with repulsion, what's most disappointing is when you come into contact with a supposed brother or sister in Christ who can hardly stand to be in the same room with you.

In all this, the Lord was making it clear that *He* alone is the *Master of the harvest.* Still, just as I had been sent to others to confirm what the Lord was already speaking to them, so too I unexpectedly found myself before a Spirit-filled minister at a small church in Lima, Ohio. Knowing hardly anything about me or my family's mission, he invited me into his office where the Spirit came upon him. Firmly he stated, "The Lord wants me to tell you that your responsibility is the seed. You are the master of the seed and it's your job to spread it wherever you go. But only the Lord is the Master of the harvest. Don't concern yourself with the harvest, because that's His responsibility."

For the word of God is living and active. Sharper than any double-edged sword, it penetrates even to dividing soul and spirit, joints and marrow; it judges the thoughts and attitudes of the heart. —Hebrews 4:12

I was cut to the heart, even speechless—a rarity for me. It's what a brother in Christ calls, *"reading your mail."* I hadn't shared anything with this pastor about the burden on my heart, yet the Holy Spirit knew what He had been trying to get through my thick skull for months. Praise be to Jesus, because He wanted me to be at peace with the knowledge that I was fulfilling my duty in sowing the seed.

He also said, "This is what the kingdom of God is like. A man scatters seed on the ground. Night and day, whether he sleeps or gets up, the seed sprouts and grows, though he does not know how. All by itself the soil produces grain—first the stalk, then the head, then the full kernel in the head. As soon as the grain is ripe, he puts the sickle to it, because the harvest has come." —Mark 4:26-29

Despite the disappointments, my family also received encouragements, enough to keep us trudging ahead. On my birthday, the Lord blessed me with one such encounter after a Sunday service we attended in Van Wert, Ohio. It was one of the few times I wasn't speaking somewhere, for the Lord had appointed me to listen rather than speak. As we stood outside the sanctuary after the service, an older man I had never met came up to me and said with excitement, "In Sunday school this morning I heard the greatest thing!"

"What's that?" I asked, recognizing the Lord's appointment.

"You know how we're always being stuck with *the lesser of two evils* on voting day?"

Knowing what he was about to say, an incredible feeling erupted in my heart. "Sure do," I replied.

"Well, all you have to do is write in *'Christ The Lord.'* Isn't that great!" he exclaimed.

"Absolutely," I told him, hardly able to contain my emotions.

"I gotta tell everyone I know about this!" He proclaimed joyfully.

That was some birthday gift! I realized he had either heard it from someone who had heard me proclaim it, or from a secondary or tertiary source that had passed it on. Do you see how one seed planted can *produce a crop—thirty, sixty or even a hundred times what was sown?*

Another witness to the Lord's harvesting ability would be given in the form of an Ohio State assemblyman whom I had met while giving a talk to a Putnam County patriot group in February 2010. With his arms folded and a smirk on his face he took me to task on the practical nature of my assertions that his constituents must vote *'Christ The Lord'* if no candidate would stand upright in Christ. I told him, "It would be good for you to lose your job over doing what is right in the sight of the Lord." As the Lord had by then told me, I specifically cited that his first and foremost priority ought to be to restore the Sanctity of Human Life to Ohio, adding, "A people who forsake their wallets to do the Lord's will first shall receive prosperity and life as well. But a people who ignore God's will, seeking first to protect their wallets, will have everything taken away from them." I made it clear to him that although he may represent Ohioans in the General Assembly, his first and foremost duty was to be a proper representative of his Lord and Savior, Jesus Christ.

This representative told me that he was firmly "Pro-Life," believing that *life* begins at conception, but asked, "Who is going to support me if I make this my top priority rather than jobs?" I turned to the group and asked them if they had heard what their representative, a fellow brother in Christ, had just asked. I told them that if they wanted this representative to fight for a restoration to God Most High and Jesus Christ, they were going to have to stand firmly behind him with their voices, their wallets and their votes. Otherwise, if even the church won't back them up, what candidate in Christ has a chance of being elected? What then will the tolerant and complacent church in America say on the day of disaster when the fierce anger of the Lord falls upon this wicked and adulterous nation? I promise you that the vast shedding of the innocent blood of the unborn now saturating this nation from *end to end* will be avenged *life for life* if we do not repent by turning from this wickedness. Yet, how can a nation that has legalized this innocent bloodshed accomplish repentance, unless it appoints leadership after the heart of Christ who will fight to abolish this terrible injustice?

> *Moreover, Manasseh also shed so much innocent blood that he filled Jerusalem from end to end—besides the sin that he had caused Judah to commit, so that they did evil in the eyes of the LORD. —2 Kings 21:16*

In the midst of all this, a professional photographer arrived at the meeting and she began snapping shots from various angles around the room. At first, I thought she might have been one of the representative's staffers, but later learned the Spirit of the Lord had called her out from her home that night, telling her to witness and record this *"important"* event. She specifically witnessed the Holy Spirit come upon me and convict our brother the representative. Even so, I felt as though I had failed to change his perspective before he left that night. I later shared with Clara my frustrations, saying, "If only they understood the value of siding with the Lord. It really is better to lose your job rather than to forsake your Savior." Again, I was looking for the harvest, but the Harvester had His own plan.

More than a year later, while my family continued the Lord's work in Arizona, that lady photographer sent me an email concerning something called the "Heartbeat Bill," which promises to ban abortions once a fetal heartbeat is detected. If passed, this proposed Ohio legislation would be the most aggressive anti-abortion law in the nation. It was championed by Lynn Wachtmann, the very representative whom the Spirit had challenged that night in Putnam County. Despite surprising opposition from Right To Life, the Ohio House passed the measure on June 29, 2011. This bill now sits dead in the hands of a supposedly Pro-Life dominated Senate.

The Lord's plans and timing are perfect. By His appointment, on September 5, 2009 I gave a keynote speech to thousands of Ohioans at the Voices of America Park in West Chester. Among those also present that day were soon-to-be Ohio Governor John Kasich and soon-to-be United States Speaker of the House John Boehner. Did they receive the seed that day? After speaking to Representative Wachtmann in February, I was also led before Ohio Senator Cliff Hite on Good Friday, April 2, 2010 at a candidate forum at the Findlay Elks Lodge. Unfortunately, the Lord's message was soundly rejected that day in favor of *money-politics,* including by Senator Hite, who was running for reelection. In another year Hite would sign on to support the Heartbeat Bill, promising to shepherd it through the Senate approval process. Yet the Lord had already shown me the Ohio Senate's forthcoming rejection.

> *"For I know the plans I have for you," declares the LORD, "plans to prosper you and not to harm you, plans to give you hope and a future."*
>
> *—Jeremiah 29:11*

After the Benevolent Protective Order of Elks had me escorted from their building that day, my heart was crushed. Still, the Lord knew *the plans He had made,* plans no man can thwart. I took my family to the local fairgrounds that afternoon where our children joined others at play on a giant sand hill at Roger Powell's Christ Resurrection Sand Sculpture, which he does annually in celebration of Resurrection Day. In the midst of their fun, little Jazelle rose up from the sand and came over to me. "Daddy, daddy, look what I found," she said, holding out a penny with a cross punched out of the center of it in the palm of her tiny hand. Her face shined bright with excitement, having found "buried treasure." Indeed it was, because as I examined it more closely, I saw a small gap in the center of the sand-filled cross in the near perfect shape of a heart. At that moment, I could feel the Spirit telling me that His heart was with me, because my heart was with Him.

But the Lord's harvest plans would get even more intriguing when in August of that same year I spoke on the phone with Ohio Right To Life's late chief lobbyist, Mark Lally, a former president and the purported "heart and soul" of their organization. The Spirit led me to this call to test their heart, directing me to ask this man a presumably silly question. So I asked, "Have you ever endorsed a candidate who was not Pro Life?"

Knowing nothing about me or my mission in Christ, he said hesitantly, "Well, when we have a *lesser of two evils* situation, we give them what's called a 'preferred status.'"

I proceeded to tell him the Lord's message about the *lesser of two evils* and stressed the urgency that the Sanctity of Human Life be made the highest law of the land—not in pieces, because the Lord has given this nation no time for that, but in one fell stroke. Not surprisingly, he rejected the Lord's will, citing "practicalities" and "fears" about a Supreme Court contest. Although he reluctantly admitted to being a "Christian," he did not see Christ as the Answer. Instead, he spoke of *"human rights."* Ultimately, he revealed that Right To Life's heart is in their organization—meaning in themselves, and not in Christ. This is not to say that volunteers do not have their hearts in the right place, because I can testify many do, but their leadership dictates where their money is spent.

Whether you serve Christ on the frontlines or in the supply camp, trust the Lord to manage His own harvest. If you march where told and plant the seeds you are given, the Lord will send the rains, as well as other workers to weed and feed as necessary. Therefore, the seeds of truth I am sowing into you are thus: In order to fulfill the Lord's requirement for repentance, the church in America must make the Sanctity of Human Life (SOHL), from conception to natural death, the highest law of the land, and Ohio, as the heart, must lead the way. There can be no exceptions! The Heartbeat Bill didn't fail because of inept and corrupt politicians. Who is man that he should oppose God? It failed because the church in America remains asleep, and because Pro-Lifers are too willing to make compromises, even though God will never accept half-measures concerning His definition of Life. How long will you listen to *experts* who cower to a Supreme Court whose walls the Lord can shake into submission over night? Does the Sanctity of Human Life belong to any political organization, or to the Church in Christ? Time is running out. If you, as part of the Church, rise up and vocally demand it, refusing to support the lesser of two evils that cares only for their wallets, then the Lord, *by His Spirit,* will deliver the harvest:

> *So he said to me, "This is the word of the LORD to Zerubbabel: 'Not by might nor by power, but by my Spirit,'" says the LORD Almighty. —Zechariah 4:6*

15

The Truth Serum

As the Lord led my family out from the *Bunny Farm* and into Ohio, it became clear that the predominant church in America does not know how to discern the lesser of two evils from a candidate in Christ. If a candidate for office says, "I'm for one nation under God!" how do you know whether they're speaking of God Most High and Jesus Christ or some meaningless universalist "god"? Even if a candidate says, "I'm Christian," is that enough? Mormon's and Jehovah's Witnesses say that, as do many whose conduct is anything but "Christian." Yet if any of these had actually "witnessed" the Living God, they would have abandoned their religious and hypocritical lies. Similarly, many so-called "Conservatives" claim to be Pro-Life, but how can you trust that when upwards of a million babies are still being slaughtered every year through abortion? In effect, the church needs a *Truth Serum*.

> *Dear friends, do not believe every spirit, but test the spirits to see whether they are from God, because many false prophets have gone out into the world. This is how you can recognize the Spirit of God: Every spirit that acknowledges that Jesus Christ has come in the flesh is from God, but every spirit that does not acknowledge Jesus is not from God. This is the spirit of the antichrist, which you have heard is coming and even now is already in the world. —1 John 4:1-3*

Because we humans cannot see into each other's hearts—save by the Holy Spirit, we must ask pointed and proving questions that can reveal true intensions. If you believe in the Lord your God and ask Him to reveal the truth, then I assure you He will. Even the most polished politician cannot successfully lie to a trained servant of Christ who is pressing him for the truth. No matter how hard the politician tries to conceal it, his true heart will be revealed.

"When you are brought before synagogues, rulers and authorities, do not worry about how you will defend yourselves or what you will say, for the Holy Spirit will teach you at that time what you should say." —Luke 12:11-12

Since leaving Texas, I have had the opportunity to testify the truth to many *rulers and authorities,* and in doing so, the Lord has exposed our nation's rebellion in three core sins: We shed innocent blood in this country and call it a *"human right."* We advocate the culture of Sodom and Gomorrah, justifying it as an *"equal right."* Finally, and worst of all, we deny our Lord and Savior Jesus Christ by denying His Name, His Word, His Cross and His Gospel from the public square under a lie called *"religious rights."* Any nation that thinks it can long survive while persisting in innocent bloodshed and sexual immorality has lost its mind, but the one that believes it can tell the King He is unwelcome on His own footstool has gone absolutely insane! What man can tell the Lord God who created the whole universe where He can and cannot walk? This rebellion is more than stupid—it's deadly. Therefore, if you want to turn your nation from disaster, before you decide to support, fund or endorse any candidate on any ballot, you must first apply the following Truth Serum, which will distinctly reveal a candidate's position on these issues:

First, any candidate competing for any office must vow to make the Sanctity of Human Life their foremost priority by stalwartly opposing any policy or law, either proposed or in effect, that permits the shedding of innocent blood. Jesus Christ is the only Way, the Truth and *the Life;* therefore one cannot be with Christ and view Life as a matter of human choice. A candidate who so much as hints that a money issue might take precedence over Life fails this test, for this is the seductive excuse that has kept Roe v. Wade standing as the highest law of the land for nearly 40 years.

"Woe to him who builds a city with bloodshed and establishes a town by crime! Has not the LORD Almighty determined that the people's labor is only fuel for the fire, that the nations exhaust themselves for nothing?" —Habakkuk 2:12-13

Secondly, any candidate seeking any office must vow that he or she will fight against any policy or law, either proposed or in effect, that promotes or in any way condones the moral depravity of Sodom and Gomorrah. God destroyed these cities because they worshipped themselves, living to please their flesh rather than to serve their Creator. America today is likewise *filled with every kind of wickedness, evil, greed and depravity.* The Lord will restore a repentant nation, but one that seeks to justify these sins, such as by passing a statute that approves "gay marriage," will be destroyed.

> *In a similar way, Sodom and Gomorrah and the surrounding towns gave themselves up to sexual immorality and perversion. They serve as an example of those who suffer the punishment of eternal fire. —Jude 1:7*

Finally, in any candidate competing for any office We The Church must seek one who has the heart of David, who demonstrates a fervent desire to fight for a restoration to God Most High and Jesus Christ, regardless of any threat Goliath spits out of his lying mouth. This means that he or she will courageously oppose any policy or law, either proposed or in effect, that seeks to remove Christ from the national public square; including the Ten Commandments being displayed within our nation's courtrooms, the teaching of the Holy Bible within our classrooms, the preaching of the Gospel on any public property, and honoring the cross of Christ anywhere within our borders. A candidate who will not honor Jesus Christ, the Author of all truth, cannot be trusted, because he honors himself. He is a *hired hand* who will abandon the needs of the flock when the wolf threatens. A servant of Christ, however, will demonstrate the heart of David, who loved the flock and risked his own life to protect it—not because he was great, but because his love for his Savior and understanding of God's judgment was great.

> *"I tell you the truth, until heaven and earth disappear, not the smallest letter, not the least stroke of a pen, will by any means disappear from the Law until everything is accomplished. Anyone who breaks one of the least of these commandments and teaches others to do the same will be called least in the kingdom of heaven, but whoever practices and teaches these commands will be called great in the kingdom of heaven." —Matthew 5:18-19*

If a candidate fails to pass any one element of the above Truth Serum then I assure you he or she is not with Christ and in reality has failed them all. Such a candidate is an evildoer, whether lesser or greater, and you must not support, fund, or endorse them in any way. It doesn't matter how good they are at anything they do, you cannot trust anyone who rebels against Christ and His teachings. To empower a person on worldly credentials alone is not wisdom:

"The fear of the LORD is the beginning of wisdom, and knowledge of the Holy One is understanding." —Proverbs 9:10

On this note, remember that every ambitious politician has to begin somewhere, so apply the Truth Serum to every candidate at every level. Today's school board candidate could be tomorrow's presidential candidate. Today's county judge could be tomorrow's Supreme Court Justice. Politicians climb government like business people climb corporate ladders, so weed out the bad seeds right from the start. Where you can find no candidate for any given office on a ballot who passes the Truth Serum, then you must instead write in *'Christ The Lord.'* In this you will cleanse your hands of the evil committed by this nation's elected leadership, taking a decisive stand for your Savior. The rest is in God's capable Hands.

To give you an example of how this Truth Serum can work, I once applied it at a candidate forum at a church in Huntington, Indiana, featuring candidates for the U.S. Senate. Citing the Truth Serum, I asked any candidate who would take a stand for the Lord to join me on stage, warning them not to equivocate. The audience was so inspired they arose to their feet in ovation, but not one candidate came forward. Actually, they were in shock. I had to pose the challenge a second time before they overcame their political paralysis and started coming forward one by one, realizing the hearts of the voters were with the Lord.

Elijah went before the people and said, "How long will you waver between two opinions? If the LORD is God, follow him; but if Baal is God, follow him." But the people said nothing. —1 Kings 18:21

Their hesitation spoke volumes, but I do not condemn them, because everyone—politician or civilian—has to make a decision about taking a stand with Christ. Perhaps this was the first occasion where someone had challenged them to do so. All my family desires is that the truth is revealed. After that, people can decide for themselves who or what to follow, such as one candidate that night did not join me on the stage. Ironically, but not surprisingly, he was a recognized "Christian conservative" and purported "constitutional expert" who had already served multiple terms in the United States Congress. In case voters that night didn't witness his misaligned priorities, during a subsequent forum in Crown Point he defiantly asserted that God is to be separated from the state and that his "master" was the Constitution. He proved the Truth Serum works.

> *Jesus called them together and said, "You know that those who are regarded as rulers of the Gentiles lord it over them, and their high officials exercise authority over them. Not so with you.* ***Instead, whoever wants to become great among you must be your servant, and whoever wants to be first must be slave of all.*** *For even the Son of Man did not come to be served, but to serve, and to give his life as a ransom for many." —Mark 10:42-45*

No piece of paper written by flawed men can make a good servant. Only the Living Word can do that. Understand that the U.S. Constitution was once used to justify slavery, it has robbed many of their civil liberties, and for forty long years it has sustained the innocent bloodshed of the unborn. It is also being used in an attempt to dispossess Christ of His own footstool. Thus, one who trumpets the "Constitution," but hardly whispers "Jesus Christ" will most assuredly *lord their authority over you.* In case you haven't noticed, they already are. Such are those who live by their own standards of morality. They are capable of any evil under the sun that meets with their selfish interests. Alternatively, a true servant of Christ will follow the heart of Jesus and submit himself to you as a *slave.* This does not mean he becomes lowly, mind you. The children of Israel, for example, did not hoist Moses upon their shoulders and honor him like a king. God was their King, and He honored Moses, but Israel abused Moses by treating him like a king, in that they grumbled against him, plotted against him, and brutalized him day and night with all of their issues and civil complaints. Moses' father-in-law, Jethro, saw this and—probably from experience—advised Moses that he ought not bear their burden alone:

> *"But select capable men from all the people—men who fear God, trustworthy men who hate dishonest gain—and appoint them as officials over thousands, hundreds, fifties and tens." —Exodus 18:21*

Do not think that because your leaders dress well, eat well and groom well they have it easy in this life. Just as the children of Israel were to Moses, so you also are a heavy burden—too much for any one man to bear! Why? Because so many in the church of America stubbornly insist upon making their own way through the wilderness instead of accepting God's. Knowing this aspect of human nature, Jethro advised Moses and Israel to choose from among them not just *"capable men,"* but also *"men who fear God."* Such men are *trustworthy* and *hate dishonest gain,* because they fear God's judgment. I'm not saying they will be perfect, because no man is, but they will perform their duty as *leaders* rather than *poll puppets,* which march to the beat of the public opinion drum. A true leader will even go so far as to defy his or her constituents by honoring what is good and righteous in the sight of Almighty God. Which do you want?

Be sure to appoint over you the king the LORD your God chooses. He must be from among your own brothers. Do not place a foreigner over you, one who is not a brother Israelite. —Deuteronomy 17:15

Though the President of the United States is not called a "king," his function is little different. He is the executive head of our nation, the arm of law enforcement and national defense, and no matter whom we have appointed, he has always been a direct reflection of the nation as a whole. Therefore, when God speaks through Moses about *not placing a "foreigner" over us,* is it a man born of a foreign country with whom He is concerned, or is He warning His Church, who is the Israel of today, not to choose a leader who is not in His Church? Yes, we are only to appoint those who are truly in Christ as Christ is in them. One who hears this word and ignores it, continuing to vote for a lesser evil, or does not vote at all, shall in the end be joined with this nation's fall. The Lord your God knows how to separate those who grieve over this nation's wickedness from those who ignore it. Along these lines, I want you to know that when that Constitution-worshipping candidate for U.S. Senate boldly declared his misaligned loyalties, he drew forth a resounding applause from the predominantly "Christian" audience. Though a natural born citizen, he demonstrated himself a *foreigner* to Israel. Yet, just like the Israel of old, the people commended his fine words:

On the appointed day Herod, wearing his royal robes, sat on his throne and delivered a public address to the people. They shouted, "This is the voice of a god, not of a man." —Acts 12:21-22

Take care that your own heart does not run after fine words, but seeks the Truth. Sadly, most people do not have a true heart for Christ, but only for themselves. Thus, the Truth Serum works not only for candidates, but also for the church. Therefore, take warning with what happened to Herod when he did not honor the Lord.

Shortly after introducing the Truth Serum to a number of groups, I was quickly shunned by political and church establishments alike. Though I had spoken no word edifying a person, a party, or an ideology, and had sought no personal benefit for my family, they ignored the Lord's call and accused me of trumpeting my own agenda. They entered into Korah's rebellion:

> *They came as a group to oppose Moses and Aaron and said to them, "You have gone too far! The whole community is holy, every one of them, and the LORD is with them. Why then do you set yourselves above the LORD's assembly?"*
>
> *—Numbers 16:3*

Everyone wants to be in charge, but few want to follow the Lord's Charge. While my family has sojourned with Christ, who had no place to lay His head, the grumblers, scoffers and backstabbers who snubbed us have continued to enjoy the comforts of their homes and purses, at least for now. They call themselves a people of *faith,* but when the Lord sends unto them not one, not two, but a whole family of six demonstrating a faith they would not dare entertain themselves, they follow the example of Satan, who frequently accuses the innocent of the very thing for which he is guilty.

God's Word tells us that a wise and prudent people seek His Face when appointing their leadership; He also warns that a foolish people seek their own way. This Truth Serum, which I have laid before you, was not merely given for my family's benefit, but for you and all the church in America. It is a simple and direct tool for distinguishing *hired hands* from true servants of Christ. You must apply it to every candidate seeking your vote. If no candidate can be found who passes the Truth Serum, vote *'Christ The Lord.'* Get an absentee ballot if you must, but do not endorse evil any longer, lest the Lord judge you as He intends to judge the whole nation.

Also, apply the Truth Serum to your family, your church and your community. It is a powerful means by which you can identify the lost—even the religious lost—in your midst. Then you can bring great glory to your Savior by testifying His Truth. Whether they accept the Truth is not up to you, but you must serve Christ as an avid witness so that all men and women have a shot at the only office that really matters—*eternal life!*

As you test your political leadership, don't forget to also test your church shepherds. Don't put yourself or those whom you love at risk by appointing a *hired hand* to any position of authority. If you find that your church is already under the yoke of a *hired hand* then out them by following the procedure Jesus taught His disciples:

> *"If your brother sins against you, go and show him his fault, just between the two of you. If he listens to you, you have won your brother over. But if he will not listen, take one or two others along, so that 'every matter may be established by the testimony of two or three witnesses.' If he refuses to listen to them, tell it to the church; and if he refuses to listen even to the church, treat him as you would a pagan or a tax collector." —Matthew 18:15-17*

But beware, for there are many church establishments who prefer dogs and swine to the Good Shepherd. In such cases, separate yourself from them, lest you share in Korah and his followers' fate:

> *As soon as he finished saying all this, the ground under them split apart and the earth opened its mouth and swallowed them, with their households and all Korah's men and all their possessions. —Numbers 16:31-32*

I assure you the day is coming when the Lord will open up the earth to swallow up the wicked. Do what you can to testify the truth to them so that they may repent. Yet, should they persist in wickedness, do not cleave to them or you too will fall subject to the Lord's firestorm, which He kindles even now against this rebellious nation.

16

The Lie We Accepted

The winter of 2010 was by far the most brutal my family had ever experienced. It wasn't because of ice storms and blizzards, but from the incessant spiritual attacks brought upon by Satan, who was desperately trying to get us to quit. In just one day we accidentally backed up into a Cadillac, cracking its bumper, and later we discovered the *Bunny Farm's* water pipes had frozen and blown while we were away. At the same time we paid for these costly mishaps, exhausting what little funds we had, false Christians slandered us, blackballed us, and deprived us of shelter for one reason or another. For example, by the Spirit, Clara once warned a woman that her daughter was harboring a sexual predator and her granddaughter was in danger. Putting her hands over her ears, she told us to leave. On another occasion our host told us not to testify Jesus to a water heater repairman. That time we decided we had to leave, but in both cases we were made homeless.

> *Three times I was beaten with rods, once I was stoned, three times I was shipwrecked, I spent a night and a day in the open sea, I have been constantly on the move. I have been in danger from rivers, in danger from bandits, in danger from my own countrymen, in danger from Gentiles; in danger in the city, in danger in the country, in danger at sea; and in danger from false brothers.*
>
> *—2 Corinthians 11:25-26*

Perhaps the worst affliction came when our children caught some strange skin infection—in a pastor's house no less, who was more interested in the

NFL playoffs than repentance. Sores broke out all over their bodies, even their faces! Clara and I were unaffected, which pretty well suggests the source.

So Satan went out from the presence of the LORD and afflicted Job with painful sores from the soles of his feet to the top of his head. —Job 2:7

You can be sure Satan knows your most tender weaknesses, so be on guard! Before you can combat a spiritual attack, which manifests itself through various temptations and afflictions of the flesh, you must recognize that you are not suffering from some random occurrence, but are actually being attacked. Sometimes Satan is given access to chastise you on account of sin. Purge that sin from your life completely and Satan will flee. Other times, as it was for Job, you have to realize that you are being tested. These are the most difficult challenges, because all you can do is submit to God's mercy and persevere in faith. When the Lord is satisfied with your refinement, which is often at the point where you can bear no more, He will deliver you.

Submit yourselves, then, to God. Resist the devil, and he will flee from you. Come near to God and he will come near to you. Wash your hands, you sinners, and purify your hearts, you double-minded. Grieve, mourn and wail. Change your laughter to mourning and your joy to gloom. Humble yourselves before the Lord, and he will lift you up. —James 4:7-10

With personal encouragement from Christ Himself we were able to persevere through all these afflictions and the *Devil did flee from us,* at least until another opportune time of testing. Moreover, our victory in faith opened the door for the Spirit to come into our lives like never before, and He blessed us repeatedly with incredible revelation; such as one morning when I awoke hearing a speech. I jumped out of bed and wrote down all I had heard. It began with, *"We accepted a lie in America called the **separation of church and state.**"*

Do you not know that your bodies are members of Christ himself? Shall I then take the members of Christ and unite them with a prostitute? Never! Do you not know that he who unites himself with a prostitute is one with her in body? For it is said, "The two will become one flesh." But he who unites himself with the Lord is one with him in spirit. —1 Corinthians 6:15-17

Who is the Church? You are, together with my family and all the people of this nation who are truly devoted to Christ. We are the members of His Body, and He is not denominated! You can be sure that when Christ *comes on the clouds of heaven in His Father's Glory,* He will not be looking at what kind of religious *hat* you are wearing; He will be looking at your *heart.*

There is one body and one Spirit—just as you were called to one hope when you were called—one Lord, one faith, one baptism; one God and Father of all, who is over all and through all and in all. —Ephesians 4:4-6

Therefore, as members of *Christ's one and only Church,* can we be separated from a government of the people, by the people and for the people? No, because We The People are the Church! Do you understand Satan's deception? If the enemy convinces you that the *Church* can and should be *separated* from its government then you will be apt to leave Christ outside the voting booth, which will make you susceptible to endorsing evil, lesser or greater. Consequently, in God's sight you will have separated yourself from Christ by joining yourself with the sin of your nation, which is the biblical definition of *uniting yourself with a prostitute.* Thus, when judgment falls upon the nation, it will also fall upon you.

Surely the arm of the LORD is not too short to save, nor his ear too dull to hear. But ***your iniquities have separated you from your God;*** *your sins have hidden his face from you, so that he will not hear. —Isaiah 59:1-2*

The Church has fallen unsuspectingly into sin by accepting a misguided theology, which denies God's Law by hearkening to the doctrines of the United States Constitution. By this doctrine, you will find "Christian" scholars on both sides of the *separation of church and state* issue arguing over man's precedent, such as Thomas Jefferson's letter to the Danbury Baptists citing a *"wall of separation between church and state,"* while ignoring God's precedent, which says:

"You shall have no other gods before me." —Exodus 20:3

"No other gods" means that you are to elevate nothing above the Lord, including a legal instrument written by flawed men, some of whom did not even acknowledge Him. Yet, through the deceptive argument that a *secular government,* which literally means 'worldly' government, is somehow superior to a *Christian government,* Satan has successfully confused and enslaved the church in America within the yoke of the *Establishment Clause* of the 1st

Amendment to the Constitution, which states: *Congress shall make no law respecting an establishment of religion, or prohibiting the free exercise thereof.*

All societies are based upon a foundation of laws, but it is the principles upon which those laws are based that determine a society's fate. Some societies thrived for many centuries, but because they were not built upon the Rock of Jesus Christ, they ultimately foundered and collapsed. In the 1971 *Lemon v. Kurtzman* case, the Supreme Court established what's been dubbed the *"Lemon Test"* in order to better define the *Establishment Clause,* as well as to further their view of the *secular* principles upon which our society was based. This test stipulates that the government's action [enacted law] must meet *all three* of the following conditions: 1) It must have a *secular legislative purpose.* 2) It must not *advance or inhibit religion.* 3) It must not *excessively entangle government with religion.*

We already know that any Supreme Court applying the Lemon Test will not pass the Truth Serum, because its first condition stipulates a *'secular legislative purpose'*—literally meaning a *'worldly' legislative purpose.* Since *the world* does not believe in or serve Jesus Christ, but serves Satan, it seeks to marginalize and regulate Christ, His teachings and His Church within the confines of 'religion.' Therefore, nothing Christ teaches concerning morality can be legislated—right? What about laws against murder, theft, and perjury; are these derived from secularism? No, these moral principles come from God, because the way of the *secular* world is to lie, rob and kill. A *secular-principled* government may implement laws prohibiting these crimes, but only against certain classes of people.

> *For the LORD your God is God of gods and Lord of lords, the great God, mighty and awesome, who shows no partiality and accepts no bribes. He defends the cause of the fatherless and the widow, and loves the alien, giving him food and clothing. And you are to love those who are aliens, for you yourselves were aliens in Egypt. —Deuteronomy 10:17-19*

Christ's Law plays no favorites. When He says innocent bloodshed, thievery and fraud are wrong and will be punished, He means for all people, of every color, culture and class—including the unborn, the defenseless, elderly and infirmed. He has also promised destruction for any society that engages in the sexual immorality of Sodom and Gomorrah and denies His Holy Name. A secular nation ignores these warnings, because its people don't believe Jesus Lives. If they did, they would repent at once! Instead, they follow the enemy, who has convinced them to *separate* their consciences from Christ and to place their trust in a false brand of morality derived from man and his reason. Since we know that God is the Originator of all morality, any *secular* model put forth to promote a moral society is worse than inadequate; it is foolishness. We must therefore conclude that the Lemon Test is a *lemon.*

> *See to it that no one takes you captive through hollow and deceptive philosophy, which depends on human tradition and the basic principles of this world rather than on Christ. —Colossians 2:8*

It is critically important that We The Church no longer accept the inane arguments of philosophers, secularists, atheists, and especially pretended Christians who desire not religious freedom, but secretly serve the enemy. If only we will obey the *principles taught by Christ* then He will raise up a government that bears His Name and His Law. Yet, so long as we allow ourselves to be bound by a cleverly articulated Establishment Clause lie, which seeks to define God in terms of religion when His is far beyond anything manmade, then we shall remain enslaved by *hired hands.* You have to reconcile in your heart that while man established religion for his own purposes, God gave mankind His Eternal Law, sealing it perfectly through Jesus Christ:

> *For by him all things were created: things in heaven and on earth, visible and invisible, whether thrones or powers or rulers or authorities; all things were created by him and for him. He is before all things, and in him all things hold together. —Colossians 1:16-17*

Since *all things were created by Him and for Him,* it is impossible to separate Jesus Christ from the affairs of any nation, and since We The Church are His Body then it is also impossible to separate us. Man may think he is establishing a secular government, but the Heavenly Government of Christ supersedes it, so man is only feeding into his vain delusions. Think about it, the whole universe has its being, its energy and order in Christ, and in Him alone is it all held together, the cells of our bodies, the underlying atomic structure, as well as all the basic elements of gravity and space that has set every world, nation and person, in its specific place and order. Since it is not possible for any force in the cosmos to separate Christ from His creation, how much less a constitutional argument? In the end, all the kingdoms of the earth, together with their establishments of government and religion will perish, but the King of kings lives forever, and so will those who abide in Him and His will.

> *Jesus knew their thoughts and said to them, "Every kingdom divided against itself will be ruined, and every city or household divided against itself will not stand." —Matthew 12:25*

Furthermore, because *in Christ all things hold together,* what nation has any hope of being united without Christ? It has none. A nation that separates itself from Christ will be divided, and that *kingdom will be ruined* no matter how vigorously lost scholars argue over matters of *"original intent"* and *"precedent."* The same applies to your own body and spirit, because you are Christ's temple. If you let any part of you become divided from your Savior, you will not be able to stand on the Day of Judgment. Consider that your salvation is not bound by the past decisions of Founding Fathers, former Presidents, Congressmen, Supreme Court Justices, philosophers and theologians who are all dead and gone. So if you cannot find a single leader in this nation, past or present, who honors Christ's sovereignty, will you join them in anarchy against the King? Do not let even the slightest lie that suggests the Constitution has any authority over your Savior's Word take root in your heart. The one who ignores the precepts of Christ in the Bible in favor of human principles is one who relies upon his own strength:

> *"When a strong man, fully armed, guards his own house, his possessions are safe. But when someone stronger attacks and overpowers him, he takes away the armor in which the man trusted and divides up the spoils."*
>
> *—Luke 11:21-22*

There is no *armor* of this world that is eternally reliable. 9/11/2001 is proof of that. How was a band of cave dwellers in Afghanistan made stronger than the United States? Because she has turned from the Lord her God and prostituted herself with the detestable ways of the other nations! America's spiritual armor has been chinked, and is spreading ever farther apart, including to your own front door. What is the Lord to do with such a people as this? Is He to accept her adulteries and spread His Tent over her, though she runs to her lovers like a harlot?

> *"Yet my people have forgotten me; they burn incense to worthless idols, which made them stumble in their ways and in the ancient paths. They made them walk in bypaths and on roads not built up. Their land will be laid waste, an ob-*

ject of lasting scorn; all who pass by will be appalled and will shake their heads. Like a wind from the east, I will scatter them before their enemies; I will show them my back and not my face in the day of their disaster."

—Jeremiah 18:15-17

To reveal to me just how long-suffering the Lord has been, He led me to a little known piece of American History. In February 1863, in the midst of the Civil War, eleven Protestant churches from seven northern states came together in Xenia, Ohio to discuss what they viewed as God's judgment upon the *Divided States of America,* and they called for a *"national repentance."* Unbeknownst to them, the day after their meeting concluded a similar conference of churches convened a meeting in Sparta, Illinois, also calling for a *"national repentance"* and coming to near identical conclusions. A year later, these two groups came together and formed the *National Reform Association.* Unified in their belief that the Founders had erred in omitting the absolute sovereignty of Jesus Christ from our Constitution, and confessing that this omission had, in part, perpetuated the blight of slavery on our national record, they adopted a proposed amendment to the preamble of the Constitution, which read:

We, the people of the United States, [humbly acknowledging Almighty God as the source of all authority and power in civil government, the Lord Jesus Christ as the Ruler among the nations, his revealed will as the supreme law of the land, in order to constitute a Christian government,] and in order to form a more perfect union, establish justice, insure domestic tranquility, provide for the common defense, promote the general welfare, and [secure the inalienable rights and the blessings of life, liberty, and the pursuit of happiness to ourselves, our posterity, and all the people,] do ordain and establish this Constitution for the United States of America.

It became known as the *"Christian Amendment,"* and notice how it cited extending *"the blessings of life, liberty, and the pursuit of happiness to ourselves, our posterity,* ***and all the people,****"* which was intended to set free the African slaves. You see, even then a remnant Church committed to upholding the precepts of Christ existed in America. They presented their amendment to Abraham Lincoln on February 11, 1864, on which occasion he seemed to express support, but reserved for himself *"time to deliberate"* on its language. Fourteen months later, on April 11, 1865, Lincoln's speech advocating voting rights for blacks incensed one John Wilkes Booth, who shot the president three days later, cancelling Lincoln's *"time to deliberate"* on anything. Ironically, in 1869, debates in Congress over the voting rights of blacks further preempted consideration of the Christian Amendment. This is not to suggest that voting rights are not important, but it does reveal that the nation's priorities have changed little in the last 150 years. Would it have been so difficult to honor Christ and extend voting rights to the people He freed?

Ultimately, the *Christian Amendment* never came into being because the will of the Church was not behind it. Similar attempts to honor Christ in the Constitution were also defeated in 1874, 1896, 1910 and 1954 for lack of Church support. I'm not trying to suggest that merely by stating "Jesus Christ" in the Constitution does this nation become better servants of our Savior. I'm saying that a people devoted to Christ would desire nothing less, and since we have not honored His Name in this manner, can it honestly be said that we are a Christian Nation? How then do we ask God to bless America?

The Lord once gave me a profound dream that placed me in the heart of a South African nation called Zambia. In this dream the Spirit revealed to me that Zambia has a Christian culture dating all the way back to a missionary visit from one of the original Twelve Apostles. When I awoke, I had to look this country up on the map. Being led by the Spirit, I then looked up their constitution, discovering that Zambia had recently undertaken an endeavor to redraft it. Following the preamble language in their 1996 constitution, the most recent draft begins:

> *We, the people of Zambia, in exercise of our constituent power:*
>
> *ACKNOWLEDGE the supremacy of God Almighty;*
>
> ***DECLARE the Republic a Christian Nation**, but uphold the right of every person to enjoy that person's freedom of conscience or religion;*

America has not been able to make up its mind about Christ from its inception, but you can say with confidence that Zambia is a "Christian Nation." According to a November 17, 2010 U.S. State Department report, nearly 87% of Zambia is Christian, which means some 13% are not. Nonetheless, the majority knows the Lord their God and desires to honor Him within the declarations of their constitution. Is this somehow wrong for the lost minority? Will the Christ-leading majority not bless them?

A 2007 Pew Forum study reported that the United States is roughly 76% Christian, which leaves somewhere in the range of 24% who are lost. Among these only 4.7% are affiliated with any religion, including just 0.6% Muslim and 0.5% Buddhist. So just who are We The Church in America trying to please by rejecting Christ?

> *Am I now trying to win the approval of men, or of God? Or am I trying to please men? If I were still trying to please men, I would not be a servant of Christ. —Galatians 1:10*

You cannot force another human being to believe as you do, not by the laws of men nor by the whip. However, a true Christian Nation led by servants of Christ can and will attest to the predominant faith by which it stands, honoring God Most High and Jesus Christ. If We The Church were to adopt Zambia's constitutional preamble, how much wind would be left in the sails of the antichrist zealots who are dead-set on eradicating Jesus from our shores and setting about our nation's certain demise? If the Church will rise and stand its ground, America's blessings would speak for themselves. They would bear witness to those who are lost, and you can believe that some of these would turn to Christ and be saved!

This nation may have abolished temporal slavery, but it remains in spiritual bondage. Consequently, millions upon millions of Americans remain chained to a freedom façade that suggests God somehow wrote our Constitution. In their hearts, they reason that the American Constitution has improved upon God's biblical system of government. They either replace Christ with freedom or attempt to meld the two together. Yes, Jesus *sets the captives free,* but not for the cause of *liberty;* such as man has defined it. He came for the glory of the Father, and to give eternal freedom to His children. Think about it, whose purpose is served by preserving a society devoted to temporal freedom, when it is perpetuating a lie that will result in eternal spiritual bondage and torment in hell?

> *"They set up kings without my consent; they choose princes without my approval. With their silver and gold they make idols for themselves to their own destruction. Throw out your calf-idol, O Samaria! My anger burns against them. How long will they be incapable of purity? They are from Israel! This calf—a craftsman has made it; it is not God. It will be broken in pieces, that calf of Samaria." —Hosea 8:4-6*

If you have ears to hear then let it be heard that the United States was formed in the cast of Ephraim. The seat of Ephraim's kingdom was Samaria, and like the Israel of old we too have established a *calf-idol* over us. We call it the Constitution. Although it is a legal document written by man's hand, this nation bows to it like it was a god. God tried to warn His people that it had no breath of life in it, but they persisted in rebellion. They consulted that calf-idol for wisdom and guidance until their day of disaster. It is pride that leads man to this madness! Must we honor the Founding Fathers more than we honor the Holy Spirit? Is God's Word somehow insufficient?

> *"I wrote for them the many things of my law, but they regarded them as something alien." —Hosea 8:12*

Remember what happened to me in *Casketville* and to Clara in Texas. Our so-called *"rights"* were completely violated by the possessed *Blown-A-Gaskets*. What value was that piece of paper called the Constitution to us? Today, servants of Christ around the country are being harassed, abused and arrested for trying to set the *souls of the captives free* by preaching the Gospel into the hearing of lost Muslims, homosexuals, women seeking abortions, and simple strangers in public squares. How is the Constitution defending their liberty? It isn't. Because the Constitution does not live and breathe, it is only as good as the hearts of those who interpret and enforce its decrees. On the contrary, the Word of God does live, He does breathe and He has real power to rescue you from any authority on this earth, because Jesus Christ is above them all:

> *Therefore God exalted him to the highest place and gave him the name that is above every name, that at the name of Jesus every knee should bow, in heaven and on earth and under the earth, and every tongue confess that Jesus Christ is Lord, to the glory of God the Father. —Philippians 2:9-11*

God the Father created all the heavens and the earth through His Son so that we, though being evil by nature, might be reconciled back to Him. We have to remember that life on this earth is short and that the earth itself, as we now know it, is destined to pass away. Therefore, what good is it to plan for the preservation of a society that is apart from God's grace?

While it's tempting to simply blame the government for separating our society from Christ, along with His blessings, the inescapable reality is that We The Church in America are guilty. 76% of Americans claim they are Christian, therefore we testify against ourselves:

> *Jesus said, "If you were blind, you would not be guilty of sin; but now that you claim you can see, your guilt remains." —John 9:41*

Once again, a nation that appoints its own leadership cannot wash its hands of the evil they do. In truth, we have stood idly by while our elected authorities have excommunicated Christ from our national public square under the guise of *constitutional principles*.

Hear O Israel and do as the Lord your God Commands: We The People of the United States of America are bound to the Constitution under which this nation *ordained* itself, though God *ordained* this nation for His Glory. If we do not separate ourselves from our nationalistic pride and unite under the Body of Christ, then we shall be destroyed as a *body* united with a calf-idol; both it and its people will be torn apart and thrown into the burning flames of the Lord's wrath. Yet, if We The Church will rise up and sanctify this nation under God Most High and Jesus Christ, then we shall be forgiven and the Lord will see to our restoration. The Lord will even pierce the most hardened hearts among our leadership. Even so, have no delusions, because we will either reduce that calf-idol to ashes ourselves or the Lord will do it for us.

> *Then I told her, "You are to live with me many days; you must not be a prostitute or be intimate with any man, and I will live with you." —Hosea 3:3*

What man would take back an adulterous wife who insisted on sustaining a relationship with her lover? Neither will God accept a people who return to Him only in pretense. Zambia's endeavor to redraft their constitution was given as an example of what We The Church in America can and must do. The United States Constitution *is not etched in stone,* proven by its built-in Amendment process. Otherwise, temporal slavery would never have been abolished. The only sacred, unchangeable Law that has ever been written is the Living Word of Jesus Christ. Therefore, do not lament the old order of things, but yearn for the new and infinitely greater order in Christ. I am not advocating a *religious government*. We already have one institution of man ruining this nation. Rather I am pleading with the Church to establish a rebirth of a nation *united in our Lord and Savior, Jesus Christ*. Moreover, I am telling you that the King will accept nothing less from a nation that declares itself to be *one nation under God, with liberty and justice for all.*

17

No Place To Lay Our Heads

Despite Satan's schemes, implemented through his willing political and religious operatives, the Lord flung open the doors of the collective Church all throughout Ohio. In a matter of months we were able to cover at least twenty-four of the state's eighty-eight counties. It happened so fast that we hardly had time to appreciate it. Cities and townships like Ottawa, Van Wert, Lima, Columbus, Kenton, Delta, Mansfield, Heath, Greenville, Wilmington, Dayton, Springfield, Akron, Cleveland, Chardon, Upper Sandusky, Celina, Troy and others came and went like a blur. When the Lord decides to open a door, it opens, and when He closes it, it is closed:

> *"To the angel of the church in Philadelphia write: These are the words of him who is holy and true, who holds the key of David. What he opens no one can shut, and what he shuts no one can open. I know your deeds.* ***See, I have placed before you an open door that no one can shut.*** *I know that you have little strength, yet you have kept my word and have not denied my name."*
>
> *—Revelations 3:7-8*

In keeping with past experience, the Lord's message was positively received in the beginning, but over time there were those who faded from the truth. No matter how hard I tried to beat away those birds going after the seed, I just couldn't get some seeds to take—at least not so far as I have seen. When we read about the missionary journeys of the apostles in Acts, especially those of Paul, we're immediately captivated by the masses that flocked to the truth. Yet, amidst those great successes were many trials and disappointments.

> *You, however, know all about my teaching, my way of life, my purpose, faith, patience, love, endurance, persecutions, sufferings—what kinds of things happened to me in Antioch, Iconium and Lystra, the persecutions I endured. Yet the Lord rescued me from all of them. In fact, everyone who wants to live a godly life in Christ Jesus will be persecuted, while evil men and impostors will go from bad to worse, deceiving and being deceived. —2 Timothy 3:10-13*

Knowing persecutions are going to occur, the important thing for a servant of Christ is that we do not quit. Paul was nearly stoned to death during his first visit to Lystra, but being a proper servant he did not give up and went back for the sake of the believers who received the Word while he was there. That's when he met Timothy, to whom he wrote the passage above and would succeed him in his ministry. Had Paul written Lystra off, because people in that city had once tried to kill him, Timothy might never have been anointed to continue Paul's work in Christ.

The truth is, despite the romanticized adventure many have conjured up in their minds, most of my family's journey has been a grueling, painful, pride-swallowing lesson about truly following the real Jesus Christ, who requires His disciples to die to themselves. Contrary to the glamorized depiction of television ministry, the real thing is dirty, it's dangerous, and it's often overflowing with tears of sorrow. People naturally want to be on a high, to swim in a pool of joy and bask in the sun of contentment. My family is no different, but we were shown that the Lord does not appreciate these sentiments when His people are regularly engaging in murder, sexual immorality and pagan idolatry. When you look around your community through the prism of the Lord's truth, do you see much cause for lightheartedness? Is there even one street in all of America that is free from idolatry? Therefore, at this late hour for our nation let repentance come before laughter. Let your joy be in the Lord's joy, not flying in the face of His grief over our rebellion.

> *Sorrow is better than laughter, because a sad face is good for the heart. The heart of the wise is in the house of mourning, but the heart of fools is in the house of pleasure. It is better to heed a wise man's rebuke than to listen to the song of fools. Like the crackling of thorns under the pot, so is the laughter of fools. This too is meaningless. —Ecclesiastes 7:3-6*

Solomon was speaking of the rebellious burning in flames. Perhaps the Spirit showed him Israel's coming disaster amid her cavalier attitude concerning sin. Similarly, my family has seen the coming disaster facing our nation, and too many members of the establishment church are disregarding it. Some ignore the Scriptures and don't believe in a judgmental God. Some misread the Scriptures and believe they will be *raptured* before the tribulation smites them. Yet, if either of these views were rooted in the truth, then why has my family suffered? Why did all the prophets, apostles and disciples of old suffer persecution, and some execution? Why did Israel have to be enslaved 400 years, then refined another 40 years after their escape from Egypt before they were allowed to possess their Promised Land? Why did God's one and only begotten Son, Jesus Christ, have to be crucified on the cross? Are any of us somehow better than these, even our Savior? Are we somehow to be spared the Refiner's fire, when none of our predecessors were spared?

They preached the good news in that city and won a large number of disciples. Then they returned to Lystra, Iconium and Antioch, strengthening the disciples and encouraging them to remain true to the faith. "We must go through many hardships to enter the kingdom of God," they said. —Acts 14:21-22

The apostle Paul understood *hardships,* and he further understood that he would not be alone in them until the hour of Christ's return. Thus, my family has been rendered penniless and homeless, we have nearly been killed, we have been plagued by infections and various physical ailments, we have been shunned by political action committees, as well as by Catholics and Protestants, we have been cast out of supposed believers' homes and thrown out from their churches, and just when we thought we could take no more, these afflictions intensified. This did not mean the Lord wasn't with us. Rather it was proof that He was:

"If the world hates you, keep in mind that it hated me first. If you belonged to the world, it would love you as its own. As it is, you do not belong to the world, but I have chosen you out of the world. That is why the world hates you."

—John 15:18-19

Though the *world hates us,* the Lord loves us dearly, and He will care for our needs when the world refuses them. So don't ever feel like the Lord doesn't love you when facing this world's harshness. He is loving you, just not in the way you might like at that moment. But if we whom He calls are going to perform to the fullest of our potential, our faith and power in the Spirit must increase while the importance we place in the flesh must diminish. So, worldly profit has been taken away that we might learn to depend upon the fruit of the Holy Spirit, that *hidden manna* sent to us from heaven above:

> *"He who has an ear, let him hear what the Spirit says to the churches. To him who overcomes, I will give some of the hidden manna. I will also give him a white stone with a new name written on it, known only to him who receives it."*
> —*Revelations 2:17*

In order to *overcome,* one must first have his or her faith challenged. Clara and I have met many on the road who long for a real and tangible burning of the Holy Spirit in their hearts, but few we have met are willing to put enough of themselves aside to let the Spirit in. On the contrary, the ones who are already suffering in this world are readily blessed by the heavenly outpouring of the Spirit, such as that homeless woman we met in the grocery store. She did nothing to earn the Spirit, but in seeing her humble heart, the Lord simply gave it. In a sense, the path to the Spirit must come through humility by way of humiliation, or humbling.

Due to a continued lack of support, my family received such humbling on February 12, 2010 when we came to a place where we had *no place to lay our heads.* We barely had enough money to feed our children lunch and dinner that day, so we could not afford lodging anywhere at any price, and no one welcomed us into their home. I suppose we could have been bolder in expressing our needs, but not at the expense of the Lord's message. The enemy has been far too successful corrupting ministry with mammon.

> *Each man should give what he has decided in his heart to give, not reluctantly or under compulsion, for God loves a cheerful giver. —2 Corinthians 9:7*

As for me and my family, our hearts led us to give our whole lives over to Christ and His harvest field, and this sacrifice led us to a motel parking lot in Findlay that night. There we sat in our Tahoe and prayed for the Lord's deliverance, looking out through the snow flurries at the warm motel rooms with an awful longing in our hearts. In our former life that motel was beneath our standards, but now we were beneath it. Our tent, *The Whale,* was still stuck in the ice at the *Bunny Farm* in Indiana, though it wouldn't have done us any good without a heater. Minutes passed by like days and sadly we realized no one was going to call or come by to offer us a roof and a warm bed. Did we have sufficient faith in the Lord? In a way, yes, but we also needed to learn the value of sustaining our faith when prayers go unanswered.

Needing to feed the kids dinner, we turned on the Tahoe and drove out in search of a fast food bargain. At the street corner we spotted a homeless man, ragged, dirty and trying to stay warm in the snow as he held his sign. Clara and I both realized how much worse off we could be. At least we still had gas in our fuel tank and a heater in the Tahoe, but where was he going to sleep?

Clara put down the window and asked, "What's your name?"

Somewhat taken aback, perhaps that someone wanted to know him, he replied, "John."

"Here John, this is from Jesus," Clara said, handing him a couple of dollars, all we could spare and still feed our kids. "He gives to us so we give to you," she said. Tearfully she then told him, "I'm so sorry you're out in this cold tonight and don't have anywhere to sleep. I wish we could do more, but we don't have a home either."

John's eyes expressed surprise. "You don't?"

Trying to control her tears, Clara shook her head and replied, "You know, when Jesus was here, He didn't have any place to lay His head. Why should we get better than He did?"

"I know I don't deserve better," John replied emotionally.

"John," Clara spoke with conviction, "I want you to know that no matter what has hurt you in your life, Jesus wants you with Him. He heals all things."

John was so moved he could not speak, but connected with his eyes. He was a man on the verge of a spiritual breakthrough.

> *As they were walking along the road, a man said to him, "I will follow you wherever you go."*
>
> *Jesus replied, "Foxes have holes and birds of the air have nests, but the Son of Man has no place to lay his head." —Luke 9:57-58*

"God bless you," Clara said as the light turned green and we slowly drove away. She then broke down crying. I was deeply pained to see her this way and reached over to comfort her, holding back my own emotions. At that moment, I felt like our suffering was in vain. For whom was I sacrificing my family's needs? Still, I had to remind myself how many times the Lord had inspired someone to come forward out of the blue to provide exactly what we needed to prevent hardships before. As much as we didn't like it, God had us in this situation for a reason. What were we to learn?

Around the corner, we found a fast food joint and used our last few dollars to get a large family pack of chicken nuggets. It wasn't exactly a balanced meal, but at least our children's stomachs would be satisfied. We immediately set a portion aside and took some back to the street corner for John. We had only left him for ten minutes or so, but he was gone. We looked everywhere for him, but he had vanished. Perhaps for the first time in a long while we had made him feel like a human being again and so he had gone somewhere to deal with those emotions privately. Either way, we weren't meant to feed him earthly food that night. We prayed the Lord would forgive his sins and heal what was broken in him. The world cannot explain the genuine love we have for our brother John, but the Lord knows.

Later that night, Clara and I settled in our Tahoe with the kids parked outside that motel. I kept looking at those warmly lit rooms with a range of emotions I had never felt in my entire life. It was so cold we hardly slept all that night. I had to repeatedly start the Tahoe to run the heater, but not for too long. We didn't have the gas money to afford that. In spite of the deep humiliation, especially considering our former prosperity, I learned a valuable lesson. I now know what it feels like to be John, albeit with a wife and four children in tow. I always had compassion for those homeless souls roaming the streets, but to walk in similar shoes was an experience beyond words.

"I know your afflictions and your poverty—yet you are rich! I know the slander of those who say they are Jews and are not, but are a synagogue of Satan."

—Revelations 2:9

18

The Fruitless Tree

After that night of nights, sleeping in our cold, cramped Tahoe, the Lord delivered shelter once more through another man and his wife in Christ who heard me speak before their group the next day. We did not tell them about the night we had just suffered, nor have we shared it with anyone before writing this book. They had never brought any strangers into their home before, let alone a family of six! Later, they confessed that they really had no idea what had come over them, and for their heartfelt obedience you can be sure they will not lose their reward.

Sleeping in warm beds again beneath that couple's roof, we thanked the Lord over and over, fervently praying for John and the many others still out in the cold like him. We could easily have suffered a great deal more, but the Lord was graceful in consideration of Clara's and my concerns for our children. The Lord never gave us more than we could bear, lest we be driven from His path, but we were stretched many times more than we thought we were capable of sustaining. Perhaps the greatest challenge in following the Lord is not trusting Him with your own life, but the lives of your loved ones. Still, we ought not forget that the Lord will not lose a one of the precious souls that has been dedicated to Him:

> *"And this is the will of him who sent me, that I shall lose none of all that he has given me, but raise them up at the last day." —John 6:39*

During the last week of February 2010, my family began a highly anticipated journey down from the frigid North to Daytona, Florida. Months before, I had agreed to speak at an event being held at the Volusia County Fairgrounds during Bike Week. Though excited to see the sun again, along with sandy beaches and the sea, I had a bad feeling in my gut. The Spirit of the Lord warned me that this event would not be fruitful. Nevertheless, we arrived in Daytona a day before the event and checked into an old beachfront hotel the organizers had arranged for the speakers. It was a bit cramped in the small room for my family of six, but it was a far sight better than the Tahoe and it was right by the beach! The last time we had taken the kids to the ocean, it had been at a beachfront resort in Naples, Florida and under entirely different circumstances. In those days we could afford to stay in a top-floor suite overlooking the gulf coast and enjoyed meals at swanky sit-down restaurants. On this trip, however, we had just enough cash after the trip down to afford another fast food feast. We were adapting, but we also weren't anticipating the challenge ahead.

After a day of fun and sun on the beach, cold rainclouds moved in the following Saturday morning. It was almost like we had been transported back to Ohio. This also didn't bode well for a good turnout at the event, just as I had been warned. The event organizers had hoped to draw thousands, but hardly more than a hundred showed up that day. Come Sunday, when I was to speak, the weather had changed little. Hopeful that I might at least reach a few people of good soil, I sought the Lord's Face that morning for a timely message by randomly opening His Word. That's when He led me to His parable of the fruitless fig tree:

> *Then he told this parable: "A man had a fig tree, planted in his vineyard, and he went to look for fruit on it, but did not find any. So he said to the man who took care of the vineyard, 'For three years now I've been coming to look for fruit on this fig tree and haven't found any. Cut it down! Why should it use up the soil?'" —Luke 13:6-7*

By the Spirit I knew this Word was indeed profound in its timing. Taking it to heart, my family ventured out to the fairgrounds, only to be disappointed by even poorer attendance at the event than the day before. Although the sun peaked out at times, there were just too many competing events offering the more seductive elements of mud bog racing, women's mud wrestling and all sorts of drunken revelry. Thus, I spoke to hardly a hundred people that day, mostly event organizers and booth operators, but as a part of the church in America they heard the Lord's call to repentance. I beckoned any who had a heart to repent for the sins of our nation to join with my family on the main floor. Of the hundred gathered, only ten joined us. Yet again, we were bearing witness to the remnant in America:

> *This is what the Sovereign LORD says: "The city that marches out a thousand strong for Israel will have only a hundred left; the town that marches out a hundred strong will have only ten left." —Amos 5:3*

Practically broke and with just one more night of shelter, Clara, the kids and I ended that day having a bite to eat in an open field away from the event. We sat on a lonely black stage, warmed by the occasional breakthrough of sunlight on an unusually chilly day in Florida. "The Lord tried to warn us," I said to Clara.

"We had to come down," she replied. Then she started laughing, "Who does this Thomas!"

The kids and I joined in Clara's laughter. Perhaps this was what the Bible means when it tells us to find joy when suffering in the service of Christ, knowing our perseverance is being trained up for the fulfillment of His purpose:

> *Consider it pure joy, my brothers, whenever you face trials of many kinds, because you know that the testing of your faith develops perseverance. Perseverance must finish its work so that you may be mature and complete, not lacking anything. —James 1:2-4*

"So what now?" Clara asked.

"Well," I began, "we can't afford to drive back to Ohio and we don't have any money for lodging after we check out tomorrow." I paused and continued, "The Lord will send someone to welcome us in, even today. Our work down here is not done. I can feel it."

No sooner had I finished saying this than a woman emerged from the auditorium some distance away. She had been one of the few who earlier joined in our prayer of repentance. Looking around, she spotted my family and came directly towards us. "Look," I said, "there she comes."

Sure enough, after complimenting our obedience to God, she promptly welcomed us to stay in her home until we were due to go back to Ohio. Like the women before her, she did this without first obtaining her husband's approval, though he followed through when we met him later. So the doors of another home of strangers, the *Marties*, were opened for my family.

The following day, my family enjoyed another rare moment of respite on the beach, after which we ventured over to the Martie's home to join them for supper. When we arrived at their house, Clara and I both prayed, "Peace to this house in Jesus' Name." Unfortunately, we both felt it return. It was a different sensation from that home in Indiana, but there was no mistaking the sense of instability in the Martie's house. The first sign of it was confirmed when we were immediately informed that we could only stay two nights, as opposed to the week for which we had originally been invited. Mrs. Martie apologetically explained that she had spoken presumptuously the day before, forgetting that their youngest son was moving out to college that week and they were just too busy planning his move. Never wanting to be a burden on anyone, we offered to find other accommodations—meaning *The Whale*, but they insisted that two days would not inconvenience them. In this, Clara and I understood the Lord did not want us in that house more than two nights. Where we would go after, I didn't know, but I trusted the Lord had a plan. We certainly knew there was work to perform in this house, so we made ourselves attentive witnesses.

For dinner that night the Marties graciously bought some steaks at the market, the first we'd had in months, and prepared a fresh tossed salad. For the salad dressing they asked our children if they would like to pick four lemons from their tree in the front yard. Naturally, they were happy to oblige. Clara and I went outside with them, followed by Mr. Martie. When we got to the tree, we saw that there were only five lemons left. "You only have five left," I said. "Are you sure you don't want us to just pick a couple?"

"Go ahead and get four. We have other trees in the neighborhood," he advised.

I motioned to the kids and they joyfully began picking.

"You know," Mr. Martie added thoughtfully, "we have another tree in the backyard, but in four years it has never given any fruit. I think we'll get rid of it."

A sudden charge of the Spirit hit me. Did I really just hear that a fruit tree in his backyard had born no fruit in four years and he was going to cut it down? Incredibly, I was bearing witness to a real-life manifestation of the *fruitless tree* parable, which the Lord had given me in His Word the day before. I looked at Mr. Martie not knowing what to say. 'Lord,' I prayed internally, 'what is it you are showing me? This can't be good for this family.'

After gathering the four lemons and heading back into the house, I whispered to Clara what had just been revealed. We both agreed to wait and listen. The Lord would reveal His truth, and when He did, we would know what our purpose was in this house. In the meantime, I followed Mr. Martie outside again to help him grill the steaks. As the meat sizzled on the grill, we engaged in some small talk. After a while he turned to me somewhat abruptly and said, "You know, I'm out of work next week. Thirteen years I've worked for that company and soon as the economy goes south they just let me go." He went on to express that he was too old to start a new career and that finding a new job in his field of expertise was going to be extremely difficult. "Anyhow, we'll be fine," he concluded, putting on a brave, yet transparent face. Like many people today, he foolishly believed that *'positive thinking'* would carry his family through this trial, but inside his heart was wallowing in hopeless despair.

Understanding my purpose, I shared my testimony about how the Lord had once lost me my job in healthcare, though it was a blessing in disguise. I related how frustrated and desperate I had been in the beginning, but in seeking the Lord's Face I had discovered what it was He wanted me to do with the life He had given me. I further explained that after obeying His will, the Lord had restored my family to greater wealth and prosperity than we had formerly known. However, when I suggested he seek the Lord's Face himself, that seed repelled off his *positive thinking* shell. As far as he was concerned, turning to the Lord for help was impractical. Was the Lord going to find him a new job, make the mortgage and car payments, and buy groceries? How little he knew.

We had a nice dinner that night, but Clara and I could feel the immense tension between the Marties. We saw the advanced signs of financial burdens driving a wedge of separation between them, an all too prevalent reality in our society. Hence, we spent the next two days trying to plants seeds of reconciliation and truth. No matter how many times we told them, "Don't worry, trust in God and obey His Commandments," they refused to receive it.

> *"Consider how the lilies grow. They do not labor or spin. Yet I tell you, not even Solomon in all his splendor was dressed like one of these. If that is how God clothes the grass of the field, which is here today, and tomorrow is thrown*

into the fire, how much more will he clothe you, O you of little faith! And do not set your heart on what you will eat or drink; do not worry about it. For the pagan world runs after all such things, and your Father knows that you need them. But seek his kingdom, and these things will be given to you as well."
—Luke 12:27-31

On the day we were to leave, Clara tearfully tried one last time to pierce Mrs. Martie's heart, since she was the one the Lord had moved to invite us in. Unfortunately, it was without success. In response to Clara's insistence upon trusting in our Savior, Mrs. Martie replied, "God does for those who do for themselves."

"And where did the Lord ever say that?" I asked.

"It's there in the Bible," she replied shortly. "Look, I admire what your family is doing. I wish you the best. Let's leave it at that."

"For this people's heart has become calloused; they hardly hear with their ears, and they have closed their eyes. Otherwise they might see with their eyes, hear with their ears, understand with their hearts and turn, and I would heal them."
—Matthew 13:15

I said nothing further and advised Clara to do the same. It is fruitless to argue against such stubborn determination not to listen—not to this man and woman from Texas, but to the Spirit of the Lord. Suffice it to say that nowhere in the Bible does it state, *"God does for those who do for themselves."*

This is what the LORD says: "Cursed is the one who trusts in man, who depends on flesh for his strength and whose heart turns away from the LORD. He will be like a bush in the wastelands; he will not see prosperity when it comes. He will dwell in the parched places of the desert, in a salt land where no one lives." —Jeremiah 17:5-6

On the contrary, from start to finish, the Lord's Word tells us to serve Him, and that those who do shall be rewarded, both in this lifetime and the next.

"But blessed is the man who trusts in the LORD, whose confidence is in him. He will be like a tree planted by the water that sends out its roots by the stream. It does not fear when heat comes; its leaves are always green. It has no worries in a year of drought and never fails to bear fruit." —Jeremiah 17:7-8

The Marties just didn't understand that their fruitless tree was a sign from the Lord meant to warn them to turn from their fruitlessness in His sight. God was not putting them out into the jobless wilderness because they had been lazy by the world's standards, but because they had been found wanting by His. Like the majority of the church in American today, the Marties believed they had to earn wages first then serve God with whatever time and resources were leftover. Is that what God wants, the scraps from your table? Of course not! This is to serve *money* over God. It may seem practical in the world, but in heaven it is absolute foolishness. God put forth His Son, Jesus Christ, as *the model* we all are to follow. His example was not about pursuing wealth in this world, but about doing His Father's business. This is the Lord's definition of fruitfulness! But what shall He do about the one who for his own sake ignores his duty to bring glory to the Father?

> *Seeing a fig tree by the road, he went up to it but found nothing on it except leaves. Then he said to it, "May you never bear fruit again!" Immediately the tree withered. —Matthew 21:19*

With deep sadness of heart, we climbed into our Tahoe with our children and left the Marties to the fate God had appointed them. Clara was still fighting back tears, knowing that what was coming would be harsh. It's hard to explain, but when you go forth serving the Lord, the Spirit quickly bonds your heart to those to whom He sends you to minister. The Lord gives you eyes to see clearly where they spiritually stand, their burdens, their pain, and sin. Yet, above all, you feel a deep and true love for them, whether they love you in return. For this reason, it hurts when they fail to receive the message the Lord has brought you into their life to deliver. They are not strangers, but brothers and sisters whom we are trying to lead to good pasture. Unfortunately, some sheep remain convinced that greener pasture exists in the world. We prayed the Lord would have mercy on them, understanding that the trials He brings forth to wake us up from this fallen world are His mercies.

> *"I am the true vine, and my Father is the gardener. He cuts off every branch in me that bears no fruit, while every branch that does bear fruit he prunes so that it will be even more fruitful." —John 15:1-2*

That day, my family was pruned in that we were made homeless again. The Marties, however, appeared to have been cut off. Upon concluding our prayer, as we sat in their driveway, the Spirit made clear to me the lesson of the fruitless tree, for it did not apply to the Marties alone. He said, 'The entire United States of America is like this family. It is a fruitless tree to Me.'

Immediately, I was concerned about our nation's deadline, realizing that tree had only four years to produce its fruit. So I asked the Lord when our nation's timeline had begun and He said, 'This presidential term of office.' I knew at that moment that no political contest could fulfill God's requirement for true repentance, which meant no individual stepping forward for the 2012 presidential race would break the *lesser of two evils* political mold. Thus, I understood that President Barack Obama had been ordained by God to serve not one, but two terms in office. It was at this time that I received something else concerning our president, but deemed it so implausible, I set it aside.

> *Land that drinks in the rain often falling on it and that produces a crop useful to those for whom it is farmed receives the blessing of God. But land that produces thorns and thistles is worthless and is in danger of being cursed. In the end it will be burned. —Hebrews 6:7-8*

Brothers and sisters, that was in February 2010. I have been warning the church in America about its fruitlessness before the Lord and our countdown to judgment ever since, but who is listening? Forget about the political implications and focus on the warning John the Baptist once gave the Israel of old, for a fruitless tree given but one more season by the Gardener must *"produce fruit in keeping with repentance."* As a member of Christ's Church and fellow watchman on the wall, I call upon you to urgently spread this alarm. Make straight your own personal walk with Christ by turning from your wicked ways, and encourage others to do the same. Forsaking the lesser of two evils and voting *'Christ The Lord'* in future elections is the easy part. The greater challenge is to truly die to yourself and begin to serve your Savior as you were born to do. Now you know why your trials have increased in these recent years, as they have for the whole of the nation. Because you didn't embrace your purpose in Christ willingly, the Lord has been mercifully bringing you closer to Him. Few will be called—or will choose—to do what my family has done, yet the Lord has a tailor-made mission for you, if you will choose to obey Him. When you do, He will teach you how to be fruitful for Him, just as He taught my family. You have no time to waste, for *the ax is already at the root of the trees:*

> *"The ax is already at the root of the trees, and every tree that does not produce good fruit will be cut down and thrown into the fire." —Matthew 3:10*

19

Which Way To Tarshish?

For as long as Clara and I can remember, our youngest daughter Jazelle has loved the story of Jonah. "Please, please, please, read me about Jonah and the big fish!" she would plead with excited anticipation. It wasn't until our sojourn down to Florida, however, that the lesson of Jonah and Nineveh really started to sink in. Although we were focused on the Spirit's leading during our encounter with the Marties, after leaving their home we felt like joining Jonah in his flight to Tarshish. But we were already in *The Whale*, stranded that very night in a shopping center parking lot amidst all the racket of Bike Week in Daytona. After our dinner expense we had just two dollars left, about a quarter tank of gas and nothing in Florida we could lean on for support—no family, no friends and no other engagements; except in Ohio in one week, which we could not get to. As far as Clara and I were concerned, we were shipwrecked. Worse yet, we had only some instant oatmeal to feed the kids in the morning. After that, we were going to be more than stranded and broke; our children would be going hungry.

Around 2 AM that night I awoke suddenly, feeling like I was suffocating in the tight space where Clara and I were sleeping in *The Whale*. Trying not to wake the kids, I stepped outside the trailer into the cold air beneath the night sky, listening to the remnant of roaring bikes heading home after last call at local bars. There were several RVs in the parking lot and oh how I lamented that I could not provide my wife and children with the least of their luxuries. Never in my life did I think a heated space, real beds to sleep in, a toilet and a small sink for brushing teeth and freshening up in the morning would be so far from reach. Looking up at the gray sky, glowing with the dirty yellow hue of city lights, I knelt down on the asphalt and prayed aloud with a desperately repentant heart, "How long O Lord must we continue to suffer this way?" If I had done something wrong, I needed to know. I knew I had not been perfect, but I had tried to be obedient. If this was punishment, I was willing to accept it, but the Lord just had to spare my wife and children from this. With tears I humbled myself and pleaded for deliverance.

Almost immediately, the Lord spoke to my spirit, saying, 'You are not here because you erred, but because you must learn to truly trust Me. This is a test and a trial you must pass.'

It wasn't easy to trust in His Voice at that moment, especially after my family had recently slept in the Tahoe during that freezing cold night in Ohio. I just wanted Him to sweep us up and place us back in our own home. I could still go forth, but at least my wife and children would have a warm stable roof over their heads. I was willing to work to provide it, but the Lord's Spirit sharply shot down that idea. I was able, I was qualified and I was sought after, but I could never go back to the world. In many ways our sacrifice was made so much harder, knowing I had the ability to earn a healthy wage in the world, but being denied any such pursuit.

Difficult as it can be to accept the Lord's will, I did. I knew there was nothing I could do for myself at that moment. I had no choice but to sit in *The Whale,* learn my lesson and trust that in due time the Lord might Command my family be spit back onto land. So, I climbed back into *The Whale* with my wife and children and did my best to get some sleep. One way or another, the Lord would have to deliver us on the morrow. He just couldn't let my children go hungry—could He?

First thing the next morning I received two different communications from Christ followers in Ohio, both sharing that the Lord had moved their hearts to reach out to support a present need my family might have. In no way had we prompted this, so I knew without a doubt the Lord had answered my desperate plea. Furthermore, they gave exactly what my family needed for the return trip to Ohio. Praise be to Jesus!

Our provision had come, but it would take a day or two for these funds to reach us, so I still had to figure out how I was going to feed my family in the meantime. We risked a little gas to get to another part of the city where we found a better, quieter place to park *The Whale* at night. There, behind a donut shop, Clara prepared the kids that oatmeal for breakfast, along with some hot cocoa we had on hand. Once again, despite their parents' heartaches, our children were as happy as can be. While Clara and I wasted time fretting about feeding and sheltering them, for them it was all an adventure, and they never doubted that Jesus would provide for their needs.

And he said: "I tell you the truth, unless you change and become like little children, you will never enter the kingdom of heaven." —Matthew 18:3

While my family ate, I headed over to the donut shop to use their Wi-Fi to see if the Lord might open any local doors for me to speak His message. After receiving His deliverance, the last thing I wanted to do was sit around waiting for funds to arrive. I felt I had to show Him I was willing to work under the most challenging of circumstances. However, the Lord was about to teach me that when you chasten your heart to His will, you needn't toil to find work. It comes right to you.

On the way over, Clara stopped me and pressed our last two dollars in my hand. "Get a coffee," she insisted. Before I could utter a word of argument, she stopped me and said, "You're going to be using their Internet, so the least you can do is buy a coffee."

Reluctantly, I agreed. A short time later, having fed the kids, Clara joined me in the donut shop. Sitting across from me, she looked longingly at my steaming, aromatic cup of coffee.

"Go and get one," I told her, handing her our last dollar.

"Oh no, is that it?" she gasped in jest.

"Oh, you're right, a whole dollar, let's save it!" I played along.

Clara started laughing, "Is it considered faith or irresponsibility to spend our last dollar on a cup of coffee that I don't need. I just want it because it smells soooo good?" She started giggling again, which can be contagious once she gets going.

Strange as it was to be giddy over our last dollar, while having no natural expectation we would be able to feed our children lunch, I told her, "To hoard our last dollar as though it will be the last we see would not be an act of faith."

With a resolute sigh, she snatched the dollar from my hand and went to the counter for her coffee, giving thanks on her way, "In faith I will get my coffee. Thank you Lord, thank you Father."

Honestly, that might have been the best cup of coffee we have shared in our lives. When you have next to nothing, it's amazing how much you can appreciate the simple pleasures in life. While we sat there together, sipping our coffees, talking about what the Lord might have in store for us next, a group of retired men came in and sat at the table next to us. They were pretty amusing to listen to, discussing everything from healthcare to world peace. They had all the answers, or so they thought.

I got up to use the restroom, leaving Clara to eavesdrop on the geriatric brigade. While I was gone, a latecomer arrived to the group and sat in a chair adjacent to Clara. As he engaged the group, for no explainable reason—beside the Lord's, he kept backing up his chair into Clara's space, pushing her further and further against the window. She didn't want to call attention to it and interrupt their discussion, which she was thoroughly enjoying, but pretty soon she had no more space to retreat. Finally, he looked back and realized what he was doing. "Oh, I'm sorry" he apologized.

"Any further and I'd be out the window," she laughed. At that time I returned and together we met Tony, who subsequently defected from his brigade to join us. We were elated. I had been so committed to find the Lord's work, yet here He had brought it to us, knowing we didn't have the fuel to get far anyhow. Thus, Tony began to share with us his burdened heart for his Christian daughter and Jewish son in-law. Because of their disagreement in religion, they had decided not to raise their children with God, but to let their children "figure out for themselves what they wanted to believe."

Why do we continue to place God in the bucket of religion? Do we honestly believe God accepts being excluded from the rearing of His children just to avoid a human dispute? Clara advised Tony to encourage them to teach their children the Lord's Commandments and to read them the Gospels at home, outside a religious establishment, and that the "grandparents" could do this themselves whenever they visited. Teaching who God is and what He Commands is not a superficial matter. While each individual must one day forge a personal relationship with Christ in order to have salvation, how we raise our children can have a dramatic effect on their ability to understand and receive the truth when their day comes.

I will open my mouth in parables, I will utter hidden things, things from of old—what we have heard and known, what our fathers have told us. We will not hide them from their children; we will tell the next generation the praiseworthy deeds of the LORD, *his power, and the wonders he has done. He decreed statutes for Jacob and established the law in Israel, which he commanded our forefathers to teach their children, so the next generation would know them, even the children yet to be born, and they in turn would tell their children. Then they would put their trust in God and would not forget his deeds but would keep his commands. —Psalm 78:2-7*

After concluding our discussion, I went and got two copies of *Things Forgotten* to present to Tony as a gift for him and his children. By this time I had received many testimonials about how that book had inspired non-believers to reconsider the Bible and to seek a relationship with God. I hoped it would do the same for his family.

Looking over the books, Tony said, "These are too nice to just give away."

"They're a gift," I asserted,

Grateful, Tony took the books, said his farewells and left the café. Clara and I began to wrap things up ourselves, but suddenly Tony reappeared with a twenty-dollar bill in hand. Before we could object he shrewdly told us, "I'm not paying for the books. This is a donation for your ministry. Now you have to take it."

We were beside ourselves. Lunch was just around the corner and we had nothing left in *The Whale* for the kids. With thanks we received his offering and from that moment on he became *Tony Twenty!* For his determination to bless us, we pray Tony's obedience be rewarded with breakthrough in Christ for his family.

In faith Clara and I spent our last two dollars on coffee and now we had twenty more! That's a 1000% return on our investment! We were able to stretch that offering into two days worth of meals for my family, including milk, bacon, eggs, and spaghetti with meat sauce, all prepared via a hotplate in *The Whale* by the sea. It was yet another lesson to us of just how adequately the Lord can and will deliver His workers. All you have to do is trust.

"Be strong and very courageous. Be careful to obey all the law my servant Moses gave you; do not turn from it to the right or to the left, that you may be successful wherever you go." —Joshua 1:7

The following day the Lord further provided me with an unexpected opportunity to deliver His message on a local talk radio program. The host had learned of our mission from his producer, whom I had met at the Sunday event. Having her hands full with the kids, Clara didn't get to hear the interview, which set up another witness as to the Lord's perfect timing.

The next morning, Clara tied up the kids in *The Whale*—with activities. She then got herself another aromatic cup of coffee, adding to it a donut, and comfortably situated herself in the Tahoe to tune in the scheduled airing of the radio interview. Meanwhile, I began a long-overdue rear brake job on the Tahoe before we pushed off for Ohio later that day. Hearing the show's introduction, I looked over from the wheel to give Clara a reassuring smile. 'Finally,' I thought, 'my wife is going to get an uninterrupted moment of peace.'

Hardly a minute into the show we both suddenly heard a woman wailing. It sounded distant at first, coming from the direction of the donut shop, but then it went quiet. Determined to listen to the interview, Clara didn't budge from her seat and I wondered if it was just some sort of strange birdcall. We were in Florida after all. Suddenly, we heard it again, then again. That's when Clara noticed a woman in tears taking a seat at a picnic table just behind the café. She probably hadn't seen us, but Clara had not missed her. I came around from behind the wheel of the Tahoe just in time to see Clara already walking over. I gave her a questioning expression and she shook her head, chuckling to herself. She knew it was the Lord's appointment and that hearing my interview wasn't as important as tending to the *Wailing Woman*.

Clara found out that this woman worked at her aunt's donut shop and was buckling under the pressure of trying to be a good steward of her relative's business while having been given no official authority to manage other employees. Clara encouraged her to let go of meaningless money matters beyond her control and to refocus herself on the Lord's purpose for her life. If her aunt wanted her oversight then she should be given the necessary authority. If none would be given, let it go. The woman's tears turned to joy, and with a renewed peace she went back to work. Her duty done, Clara came back just as the interview ended. You see, perfect timing!

Like Jonah, after three days the Lord had restored us, unharmed and well fed, and just as Jonah surely never forgot the smell from inside that fish, we would never forget the feeling of being stranded in *The Whale*. We also walked away from that experience with a greater faith and understanding of God's will. Had we received our provision a day or two earlier, *Tony Twenty*, that radio audience and the *Wailing Woman* would not have received the Word the Lord had desired them to hear through us; neither would my family have learned a deeper trust in the Lord's providence. While various situations that fall upon you may seem like a plague of misfortune, remember that the Lord knows precisely what He is doing. Moreover, everything the Lord does is for our good, and the good of our brothers and sisters to whom we have been sent, or perhaps rendered still until the moment they cross our path.

Jonah attempted to flee to Tarshish because he did not want to leave home, nor did he believe the Ninevites were deserving of God's mercy. After all, they were not the children of Israel. We make the same mistakes today when we judge someone's book by their cover. We don't like their appearance, how they dress, the way they speak, where they live, or the religion they espouse, so we save our preaching for the choir, which amounts to nothing. We make judgments, not about sin, but about whom the Lord is willing to forgive and restore, forgetting that a servant is not the Judge or the King. We can also ignore someone in need, deeming their issue to be trivial when to them it feels like an earthquake. It is enough that a good and faithful servant obeys the Judge and the King, performing the tasks given to the best of his or her ability, whether he or she approves.

20

The Prodigal Son

Though it took every last dollar we had been given to get back to Ohio, on March 11, 2010 we arrived precisely on time before another gathering of the Lord's Church in Celina. They received the Lord's message well, and through them the Lord funded another trip to Jefferson City, Missouri, where I had been asked to deliver the keynote speech before the Callaway County Republicans. On the drive out I told Clara, "I really don't know why they're having me. Don't they know what I'm going to say?"

Indeed, I never advocated voting *'Republican.'* On the contrary, I strictly advised Christian voters to forsake the lesser of two evils candidates, Republican or Democrat, and write in *'Christ The Lord.'* It seemed to me that this message would not be well received by this forthcoming group of Republicans, especially heading into the 2010 election season. That's when I committed an error, because I considered how I might 'shrewdly' plant seeds that might eventually lead the audience to the ultimate truth. As I would soon discover, a servant of the Lord has no business altering the message he has been given to fit the ears of those to whom he has been sent to proclaim it. God's Word is fully capable of piercing all barriers, but we must be willing to use its full force. If a man or woman will not hear the bold truth, they will not hear it softly, at least not until the Father has humbled them.

On the night of March 15, 2010, we arrived at a banquet hall in Fulton where my family sat and supped with a houseful of Republican politicians, party organizers, boosters and volunteers. *Windex Woman* would have felt right at home, at least in the beginning. After Clara, the kids and I listened to a series politicians vie for support, the host introduced me to the crowd and I shortly ascended the stage to deliver the keynote address. Despite the Spirit's warnings, I began down the shrewd course I had conjured in my own mind on the drive over. Consequently, about five minutes into my speech, my slate was wiped clean. My mind drew a complete blank and for the first and only time on our journey, I was rendered speechless. No one gathered seemed to notice anything was wrong, but all I could see were their curious faces staring back at me, expecting words that weren't coming. Realizing what had happened, I excused myself from the audience and turned aside to have a private word with the Lord. 'Forgive me Lord, I understand,' I silently prayed. 'Tell me what you want and I will obey.'

> *Therefore this is what the LORD says: "If you repent, I will restore you that you may serve me; if you utter worthy, not worthless, words, you will be my spokesman. Let this people turn to you, but you must not turn to them."*
>
> *—Jeremiah 15:19*

Along these lines, the Spirit said, 'Give them the hard truth and subtract nothing from it. It is all or nothing.'

I looked at the audience then over to Clara and the kids, honestly asking, 'Is my family in danger, Lord?'

'Trust in Me,' He replied.

Weak in spirit, but emboldened by the Holy Spirit, I turned back to the group and delivered the Lord's message, abandoning my own. I told them that We The Church, regardless of party, were responsible for the sad state of our nation, because we had forsaken the God of our fathers. I explained that at one time both political parties could at least agree on God, but today both have fallen away on account of greed. I then boldly challenged them with the *Truth Serum* and voting *'Christ The Lord.'* Finally, being led by the Spirit, I shared the account of Jonah's preaching at Nineveh, explaining that politics, ideology and money cannot heal our nation, but only a demonstration of true repentance where we turn from our wicked ways. Although the Ninevites were not what Jonah considered to be the Lord's people, called by His Name, they were spared by virtue of their obedience to His Word:

On the first day, Jonah started into the city. He proclaimed: "Forty more days and Nineveh will be overturned." The Ninevites believed God. They declared a fast, and all of them, from the greatest to the least, put on sackcloth.

—Jonah 3:4-5

That's when the Spirit convicted me to speak something I would never have planned. The Lord had revealed His parable of the fruitless fig tree through the Marties' lemon tree in Florida. He had further told me that our nation's four-year trial was commensurate with *'This presidential term of office.'* Now, as I stood before a large group of dedicated Missouri Republicans, He made clear to me that the order of the mass repentance at Nineveh was the key to the restoration of the United States:

When the news reached the king of Nineveh, he rose from his throne, took off his royal robes, covered himself with sackcloth and sat down in the dust.

—Jonah 3:6

That *news* reached the king, because all the people of his city *from the greatest to the least* were in repentance after hearing Jonah's preaching. Had the king not seen his people already embracing repentance there would have been no provocation for him to join them. Thus, it was revealed to me that when the church in Nineveh repented, the Lord had mercy on them and humbled their king:

Then he issued a proclamation in Nineveh: "By the decree of the king and is nobles: Do not let any man or beast, herd or flock, taste anything; do not let them eat or drink. But let man and beast be covered with sackcloth. Let everyone call urgently on God. Let them give up their evil ways and their violence. Who knows? God may yet relent and with compassion turn from his fierce anger so that we will not perish." —Jonah 3:7-9

Resisting the incessant assault from the enemy that tempts us to question the Lord's truth, I proclaimed to that crowd of dedicated Republicans that when the church in America awakens, so shall President Barack Obama. He will come to know the truth and with a new heart he will gather together with Congress and descend the Capitol footsteps to declare a national repentance. "We all need to be in Nineveh tomorrow in sackcloth and in ashes," I concluded.

Although I had braced myself for rejection, these sworn political enemies of our president erupted with a standing ovation of praise to the Lord. It was beautiful, a political body transformed into the Body of Christ, setting aside their worldly proclivities in devotion to their Savior. When I heard these least likely of voices lift up praises to the Lord that President Barack Obama might be awakened to the truth and lead our nation to the Lord's restoration, I was overwhelmed. I felt joy, because they believed, but also shame, because I had tried to give these people something I deemed *'palatable.'* Thanks be to God, because He prevented me from dishonoring Him. He knew this audience was going to receive His message long before we had set out from Texas. No matter how fantastic and implausible it may seem, who are we to question God?

That night, the Lord refilled our coffer yet again, and through the least likely of subjects—politicians. One after another, they thanked me for reminding them that their first allegiance is to Jesus Christ. It taught me that We The Church don't need to replace every seat in every office in the nation, but if only we would set aside our money concerns and cry out urgently on the Lord, ceasing our rebellion against His Word, then He would heal us in every way.

> *"'After this I will return and rebuild David's fallen tent. Its ruins I will rebuild, and I will restore it, that the remnant of men may seek the Lord, and all the Gentiles who bear my name, says the Lord, who does these things' that have been known for ages." —Acts 15:16-18*

The next day, we started back for Ohio and I began to process all the Lord had spoken through me and to me. I once thought it challenging to proclaim *"Vote 'Christ The Lord.'"* Had I now been sent forth to proclaim the reelection and awakening of President Barack Obama? I was numb, realizing the scope and gravity of what I had been given. I could never have conceived this. It is so beyond me. The pages of the Bible are springing to life for all to witness, and though so many have taken the Lord's Word for granted in this so-called modern age of reason, by His grace and authority shall we be given this gift, so long as the nation embraces repentance.

The Lord knows that certain truths He is going to give us will be difficult to accept. For this reason, God has declared that every matter of His truth shall be established through two or more witnesses:

> *This will be my third visit to you. "Every matter must be established by the testimony of two or three witnesses." —2 Corinthians 13:1*

We have multiple examples of this recorded in the Bible, such as when Gideon twice put out a fleece to test if it was indeed the Lord who was telling him to deliver Israel from the oppression of that vast army of Midian. Remember that John the Baptist came to prepare the way for Christ as a confirming witness in the *spirit and power of Elijah.* Not one wise man, but *wise men* witnessed the birth of Christ. Two prophets, Simeon and Anna, witnessed baby Jesus' consecration at the temple. Christ sent forth His workers *two by two* into every town and village of Israel. Our Lord also appointed Twelve Apostles to serve as eyewitnesses of His Gospel, including His resurrection.

In keeping with His Word, the Lord also sent my family multiple witnesses concerning the awakening of President Barack Obama. Among the first, an attorney and advocate for introducing Bible studies into Ohio public schools called me almost immediately upon our return from Missouri. A pastor had suggested we speak nearly a month prior, but we had not been able to connect. Yet again, it was the Lord's timing. After only briefly sharing my family's mission with this sister in Christ, the Holy Spirit moved her to interrupt me and ask if I had read a book about a president who comes to office an unbeliever, but while facing a national crisis he has a profound awakening in Christ. I had told her nothing about our newfound understanding that Barack Obama was to have such an awakening while in office.

> *Then Jesus told him, "Because you have seen me, you have believed; blessed are those who have not seen and yet have believed." —John 20:29*

Another witness, perhaps the most powerful, was delivered on the evening of May 6, 2010. For many, this was the National Day of Prayer, but for my family it was the day the Spirit had appointed for Ohio to initiate a national repentance. Led by the Spirit, my family had labored intensely all throughout April to organize the disparate and denominated church across Northwest Ohio to unite for an all-day caravan of fasting, prayer and repentance across seven counties. In each county we planned to stop in a key city to bow down and humble ourselves before the Lord, in order that we might beseech His Healing Hand for our nation. After alerting the Church Body in the region, I spent the day before the event seeking the Lord's Face about how I should teach His Church to pray for our lost president. As I began to write what was given, my heart was unexpectedly crushed by an immense sorrow. An understanding of the Lord's infinite heartache for His lost children was being planted within me.

Consider the vastness of God's creation, from the outer reaches of the universe to the smallest particles of matter our feeble human eyes have barely seen. When we compare our creative skill to the Lord's, it's laughable. The greatest of our engineering feats is less than a spec on a spec in the spectral dustbowl of the universe Almighty God breathed into being. In the same way, our capacity for love is equally infantile. As much as we love our children, we cannot fathom the measure of the Lord's love unless we multiply our love by the infinite vastness of His creation. That is how big His Heart is. Now, consider closely how you would feel if one of your children suddenly went missing. Really take time to imagine it and let those feelings set in deep. How great is the desperation, despair and grief in your heart at the mere thought of it? Even if this has been a real tragedy in your life, your anguish is less than a spec on a spec on the scale of the Lord's heartache for one of His lost children. Like you, our Father in heaven longs to embrace His children again, but His longing is far beyond human comprehension. Perhaps there are no greater words to express the measure of God's love for His children than these:

> *"For God so loved the world that he gave his one and only Son, that whoever believes in him shall not perish but have eternal life." —John 3:16*

What the Lord was sharing with me that day was less than a spec of the measure of His Heart and the pain He bears for His lost son, Barack Obama, and it was more than I could bear. Through this, I realized just how real the parable of the prodigal son is to our Father in heaven:

> *Jesus continued: "There was a man who had two sons. The younger one said to his father, 'Father, give me my share of the estate.' So he divided his property between them.*
>
> *"Not long after that, the younger son got together all he had, set off for a distant country and there squandered his wealth in wild living." —Luke 15:11-13*

After traveling through six cities the following day; Celina, Indian Lake, Kenton, Findlay, Ottawa and Van Wert, we finally drove to a church in the seventh city of Lima after a long day filled with prayer, fasting and tears of repentance. Before I spoke to the gathered, two pastors of different religious orders, united in Christ, took their turns at the pulpit to share the messages the Lord had placed upon their hearts. Neither pastor knew of the prophecy the Lord had given me concerning our president nor had they consulted each other on their messages, but had sought the Spirit independently.

The first pastor stepped forward and began, "God accepts repentance..." He then went on to describe the *parable of the prodigal son* to illustrate his point.

"Oh great," said the other pastor, sitting beside me, "the *prodigal son* was going to be my theme."

> *"When he came to his senses, he said, 'How many of my father's hired men have food to spare, and here I am starving to death! I will set out and go back to my father and say to him: Father, I have sinned against heaven and against you. I am no longer worthy to be called your son; make me like one of your hired men.'" —Luke 15:17-19*

Recounting the parable of the prodigal son, both pastors gave near identical messages about God's love for His lost children. By the time they had concluded, I was overwhelmed. Truly, the Spirit was speaking to any who would listen. So, I stepped forward and told them how the Lord had made clear to me that our lost president was the embodiment of the *prodigal son*, whom the Lord longs to draw home.

> *"So he got up and went to his father. But while he was still a long way off, his father saw him and was filled with compassion for him; he ran to his son, threw his arms around him and kissed him." —Luke 15:20*

None should doubt the Lord's ability to awaken our president, for He has humbled more prideful men before. Was Nebuchadnezzar able to resist His call? Was Saul of Tarsus? Consider what great enemies of God's people both of these men were. Nebuchadnezzar sacked Jerusalem, slaughtered the people and burned the Temple to the ground. Saul of Tarsus was an admitted persecutor and murderer of the *followers of the Way,* the original Christian church in Judaea. Yet, one day while honoring himself, Nebuchadnezzar heard a voice from heaven decree his judgment. Shortly thereafter he found himself eating grass like cattle and wandering the wilderness like an animal. Likewise, Saul of Tarsus heard a voice from heaven—Jesus, whose burning Glory caused him to go blind. When the humbling of both these men was achieved, the Lord restored them, and they both gave great glory to the Name of the Most High God.

At the end of that time, I, Nebuchadnezzar, raised my eyes toward heaven, and my sanity was restored. Then I praised the Most High; I honored and glorified him who lives forever. His dominion is an eternal dominion; his kingdom endures from generation to generation. All the peoples of the earth are regarded as nothing. He does as he pleases with the powers of heaven and the peoples of the earth. No one can hold back his hand or say to him: "What have you done?"

—Daniel 4:34-35

Like Nebuchadnezzar, our president shall first be humbled and then he will come to acknowledge the absolute sovereignty of the Lord his God. It may even begin with a dream of a tree that was cut down. It is no coincidence that President Barack Obama models his presidency after Abraham Lincoln's. Indeed, he will follow after Lincoln's trials. Lincoln thought his ultimate duty was to uphold the Constitution of the United States, so he sought to make compromises on the issue of slavery. Consequently, the people of the Divided States of America and Lincoln were bound to the same fate. What the nation suffered upon the battlefields of the Civil War, Lincoln suffered personally in the White House. When the nation was humbled into accepting the abolition of slavery, so was Lincoln. So shall it be for Barack Obama, only his *Emancipation Proclamation* will be the abolition of abortion. This is how you will know our president's awakening is genuine, and that it came from God, for he will turn from his wicked ways and seek to make the Sanctity of Human Life the highest law of our land. When that day comes, who will say this was man's doing? Surely the whole world will see this as an act of God for the glory of His Great Name.

Therefore, take care that you do not let selfishness, or your own worldly concerns and prejudices harden your heart. Jonah once sat atop that hill overlooking Nineveh, becoming *"angry enough to die"* when the people of that great city received the Lord's grace. If the Lord has decided to call one of His lost children home and subsequently honors him, what is that to you? If you are truly a member of the Body of Christ, should you not rejoice as your Father in heaven rejoices?

"The older brother became angry and refused to go in. So his father went out and pleaded with him. But he answered his father, 'Look! All these years I've been slaving for you and never disobeyed your orders. Yet you never gave me even a young goat so I could celebrate with my friends. But when this son of

yours who has squandered your property with prostitutes comes home, you kill the fattened calf for him!'" —Luke 15:28-30

If you should find yourself sharing the sentiments of the *older brother,* it would be good for you to find a mirror and have a close look at yourself. If you know your Savior, you might remember that He once took pity on you, cleansing you of your sinful ways, though you deserved no better. He did this not only for you, but for His own Name's sake, knowing that your transformation from death to life would shine as an indelible witness of His Glory, thus attracting others to His salvation. Is there any greater witness of this than Saul of Tarsus, whom Jesus transformed into Paul the apostle?

Then Ananias went to the house and entered it. Placing his hands on Saul, he said, "Brother Saul, the Lord—Jesus, who appeared to you on the road as you were coming here—has sent me so that you may see again and be filled with the Holy Spirit." Immediately, something like scales fell from Saul's eyes, and he could see again. He got up and was baptized. —Acts 9:17-18

Paul would go on to become perhaps the greatest missionary of all time, but many Christians in his day could not accept him as a brother. Likewise, there will be Christians today who will resist accepting our president's awakening, even when the scales fall from his eyes. Once a false shepherd wrote me that President Obama was among *"Satan's Children,"* adding, *"Not everyone shares your burden for Barack Obama, nor for repentance."* On another occasion, an African-American pastor confessed to me that he too had desired Barack Obama's downfall. He was mortified that on account of his being black other pastors in his community and members of his own congregation automatically assumed he voted for an enemy of Christ. Of course, given the lesser of two evils on the 2008 presidential ballot, for whom did his peers vote? Notwithstanding, he plaintively questioned, "How can the first black president of the United States be this man?" Thankfully, after hearing my testimony, my African-American brother repented, being reminded of his duty by the words the Spirit inspired through none other than the apostle Paul:

I urge, then, first of all, that requests, prayers, intercession and thanksgiving be made for everyone—for kings and all those in authority, that we may live peaceful and quiet lives in all godliness and holiness. This is good, and pleases

God our Savior, who wants all men to be saved and to come to a knowledge of the truth. —1 Timothy 2:1-4

Following that night in Lima, my family took a long awaited three-day Sabbatical. During this period we prayed constantly for the Lord's guidance and sought clarity in His Word. It was an incredibly Spirit-filled time. We were given dreams, visions, and Scripture was revealed to us in ways we had never before understood. I continually asked the Lord to confirm that we were properly hearing His Voice, that the mass repentance at Nineveh was the key to our national restoration, and that our president would indeed awaken to lead our nation back to God Most High and Jesus Christ, just as Nineveh's king led them. On the evening of the third day, exhausted from all the Lord had been sharing with us, I decided to turn on the television for the first time in months. Before the picture on the screen came alight, I heard the voice of a narrator say, "So just what kind of fish was it that swallowed Jonah?" Incredibly, I had turned on a documentary exploring the validity of the biblical account of Jonah. We heard the Lord's Voice loud and clear, 'It is the truth.'

21

"God Bless the Children!"

Before the spring thaw, I spoke on a Sunday night before a church in Findlay whose pastor I had met some weeks before. I was wary about that night, because during my meeting with this pastor I had felt the Holy Spirit come upon me and saw his face split into two. I blinked my eyes, but his face remained split for an eerily long moment as he went on and on about his ministry. I understood the Lord was showing me that he was 'two-faced.' Yet, I also realized the Lord had sent me to his church for the benefit of the flock, which did not belong to the pastor, but to God.

After delivering a message I pray has taken root for Jesus, Clara and I took the kids to a nearby diner to treat them to ice cream. We wanted to spend some quality time with our children, but the Lord had other plans. Soon as we pulled into the parking lot, Clara and I both spotted a stranded conversion van with two women and their five sons standing beside it in the cold while a roadside service guy futilely tried getting it started. When I parked, Clara told me assertively what I already knew, "You need to go help them."

"I know," I agreed.

As Clara and the kids walked inside the warm diner, I walked through snow flurries to meet the family and see how I could help. The story behind their situation was that these women had taken their boys on a vacation road trip down to Florida. On the way back home to Michigan their van's alternator suddenly conked out on the freeway. They managed to get it to the parking lot, but now it wouldn't start. Having expended all their money on their trip, they couldn't afford to fix it, nor could they afford a room for the night. When I asked them if they had any nearby family or friends they could stay with, they replied, "No, we'll just sleep in the van."

"Oh no, you're not gonna do that!" I insisted, pointing to the snow flurries. "You'll freeze out in this cold." I realized how profound this encounter really was. Just across the street from the diner was the motel where my family had slept in our Tahoe in the January cold. How could I let this family to do the same, especially since the Lord had placed the ability to shelter them within my pocket through that evening's *love offering?*

I asked the roadside assistance guy if they had any deals with nearby lodging, and he confirmed that they did with a brand new hotel right across the street. In short order, we set this family up with a suite, along with some extra cash for breakfast in the morning. I then turned my attention to the alternator. I was prepared to pay for it to be replaced or repaired, but the Lord stepped in with another solution. The roadside service guy knew the hostess in the diner and her boyfriend, a mechanic. Between them, they arranged for the alternator to be fixed right there in the parking lot the next morning! That's what the Lord can do when just one of His workers snaps into action. Though I was prepared to give all I had for this family, the Lord simply used me to start another *Jesus-reaction* of blessings. It was awesome to watch it all unfold. I'll never forget the way the roadside service guy, those two women and their sons looked at my family. They just couldn't believe the Lord had sent these strangers to deliver them. But we weren't strangers. We were and remain servants of Christ Jesus, their brothers and sisters, whom the Lord had placed in their path at precisely the right time. We especially pray those young men will remember the encouragement I gave them to take up their own personal service in Christ.

When I finally made it inside the diner, I found my children sitting in a corner booth joyfully slurping the last of their sundaes and shakes. Their mother, however, was tending to a homeless man at the breakfast bar. When the hostess had first led Clara and the kids past him to their booth, he had boisterously called out, "God bless the children! God bless the children!" Naturally, Clara engaged him to see if he was mocking the Lord or was he a divine appointment. He turned out to be an appointment. Seeing me approach, Clara introduced me to *Harley*, who was very drunk. Swaying in his seat, he greeted me in a slurred voice, "Nice to meet you."

"You need to talk with him," Clara said, giving me the handoff, but first we waited for Harley to finish a large glass of milk the waitress had just served up. Earlier our children overheard him ask about the cost of a glass of milk, which he couldn't afford. So, they took it upon themselves to gather the money needed from their own pockets and ordered it for him. As Harley had explained, he had grown up on dairy farm and drank milk *"fresh from the teat!"*

After he guzzled the last of his milk, I helped Harley to his feet and started walking him out of the diner. "Let's go Harley."

"Where are we going?" he asked, his legs dangling beneath him.

"Outside," I said, "where we can talk."

"I don't wanna go outside. It's cold out there," he complained, swearing like a sailor, but not in a disrespectful manner.

"It'll be good for ya," I assured him. "Besides, I want to make sure you're awake enough to hear what I have to tell you."

Soon as we emerged from the warmth of the diner into the snow flurries outside, Harley complained again, "You see, it's cold."

"Oh, it's not so cold," I told him, fighting back the shivers in my Texan blood.

Together, we sat on the curb and I asked him, "Harley, what happened to you?"

"I'm just a big screw-up," he groaned. He began telling me his life story, how he had always been a drinker and how it had ruined his marriage and his children. He was all torn up over his daughter, who was working as an exotic dancer. He knew that his drunken example during her youth had led her to that life. He began to weep, further explaining that he had been homeless for some time. "I wanna give it up, but I have to drink or I'll freeze," he insisted.

"You know that's a lie," I told him. "The enemy wants you to make excuses to drink yourself to death. That's his goal."

"I know, I know," he cried. "But what am I gonna do? I have a job, a real job. I'm supposed to start tomorrow, but I can't even take a shower. I can't show up like this," he cried out in despair.

"You know Harley," I began, "the Lord will help you out of this, but you're going to have to make a commitment yourself. You've got to ask Him for forgiveness for all you've done. Then you have to decide that you're done with this life and you're not going back. If you do, the Lord will give you strength to stay the course."

"I do—I do want out. I want the Lord to forgive me." With that he aggressively took my hand in his, squeezing it tight. "Let's pray. Pray that God forgives me."

So we began to pray and I've never seen a man so repentant in all my life. Tears were flying out from his eyes as he wailed and he cried out, "God forgive me! I don't want to live like this anymore! In the name of the Father, the Son and the Holy Ghost! Forgive me God! Forgive me, forgive me Jesus..." His plea was so powerful it brought me to tears. I had never witnessed so deep and heartfelt a prayer, offered by a man so broken. If only the whole church in America had a heart to repent like this man did!

When finally we said, "Amen," Harley recomposed himself and opened his eyes wide for the first time since I'd met him. It was though he became instantly sober. But that wasn't all. "Harley, can you feel it?" I asked, as he continued to firmly squeeze my hand.

He thought for a moment, looked around at the snow flurries and said, "Yeah, yeah I feel it."

"It's warm," I laughed. "I told you we'd be alright."

He began to laugh with me. "It really is warm."

I embraced him and said, "I love you and the Lord forgives you."

"I love you too," he answered and squeezed me tight.

After a long moment, we finally let go of one another and I helped him to his feet, "Now let's get you that shower."

"I'll be fine," he said. "You've done enough."

"No way you're sleeping out in the cold tonight," I asserted.

I walked him back into the diner and sat him down. Then I found the roadside service guy and told him to get us one more room at the inn. He had a full load with the van family, so he called one of his buddies to come pick up Harley. While we waited for his ride, Harley sat with Clara and me on either side of him inside the diner in the waiting area. He held each of our hands and asked if we would pray with him some more. We did, and afterwards he gave a deep cleansing sigh, "Wow..." He looked at Clara and me and asked, "Can you feel that?" He lifted up our hands, squeezing them tighter. "That's power!" The Spirit was overwhelming him.

"It's the Lord, not us," we told him. "We're just His servants."

It wasn't long before Harley's ride pulled up and a man and woman got out of their pickup.

"Here they are," I told him. "They're going to take you to the hotel where you can have that shower."

Harley thanked us profusely, but when he saw his driver's face, he said, "Aw, he's just like me."

"What do you mean?" Clara asked him.

"He's a drunk just like me," he said as a matter of fact.

Clara and I went outside to greet the couple, somewhat concerned. Without wasting time, Clara got right next to the man and said, "When we seek the Lord earnestly He heals everything."

He expressed no anxiety about being confronted, but admitted, "I used to have a problem, but I've been clean for a while now."

Without being pejorative, Clara replied, "I just wanted to make sure we were putting Harley in good hands."

"I understand," he replied with genuine appreciation.

I gave him the money for the room and something extra for their time and trouble. He and his girlfriend then helped Harley into the backseat of their pickup. I reminded Harley, "When you wake-up tomorrow morning, go into that bathroom and take a long look in the mirror. Don't forget what it felt like to sleep out in the cold. Don't forget that God sent us to you tonight to give you another chance. Don't squander this opportunity to set your life straight. From this day forward, make a vow to the Lord never to return."

"I won't forget," he assured me.

As they drove off to the hotel, Clara and I finally rejoined the kids. Two hours had passed since our arrival, and now it was past midnight. Yet we were hardly tired, because the Lord's Spirit was moving. Before we left the diner, the couple that had taken Harley to the hotel returned with some leftover money in hand. They didn't feel right about keeping anything for themselves. More importantly, they wanted to share with us how Harley had reacted when they showed him to his room. First, he tried to convince them to take him to the cheap motel where my family had spent that night out in the cold, sleeping in our Tahoe. He just didn't think he was worthy to stay at that brand new hotel. When he got to his room, he fell into tears. It might have been the nicest space he had ever had the privilege of sleeping in. Then he got a view of the bathroom, to which he proclaimed, "I'm gonna take five showers in the morning!"

We have no knowledge of what happened to Harley after that night. We pray for him from time to time, remembering his prayer of repentance and beseeching the Lord's blessings for this man who came to us lost, but left us found. We also remember John, the homeless man we had met that night we had slept in the Tahoe in the cold. We often wonder if either John or Harley, or perhaps both, weren't men at all, but angels sent to remind us that restoration comes one soul at a time. Yes, the Lord will bring down the walls of Jericho, but we the servants of Christ are still going to have to march round about it seven times, trumpeting His truth.

Do not forget to entertain strangers, for by so doing some people have entertained angels without knowing it. —Hebrews 13:2

22

What Is Truth?

If you were walking on the street and narrowly avoided a sinkhole, you would want to warn others to stay clear of it as well, and they would most likely heed your warning. Yet, when you try to warn someone against sin, because the Holy Bible calls it sin, not even many Christians will listen, instead they fall right in. The problem is the church in America has become conceited, believing it knows better than the Word of God. Either it disregards the Word as having been written merely by men, or it takes it to mean what it wants it to mean, rather than what it actually says.

> *Do you see a man wise in his own eyes? There is more hope for a fool than for him. —Proverbs 26:12*

Those who relish their own wisdom have effectively distorted what has been called the *Golden Rule* from its original intent to create a new religion called *To Each His Own.* Its followers do whatever they desire in the privacy of their own space and expect that everyone else will respect it, even when what they do may be harming others as well as themselves. When called out on it, such people quickly justify their wrongdoing, saying, "Who are you to judge?"

> *"Son of man, speak to your countrymen and say to them: 'When I bring the sword against a land, and the people of the land choose one of their men and make him their watchman, and he sees the sword coming against the land and*

blows the trumpet to warn the people, then if anyone hears the trumpet but does not take warning and the sword comes and takes his life, his blood will be on his own head.'" —Ezekiel 33:2-4

No man or woman is the Judge, but as good and faithful watchmen on the wall we are witnesses sent forth to cite the Eternal Law of God Most High and Jesus Christ. You can ignore the witness, but the Judge will hold you accountable to their testimony. He won't bother to hear inane excuses; neither will He consult a jury made up of lawless peers, because He is the source of all truth.

"You are a king, then!" said Pilate.

Jesus answered, "You are right in saying I am a king. In fact, for this reason I was born, and for this I came into the world, to testify to the truth. ***Everyone on the side of truth listens to me.****" —John 18:37*

When summer finally arrived, by the Lord's providence my family found ourselves staying on a milk farm, enjoying milk just like Harley in his youth. One Saturday, the farmers invited us down to their market in Dayton. There, Clara and I met a man named James who perfectly illustrated the Power of Truth. He was the quintessential syncretist, one who believes in the lie that *all roads lead to heaven,* or more precisely that man can make his own way to heaven. The Lord first led him to Clara, and as they began to talk, she asked him, "So James, do you love the Lord?"

Rather put off, James replied, "I don't believe like you do."

"What do you believe in?" Clara asked.

"I find something peaceful about eastern religions."

Clara sincerely disagreed, "There's nothing peaceful about dead-end paths, there is only one Way and His Name is Jesus Christ."

"Well, you're entitled to believe what you want to believe and I'll believe what I believe. We'll just have to agree to disagree."

Clara told him plainly, "No James, I won't 'agree to disagree.'"

James became ruffled. "No? That's the problem with you Christians. You just can't let people believe what they want. I have my opinion and you have yours. Why can't you leave it at that?"

"Because I know where I'm going and I would like to see you in heaven too. You're lost, James, and I love you too much not to tell you the truth." Intrigued by her sincerity, James remained engaged. People generally sniff out phonies, but a sincere truth pierces the heart. They may not like what the truth says, but they listen, because the Lord has built within each of us a natural desire for His Voice. After all, even a compulsive liar wants to hear the truth.

I arrived in the midst of their debate, and Clara introduced me to James, saying, "This is James. He's been burned by the church."

James was in shock, because he hadn't shared that with Clara.

"Well, can't blame you there," I told him, reaching out to shake his hand. Immediately, James was put at ease. I like to describe it as the *meat tenderizer* approach. First, Clara comes in and *BAP, BAP, BAP,* she tenderizes the subject to receive the truth. Then I come in with the soothing salve, to which the subject says, *"Ahhh..."*

Without missing a beat, I asked, "So what did the church do?"

James explained that he had been with a particular church denomination, but was kicked out. "I might have been an adulterer," he remarked sarcastically, but Clara and I understood he was confessing. He then proceeded to outline his disagreements with Clara.

"You may not agree with me," I told him, "but there is only one Way and that's Jesus Christ."

"That's what your wife said," he muttered. "But that's because you don't know the richness of eastern religions."

"What makes them rich?" I asked.

"My belief," he began, "is that any religion that applies the *Golden Rule* has merit."

"What's the Golden Rule?"

"You know," he asserted, "do unto others as you would have them do unto you."

> *"So in everything,* ***do to others what you would have them do to you,*** *for this sums up the Law and the Prophets." —Matthew 7:12*

Interestingly, James denied having any faith in Christ, but somehow he was comfortable quoting the Lord to justify his pagan beliefs. This has become standard practice among the lost, including among proclaimed "Christians," and it is a tactic of Satan. However, you can defeat these hollow arguments by driving to God's deeper truths, which apply the *whole Word.* Following the Spirit, I told him, "But that's not the Golden Rule."

"Sure it is," he argued.

"What Christ said to His apostles was, *'As I have loved you, so you must love one another.'"* I paused as that got him thinking.

"My command is this: Love each other as I have loved you." —John 15:12

"You see James," I continued, "there are plenty of sadistic people out there who would be all too happy to brutalize one another and have the same done unto them. That's not love. To love one another as our Lord loves us sets an entirely different standard."

Not surprisingly, James was struck by the truth and nodded his head. "Yeah, I agree with that."

Of course he would agree, because when Jesus put forth *The Beatitudes* concerning how people are to treat each other, as described in Matthew 7, He was speaking from a foundation of God's righteousness, not man's. Jesus had already explained this to those who had gathered for His *Sermon on the Mount,* so they would not have misunderstood Him to be applying any human standard:

"You have heard that it was said, 'Love your neighbor and hate your enemy.' But I tell you: Love your enemies and pray for those who persecute you, that you may be sons of your Father in heaven. He causes his sun to rise on the evil and the good, and sends rain on the righteous and the unrighteous."

—Matthew 5:43-45

That is God's measurement for righteousness, and this concept shifted our discussion into a whole new gear. Next thing, we were agreeing that there is a God, though he was not prepared to identify *who* God is. All I could do was point him in the right direction and say, *"You see, God is right there."* After that, James was going to have to open his eyes and accept the truth. "So James," I continued, "you strike me as a man who is seeking the truth."

"Yes I am," he confirmed.

I already knew that James wasn't ready to accept the truth of Jesus Christ at face value. Instead, he was convinced that there was no way to know the truth for sure. So I asked him, "James, do you believe that truth is dependent upon the intellect of man, or is truth derived from another source?"

James thought it over for a moment and replied, "No, truth has to come from another source."

"That's right," I agreed, "because if it were dependent upon man, none of us would be here right now. Man would have self-destructed long ago."

James was following. "So truth has to come from something that is beyond man and even beyond creation itself, because the natural order of things doesn't come from nowhere. That would be illogical. The truth that set the order of all creation and mankind has to come from somewhere or someone."

James smiled, "I see what you're saying, but I'm not so sure about God."

"I know, but His existence is not dependent upon your acceptance of Him. He's real. He's just waiting for you to figure that out."

James shrugged, "Yeah, but who can be sure."

I put my hand on his shoulder and smiled sincerely. "If you really are about seeking the truth then when you find it, you're going to find Christ waiting there for you." With that I politely excused myself, disengaging the debate. Sometimes you just have to let the seeds do their job. Good thing Clara had meat tenderized James first, otherwise we might never have gotten any to take!

When applied properly, without any human agenda, the truth works. Truth is hard to argue against if given without prejudice, but with honesty, integrity and love. In reality, no one can be intellectually honest and refute the truth. All they can do is reveal their bias and the lies in which they have falsely placed their trust.

During our time on that dairy farm, our children thoroughly enjoyed *farm chores,* which confused the farmers' kids. At the same time, Clara and I added *'milking cows'* to our résumés, which confused us. Early one Sunday morning, the kids also got to see a calf being born, or *"baby caf!"* as Jazelle and Justin would say. The night before, I had a strong feeling that calf was coming the next morning. Before first light, the Lord awakened me suddenly with the distinct smell of cow in my nose. Quickly, I rustled the family together from their sleep and got out in time to witness the birth. It was one of those rare moments in our children's lives they'll never forget, and I praise God we didn't miss it.

Perhaps our favorite pastime on that farm, however, was chasing some rebellious sheep back into their pen. Their sheep had divided themselves into two distinctive groups, the obedient sheep and the rebellious sheep. On a daily basis the rebellious sheep would exploit a section of fence line in disrepair, seeking what they perceived was greener pasture on the other side. The obedient sheep, on the other hand, remained in their pen and would bleat at the rebels to return to where they belonged. The rebellious sheep yelled back dismissively and continued to mow down the forbidden pasture.

When Clara, the kids and I caught the sheep out, we'd all run into the field laughing and yelling, "The sheep are out! The sheep are out!" Right away, those rebellious sheep ran back to their proper pasture, but not without giving us some *lamb-lip* as they ran. In their indignant bleating, we could almost hear, "Leave us rebellious sheep alone you pesky Tabbacks, we're happy in the forbidden pasture!"

Although this was amusing, we found out that in times past some of those rebellious sheep had been killed outside the safety of their pen. One in particular had wandered out onto the road in the middle of the night and was struck by an automobile. Not only had that sheep foolishly put its life at risk, but it also endangered the life of the driver. In this typical sheep-like behavior, we understand why our Lord and Savior referred to us as sheep:

> *Jesus answered, "I did tell you, but you do not believe. The miracles I do in my Father's name speak for me, but you do not believe because you are not my sheep. My sheep listen to my voice; I know them, and they follow me. I give them eternal life, and they shall never perish; no one can snatch them out of my hand." —John 10:25-28*

Like the Israel of old, Christians today behave like rebellious sheep, for though they are familiar with some Scripture, they do not do what the Holy Bible says. Why? Because they do not believe it is actually God's Holy Word. Incredibly, a great many shepherds are perpetuating this lie of Satan, treating the Bible as merely a guidebook written by priests, subjecting it to rash and ignoble interpretations based upon man's desires, as opposed to the Truth.

For example, on July 4, 2010, my family called upon the church in Ohio to put their flags at half-staff in mourning, and to gather with my family at the capital in Columbus to repent before God for the sins of our nation. Out of the thousands invited, just 23 took time away from their usual patriotic revelry to submit themselves to God, and one of these was a man who joined us from the bus stop! We wondered what a turnout of so few might mean for Ohio and the nation, so my family prayed for the Lord's guidance, and afterwards we opened the Bible randomly to this Psalm:

The LORD is my shepherd, I shall not be in want. He makes me lie down in green pastures, he leads me beside quiet waters, he restores my soul. He guides me in paths of righteousness for his name's sake. —Psalm 23:1-3

We were encouraged. That day, the Lord also conspicuously directed our path by a worker's compensation government building. Its flag stood at half-mast—the only such witness we saw that entire day. Nothing is impossible for God!

That evening, my family went to a hotel in Dublin and turned on the TV. Since July 4th fell on a Sunday that year, a well-known Christian mega-church pastor appeared on screen, giving a message about people discovering their "life's purpose." Money and self-gratification was his chief objective, but I became incensed when he misquoted God. He said, "I knew you before," specifically omitting *"the womb"*:

"Before I formed you ***in the womb*** *I knew you, before you were born I set you apart; I appointed you as a prophet to the nations." —Jeremiah 1:5*

Wolves in shepherd's clothing, such as that pastor, distort God's Word for their own selfish ends, leading a great many lost sheep into a forbidden pasture where their *Life appointment* is put in grave danger. They say, "If you're a good person, respecting and loving one another, and doing what you feel in your heart is right, then you have a place in heaven." Yet, because they ignore the greater definitions of goodness, love and righteousness as defined in the Bible, one by one the sheep fall prey to the enemy. The Lord is graceful, so He repeatedly sends true watchmen to warn them. Still, many will not listen, even if he yells, "The sheep are out!"

"Why do you call me good?" Jesus answered. "No one is good—except God alone." —Luke 18:19

People steeped in the universal virtues of *charity* and *humanity* will suggest that human nature is basically good, and they will speak much about their concept of *love*. However, a self-examination under the Ten Commandments reveals that none of us are inherently good. After all, who among us has not coveted something belonging to our neighbor, if not worse? The truth is that *righteousness* is almost entirely a foreign concept to mankind. It certainly cannot be attributed to biology or any genetic trait. The people exampled in the Bible proved that case beyond any shadow of a doubt. Righteousness, such as the Lord defines, must be taught, and the only reliable source for this instruction is the Holy Bible. Those who care to learn it inevitably find themselves at the foot of the cross of Christ where *righteousness that is by faith* is rewarded with salvation:

> *But whatever was to my profit I now consider loss for the sake of Christ. What is more, I consider everything a loss compared to the surpassing greatness of knowing Christ Jesus my Lord, for whose sake I have lost all things. I consider them rubbish, that I may gain Christ and be found in him,* ***not having a righteousness of my own that comes from the law, but that which is through faith in Christ—the righteousness that comes from God and is by faith.***
>
> *—Philippians 3:7-9*

As a member of the Body of Christ, or one considering joining the only Way, the Truth and the Life, you must come to recognize that no one shall be self-justified before God. Everyone seeking the gift of eternal life must present themselves *in Christ* or they will be put to shame, just as the Word of God declares:

> *"All things have been committed to me by my Father. No one knows the Son except the Father, and no one knows the Father except the Son and those to whom the Son chooses to reveal him." —Matthew 11:27*

True human nature is not revealed under temperate conditions, but under extremes. You really don't know a person until you have seen how they operate under great temptation, pressure and stress, or until they have been given great authority. Under the worst of circumstances, some of the *"nicest, most peaceful people"* will suddenly and unexpectedly commit violent murder:

> *Because of the suffering that your enemy will inflict on you during the siege, you will eat the fruit of the womb, the flesh of the sons and daughters the LORD your God have given you. Even the most gentle and sensitive man among you will have no compassion on his own brother or the wife he loves or his surviving children. —Deuteronomy 28:53-54*

Is this the outcome of their good human nature or were they a murderer at heart all along? Contrary to popular opinion, a heart that does not bear the seal of Jesus Christ is a heart that has no concept of goodness. Without warning, Satan can come into that person's heart and drive him or her to the most vile deeds.

Jesus answered, "It is the one to whom I will give this piece of bread when I have dipped it in the dish." Then, dipping the piece of bread, he gave it to Judas Iscariot, son of Simon. ***As soon as Judas took the bread, Satan entered into him.***

"What you are about to do, do quickly," Jesus told him. —John 13:26-27

The Lord once sent me to witness to a "Christian" man right after that Hindu woman in *Casketville* attacked my family. I impressed upon him the importance of testifying the Name of Jesus Christ, saying, "There is no other way to heaven."

"I'm not so sure about that," he questioned. "I have a Hindu guy working for me, and I just have to say that they are some of the nicest, most peaceful people."

He had no idea what he was saying. I pray he gains greater wisdom in Christ before the day of disaster befalls this nation, because on that day, naïve Christians will not survive true human nature. Fact is, those absent of Christ are mastered by their flesh, and such as these will not hesitate to lie, rob, bruise, batter, abandon, and even kill their fellow human beings, whether strangers or the members of their own families, in order to satisfy their desires. Alternatively, those who know the Spirit of our Savior will feel urged to give whether they have little to nothing to spare, to lift up the weak whether it slows them down, and to sacrifice themselves in order to save the life of another—especially if saving that life means testifying the only Name that gives Life!

All Scripture is God-breathed and is useful for teaching, rebuking, correcting and training in righteousness, so that the man of God may be thoroughly equipped for every good work. —2 Timothy 3:16-17

Why does mankind incessantly doubt God's Word? As Creator of the entire universe, is it so hard to believe that God has the authority to override the will of man and preserve His Word? So that man would not blindly walk into a pit of destruction, God ordained that through His people Israel an ultimate source of truth would be drafted and maintained throughout the generations. For this task, He set Israel aside, raising up and refining a nation of priests whom He taught to meticulously record His Word, although they struggled to obey it. The strictness of God's Law, as delivered through Moses, and Israel's many sufferings for violating His Decrees were all for our benefit today, that we might see clearly our inequities and therefore accept salvation through Jesus Christ. Without Christ, we remain bound to sin and therefore cannot measure up to God's standard of righteousness.

> *For God has bound all men over to disobedience so that he may have mercy on them all. —Romans 11:32*

Some will say, "If God is real, why hasn't He revealed Himself to me?" During our travels, the Lord showed us repeatedly how gracious He is with such requests. An unbeliever need only ask humbly, "Lord Jesus, if you're real, please show me and I will follow you."

To emphasize this reality, the Lord led my family to a spectacular witness one day while we were driving up I-17 in Arizona. Incredibly, as we looked out at the beautiful sunset to the west, we were stunned to see the glory of what appeared to be another sun rising in the east! It was so fantastic our whole family gave praise to the Lord.

A few days later, we met a Messianic Jew who eagerly described himself as "the most sarcastic Jew" in his entire family. Before Christ found him, he said he used to go to Christian functions just to mock. On one such occasion, he found and lifted up a copy of the Holy Bible over his head. Before the gathering of Christians he declared, "Jesus if you are real, you are going to have to show me!" After that, he opened the Bible randomly and found himself staring in disbelief at Isaiah 53:

> *But he was pierced for our transgressions, he was crushed for our iniquities; the punishment that brought us peace was upon him, and by his wounds we are healed. —Isaiah 53:5*

He was absolutely stunned by what he had stumbled upon, and for the first time in his life he feared God. Having been shown this passage before by servants of Christ as proof that Jesus is the Messiah, he knew its significance. He said, "What are the odds, out of all the pages in the Bible that I would open it up to this?" For the next few days, he tossed and turned over the possibility that Jesus might really be the Christ. Finally, he decided that he was going to believe in Jesus, but he prayed, "God you're going to have to show me that I am making the right decision."

The next evening as he drove on the freeway, he noticed that while the glory of the sun was setting in the west, incredibly another glory of light was rising in the east! He couldn't explain it, because there was no logical source for that light. He went to bed that night restlessly trying to make sense of what he had seen. Early the next morning, as he drove to work, he looked out to the east and saw the glory of the sunrise. At that moment, he knew God had answered him, for its brilliant light looked just as it had the evening before. "I got affirmations all over me," he said, pointing out the goosebumps on his arms. "I get these every time I tell this story, but that day I felt like they were going to burst out my cheeks!"

"Let us acknowledge the LORD; let us press on to acknowledge him. ***As surely as the sun rises, he will appear;*** *he will come to us like the winter rains, like the spring rains that water the earth." —Hosea 6:3*

From the beginning of time the Lord our God has gone to extraordinary lengths to reveal Himself to us all. Dare to seek Him with the same kind of zeal you sought your last paycheck and you will surely discover the real Jesus Christ for yourself. Forget about what the skeptics say, because if they had truly sought after Jesus they would have found Him. He is not hiding. He lives and is waiting for His children to open up the doors of their hearts for Him. When you do, He will speak to your heart in ways you cannot deny, so conspicuous in timing and circumstance that all the scholarly arguments about biblical translations, dates and priestly motives will dissipate in place of your newfound conviction in the Truth. In that day, you will understand why Jesus and the Word are inseparable:

In the beginning was the Word, and the Word was with God, and the Word was God. He was with God in the beginning. Through him all things were made; without him nothing was made that has been made. In him was life, and that life was the light of men. The light shines in the darkness, but the darkness has not understood it. —John 1:1-5

This is where Jehovah's Witnesses fall, because they don't understand the Word. Once the Lord appointed for Clara and me to meet a pair of Jehovah's Witnesses, a man and a woman, who showed up one day at a house we were staying at. By the Spirit we recognized the appointment and so we welcomed them in. We sat together in the living room and I proposed we pray before entering into a discussion about God's Truth. They quickly declined. Knowing little to nothing about their doctrine, this surprised Clara and me, so we asked them why. "We don't worship Jesus," they replied. Satan has convinced these lost souls that they are honoring God, when in reality they are rejecting Him by refusing to bow down and *worship* the Son. We wound up witnessing to the *Witnesses* that you cannot separate the Son from the Father; they are One. As the Word testifies:

> *Then I heard every creature in heaven and on earth and under the earth and on the sea, and all that is in them, singing: "To him who sits on the throne* ***and to the Lamb*** *be praise and honor and glory and power, forever and ever!"*
>
> *The four living creatures said, "Amen," and the elders fell down and* ***worshipped.*** *—Revelations 5:13-14*

You see that all creation is *worshipping* Him who sits on the throne *and the Lamb.* They are not separate, but One! Neither are the proclamations of *"praise and honor and glory and power"* distinguished between the Father and the Son—they are honored as One, and by the *elders!* This is a heavenly truth, which may be difficult for the human mind to fully comprehend, but it is no less the Truth. As Jesus said:

> *"I tell you the truth, we speak of what we know, and we testify to what we have seen,* ***but still you people do not accept our testimony.*** *I have spoken to you of earthly things and you do not believe; how then will you believe if I speak of heavenly things?" —John 3:11-12*

When Jesus spoke this Word to the Pharisee Nicodemus, He was fulfilling the Word He had once spoken to the prophet Isaiah:

> ***Who has believed our message*** *and to whom has the arm of the LORD been revealed? —Isaiah 53:1*

It was not Moses who led Israel from Egypt; it was Jesus Christ. This is a heavenly mystery, but if you have ears to hear it then receive the truth that every Word uttered by God the Father was spoken through Jesus Christ. No prophet ever heard a Word from God, or saw an image of God that wasn't delivered through the Son. In this manner, God has established that everything created must come to Him *through the Son:*

> *"For God did not send his Son into the world to condemn the world, but to save the world* ***through him.*** *Whoever believes in him is not condemned, but whoever does not believe stands condemned already because he has not believed in the name of God's one and only Son." —John 3:17-18*

This is where the Jews fell as well. Because the time had not yet come when *the arm of the Lord should be revealed* to them, they could not conceive of a God consisting of a Father and a Son, even though all of their teachings had been revealed through His Holy Spirit. After all, where did their prophets learn God's Word, since no Book of the Law existed before Moses?

Jesus answered, "My teaching is not my own. It comes from him who sent me. If anyone chooses to do God's will, he will find out whether my teaching comes from God or whether I speak on my own." —John 7:16-17

The concept of the Holy Trinity is difficult to grasp, especially for monotheist Jews and Muslims, but it should not be difficult to understand that the One True God has revealed Himself by *two or three witnesses: The Father, the Son and the Holy Spirit.* Even so, God is One, proven by the fact that neither Jesus nor the promised Holy Spirit have spoken on their own, but only what the Father has spoken to His children through them:

"But when he, the Spirit of truth, comes, he will guide you into all truth. He will not speak on his own; he will speak only what he hears, and he will tell you what is yet to come. ***He will bring glory to me by taking from what is mine and making it known to you. All that belongs to the Father is mine.*** *That is why I said the Spirit will take from what is mine and make it known to you."*

—John 16:13-15

Just as Jesus, the Living Word, declared, *when you choose to do God's will,* this truth will become an indwelling reality by virtue of His Holy Spirit. You may not be able to articulate it in human terms, but you will know it to be true in your heart, and you will be led to live a life glorifying to your Savior.

Many times over the course of our journey, people have asked us, "How should I read the Bible?" because they can't make sense of the parables. As the Lord has taught my family, His Word is both literal and symbolic, all perfectly knit together as a complete witness of His eternal Truth; such as the Lord created both *the heavens* and *the earth.* The first is spiritual and the second is temporal, and both testify to God's surpassing greatness. In fact, just about anything you can think of in this natural earth has a spiritual witness. Have you ever wondered why we have two eyes and two ears, yet one tongue? This reflects two witnesses of the truth who speak with One Voice, the Father and the Son. Likewise, servants of Christ are called to speak the truth by virtue of the Holy Spirit, testifying to the nature of the Father and

Son's unity. Alternatively, people who double-speak reflect a fork-tongued serpent, which is indicative of Satan, whose goal is to divide people from the Truth.

Unfortunately, many people think they are hearing the truth and teaching it, when they are actually being deceived and go forth deceiving. My family can testify that we have a genuine love for the Jehovah's Witnesses we've met. We deeply care for their salvation. Still, the hardest people to share the truth with are those who are sure they already know it, and this applies to all religions. Consequently, you can speak the truth to a multitude of people and find that many will struggle to understand it, and some flat out reject it. This dynamic reflects the Word Christ spoke to the prophet Isaiah, warning the ancient Jews, and future Christian's to come, that because of their devotion to wickedness, God's Truth would seem like a foreign language to them:

He said, "Go and tell this people: 'Be ever hearing, but never understanding; be ever seeing, but never perceiving." —Isaiah 6:9

The Word is just as applicable today and to this modern era as it was in the days it was walked out by the ancient prophets, apostles and disciples who by the inspiration of the Holy Spirit wrote down their personal testimonies for our benefit. So, if you want to know the real Jesus, you must begin by doing the simple things the Word Commands. Start by expunging from your life anything the Bible explicitly condemns as sin:

Once I was alive apart from law; but when the commandment came, sin sprang to life and I died. —Romans 7:9

That *commandment* of which Paul was speaking was the very first:

And the LORD God commanded the man, *"You are free to eat from any tree in the garden; but you must not eat from the tree of the knowledge of good and evil, for when you eat of it you will surely die." —Genesis 2:16-17*

This was the first and only prohibition issued from God before *The Fall.* It also presented the first opportunity for mankind to sin, and for Satan to arouse that temptation. When Adam and Eve fell into temptation and disobeyed this Commandment, they realized they were naked, which was literal and symbolic. They were unclothed and they were in sin:

And he said, "Who told you that you were naked? Have you eaten from the tree that I commanded you not to eat from?" —Genesis 3:11

God did not tell His first children that exposing their nakedness was wrong. Their newfound *knowledge of good and evil* brought forth this revelation. The fruit they ingested was *sin,* and it became a part of their spiritual being. For this reason, you cannot pretend to be ignorant of what is sinful behavior in your own life. That *knowledge* has been passed down in spiritual DNA from your original ancestors. You may have trained yourself to ignore guilt, but the *knowledge of good and evil* is still there. Sin *springs forth* from a rebellious spirit, that same spirit that resides in us all. Therefore, we must train ourselves to hearken to the biddings of the Holy Spirit, so that we will not perish in our sins, but *live* in obedience to God's Commands. This is the purpose for which the Lord has given us His Word, to bolster our spiritual defenses against our inherited sinful nature.

If you already know all this, along with the real Jesus, I challenge you to dig deeper. Even the apostle Paul, in spite of all his sacrifices and testimonies, did not believe that he had arrived at a perfect knowledge of Christ Jesus:

> *Brothers, I do not consider myself yet to have taken hold of it. But one thing I do: Forgetting what is behind and straining toward what is ahead. I press on toward the goal to win the prize for which God has called me heavenward in Christ Jesus. —Philippians 3:13-14*

Those who do not constantly seek God's Face in His Holy Word, challenging themselves to do what He Commands, will fall for one or more of Satan's deceptions, which are intended for one purpose: To lead you to death and destruction. Remember the Marties were certain the Bible says, *'God does for those who do for themselves.'* Had they been reading the Word frequently, studying it as though their next paycheck depended upon it, perhaps they would have discovered their error and repented. How many errors in judgment have you made? Don't wait until Judgment Day to find out whether you are pleasing your Savior.

When you read the Bible, ask the Father, in Jesus' Name, "Lord, help me understand and obey your Word." Then when you read a verse you don't understand, ask God to reveal it to you. Somehow, someway, whether in the wind, the way the sun shines, or by some other witness, He will answer you, so long as you trust in Him and strive to make His Truth the highest order for your life.

"I tell you, though he will not get up and give him the bread because he is his friend, ***yet because of the man's boldness he will get up and give him as much as he needs.***

"So I say to you: Ask and it will be given to you; seek and you will find; knock and the door will be opened to you. For everyone who asks receives; he who seeks finds; and to him who knocks, the door will be opened." —Luke 11:8-10

Every conclusion put forth in this chapter, and this entire book, has been derived from three united sources: The Living Word of Jesus Christ, His Holy Spirit, and the Father who sent them unto us so that we would know the Truth, and live by it.

To the Jews who had believed him, Jesus said, "If you hold to my teaching, you are really my disciples. Then you will know the truth, and the truth will set you free." —John 8:31-32

23

Defeating Death

By September of 2010, my family had been on the road nearly a year and a half—far longer than I thought we could sustain. Since directing us to Isaiah 51 and convicting Clara and me to totally trust in Him alone, we had been shown much revelation and prophecy, including the impending awakening of President Barack Obama. How exactly this impossible puzzle might come together remained something of a mystery to my family, until the Lord had made clear to me one day, *'Life will lead the way.'*

To better understand how God regards the Sanctity of Human Life, read what He spoke to Ezekiel:

> *"And you took your sons and daughters whom you bore to me and sacrificed them as food to the idols. Was your prostitution not enough? You slaughtered **my children** and sacrificed them to the idols." —Ezekiel 16:20-21*

When the Lord says *"my children,"* He means it. The children we bear unto Him do not belong to us, they belong to the Father who *knitted them in the womb*. He gives us these precious gems to be their good stewards only for a time, to raise in His Word and wisdom in preparation for the day when He shall call them individually, just as He calls all His children. This is why no man or woman has any *right* to destroy the innocent seed God gives on account of our selfish nature, no matter the circumstance. Even in a supposed case of *'endangering the life of the mother'* you have to understand that God's design is perfect. He specifically tied the life of the mother to the life of the child. If the mother dies, so does the baby in her womb. Therefore, any effort to preserve the mother's life must be extended to the unborn infant. You will not find a viable argument to the contrary, because God does not view the unborn as parasites. They are His children!

One day in mid-September, God's view of the Sanctity of Human Life was further revealed as my family drove down to Kettering, Ohio, where I would be speaking to a Pro-Life group. Clara and I had been fasting and praying for the last three days, seeking the Lord's Face on several matters, yet I did not anticipate the revelation He would deliver in response. We had just reached Dayton, when the Holy Spirit unexpectedly spoke, 'They chose death.'

> *The woman said to the serpent, "We may eat fruit from the trees in the garden, but God did say, 'You must not eat fruit from the tree that is in the middle of the garden, and you must not touch it, or you will die.'" —Genesis 3:2-3*

On the road I have said many times that one Word of the Lord is like a thousand words in any of the tongues of man, like a fruit that perpetually bears good seed. In pointing me to Genesis, the Lord reminded me that He had planted not one, but two trees in the center of the Garden of Eden. While He told Adam and Eve the tree of the knowledge of good and evil was a *tree of death,* He never told them they could not eat of the fruit of the Tree of Life. Nevertheless, the first man and wife, having been tempted by the serpent to eat the forbidden fruit, turned their backs on Life and chose death.

> *"You will not surely die," the serpent said to the woman. "For God knows that when you eat of it your eyes will be opened, and you will be like God, knowing good and evil." —Genesis 3:4-5*

For the first time in history, mankind was convinced that he could be *"God,"* and somehow the fruit of the Tree of Life didn't look so appealing next to the idea that he could rule his own universe. This is at the heart of the Mormon deception, but it has also infiltrated practically every mainstream denomination of Christianity, such as my family experienced while witnessing the Sanctity of Human Life to countless people along the way. Many "Christians" expressed personal reservations about abortion and euthanasia, but were unwilling to support a law banning such action. Instead, they were quick to espouse *"human rights,"* meaning they believed people should be able to *'play God'* by making up their own rules about life. God never said man had the *'right'* to shed innocent blood. Man has taken this *'right'* upon himself in rebellion against God. Anyone who exercises self-given *'rights'* in violation of God's Law shall be punished in the end. They will not escape the Judge. Thus, Christians who insist upon upholding *human rights* in contradiction to God's Word reflect Eve, who was the first to fall in order to serve as a witness of the adulterous church to come, just as Mary the mother of Jesus was an example of the faithful and obedient church.

When we asked *the lost* if they believed in the Sanctity of Human Life, they were even bolder, answering, "No, because I'm my own god." It was disturbing just how many times we received this response. They further insisted that God had lied to Adam and Eve, believing they had not died from eating that forbidden fruit. So I would ask them, "Are Adam and Eve alive today?" Seeing they were stumped, I concluded, "No, because they died."

The enemy's essential strategy to separate mankind from God has not changed since the Garden of Eden. His device is to convince us that we ought to be our own gods, being served rather than serving, and deciding for ourselves what is good and evil. Those who fall for this trap become slaves to the desires of their flesh. In turn, they forsake life and embrace death, which is no more evident than in how our society has declared the shedding of innocent blood, born or unborn, a *human right.*

Shortly after Kettering, the Lord sent me before two long-time ministers at a local church in Dayton. One was white and the other black, and both had been offended when I had delivered the Lord's message before their ministerial group a week prior. To settle the matter righteously before God, I proposed we meet to discuss their disagreements, which primarily revolved around my having declared that our president was "lost" on account of his support for abortion. As the Spirit had already shown me, they had not taken offense for the sake of our president, but for themselves, because they too supported abortion. In essence, by calling out the *tree of death,* I had exposed their fruit, and they were not happy about it. Such is how the Holy Spirit reveals all things:

> *"For whatever is hidden is meant to be disclosed, and whatever is concealed is meant to be brought out into the open." —Mark 4:22*

Sitting with the two of them in the black reverend's office, I opened up a Holy Court of Law by asking them to explain their grievances in Jesus'

Name. Taking turns, they proceeded to accuse me of trying to be "the Judge," they mocked and sneered at my "ministry credentials," and they rebuked my words as "divisive and damaging to their attempts to unify the church." When they had laid out all their complaints, I simply told them the truth, "You cannot be with Jesus Christ and view life as a matter of human choice. Do you believe a woman has a right to abortion?"

"Yes, because she does!" the black reverend snapped at once and his white counterpart agreed.

"Then like our president, you too are lost!" I told them.

The reverend jumped to his feet, as if ready to strike me. I stood as well, and when he saw I was not going to back down, he reached over and grabbed a white ball cap with the words *'Jesus Loves Me'* printed on the side of it. He placed it firmly on his head and sat back down. The Spirit told me, 'That's his happy cap.'

Recollecting himself, he said, "A long time ago the Lord showed me abortion was wrong. So when a woman comes to me seeking counsel, I tell her, 'You should keep the baby.'"

By the Spirit I saw the divided heart in him and asked, "But do you also tell her she has a right to choose an abortion?"

"I do," he proclaimed defiantly, "because she does!"

"You're a minister of Jesus Christ!" I fired back. "You cannot tell a woman she has any right to destroy the seed God gave her. She has no right in God's sight and she will suffer the consequences—and so will you for telling her it was her right."

That put him on his feet again and I followed suit. This went on for about four hours to no avail. Though the white minister played the role of peacemaker, the Spirit told me plainly, 'He's a Judas.'

Such is the predominant church in America today. Like Judas Iscariot, the establishment church has given their souls over to mammon. No matter how many facts and figures you throw at them, none of it will be heeded. Not until they are severely humbled will they bother to awaken and repent.

After he drove the man out, he placed on the east side of the Garden of Eden cherubim and a flaming sword flashing back and forth to guard the way to the tree of life. —Genesis 3:24

God banished Adam and Eve from the Garden of Eden for their disobedience. What we need to understand is that Eden is symbolic for heaven and the flaming sword is both the Word of God and His Holy Spirit, which guards access to the Tree of Life whose fruit gives eternal life.

> *Then the angel showed me the river of the water of life, as clear as crystal, flowing from the throne of God and of the Lamb down the middle of the great street of the city. On each side of the river stood the tree of life, bearing twelve crops of fruit, yielding its fruit every month. And the leaves of the tree are for the healing of the nations. —Revelations 22:1-2*

At His appointed time our Heavenly Father revealed to us all the Tree of Life by sending *His only begotten Son* into the world. He is the foretold Messiah, the *bread that came down from heaven* to give eternal life to all who receive Him. He is Jesus Christ.

> *"Make a tree good and its fruit will be good, or make a tree bad and its fruit will be bad, for a tree is recognized by its fruit." —Matthew 12:33*

Jesus Christ sacrificed Himself upon the cross and resurrected Himself on the third day to fulfill the Scriptures and fully reveal His fruit, proving He is indeed the Tree of Life. This is why Jesus Christ and the Sanctity of Human Life are inextricably linked, and why the Jews were taught from the very beginning that they serve the *"Living God."* Furthermore, in *defeating death* upon the cross, Christ demonstrated His ultimate victory over Satan, for at the core of the spiritual war for the souls of all mankind is the battle between life and death. Therefore, you cannot claim to have life in Christ and in the same breath defend America's present culture of death, excusing the shedding of innocent blood as a human right! Any who persist in this lie are eating a rotten fruit from the tree of death. Such people have not humbled themselves before the cross of Christ, but stand in rebellion against God. Like their forebears, the men and women of this age who persist in death will be brought to shame.

Sadly, like Adam and Eve, many today continue to covet worldly wisdom and knowledge, exposing their nakedness before God. Consider how, in our veracious pursuit for knowledge, the elite establishments of education in our society have decided that God is an unnecessary fable, that Genesis is less plausible than Evolution, and that eternal life will become a scientific reality in the near future. Eventually, the forbidden fruit-eating geniuses of every age, including the present, will fall at the feet of Christ and mourn, realizing they wasted their brief lives on the illusion of their own grandeur.

The fear of the LORD is the beginning of knowledge, but fools despise wisdom and discipline. —Proverbs 1:7

If you follow the rotten fruit of death back through American history, you will inevitably stumble upon *eugenics,* which lies at the root of modern genetic research and engineering. Sir Francis Galton invented the term in 1883 while engaging in a study of human genetic traits, through which adherents have proposed that mankind ought to stop fostering certain *ill-favoured* races of man and start selectively breeding a *master race.* Aside from Satan, Galton's inspiration derived from his cousin Charles Darwin's *Evolutionary Theory,* which argues that mankind was not created in God's image, but evolved from apes, and further posits *natural selection,* meaning *survival of the fittest.* Eugenics Societies sprang up all over Europe, and sadly their blighted seeds also took root in the bloodied soil of the post-Civil War United States. Essentially, white American elitists, concerned their superior gene pool was being polluted by former slaves, began implementing *applied eugenics* through various forms of *population control.* These programs included forced sterilization, birth control, and euthanasia, which is just a pretty term for extermination. Their targets were primarily blacks and other peoples of color, as well as the blind, deaf, dumb, those suffering from epilepsy or some other mental or physical disability, anyone deemed a financial *burden upon society,* and criminals. Already you should know the origin of the *Eugenics Tree,* because all the people they sought to exterminate were those for whom Jesus of Nazareth had mercy, fed, healed and gave the gift of eternal life. Remember that even that repentant criminal who was crucified beside Christ was saved!

"This is what the LORD says: Do what is just and right. Rescue from the hand of his oppressor the one who has been robbed. Do no wrong or violence to the alien, the fatherless or the widow, and do not shed innocent blood in this place."
—Jeremiah 22:3

If you believed our country was a "Christian Nation" then it will grieve you to explore the toll of life destroyed by Satan's prideful and gullible American eugenicist disciples. For example, in the 1927 case of Buck v. Bell, in an 8-1 decision the U.S. Supreme Court ruled to uphold Virginia's compulsory sterilization law, then targeting Carrie Buck, a white woman. At age 17, Carrie was raped and became pregnant by a member of her foster family, which subsequently institutionalized her in a vain attempt to protect their reputation. Dr. James H. Bell of the Virginia Colony for the Epileptic and

Feebleminded subsequently labeled Carrie *"a genetic threat to society."* The U.S. Supreme Court ultimately agreed. The majority opinion, written by Justice Oliver Wendell Holmes Jr., serves as a horrifying reminder of our speckled national history. In part, he wrote:

> *"It is better for all the world if, instead of waiting to execute degenerate offspring for crime or to let them starve for their imbecility, society can prevent those who are manifestly unfit from continuing their kind. The principle that sustains compulsory vaccination is broad enough to cover cutting the Fallopian tubes."*

On October 19, 1927 the United States of America did indeed cut Carrie Buck's Fallopian tubes. In subsequent decades upwards of 65,000 supposedly *unfit* Americans in 33 states were also forcibly sterilized, many without their knowledge or consent. Incredibly, it was this United States' precedent after which the Nazis claimed they had modeled their eugenics pogroms. They sterilized more than 400,000 people, but later decided euthanasia was a more efficient solution for eradicating *"unfit"* races from their society. Consequently, they went on to exterminate some 17 million people, including 6 million Jews. This is what happens when the people of the light fall silent, and for this, America ought to be ashamed, because we have gone far beyond Nazi *"crimes against humanity"* as a result of legalized abortion. In fact, just as compulsory sterilization laws were being weeded out from our society, in 1973 Roe v. Wade was being ushered in. In August 2011 the eugenicist-founded Guttmacher Institute reported that since 1973, We The People of the United States have shed the innocent blood of more than 50 million unborn babies. Have we no shame? We judge the Nazis, but we do even worse! Where is the Church?

> *"You blind guides! You strain out a gnat but swallow a camel."*
>
> —*Matthew 23:24*

African-Americans have been among the hardest hit by this fruit of death. In 2008, as reported by the CDC, an astonishing 501 black babies were aborted for every 1000 born. That's over one-third of the black population exterminated! Leading this charge is Planned Parenthood, an organization claiming to be a women's health advocate! It should surprise no one that its founder, Margaret Sanger, was a committed eugenicist. What you may not know is that her ultimate achievement in pursuing the eradication of *feebleminded* races, and particularly blacks, was the development of *the pill*.

Americans have been duped for the last 50 years into believing *the pill* is innocuous, but it is not. Consider the tree from which it comes! Not only can the synthetic hormones in *the pill* endanger the life of the mother, such as dramatically increasing the risk of breast cancer, but if you consult the Physicians Desk Reference (PDR) and other sources you'll find that all birth control medications are *"abortifacients,"* meaning they cause abortions. This happens as a result of what's called *"breakthrough ovulations,"* where a mother still produces an ovum that can be fertilized by the father's sperm, thus completing the biblical definition of *conception.*

For you created my inmost being; you knit me together in my mother's womb.
—Psalm 139:13

Today, modern science has finally caught up with what the Bible declared three thousand years ago: *The life of a unique human being begins at conception.* Even so, did the Church need geneticists to prove to us what we should already have accepted in God's Word? At any rate, this is why *the pill* and its various offshoots are called "birth control" and not "pregnancy control." They don't prevent pregnancy! Instead, these medications prevent the mother's living baby from successfully implanting in her uterus. Consequently, the baby dies and is expelled in the mother's menses. These are known as *medication abortions,* the same function you find in the abortion drugs called Plan B and RU-486. There have been various studies conducted to assess the number of infant deaths due to abortifacients, some estimating more than a million each year, but what you need to know—and tell others—is that the invention of *the pill* was a deception of Satan designed to trick you into murdering the Lord's children. If a doctor was to tell you, "Here, take this pill. It will save you stress and money, but it might kill you." Would you take it? Sadly, many Christians do. But you, now having read the truth, should never again be willing to accept any risk of committing murder against a child planted in your womb by the Lord your Judge.

"If I had not come and spoken to them, they would not be guilty of sin. Now, however, they have no excuse for their sin." —John 15:22

If you have ears to hear, then hear the truth about the plague coming upon our nation, for it began at the *tree of death,* it became an applied science under the label of *eugenics,* but it will achieve its awful purpose under the banner of *genetic research and engineering.*

God saw all that he had made, ***and it was very good.*** *And there was evening, and there was morning—the sixth day. —Genesis 1:31*

God did not create genetics for man to tinker with. When God sees something He has made as *"very good,"* He means it cannot be improved. His Creation is perfect, though sinful man has introduced much corruption—to himself, his offspring, and everything he tries to reap and sow in the earth, which was *"cursed"* as a consequence of his rebellion in the Garden of Eden. Nevertheless, the Lord promised to bless Israel in their Promised Land, so long as they did not engage in the sinful practices of those whom they dispossessed:

He will love you and bless you and increase your numbers. He will bless the fruit of your womb, the crops of your land—your grain, new wine and oil—the calves of your herds and the lambs of your flocks in the land that he swore to your forefathers to give you. You will be blessed more than any other people; none of your men or women will be childless, nor any of your livestock without young. The LORD will keep you free from every disease. He will not inflict on you the horrible diseases you knew in Egypt, but he will inflict them on all who hate you. —Deuteronomy 7:13-15

Somehow, the church in America has forgotten this. Is it beyond the Lord to free our society from disease, blight, plague and pestilence? Of course it isn't, but our sin is keeping us from His blessings. In an attempt to escape God's judgment, people run from His Voice, which is beckoning repentance, and instead nakedly turn to scientists who promise drugs to cure their diseases, and genetically modified organism (GMO) crops to stand against plague and pestilence. Yet, in all man's efforts to escape his Creator, he is only deceived all the more. Who is the chief propagator of disease, plague, pestilence; even the weeds in the fields?

Jesus told them another parable: "The kingdom of heaven is like a man who sowed good seed in his field. ***But while everyone was sleeping, his enemy came and sowed weeds among the wheat,*** *and went away. When the wheat sprouted and formed heads, then the weeds also appeared.*

"The owner's servants came to him and said, 'Sir, didn't you sow good seed in your field? Where then did the weeds come from?'

"'An enemy did this,' he replied." *—Matthew 13:24-28*

Since we know that eugenics spawned from the enemy, and genetic research and engineering was born from eugenics, then the fruit is one in the same. It's rotten! People will say, "How can genetic research be bad? Look at all the diseases they have cured." Many diseases have been *treated,* but has man *eradicated* even one? In reality, people run to the world for a cure and catch another disease along the way—sometimes more deadly than the original. Consider that antidepressants, among the bestselling drugs in America today, have side effect warnings in the PDR that plainly state "worsening of depression" and "suicidal thinking." How can we be so gullible? Therefore, when you take a medicine God did not make from the natural earth, but something man made in a laboratory, how do you know all that it is doing? Can you attach a camera to a molecule designed by man to treat your deficient pancreas and watch it work its way to your brain? What about the food we eat? When man crosses genes from two different plant species and creates something new, even if that ear of corn looks, smells and somewhat tastes the same as the one God made, are you really sure it's not doing something inside of you God never intended?

"Keep my decrees. Do not mate different kinds of animals. Do not plant your field with two kinds of seed. Do not wear clothing woven of two kinds of material." —Leviticus 19:19

God put forth these decrees, knowing Satan would come along to tempt us into corrupting His Holy natural order. Just because scientists claim to have mapped the human genome does not mean they really know what they are dealing with. They cannot see all the hidden properties the Lord has applied to His creation so that we, His children, would be balanced in *heart, mind, soul and strength*. Therefore, despite all the good this world will attribute to genetic research and engineering, as a member of the Body of Christ you can be sure such manmade creations are being fed to you to throw off your moral compass. When you look into some of the shocking and grisly crimes now being committed across our nation, you will likely find a drug connection, often physician-prescribed. Some in the world will argue these people weren't on the right drugs, but I assure you they were possessed by more than synthetic chemicals.

Take heed, for the medicines you have been ingesting and injecting into your body are systematically weakening your inhibitions against sin. Through sin, Satan and his demons are able to possess a man or woman, even a child, and lead them to engage in great evil. In some cases the host will kill others, and sometimes himself. This the Lord tragically witnessed to my family when a devoted churchgoing man committed suicide due to side effects from Parkinson's medicine. Incredibly, the mega-church pastor assured congregants that their lost brother had gone to heaven, in spite of committing self-murder. Who knows what goes through a sinner's heart as his life ebbs away? Perhaps he repented and was saved at the last second, for the Lord is graceful, but let no true shepherd in Christ suggest that your last living act can be one of outright rebellion and your subsequent reward be the crown of life. That pastor put forth a terribly poisonous witness. At the funeral reception, one of his congregants, suffering from his own ailments, remarked of his deceased friend, "I wish I had a gun, so I could go and join him in heaven."

The Lord has brought the connection between sin, drugs and death to my family's attention through multiple military veterans sent to us along the way, spanning from Vietnam to the latest wars in Iraq and Afghanistan. These veterans all suffered from Post Traumatic Stress Disorder (PTSD), but the world misunderstands their plight. One Iraq veteran we met, who had suffered a brain injury from an improvised explosive device (IED), was assaulted again when the military shrink at Fort Hood, Texas accused him of "murdering Muslims." This, combined with the drugs they prescribed him, put him on the brink of suicide. Our prayers and testimony have helped to relieve his spiritual burdens, but he will need constant therapy in Christ the rest of his life.

When a soldier, on either side of a conflict, engages in or experiences violent bloodshed of human beings made in God's image, demonic forces besiege their souls. Unfortunately, the world's answer to this problem is *shrinks and drugs,* both of which are a Satan-inspired ploy to numb the minds of the afflicted. Psychiatrists do this by attempting to deal with moral dilemmas through worldly justifications and explanations that exclude Christ. Drugs accomplish the same result chemically. Because these poisons have been made more available than ever before, the result is a staggering death and suicide rate among veterans returning home from the warfront. As my family was finalizing this chapter while staying at a remote farm in Ohio, the Lord put forth a poignant witness on October 1, 2012, delivering to our doorstep the Springfield News-Sun, which had curiously published an investigation conducted by the Austin-American Statesmen, our home newspaper in

Texas! This investigation reported that "nearly two-thirds" of Texan casualties on the warfront had been matched at home by returning Texan veterans that have subsequently died due to "prescription drug overdoses, toxic drug combinations, suicide and single car crashes." These embattled souls need spiritual healing in Jesus Christ, but who's to provide this benefit if the Church won't step up?

No matter the size and flavor of the fruit, if it leads to death, it comes from the tree of death. Unfortunately, the predominant church in America accepts the rotten fruit and propagates its lies, even though they are supposed to be ambassadors of the Truth.

> *"Watch and pray so that you will not fall into temptation. The spirit is willing, but the body is weak." —Matthew 26:41*

Satan knows your flesh is weak. This is why Jesus said, *"Watch and pray,"* for one falls into temptation when he drifts apart from his source of strength—Christ The Lord. To *"watch"* is not to stand around looking at things, but to be a *"watchman"* for your Savior by being a testifier of His Word and Truth, as well as a proper caretaker of your afflicted brethren. To *"pray"* is not merely to recite memorized prayers or to pray over your food, but to be in constant spiritual communion with the Lord your God. You do this by tirelessly seeking His will and striving to obey it.

When the Church falls asleep, as Jesus' disciples did in the Garden of Gethsemane, the lies of this world take root. Look at the drug industry. Hardly a century ago it was little more than a band of 'snake oil' scam artists. Are we to believe they have changed their venomous ways? Look at the symbol of the American Medical Association. Whom do they serve? Whether they brandish the Caduceus [winged staff with two snakes], representing the god of liars and thieves, or the Asclepius [single snake], representing the mythical god of healing, both are satanic distortions of the biblical account where Moses lifted up the *bronze snake* in the wilderness to heal the rebellious Israelites from their snakebites:

> *Then the LORD sent venomous snakes among them; they bit the people and many Israelites died. The people came to Moses and said, "We sinned when we spoke against the LORD and against you. Pray that the LORD will take the snakes away from us." So Moses prayed for the people.*

The LORD said to Moses, "Make a snake and put it up on a pole; anyone who is bitten can look at it and live." —Numbers 21:6-8

The Spirit once took me to the east side of the Temple Mount in Jerusalem in a dream, where He revealed the true meaning of the *bronze snake.* I found myself standing with priests in ancient robes. One of them explained the layout of the Temple, including how it was designed with a cemetery plan that stretches southeastward down a terraced mount along a ravine, winding down into a valley. Each tier had a gravesite design and this was "part of the Temple plan." I wondered why this was, though no explanation was given. Then I realized that the winding path down the ravine into the valley resembled a river route. Suddenly the Holy Spirit spoke to me that it was 'serpentine' in nature, resembling 'the *bronze serpent* Moses had lifted up in the wilderness.' Furthermore, I understood that the serpent stands for *death,* because it was the *serpent* who led Adam and Eve, and all mankind, to their *Fall.* Thus, *death* was lifted up on a pole to heal Israel, for it was *death* that the coming Messiah would one day defeat upon the *cross:*

"Just as Moses lifted up the snake in the desert, so the Son of Man must be lifted up, that everyone who believes in him may have eternal life." —John 3:14-15

The significance of all this is that when you look upon the cross of Christ, you must acknowledge and repent of the instrument of your death, the serpent, which represents your sinful rebellion against God. Then, by the precious blood of Christ, you will be cleansed of the serpent's poison and be redeemed. The Lord's Temple has been crafted from the very beginning with both death and resurrection in mind; such as the *dead in Christ,* symbolically entombed within the *train* of the Temple, will rise on the last day:

This is why it says: "When he ascended on high, he led ***captives in his train*** *and gave gifts to men." —Ephesians 4:8*

This expression, illustrated by Paul, was made clear to me when, after a sudden event, *living water as clear as crystal* sprang forth from the Temple, filling the whole valley, including the terraced mount. On the first tier the water was ankle-high, on the second tier it was knee-deep, then waist-deep, and finally one was totally immersed in water on the last tier.

As the man went eastward with a measuring line in his hand, he measured off a thousand cubits and then led me through water that was ankle-deep. He measured off another thousand cubits and led me through water that was knee-deep.

He measured off another thousand and led me through water that was up to the waist. He measured off another thousand, but now it was a river that I could not cross, because the water had risen and was deep enough to swim in—a river no one could cross. —Ezekiel 47:3-5

I have not physically been to this site in Jerusalem, but the Lord later led me to the above Scripture to confirm its validity. I have also come to understand that Satan has been setting up false witnesses of biblical symbolism, expressing them in various pagan traditions from the very beginning of time. Archeologists are mystified by the mythology parallels between disparate ancient cultures on opposite ends of the earth, because they fail to understand that the demonic realm, having knowledge of God and His Truth, has taken the same bag of tricks to every society. In all this, the enemy's ultimate goal is to confuse God's children into unwittingly rejecting the cross:

When you were dead in your sins and in the uncircumcision of your sinful nature, God made you alive with Christ. He forgave us all our sins, having cancelled the written code, with its regulations, that was against us and that stood opposed to us; he took it away, nailing it to the cross. And having disarmed the powers and authorities, he made a public spectacle of them, triumphing over them by the cross. —Colossians 2:13-15

I'm not saying all medical practitioners are evil, because some do have a love for Christ, but the original Hippocratic Oath invoked the names of false gods. Is it any wonder they follow this oath by posting idolatrous symbols on the doorposts of their offices? Does an MD or PhD somehow preclude an individual from Satan's deceptions? Therefore, you go into a doctor's office to be delivered from poison, but receive a prescription that poison's you further. This is why you should entrust your life only to *the Doctor,* for Christ alone tramples upon all of Satan's schemes. Consult Him before you accept any doctor's advice, lest you fall into the hands of charlatans. The difference between a pharmacist and a street corner drug dealer is a license and a white lab coat. Thus, the Lord sees some of His children dealing drugs for money, while others beg for them—some for fear of death and disease, and others to feed their addictions.

There is also nothing coincidental about the fact that pharmaceutical corporations are the same that are manufacturing GMO seeds, as well as dangerous pesticides and herbicides. The first manufacturer of *the pill,* Searle, was once acquired by biotech giant Monsanto. Bioscience corporations like these merge because they have synergies, elements that complement each other, and they come from the same tree. *The pill* was developed to destroy human life in the womb, treating God's planted seed as an invader. Pesticides and herbicides have been developed to destroy God's created insect and plant life, which may invade crops. GMO seeds were developed to grow food that would be immune to the toxins used to destroy those natural invaders. Various drugs are developed to kill invaders that come into the body, yet as we have seen with synthetic antibiotics, they can weaken our immune systems. Therefore, what happens when America consistently eats food designed to be resistant to anti-invader toxins? Since you are what you eat, America will become anti-invader toxin resistant. In other words, she will become resistant to her own immune system. She will become divided against herself, a kingdom that cannot stand—all because she has separated herself from Christ. She is a God-given seed the world has treated as a disease, and she welcomed it upon herself.

Then the dragon was enraged at the woman and went off to make war against the rest of her offspring—those who obey God's commandments and hold to the testimony of Jesus. —Revelations 12:17

And for what have we invited this ruin upon ourselves? *Mammon.* For money, we enable corporations and the government together to corrupt our bodies by tainting our food supply, our water, even the air we breathe. Then, for more money, we buy their medicine to treat the very conditions these environmental poisons initiated. Yet, because those medications come with side effects, we continue to accept the advice of worldly doctors and buy more drugs to counteract them. Insane as it sounds, these additional medications come with their own host of side effects, which require even more drugs to treat. The drug cartels have nothing on the international healthcare industry. The one is a kitten and the other a ravenous lion! Just look in your parent's medicine cabinets and you will see.

"Who of you by worrying can add a single hour to his life?" —Matthew 6:27

Since Jesus has said you cannot *add a single hour to your life,* why trust a physician who speaks differently? At the very least, why poison yourself with the drugs they prescribe and administer to the very end of that last hour of your life? In a futile effort to add an imaginary hour, not only will death still come at the appointed time, you will also have exhausted every ounce of your nation's wealth in a vain attempt to defy God's Word. This is how the *Greatest Generation* began this nation's freefall into debt, and their *Baby Boomer* children and grandchildren are seeing to its finality. A *spirit of stupor* has come over the whole nation on account of sin. Consequently, America lies in a pit so deep she can hardly see a pinprick of light above.

No man has power over the wind to contain it; so no one has power over the day of his death. As no one is discharged in time of war, so wickedness will not release those who practice it. —Ecclesiastes 8:8

Our nation's widespread culture of death is daunting; it reaches into the womb, the battlefield, the farmer's field, the grocery store, the doctor's office, and perhaps your own medicine cabinet. So my family would have no doubt about the new *Dionysus cult* of intoxication that has swept across our nation, the Lord sent a man to our doorstep on that remote Ohio farm, again as we were finalizing this chapter. Soon as we began to talk, the conviction of the Holy Spirit struck him, and he shortly confessed his addictions to alcohol, tobacco, and finally to a powerful pain medication. He feared people might look at him like a crack addict. He also admitted that this *prescribed* medication was causing him memory loss. Sadly, he was convinced that an operation his doctor had recommended would solve his pain problem. All too often, worldly doctors propose expensive surgery to alleviate pain, but in reality they create new pain, which leads to more pain-med dependency. My family prayed for this struggling brother and told him the same thing we will tell you: Purge these drugs from your life! They are not helping you, and they could kill you—not only your flesh, but also your spirit. Any kind of intoxicant, prescribed or illegal, opens the door for demonic forces to enter your heart and destroy your inhibitions against deadly sins:

Do not get drunk on wine, which leads to debauchery. Instead, be filled with the Spirit. —Ephesians 5:18

Remember our testimony about the woman with the *celebrity tote bag.* Turn to Christ with all your heart and you too will be delivered from even the most potent chemicals Satan's servants have conjured up on the face of this earth. It's not what you eat or drink that defiles you, but what comes out of you. Therefore, when you bombard your body with intoxicants, you weaken your inhibitions against sin. That's what happened to the man who poisoned his mind with Parkinson's medications. He knew the Truth, but his weakened flesh led him to commit suicide. Do not let the worries of this world deceive you. Your Father in heaven will call you Home at precisely the right time, not an hour too late or too early, and you will not be disappointed in the eternal dwelling He has prepared for you.

At the same time We The Church make our personal paths straight, let us also make straight the way of our nation by heeding the call of the Holy Spirit, who clearly says, *'Life will lead the way.'* Our national repentance cannot be fulfilled unless our nation turns from its culture of death by making the Sanctity of Human Life the highest law of the land. We must demand it of our elected officials, and we must refuse to support any who will not make this their foremost priority. Any *call to repentance* that falls shy of this goal is paying the Lord lip-service, and He will not restore us. However, if the Church follows through on this Command, all the other pillars of evil the enemy has erected in our nation will begin to topple. The Spirit is more than capable of reducing whole nations to their knees, beginning with one stubborn subject at a time.

The Lord demonstrated this one Sunday when He sent my family before a church in Springfield, Ohio to issue His call to repentance through the Sanctity of Human Life. When we gathered in a repentant prayer huddle, a woman of the *Baby Boomer* generation towards the back of the group unexpectedly confessed, "I have paid careful attention to the testimony given here today and I find it to be the truth. So with my brothers and sisters here as witnesses, I ask you to forgive me Lord for believing that a woman should have the right to an abortion." That woman also rebuked euthanasia. How merciful is the Lord that He would bring this threat upon the same generation that ushered in Roe v. Wade, so that their hearts might turn from death and again cleave to Life. The astonished pastor later told me that she was the most liberal member of his congregation, a staunch women's rights activist!

After her confession, the entire congregation felt what the Bible calls the *Oil of Joy* descend upon us. All together we began to rejoice, for the Lord was pleased to forgive our sister, and oh how the heavens celebrate when a lost sheep is welcomed home.

> *You love righteousness and hate wickedness; therefore God, your God, has set you above your companions by anointing you with the oil of joy. —Psalm 45:7*

There is hope, but first the church in America must awaken to the threat our culture of death has already kindled. Twice on my family's journey the

Lord has awakened me, speaking into my hearing words of warning concerning His forthcoming punishment. The first word He spoke was "Topheth":

> *"So beware, the days are coming, declares the LORD, when people will not longer call it Topheth or the Valley of Ben Hinnom, but the Valley of Slaughter, for they will bury the dead in Topheth until there is no more room."*
>
> *—Jeremiah 7:32*

The Lord's warning to Judah is being issued against the United States at this hour. If we do not turn from our obsession with death, then blood for blood and bone for bone the men and women of this nation shall fall, and the dead shall lie in heaps with no one to bury them. The fertile field shall be made desolate, and the imposing city will be laid low.

The second word the Lord spoke to me was "Sepharvaim":

> *The king of Assyria brought people from Babylon, Cuthah, Avva, Hamath and Sepharvaim and settled them in the towns of Samaria to replace the Israelites. They took over Samaria and lived in its towns. When they first lived there, they did not worship the LORD; so he sent lions among them and they killed some of the people. —2 Kings 17:24-25*

When Ephraim and the ten tribes of Israel were conquered and deported from their homeland, the Assyrians resettled five pagan kingdoms in their lands. These peoples brought with them all sorts of detestable religious practices, but the Sepharvites were among the worst, sacrificing their children in the fire to false gods:

> *The Avvites made Nibhaz and Tartak, and the Sepharvites burned their children in the fire as sacrifices to Adrammelech and Annamelech, the gods of Sepharvaim. —2 Kings 17:31*

Adrammelech was in no coincidence the name of the son who murdered his father, Sennacherib, the king of Assyria, whose death Isaiah had predicted:

> *One day, while he was worshipping in the temple of his god Nisroch, his sons* ***Adrammelech*** *and Sharezer cut him down with the sword, and they escaped to the land of Ararat. And Esarhaddon his son succeeded him as king.*
>
> *—2 Kings 19:37*

This is a warning to America about what our culture of death has already bred. The generation that has survived abortion has learned from our nation's disregard for life. They seek to euthanize their aging fathers and mothers, deeming them an undo financial *burden upon society*. The Lord is also gathering lions to send against our nation, lions bearing the mark of *Babylon The Great.* Still, the grace of the Lord will supersede this evil, if the nation repents. I am among that generation of Roe v. Wade survivors, born exactly three months and three days after the U.S. Supreme Court issued that fateful ruling. I was raised to view the world through the prism of financial concerns, but God awakened me to His Truth.

Turn from death America, before it is too late! The mortal life of a human being is but a whisper and a mist, here today and gone tomorrow. Consider the ages of those who are implementing policies of death for their own selfish gain. Are they not already on the tail end of their human lifespans? Does it make sense to exterminate future generations for the selfish whims of those who will be dust in a decade or two? This vanity all began when mankind denied Jesus Christ and decided he would rather be his own god. Understand that our Creator did not give Adam and Eve a *choice* between life and death, but Commanded they cleave to Life.

In all things, follow the fruit and use the Word of God to discern its nature. If the fruit is bad then so is the tree from which it came, and no bad tree can produce good fruit, least of all one that has been genetically modified in a foolish attempt to outdo God. So remember, *'Life will lead the way'* to our restoration, because Jesus Christ is the only Way, the Truth and *The Life.*

24

Breaking Idolatry

By the time we entered into our second holiday season on the road with no home, no money and no provision, except what the Lord provided, my family had been introduced to nearly every denomination of the Christian faith you can think of. Unfortunately, in all of them we found symptoms of a common disease. It has multiple forms and affects various parts of the body, but it all can be categorized under a voracious cancer called *idolatry.*

> *But if your heart turns away and you are not obedient, and if you are drawn away to bow down to other gods and worship them, I declare to you this day that you will certainly be destroyed. You will not live long in the land you are crossing the Jordan to enter and possess. —Deuteronomy 30:17-18*

All idolatry stems from man worshipping himself, believing he can ignore what the Word of God says and make up his own rules. This is a fatal mistake. God never once approved the keeping or worshipping of idols anywhere in His Word. So how is it that this supposedly "Christian nation" is filled with them? Consider the Statue of Liberty, modeled after the pagan Roman goddess Libertas, the goddess Justitia sitting outside the U.S. Supreme Court, the goddess Columbia atop the Capitol Building, and the most recent Martin Luther King Jr. statue in the National Mall. There is nothing about these idols the Lord our God finds edifying. Did Libertas free the slaves? Did Justitia give mankind the Law? Did Columbia give birth to the United States? Was Martin Luther King Jr. the rock cut out of the mountain that turned the heart of a nation against racial prejudice, or was it Jesus Christ? You can be sure that Joshua and the Israelites whom the Lord brought out of His iron-smelting furnace would have destroyed all these false images if this had been the land of Canaan they were promised. Why then has the church in America done nothing? I am not proposing vandalism. I am suggesting that a government of, by, and for Jesus Christ could have and should have ordered their dismantling. If we had any fear of God whatsoever we would tear down that Freemasonry obelisk dedicated to Washington and replace it with a giant cross dedicated to Christ.

Our nation's blasphemous monuments represent just one of Satan's deceptions by which he dupes the church into accepting idolatry, disguising an act of *worship* beneath a veil called *"symbolism."* A sculptor, commissioned by our elected government and paid for by We The Church, carves a marble statue in the image of an ancient Roman god or goddess. He unveils his masterpiece and says, "The inspiration for this sculpture was to *symbolize* 'truth.'" Now if that were the truth he would have carved a cross. Anyone who is being inspired by the Spirit of Truth is led to this conclusion, but anyone being led by Satan seeks to honor a dead god from a dead society of dead people. Satan doesn't lead these people to such lies for no reason, for he knows that when a society honors an idol they dishonor Christ. This errant behavior meets the biblical definition of *idol worship,* which is *a sin that leads unto death:*

> *If anyone sees his brother commit a sin that does not lead to death, he should pray and God will give him life. I refer to those whose sin does not lead to death.* ***There is a sin that leads to death.*** *I am not saying that he should pray about that. All wrongdoing is sin, and there is sin that does not lead to death.*
>
> —*1 John 5:16-17*

You cannot pray that *sin leading unto death* simply goes away; the sinner must himself turn away from it. Sadly, Satan has succeeded in immobilizing much of the church by convincing it to rely upon prayer alone. Yes, pray the Lord strengthens His Church, but for what? Pray that we are encouraged and emboldened to take action—especially against the idols in our midst.

Perhaps the most prevalent of Satan's deceptions concerning idolatry is the one that disguises the meaning of *worship* beneath a veil called *"tradition."* Take Christmas for example, which did not originate with Christ's birth, but the popular Roman pagan holiday of Saturnalia, a drunken seven-day celebration of lawlessness from December 17th through the 25th. These early Roman festivities encompassed everything from gluttony and sexual immorality to a rampage of rape and human sacrifice! Is it any wonder why Christmas in America has strayed progressively further from Christ and become more of the drunken, gluttonous, shopping-frenzied, Santa Claus-worshipping abomination we see year after year? Consider the tree from which this rotten fruit comes! Knowing this history, the early American Puritans actually banned Christmas in Massachusetts. You can be sure their children weren't writing gift wish lists that amounted to idolatrous prayers to a fairytale fat man in a red suit. Neither did they erect Christmas Trees, a practice modeled after Ashtoreth worshippers who idolized trees much like witches and wiccans do today.

> *"They adorn it with silver and gold; they fasten it with hammer and nails so it will not totter." —Jeremiah 10:4*

The Bible does not condone Christmas Trees, nor does it specify the day on which Jesus was born. There are different theories about that day, though you can be sure it wasn't December 25th. At any rate, as the Spirit once spoke to me, Christ's Nativity was not the date on which the Father wanted His followers to focus. The date He specifically caused to be recorded in the Bible was the birth of His Body, or Church, which took place on the Day of Pentecost:

> *When the day of Pentecost came, they were all together in one place. Suddenly a sound like the blowing of a violent wind came from heaven and filled the whole house where they were sitting. They saw what seemed to be tongues of fire that separated and came to rest on each of them. —Acts 2:1-3*

This is the event of which Christ foretold after His Resurrection—yet another day gullible Christians have been led to pervert. Like Christmas, Easter also derives from pagan *traditions* representing spring and fertility rites, hence the bunnies and eggs theme. When seeking the Lord about Easter, He gave my son Austin a vision wherein he saw Egyptian pyramids painted like Easter eggs. The Spirit also gave the interpretation, 'The pyramid is a tomb and Easter eggs are dead. Therefore, Easter is a ritual of death.' So much for all those wasted Sundays in our youths when we spent one hour in church and the rest of the day chasing the Easter Bunny, hunting for dead eggs and devouring loads of GMO-sweetened candy. Why subject your children to the same, especially now that you know this behavior offends God? Everything about "Resurrection Day" ought to be about our Savior. There should be room for nothing else, because He is that great!

Since having our eyes fully opened, my family has dropped these holidays like the bad habits they are, and Halloween was the easiest. The only thing frightening about this festival of death is how many of us have been tricked into celebrating it. Christmas was much tougher to wean ourselves from. Nevertheless, before Jazelle and Justin were born, Clara and I had already given Santa Claus the boot, because Rielle and Austin felt so betrayed that we had lied to them about that fat man fable. The tree was more difficult to toss, but once it was gone we never missed it. Oh the needless fortune we burned on ornaments and other Christ-less decorations—*most made in China!* We now spend December 25th celebrating Christ, reading the Bible and reflecting on His Gospel. We'll even sing Christmas songs that are actually about Christ, and we celebrate Him all throughout the year.

Aside from holidays, Satan's idolatry deception has infiltrated and bound countless Christian homes by disguising *worship* under a canvas of *"art."* This was fully revealed when we went to buy Austin some shoes at a discount department store. We found a nice pair that fit his feet—and our tight budget, but the Spirit pointed out a pair of Buddha idol bookends sitting on one of the store shelves. Convicting our hearts that we could not give our pearls to swine, we took those idols up to the checkout and I asked the manager if she would remove them from the store. If so, we would buy the shoes. If not, we'd have to buy a more expensive pair elsewhere, even at the risk of depleting grocery money. The manager thought I was joking at first, but she quickly realized we were serious. I asked her if she was a "believer in Jesus." She acknowledged she was. With patience and conviction I told her, "These are false gods that sadly lead a lot of people to their deaths. We serve Jesus Christ, so we take these matters seriously."

"I understand," she replied, blinking her eyes.

I could see that she was torn. By the Spirit, I also understood that she was a churchgoing woman, and this might have been the first time anyone had challenged her concerning her faith. So I told her, "Just because you can sell something, doesn't mean you should."

Shaking her head, she said, "You know, I—I'm speechless."

"I know," I told her, recognizing the listening ears of her colleagues. If she let slip one wrong word, she could easily lose her job.

"I'm proud—" she began then hesitated a moment, realizing the Lord was listening. Finally, she shrugged and concluded, "I'm happy to have my job."

With compassion I told her, "God is a very good provider, but obedience must come first."

Is a paycheck of any amount worth angering your Maker? Look around your home. What do you see? Has Satan infiltrated your house with idols of various sorts, hiding beneath the guise of symbolism, tradition, art or décor? The problem with the church in America is that we are still dealing with bad teaching carried over from the old world school of religion. So much of what we claim to be American tradition is actually European, and so much of that is actually Roman. This is why it is so important that you personally seek God's Face in His Word. Otherwise, you might think you are doing something the Lord finds appreciable, when in reality He finds your conduct detestable.

It seemed good to the Holy Spirit and to us not to burden you with anything beyond the following requirements: You are to abstain from food sacrificed to idols, from blood, from the meat of strangled animals and from sexual immorality. You will do well to avoid these things. Farewell. —Acts 15:28-29

My family has repeatedly encountered Christians, regardless of religion, who either forget or are completely unaware that the original Church strictly forbade consumption of anything *"sacrificed to idols."* In today's environment you must apply this rule to everything you consume (or buy) in the marketplace. Are you going to a restaurant, a grocer, furniture, clothing or department store that has propped up an idol outside or inside its doors? Don't defile yourself by sacrificing any of your wages to them. Instead, ask them to remove the idol in return for your patronage. What about music, movies and other forms of entertainment you consume, whether at the theater or at home? Is there anything in these that is promoting death, Sodom and Gomorrah or is defamatory towards Christ? Why buy anything called "Devil" or bearing any satanic image? Is hell somehow a joke? Purge these things from your life and stop sharing your pearls with dogs and swine, because they are tearing you, your family and your nation to pieces.

Be careful, however, that the exercise of your freedom does not become a stumbling block to the weak. For if anyone with a weak conscience sees you who have this knowledge eating in an idol's temple, won't he be emboldened to eat what has been sacrificed to idols? —1 Corinthians 8:9-10

Anything unedifying to Christ that you consume is a bad witness to those who are falling. For instance, a man who drinks wine in moderation, mindful of Christ's blood, is approved by the Lord. On the contrary, a man who drinks wine in front of a man who battles with alcoholism is not only inconsiderate, he is a man who is contributing to the fall of his brother. Such a man is guilty for leading his brother into sin.

So this weak brother, for whom Christ died, is destroyed by your knowledge. When you sin against your brothers in this way and wound their weak conscience, you sin against Christ. —1 Corinthians 8:11-12

Once, while staying at a farm in Central Ohio, a man showed up, banging at the door around midnight. "Is there a preacher in this house!" he yelled. Before I could get to the door, he let himself in and I met *Wild Bill.* It turned out he had learned about my family's mission from another and came to be healed of his addiction to alcohol. What led him to this addiction was something called *false grace,* which I'll cover later. Because he came with a humble heart, the moment I shook his hand he was struck by the Spirit. "Wow!" he exclaimed. He had felt the Spirit in his youth, but his drunken disobedience had driven the Spirit away.

And do not grieve the Holy Spirit of God, with whom you were sealed for the day of redemption. —Ephesians 4:30

After correcting his false concept about grace and revealing to him that he had been a "bad witness" to all the alcoholics in his community, he repented and was healed of his addiction—including the buzz with which he arrived. *Wild Bill* became *Sober Bill*—for a while, but later fell away again to Satan's lies. I pray this is not the conclusion of his walk. I do know that by the true grace of the Lord, *Wild Bill* can no longer drink beer without getting "the runs."

Therefore, if what I eat causes my brother to fall into sin, I will never eat meat again, so that I will not cause him to fall. —1 Corinthians 8:13

Idols are nothing. They have no breath, no power and no authority over you. However, when you consume things dedicated to idols, or worse, prop their inspired *art* up in your home, you open a gateway for Satan and his demonic legions to enter into your life and chastise you with all sorts of maladies. Once a brother in Christ shared with my family a testimony about a couple that had owned a high-end antique store. Despite being "Christian," they sold him a chest with a pentagram etched into its base. By God's grace, he discovered the satanic symbol before he took it into his home. Being a good witness, he took it back to the "Christian" dealers. They apologized, said they had overlooked it and promised to get rid of it. However, they painted over that pentagram and sold it again. Within a year, those "Christian" dealers went bankrupt, got divorced and the man died from cancer. Don't let this happen to you. Treat idols like the plagues they are and cut them from your lives, and don't lament their dollar value. Destroy them! Do this and you will prosper for your obedience, but if you treat idols and other satanic objects with the same cavalier attitude as the rest of the world, you and your money will perish together.

When you take a close look at our society today through the idol-detecting scope the Lord provides in His Word, you will be astounded by what you see. Idolatry is everywhere! Even Christian stores, radio and television are filled with it, if not in their programming then in their advertisers. You may not be able to find one grocery store in all of America that is not selling food alongside something idolatrous and satanic. Just look in the book section of your local grocer. Are they selling vampire, zombie, witchcraft and other illicit books inspired by Satan? Remember that anything that glorifies death or sin is idolatrous in the sight of the Lord. Likewise, things that promote any perversion of God's creation are idolatrous. This includes the alien and super hero craze now flooding movie theaters, television, bookstores and toy aisles. The ancient Greeks had the same problem. As God has taught my family, 'I did not create an *animal-man* or a *bug-man.* I created *mankind* in My image.'

> *The coming of the lawless one will be in accordance with the work of Satan displayed in all kinds of counterfeit miracles, signs and wonders, and in every sort of evil that deceives those who are perishing. They perish because they refused to love the truth and so be saved.* ***For this reason God sends them a powerful delusion*** *so that they will believe the lie and so that all will be condemned who have not believed the truth but have delighted in wickedness.*
>
> *—2 Thessalonians 2:9-12*

Perhaps the most potent of Satan's deceptions is when an idol appears to come to life. All too often this *powerful delusion* succeeds in blurring the line between *worship* and *"prayer,"* because people don't realize that everything supernatural does not automatically come from God.

*"For false Christs and false prophets will appear and perform great signs and miracles to **deceive even the elect**—if that were possible." —Matthew 24:24*

Satan and his demons can perform miraculous signs and wonders in order to *deceive even the elect*. The Lord permits this, because He has fully revealed His Word through Jesus Christ. Therefore, what better way to sort out the goats from the sheep than to let them sort themselves by those who obey His Word as opposed to those who rebelliously insist upon making their own rules concerning worship:

*The LORD says: "These people come near to me with their mouth and honor me with their lips, but their hearts are far from me. **Their worship of me is made up only of rules taught by men.**" —Isaiah 29:13*

I once met a man in Cleveland, Ohio who was dangerously suffering from obeying *rules taught by men*. He and his family had welcomed my family into their home for the week of Thanksgiving 2010, but as I fellowshipped with him one night in his study, he discretely shared with me that a demon had recently tried to smother him in his bed with his pillow. His wife and children were away at the time, and he was clearly shaken. He further explained that these kinds of attacks had consistently followed his *"conversion experience"* during a pilgrimage to Medjugorje in Bosnia-Herzegovina. There he witnessed firsthand a supernatural appearing of the *Blessed Virgin*. He was so convicted by this miraculous event he recommitted himself to the religion of his youth—Catholicism. As he related to me, and I later confirmed, Medjugorje is a modern-day recurrence of 1917 Fatima, Portugal, where apparitions of the Blessed Virgin appeared consistently over the course of several months. This apparition reportedly revealed herself to three children, giving them *"Three Secrets"* and leading them to engage in various self-mortifications, such as painfully binding their waists with tight cords, self-flagellation using stinging nettles, fasting from water on hot days, and other supposed acts of penance. The final *"sign"* took place on October 13, 1917, called the *"Miracle of the Sun,"* which is what this man had seen in present-day Medjugorje. He said the sun literally "danced" in the sky, "spun like a top," and came "crashing" down to the earth, stopping just above the heads of the spectators. He testified that they could actually feel the heat!

*And he performed great and miraculous signs, **even causing fire to come down from heaven to earth in full view of men**. —Revelations 13:13*

All of this was incredible, but what really pierced him was the shadow of the Blessed Virgin in the midst of the sun, for as he stared at this image in wonder it suddenly transformed into a fetus. It cut him to the heart, because in his youth he had shamefully encouraged a girlfriend to get an abortion. His continued guilt was plain to see, and I had compassion for him. I explained to him that if he was truly repentant in heart, Jesus forgave him, but he was convinced that fetus image was a personal *"sign"* from the Blessed Virgin that he needed to satisfy his own penance. This was why he had been so gravitated by my testimony concerning the link between the Sanctity of Human Life and our nation's restoration.

You cannot underestimate the complexity of Satan's deceptions, but you will expose them if you follow the nature of the fruit. After staring at the *"Miracle of the Sun,"* the Catholic priest told this man to look upon the Virgin Mary statue standing in the courtyard. He was astonished to see that it had transformed into *"pure gold."* Overwhelmed, and encouraged by the priest, he and the other onlookers bowed down before the statue and worshipped.

> *As Peter entered the house, Cornelius met him and fell at his feet in reverence.* ***But Peter made him get up. "Stand up," he said, "I am only a man myself."*** *—Acts 10:25-26*

Peter understood that what Cornelius was doing was *worship,* so he made him get up. The Bible puts forth this detail as a warning to the Church, and relates a similar example through the apostle John:

> *At this I fell at his feet to worship him.* ***But he said to me, "Do not do it!*** *I am a fellow servant with you and with your brothers who hold to the testimony of Jesus.* ***Worship God!*** *For the testimony of Jesus is the spirit of prophecy."*
>
> *—Revelations 19:10*

Notice how John's angelic guide also correlated his falling at his feet with *"worship."* Sadly, many Catholics follow in this error by worshipping both Peter and John, as well as many other "beatified [deified] Saints," including Mother Theresa and John Paul II. They won't call it "worship," but will say, "I only pray to him (or her) for intercession with Christ." They do not realize that prayer is a greater form of worship than falling at one's feet, because it bears with it the expectation of a supernatural answer to that prayer. This is not the same as asking a living person to pray for you, as was asked of the biblical prophets and apostles during their mortal lives. Petitioning the dead is an invitation for Satan to come in and deceive:

> *When men tell you to consult mediums and spiritists, who whisper and mutter, should not a people inquire of their God?* ***Why consult the dead on behalf of the living?*** *—Isaiah 8:19*

We serve a Living God—a jealous God, and He clearly declares that you are not to pray to anyone but Him:

> *"You shall not make for yourself an idol in the form of anything in heaven above or on the earth beneath or in the waters below.* ***You shall not bow down to them or worship them; for I, the LORD your God, am a jealous God,*** *punishing the children for the sin of the fathers to the third and fourth generation of those who hate me, but showing love to a thousand generations of those who love me and keep my commandments." —Exodus 20:4-6*

Following the Spirit, I asked the man if his life had been made better after his *"conversion experience."* I did not correlate "better" with worldly benefits, but "spiritual blessings." Without hesitation, he said, "No, worse!" Not only had he suffered from demonic attacks, but he had also fallen into drug abuse and depression, which nearly cost him his marriage and family. These issues had recently peaked subsequent to a disturbing meeting he had with his priest. He went to him vying for "Church support" to help make the Sanctity of Human Life the highest law in Ohio. Shockingly, his priest told him, "We [the Catholic Church] are definitely in favor of the Sanctity of Human Life, but I don't think it should be a law." Thus, the hypocritical nature of religion crushed this man's faith. I grieved for him, because he couldn't yet see that the grace of the Lord was attempting to shake him loose from the religious hypocrisy in which he had near fatally placed his hope. He needed to place his trust in the Rock personally, but first he had to recognize that Satan's idolatrous deception was at the heart of his problems.

Concerned that we might offend this family, Clara and I seriously took this matter before the Lord. We wanted to help them, not drive them away, but a true servant of Christ speaks the hard truths and lets the Lord sort His people out. Therefore, as Clara and I prayed in their living room one night, while the man and his wife were out to dinner and all our children were asleep upstairs, the Lord boldly revealed His will. We prayed, "Lord, please confirm the source of these demonic attacks." As soon as we said, "In Jesus'

Name, amen," all the lights in the house suddenly went out, except for one in the corner of that room. We looked over and found ourselves staring at the illuminated statuette of a Virgin Mary shrine. I could almost hear Satan laughing through that idol and I knew we had no choice but to combat this evil head on! I also knew at that moment how my family was going to suffer as a result.

When the man and his wife came home, we sat with them in their living room and shared the revelation the Lord had delivered unto us. To help them understand the truth, I related a similar experience recorded in the Bible by the prophet Jeremiah:

> *"We will not listen to the message you have spoken to us in the name of the LORD! We will certainly do everything we said we would: We will burn incense to the* ***Queen of Heaven*** *and will pour out drink offerings to her just as we and our fathers, our kings and our officials did in the towns of Judah and in the streets of Jerusalem. At that time we had plenty of food and were well off and suffered no harm. But ever since we stopped burning incense to the* ***Queen of Heaven*** *and pouring out drink offerings to her, we have had nothing and have been perishing by sword and famine." —Jeremiah 44:16-18*

Anyone connected with Catholic culture knows that the official title of the Blessed Virgin is the "Queen of Heaven," the same unclean spirit—*not the real Mary*—that had deceived and corrupted the Israel of old. It's not hard to understand how a deception of this magnitude could pierce the highest ranks of the single largest Christian denomination in the world. Didn't Satan pursue the Jewish Sanhedrin with the same vigor, convincing them to murder Jesus? Didn't he get to Judas as well, one of the Twelve? Surely, it was Satan's goal from the beginning to enter into the hearts of every willing bishop and pope in order to plant his dastardly seeds. He knows this is the best way to get his filthy claws on the flock. This is why you should not lean on religious traditions and teachings alone, but must test them with Jesus' Word and His Holy Spirit, throwing out anything conflicting with these ultimate sources of Truth.

> *"And I will do whatever you ask in my name, so that the Son may bring glory to the Father." —John 14:13*

Not every Catholic worships Mary and the Saints, but a great many do. My family's concern is not religious. We have no stake in that race. Our sole concern—as yours should be—is to reveal the truth, because no idolater is getting into heaven:

Do you not know that the wicked will not inherit the kingdom of God? Do not be deceived: Neither the sexually immoral ***nor idolaters*** *nor adulterers nor male prostitutes nor homosexual offenders nor thieves nor the greedy nor drunkards nor slanderers nor swindlers will inherit the kingdom of God.*

—1 Corinthians 6:9-10

For any who would argue, consider that the Word says Jesus is your sole intercessor before God. There is no other. He is the One who tore that veil and went into the Holy of Holies forevermore. He is the only One who sits at the right hand of Power, and it is beneath Jesus to suggest He doesn't have the desire or ability to hear and answer every single prayer lifted up to Him. Furthermore, you can be sure that His decisions are final. No one, not even Mary, can change His mind, because He only does the will of the Father.

"For I have come down from heaven not to do my will but to do the will of him who sent me." —John 6:38

Mary, the mother of Jesus, was a faithful servant of God. We should have every expectation that she is indeed in heaven, endlessly showering her praise and worship upon the Lord her God, even the Son. She has no time therefore to spare for earthly woes and complaints. Beseeching her intervention with endless tears and petitions is at the least a complete waste of your time. At the most it is blasphemy. The Lord has mercifully wiped every tear from her eyes and kept her shielded from our miserable affairs.

"He will wipe every tear from their eyes. There will be no more death or mourning or crying or pain, for the old order of things has passed away."

—Revelations 21:4

A loving God does not say to His good and faithful servant who just finished a long, hard race, "Well done, now go run another marathon!" Along with the rest of the saints, Mary's burden with this world has been fulfilled and now she is at rest. The same awaits any man or woman who is anointed by the baptism of the Holy Spirit. Like Mary, once the Spirit has been poured out on you from heaven, you've been *saint-i-fied!* This is the seal of your appointment in Christ, and it is given without vote or approval from any religious authority on earth.

There is a spiritual realm out there, well beyond human understanding, though the Word warns us of its existence. Unclean spirits can manifest themselves as dead relatives, Saints, the Blessed Virgin, animals, gods, Santa Claus, the Tooth Fairy, the Easter Bunny and even an *angel of light* in order to deceive you. This is why you must *test every spirit* with the Word of God—and learn it well, so you can combat Satan's lies with the Sword of Truth, as Jesus Himself did:

> *The tempter came to him and said, "If you are the Son of God, tell these stones to become bread."*
>
> *Jesus answered, "It is written: 'Man does not live on bread alone, but on every word that comes from the mouth of God.'" —Matthew 4:3-4*

Satan's deceptions are complicated and confusing, which is why having *a good and faithful shepherd* is helpful, but all you really need is the Head Shepherd. Beseech Jesus Christ in earnest prayer and petition, asking Him to "reveal the truth," and He will. Just be sure you are willing to accept those truths you may not want to hear.

Unfortunately, when I exposed the *"Queen of Heaven"* deception that night, that Catholic man rebuked me as a "messenger of Satan" and cast our whole family out from his home at 1 AM in the morning! Compassionately, I told him, "The hardest thing for you after this night will be to reconcile that if your priest, who denied Christ by denying Life, were to come into your home, you would welcome him with open arms. But when God sends you a man who tells you the truth about Satan's lies, you drive me and my family from your home, calling me 'Satan's messenger.'"

"I can't hear this!" he cried out and stormed off, holding his hands over his ears.

My family subsequently spent Thanksgiving homeless, and Clara and I fasted for the Lord's deliverance—not just for that family and ours, but also for this idolatrous nation. We genuinely love that family, so much so that we were willing to suffer in order that they might learn the truth. As for you, whether Catholic or Protestant, if you have a heart for your Savior, repent from your own idolatry. Break them, burn them, throw them away and do so quickly. Turn from these wicked things like you would the plague. Separating yourself from objects of your affection can be difficult, but it so worth honoring your Savior.

Put to death, therefore, whatever belongs to your earthly nature: sexual immorality, impurity, lust, evil desires and greed, which is idolatry. —*Colossians 3:5*

The Lord knows we must eat, clothe and shelter ourselves, but do not use this as an excuse. Seek wages and goods that are free from the stain of idolatry. Is money worth polluting yourself when the eternal cost is more you can afford? By now this book should have opened your eyes enough to understand that God does not accept man's way. It's either Jesus Way or the pit of burning sulfur. There is no in-between. Either you will love the Lord your God, make Him your sole Master and prosper, or you will love the world and serve Satan by running after *the deceitfulness of wealth.* Those who choose the latter are possessed by demons of *greed*, and these demons invariably lead their subjects to all forms of *idolatry.* Whether man sees an idol as *'symbolic,'* or finds it acceptable under the pretense of *'tradition,'* or celebrates it under the classification of *'art,'* or beatifies it and justifies its worship under a semantical definition of *'prayer,'* to God it is all rebellious sin that will only lead you to *death and destruction*.

25

More Than Milk

After depriving us of our Thanksgiving holiday, the Spirit finally released my family from Ohio and sent us out West to Arizona. Ironically, I had been invited to speak to a Pro-Life group at a Catholic church near Chandler in early December. Although we did not celebrate Thanksgiving in the traditional manner, we did give thanks to the Lord through prayer and fasting. The long drive also gave us plenty of time to reflect on our journey, our trials, and all the revelations we had thus far received. Apparitions of the Blessed Virgin are disturbing, but the underlying problem crippling the church in America, Catholic and Protestant, is *milk:*

> *In fact, though by this time you ought to be teachers, you need someone to teach you the elementary truths of God's word all over again. You need milk, not solid food! —Hebrews 5:12*

Milk is to know that Jesus is the Christ, Messiah and Savior who died upon the cross for our sins, was resurrected on the third day, now sits at the Right Hand of God the Father, and is the only Way, the Truth and the Life who will one day return in His Father's Glory to judge the whole earth as King of kings and Lord or lords. Incredibly, as my family has witnessed, much of the collective church in America needs to relearn this most essential Gospel fact.

Anyone who lives on milk, being still an infant, is not acquainted with the teaching about righteousness. But solid food is for the mature, who by constant use have trained themselves to distinguish good from evil. —Hebrews 5:13-14

The problem with a strictly milk diet is that it is insufficient to expose Satan's artful deceptions which are leading the church headlong into sin. The *teaching about righteousness* originates with the Word of God, but in order to effectively *distinguish good from evil* you must graduate to the *solid food* of the Holy Spirit of Truth, that *hidden manna* from heaven. Without the Counselor it is impossible to unlock the full meaning of the Scriptures, and this is why a significant proportion of the church in America has gone astray. Satan shows up with a Word-based lie and people fall for it.

"If you are the Son of God," he said, "throw yourself down. For it is written: 'He will command his angels concerning you, and they will lift you up in their hands, so that you will not strike your foot against a stone.'"

Jesus answered him, "It is also written: 'Do not put the Lord your God to the test.'" —Matthew 4:6-7

The important lesson above is that Satan is not forbidden from quoting Scripture to suit his own purposes, but did he really think he was going to trick the Living Word? We can be sure that Christ put forth this witness so that we would understand how Satan seeks to confuse the Church by twisting the meaning of the Word. Jesus also teaches us how to counter this action by applying the *full meaning* of His Word. Unfortunately, legions of pastors and priests have graduated from Bible College without learning this skill. They become experts in church history and theology, but since they have not the Holy Spirit living within them, they do not understand the Word they study and preach. As a result, they are little better than infants crawling along the floor, futilely trying to teach other infants how to walk. Together they stumble.

"I have listened attentively, but they do not say what is right. No one repents of his wickedness, saying, 'What have I done?' Each pursues his own course like a horse charging into battle." —Jeremiah 8:6

They ask, *"What have I done?"* not because they do not understand the truth, but because they reject it. Their calloused hearts have muted their ears and blinded their eyes. This lesson the Lord made clear during our journey throughout the State of Arizona.

At first, we had only anticipated spending a few weeks in the West, so my family had packed just one bag each and left *The Whale* behind at a farm in Ohio. As it turned out, the Lord had other plans and we wound up spending several months engaging the disparate church throughout the state. With little-to-no funds, just a couple changes of clothing, some toiletries and absolutely no homemaking supplies, we learned just how well the Holy Spirit really will provide anything you lack!

Our lesson began as the Lord exposed the church's milk-drinking hypocrisy. Christians don't just wake up and say, "I'm going to be a hypocrite today." Instead, they set their hearts on themselves. Feeding this lie is a rotten seed Satan planted among the ranks of the Church going all the way back to the beginning. It's called *false grace:*

> *How much more severely do you think a man deserves to be punished who has trampled the Son of God under foot, who has treated as an unholy thing the blood of the covenant that sanctified him, and who has insulted the Spirit of grace? —Hebrews 10:29*

One hot summer day in Chandler as my family checked out of a hotel, I found the Tahoe's gas tank bone dry. Four times I tried to start it before I stepped aside to have a word with the Lord. I was on the verge of loosing my temper. As a servant of Christ, it always seems that when your fuse is short, Satan is standing right there lighting a match. Fighting back the old me, the one who thought I was in control, I prayerfully accepted the Lord's will. After this, He told me, 'Load up your family, put your hand on the dashboard and ask Me to provide the fuel you need. I will deliver you.' Doing as I was told, I crammed my family into the baking oven of the Tahoe, put my hand on the dashboard and led them in a prayer as we sweat. After we said, "Amen," I turned the key and—praise be to Jesus—it started right up!

Without delay we went to the nearest gas station three miles up the road where I thankfully filled up the tank. At the same time, Clara and I were wondering what was the point of all that? As if just on cue, a young man walked up and, noticing our Texas plates, asked, "Are you from out of state?"

'Appointment,' said the Spirit, so I replied, "We've been serving Jesus on the road for the last two years."

"Really," he seemed intrigued, "how do you do that?"

In short order, I learned that he was a windshield replacement salesman, so he cased gas stations for business. He also confessed that he felt he had been called by God and had gone to an evangelism training school in New Zealand, but had been turned off by fake witnesses of the Holy Spirit. "I just didn't buy everyone being slain in the Spirit right on time each morning," he said.

"So you put aside the Lord's calling because of a few fakers?" I questioned.

He shrugged and replied, "Well, since we're saved by *grace* and not works, I figured I got my foot in the door of heaven, so why not do something for myself?"

His foot! What about the rest of him? So I asked him, "When you get to heaven, don't you want to hear *'Well done, good and faithful servant!'* Or are you willing to risk your place for some worthless pursuit of money?"

He shrugged again, this time not knowing what to say.

"How much money are you making?" I asked.

Proudly he replied, "I made $890 last week."

My heart sank for him. He had no idea that he was saying to God, 'For a measly $890 a week I neglected your call.'

"Do you read your Bible?" I asked.

"I have," he replied. "I mean, it's basically just a self-help book, right?"

I shook my head in astonishment, lamenting all the lies this guy had ingested from the religious establishment. Assertively, I told him, "The Bible is all about service. By serving and loving one another as Christ loves us, we help ourselves, and when our work is finished, we receive our treasure in heaven—the crown of life. But a branch who bears no fruit is good for nothing, except to be thrown away and burned."

> *"I am the vine; you are the branches. If a man remains in me and I in him, he will bear much fruit; apart from me you can do nothing. If anyone does not remain in me, he is like a branch that is thrown away and withers; such branches are picked up, thrown into the fire and burned." —John 15:5-6*

Seeing he was somewhat convicted, I prayed for this young man, asking the Lord to show him the real Spirit. I also had him promise he would start searching the Scriptures daily. I pray he has followed through. If not, he might not discover that his election by *grace* is in grave danger before it's too late.

So too, at the present time there is a remnant chosen by grace. And if by grace, then it is no longer by works; if it were, grace would no longer be grace.
—Romans 11:5-6

Do you see how Satan twists the Scriptures to lead the sheep astray? Did Christ offer up Himself as a sacrifice so that you could go on being a sinner? Absolutely not, which is why the apostle Paul warned the Church about Israel's history:

Consider therefore the kindness and sternness of God: sternness to those who fell, but kindness to you, provided that you continue in his kindness. Otherwise, you also will be cut off. —Romans 11:22

God chooses His *elect*. We did not choose ourselves, but God chose us, just as He chose His Twelve Apostles. However, one of those *chosen* fell away and suffered death and destruction to serve as a warning to the Church of every age. Judas saw all the miracles, and he likely participated in some himself—by the Spirit of Grace—when Jesus sent His apostles *two by two* into all the villages and towns of Israel. Therefore, to the one who persists in innocent bloodshed, sexual immorality and a denial of our Lord Jesus Christ, grace can no longer save him, because he has not *continued in His kindness.* Instead, he has turned his back on God's gift.

Everyone who sins breaks the law; in fact, sin is lawlessness. But you know that he appeared so that he might take away our sins. And in him is no sin. No one who lives in him keeps on sinning. No one who continues to sin has either seen him or known him. —1 John 3:4-6

After the *Grace Man* appointment at the gas station, the Lord led us to several churches throughout North Phoenix in keeping with the custom of Jesus and His apostles. We specifically targeted Sunday Schools and Bible studies where we could speak freely and avoid causing offense by disrupting religious services. Through these engagements the Lord further illustrated the pervasive effects of *false grace,* which manifests itself primarily in the form of *false love*. This is the same kind of love the Israel of old expressed towards the Lord. They said, "I love you." Then they went and committed adultery.

One of the first churches we visited made this witness of *false love* explicitly clear. Before we went there, the Spirit warned me that this establishment had recently 'split' and had 'no shepherd.' When my family arrived for their Sunday School we first met *Rusty,* the class leader, who quickly disclosed, "We just went through a split and we're always looking for good shepherds." Their troubles were made evident when only three others attended the class. My family tripled their number! Despite the poor attendance, the Spirit came upon us in force. In the midst of sharing testimony, the Lord directed my attention to the woman sitting beside Clara and said, 'She needs healing. Go and do it.' I was convicted in heart and knew I had to obey. So, I walked over to her and said, "The Lord says you need healing." She instantly broke into tears and received the Lord's Healing Hand. As I felt the power of the Lord flow through my hands into her shoulders, I asked, "Can you feel that?"

"Yes," she replied, and gestured with her hand between her breasts, "I feel heat right here."

I didn't know it, but before the Lord had prompted me, she had whispered to Clara that she was suffering from breast cancer.

Later, my family attended the church service and that's where everything went south. The pastor came on *stage* in flip-flops, designer jeans, his shirttail was hanging out, and he casually held a coffee mug in one hand and laptop in his other—no Bible. *Pastor Flip-flops* set his laptop down on a clear plastic podium and began preaching about *agape love,* specifically citing a 'Christian book' he had recently read that chastised Christians' anti-abortion and anti-homosexual beliefs. To the recently *split* flock he said, "God is love, and we have to show people another side of the love of Christ." He went on to describe God's love as an "orgasmic" kind of love and made an intentional pun about a cable series that glorifies polygamy.

My family was appalled. Clara wanted to get up and walk out with the children and I wanted to stand and denounce Satan, but the Spirit told us to hold our peace. Afterwards, as the Spirit led, I confronted *Flip-flops* privately. "God is love," I told him, "but love without truth is really not love at all. The reason true servants of Christ are against homosexuality and abortion is that we know these sins torment those who practice them and lead unto death. What good are we to God if we ignore these issues or attempt to excuse them in any way, knowing these people will suffer and die by their sins?" I concluded by saying, "We have to love the sinner, but hate the sin. To love the sin and the sinner together is not love, but a lie."

"Okay, well thank you," he said dismissively, leaning all the way back in his chair and receiving nothing. The Spirit had spoken the truth, for this was 'no shepherd.' Ignoring my pleas to embrace the whole truth, he invited me to leave with a plastic smile. While it is easy for Clara and me to love all kinds of sinners, phonies are really hard to stomach, and hypocrite pastors are the worst.

> *"Woe the shepherds who are destroying and scattering the sheep of my pasture!" declares the LORD. Therefore this is what the LORD, the God of Israel, says to the shepherds who tend my people: "Because you have scattered my flock and driven them away and have not bestowed care on them, I will bestow punishment on you for the evil you have done," declares the LORD.*
>
> *—Jeremiah 23:1-2*

After two months of witnessing to one hypocrite church after another, we finally encountered a pastor who seemed to have a true heart for Christ. His teachings were biblically sound, yet he did not have the Spirit. I call him *Pastor Wow,* because he said, *"Wow!"* every time I shared a revelation in God's Word. Curiously, he was soon leaving the church he had planted for another church hiring him out of state. His current church was interviewing for his replacement, and they suggested I apply for the job, to which I replied, "I have a job." Following the Spirit, I did offer to shepherd them for a transitional period, but this they rejected. Their elders were adamant about seeking a typical applicant with a Bible College degree and a genuine interest in their salary and benefits package, including a new home in the area and retirement plan. Isn't it odd to consider that God's shepherds can be hired? It's stranger still that supposed shepherds actually do retire. I thought that was up to God, in which case He takes His servant home to heaven.

At any rate, my family was inclined by the Spirit to join with *Pastor Wow* and his flock in fellowship, Bible study, and we attended three of their Sunday services. They were all greatly intrigued by my family's testimony and many believed I was the shepherd they had prayed for the Lord to send, but the *elders* still sought that typical pastor mold. On the last Sunday, before *Pastor Wow* was to leave the state, the elders invited their primary 'ordained candidate' to come and deliver a sermon as a guest pastor. Ironically, he too was from Texas, but like a good pastor, he had applied for the "job." We call him *Pastor Slick.* He was well-groomed, witty and down with all the latest trends and technology. He was also a reader. He began his sermon by telling the gathered congregation about a book he had recently read that surveyed people's negative impressions of Christians, highlighting our anti-abortion and anti-homosexual beliefs. Did you catch that? Indeed, he gave almost the identical sermon about unaccountable *agape love* as *Pastor Flip-flops*. He concluded by reflecting on his college days when he had told a homosexual friend, "I'm sorry, but I can't condone your lifestyle." This friend never spoke to him again and he expressed regret, suggesting he could have said something different. Then he said, "So you see, we have to show people another side of the love of Christ."

The Spirit in me was incensed that the elders had invited this poisonous snake right through the front door of their house! I tried warning *Pastor Wow,* but he ultimately proved his lack of the Spirit by rejecting my testimony.

In the midst of these disappointments, Clara and I took our children to the local park and spotted a young man walking in front of us. Immediately the Spirit said, 'Homosexual needs witnessing.' Clara and I both heard the Spirit at the same time. Almost fumbling over each other, we called out to him, "Do you love Jesus?"

Looking back with a grimace, he asked, "Isn't that personal?"

"Very," we agreed. Though apprehensive, he was strangely compelled to sit with us while our children enjoyed the playground. We introduced ourselves and learned his name was Adam. Beyond coincidence, we were the second witness to approach him out of the blue about Jesus in the last week. It was also his tenth day coming off a heroine addiction.

"We know what you do," Clara said firmly, referring to his homosexuality. "We hate it, but we love you."

"We hate what you do, because it's destroying you," I added.

Adam seemed convicted at that moment. It's hard to explain, but he could actually feel the genuine love emanating from the Spirit within us. That's when I asked him, "If you want to be made clean and put this sin behind you, you can accept Jesus Christ right now."

"I'm not ready for God," Adam quickly retracted. "I'm going to get my life straight for myself." He had insisted that he did not believe in God, but we knew that God was calling him. Unlike other hypocrites he had encountered throughout his life, Adam felt the sincerity of our love. What a crime it would have been had we told him, "Just accept Jesus as your Savior and you can go on destroying yourself in sin." *Flip-flops, Wow, Slick* and many false witnesses would likely have done so. What then would have been Adam's incentive to accept Jesus? If sin doesn't matter, why bother repenting before the cross of Christ?

If we deliberately keep on sinning after we have received the knowledge of the truth, no sacrifice for sins is left, but only a fearful expectation of judgment and of raging fire that will consume the enemies of God. —Hebrews 10:26-27

Because sin is stinging to the point of death, true repentance in Jesus Christ—in which a sinner turns from his wickedness—is necessary. Therefore, be cautious that you never appease or accept evil, for woe unto the sinner, but greater is the woe unto the one who causes him to sin:

"Woe to the world because of the things that cause people to sin! Such things must come, but woe to the man through whom they come!" —Matthew 18:7

The world is filled with liars who will tell you all kinds of flatteries as they attempt to lift your wallet from your vest pocket. They belong to a 'sheep-shearers anonymous club,' though they're not interested in turning from their wicked fleecing habits, just in hiding their true identity—*hired hands.* The one who truly loves you, however, is he who refuses to ignore any sin that is leading you unto death. Even if you say, "You're not the judge of me," or "All sin is sin," or "I'm saved by grace," or "I just don't believe in judgment," understand that any false belief harbored in your heart will be revealed to your shame on Judgment Day.

For we know him who said, "It is mine to avenge; I will repay," and again, "The Lord will judge his people." It is a dreadful thing to fall into the hands of the living God. —Hebrews 10:30-31

Lost people will say anything to justify themselves, but those truly in Christ are required to understand the difference between sin that results from a lack of discipline, as opposed to sin that stems from disobedience, which is rebellion. Salvation comes not by faith alone, but also through *obedience,* which is demonstrated both in dying to our former sinful nature and by testifying the Truth. This doesn't mean you do not stumble at times or that you are in any way perfect, but you continue to fight the good fight and tirelessly strive to become like Christ. Some who have been invested in evil their whole lives may be granted the Lord's grace with their final repentant breath, but one who defiantly says to God, "You made me a sinner, now accept me as I am," will *fall* into the burning pit of sulfur. He does not cease to exist, for what fear is there in that? No, his spirit goes into an eternal prison:

"Where their worm does not die, and the fire is not quenched." —Mark 9:48

Even so, this warning is not for unbelievers alone. It also applies to unrepentant "Christians":

> *"But when the king came in to see the guests, he noticed a man there who was not wearing wedding clothes. 'Friend,' he asked, 'how did you get in here without wedding clothes?' The man was speechless.*
>
> *"Then the king told the attendants, 'Tie him hand and foot, and throw him outside, into the darkness, where there will be weeping and gnashing of teeth.'"*
>
> *—Matthew 22:11-13*

That man of whom Christ spoke was a Christian who received the *grace* of the Lord, but forfeited the fight against his sinful nature. He accepted a lie that told him he could get into heaven with his sin still attached to him, thus soiling his *wedding clothes* after they had been *washed clean by the blood of the Lamb.* God will never introduce rebellion into heaven. He had that problem once, and that is why you have an *accuser* constantly tempting you to follow him in his fate. Therefore, persevere in righteousness, so that you may partake of the Lord's Wedding Banquet.

> *"Not everyone who says to me, 'Lord, Lord,' will enter the kingdom of heaven, but only he who does the will of my Father who is in heaven. Many will say to me on that day, 'Lord, Lord, did we not prophesy in your name, and in your name drive out demons and perform many miracles?' Then I will tell them plainly, 'I never knew you. Away from me, you evildoers!'"*
>
> *—Matthew 7:21-23*

The grave danger for a majority of Christians is that they do not seek the Counselor to guide them, but blindly trust in a priest, pastor, or some purported theologian claiming to be Holy Spirit inspired. Worse yet, a great many establishment churches staff a board of milk-drinking elders who *hire* their shepherds. Why do they expect anything besides a *hired hand?* Instead of seeking a Spirit-filled man of God, they require an applicant who shares their craving for milk, as well as a certified milk-drinking degree. Whether misled or misleading, the predominant church in America is simply not walking in obedience before God.

As for you, since you cannot ride any lie into heaven, you must have the Counselor for yourself so you can steer clear of lies and invest yourself in the whole truth of Jesus Christ. The Good News is that the Holy Spirit is yours for the asking. Although, many may find themselves asking, "Where is He?"

"For my flesh is real food and my blood is real drink. Whoever eats my flesh and drinks my blood remains in me, and I in him. Just as the living Father sent me and I live because of the Father, so the one who feeds on me will live because of me. This is the bread that came down from heaven. Your forefathers ate manna and died, but he who feeds on this bread will live forever."

—John 6:55-58

To better grasp the reality of the Spirit, you must unravel this mysterious Scripture. Given their lack of understanding, the religious Jews who first heard it were appalled. The Law given to Moses clearly forbade drinking blood of any kind, let alone a man's. How then could this instruction have come from the Christ? Aware of His disciples grumbling, Jesus explained Himself:

"The Spirit gives life; the flesh counts for nothing. The words I have spoken to you are spirit and they are life." —John 6:63

Despite making His intent clear, pointing out *"the flesh counts for nothing,"* many of Jesus' disciples abandoned Him at this *hard teaching.* They just couldn't understand that when He spoke of His flesh and blood as real food and drink, He meant the filling of the promised Holy Spirit that would come into the hearts of each of His faithful followers, sealing their election to heaven. Once again, Christ was fulfilling Scripture, proving that *understanding* of His Word is reserved for those whom the Father will *draw.* As He said to those who were grumbling:

"It is written in the Prophets: 'They will all be taught by God.' Everyone who listens to the Father and learns from him comes to me." —John 6:45

Therefore, all others will either reject Christ's Word or will attempt to pervert it. The Catholic religion, for instance, will argue that the *Communion [Eucharist]* they consume at every Mass *mystically transubstantiates* into the literal body and blood of Jesus. In other words, they believe they are actually eating Christ, and are being saved by it.

*Then Jesus declared, "I am the bread of life. He who comes to me will **never go hungry**, and he who believes in me will **never be thirsty**." —John 6:35*

Can a person believe with his or her stomach? Surely not, which is why no matter how many times a Catholic has the Eucharist, he or she *will hunger and thirst again*. This further proves Christ's *spiritual* meaning. After the stomach has perished along with the rest of the flesh, only the soul will remain, but where will it go without the Holy Spirit? In this, Satan's deception is exposed, for he has convinced a great many Christians, now under the Catholic tent, that they have been *filled* by something other than the Holy Spirit, even though the Spirit is the only *filling* that can truly save you. As the Lord has shown my family, many of our Catholic brothers and sisters are not even aware of this *false grace* lie; neither do they understand that when the priest lifts up the Communion Host, he is also performing what he believes to be a literal sacrificial offering of the Body of Christ. This violates God's Word:

> *For Christ did not enter a man-made sanctuary that was only a copy of the true one; he entered heaven itself, now to appear for us in God's presence.* ***Nor did he enter heaven to offer himself again and again,*** *the way the high priest enters the Most Holy Place every year with blood that is not his own. Then Christ would have had to suffer many times since the creation of the world.* ***But now he has appeared once for all*** *at the end of the ages to do away with sin by the sacrifice of himself. Just as man is destined to die once, and after that to face judgment, so* ***Christ was sacrificed once*** *to take away the sins of many people; and* ***he will appear a second time, not to bear sin,*** *but to bring salvation to those who are waiting for him. —Hebrews 9:24-28*

Christ, the unblemished Lamb, was the eternally atoning sacrifice for all mankind *once for all.* When He *appears a second time* in the flesh, He will be as our Judge. So how can the Catholic Church supposedly hold Christ's flesh up as a sacrifice at each Mass? The answer is they can't. They have been deceived. Communion, as Christ presented it to His disciples at the Last Supper, is proper and should be honored, but *in remembrance*, not as a sacrifice:

> *And he took bread, gave thanks and broke it, and gave it to them, saying, "This is my body given for you;* ***do this in remembrance of me.*** *" —Luke 22:19*

Once again, it goes back to the tree of death, where Satan has said, "Here, eat this fruit and become God." Just as the Israel of old quickly turned away from God after Joshua and the generation he led into the Promised Land died, so it was with the Christian Church. Even before the passing of the original apostles, strange teachings emerged, and have been sustained over the centuries. This is how a rotten seed of Satan can become *sacred church tradition,* and how a people called by Jesus' Name can stain their clothes by embracing practices the Lord finds unedifying to His Name.

Do not be carried away by all kinds of strange teachings. It is good for our hearts to be strengthened by grace, not by ceremonial foods, which are of no value to those who eat them. —Hebrews 13:9

Whether by religious ritual or philosophical preaching, a great many Catholics and Protestants are practicing a *false grace* lie that attempts to place Jesus on the cross to be sacrificed over and over again. They do this by appeasing sin. It may surprise you, but the Spirit has revealed to my family that this is why some Christians prefer the crucifix [Jesus on the cross]. Subconsciously, they are dwelling in Jesus' death, when the Father wants us all to dwell in His Resurrection. Jesus *defeated death* upon the cross and was taken up to heaven, so how is an image crafted by man's hands and nailed to a cross in any way edifying to our Savior's victory? Let us look upon Christ as all the angels in heaven see Him in His Father's Glory, and let us dwell in His victory. Everyone stumbles, but there is a difference between recognizing the fact that we are all sinners—yet striving to live righteously in Christ, as opposed to embracing sin and perpetually excusing it. The ancient Jews and Israelites had the same problem. They sinned and they made sacrifices. The committed the same sins again, and they made more sacrifices. So long as they could afford to make the offerings to the priests, they had little to no incentive to turn from their wickedness. This worked out well for the priesthood, because the more Israel sinned, the more they were fed by the offerings. However, this did not sit well with God:

"Will you steal and murder, commit adultery and perjury, burn incense to Baal and follow other gods you have not known, and then come and stand before me in this house, which bears my Name, and say, 'We are safe'—safe to do all these detestable things? Has this house, which bears my Name, become ***a den of robbers to you****? But I have been watching! declares the LORD."*

—Jeremiah 7:9-11

Jesus fulfilled this Scripture by driving the merchants from the Temple, demonstrating what He will do on the *last day* to all who seek to come unto Him with false humility and worldly devotions:

And as he taught them, he said, "Is it not written: 'My house will be called a house of prayer for all nations'? But you have made it ***'a den of robbers.'"***

—Mark 11:17

It was this chastisement that led the Jewish priests and teachers of the Law to seek a way to kill their Messiah. They saw the Temple as their possession, when it has always belonged to Christ Jesus. So too the religious establishments of this era mistakenly see the Church as belonging to them. You, however, must come to the Lord with a genuine repentant heart, proven when you turn from your sin. It doesn't matter how much you give to the priests, pastors, churches, poor and needy, because you cannot *buy* your way out of hell. You have to come to a place of humility, usually by way of humiliation, so that you surrender your whole life to God. Then, if the Lord tells you to rid yourself of all your wealth and belongings and come follow Him into the wilderness, you will. This is what a true acceptance of the cross of Christ looks and feels like, and it's the kind of commitment that is desperately lacking in the predominant church in America. For this reason, a great many "Christians" don't really know the Spirit of their Savior.

Sin separates us from God. Therefore, how can we receive the indwelling of His Spirit when we are dwelling in Satan's lies? Don't let personal or religious loyalties stand in your way. Let yourself be *taught by God,* for an hour is coming where the terrible betrayal of Judas, who also partook of the Lord's bread, will be repeated against the modern-day Body of Christ—His Church. That will be an especially dark day for those who only know the Spirit as a biblical concept, and not as a spiritual reality, burning in your soul.

> *"When the Counselor comes, whom I will send to you from the Father, the Spirit of truth who goes out from the Father, he will testify about me. And you also must testify, for you have been with me from the beginning."*
>
> *—John 15:26-27*

The most direct path for coming into true communion with the Lord's Spirit is *testimony*. A man or woman who is willing to openly confess his or her faith in Jesus Christ and share the wonderful things Jesus has done for them will most assuredly receive the Spirit of Truth, because you have embraced the purpose for which you were reborn—to bring God glory!

> *Behind the second curtain was a room called the Most Holy Place, which had the golden altar of incense and the gold-covered ark of the covenant. This ark contained the gold jar of manna, Aaron's staff that had budded, and the stone tablets of the covenant. Above the ark were the cherubim of the Glory, overshadowing the atonement cover. But we cannot discuss these things in detail now.*
>
> *—Hebrews 9:3-5*

The most prized and mysterious article of the ancient Tabernacle, and the First Temple after it, was the Ark of the Covenant, also called the Ark of the Testimony. The Ark itself was representative of God's Throne in heaven. From between the worshipping cherubim above the *mercy seat* the Holy Spirit appeared before the High Priest and issued forth instructions to Israel, but now we have a Son who asks the Father to send His Holy Spirit into the hearts of His faithful servants, where He now instructs us concerning the Father's will. The articles inside the Ark, the gold jar of manna, Aaron's staff—which budded, blossomed and fruited with almonds, and the tables of the Testimony [The Word], were all representations of Christ The Lord. As you have already read, Jesus is the manna that comes down from heaven, he is the Tree of Life in the Garden of Eden—*the Branch* spoken of in the Prophets, and He is the Living Word. Roughly twelve hundred years after Moses constructed the Ark, Christ was sent to the earth to establish His Covenant. At that time, Jesus taught His disciples how they should pray:

> *"This, then, is how you should pray: 'Our Father in heaven, hallowed be your name, your kingdom come, your will be done on earth as it is in heaven."*
>
> *—Matthew 6:9-10*

He did not suggest we pray for a Kingdom that was *yet* to come, but a Kingdom that had *already* come:

> *Once, having been asked by the Pharisees when the kingdom of God would come, Jesus replied, "The kingdom of God does not come with your careful observation, nor will people say, 'Here it is,' or 'There it is,' because the kingdom of God is within you." —Luke 17:20-21*

On another occasion Jesus also told them:

> *"But if I drive out demons by the Spirit of God, then the kingdom of God has come unto you." —Matthew 12:28*

We The Church are the vessels through which God's Kingdom is made manifest on this earth by virtue of our *testimony*. In fact, we are the bearers of God's throne, made clear through the prophet Ezekiel:

> *As I looked at the living creatures, I saw a wheel on the ground beside each creature with its four faces. This was the appearance and structure of the wheels: They sparkled like chrysolite, and all four looked alike. Each appeared to be made like a wheel intersecting a wheel. As they moved, they would go in any*

one of the four directions the creatures faced; the wheels did not turn about as the creatures went. Their rims were high and awesome, and all four rims were full of eyes all around. —Ezekiel 1:15-18

The living creatures shown to Ezekiel had four faces, a man, lion, ox and eagle. These represent the Lord's *testifiers* upon all the face of the earth. Whether they want to, anything that lives and breathes proclaims the Glory of Him who made them. The wheels are covenants, two concentric rings—one within the other—without beginning or end. These represent the Old Covenant through Moses and the New Covenant through Christ. The chrysolite represents the Church; such as it shines in heaven. This is why the Lord asked Abraham to number the stars, if he could count them, for such would his offspring be. Lastly, the eyes are witnesses, which is what every member of the Church in Christ is born to be. Moses understood all this, for he testified to the Israel of old:

Now what I am commanding you today is not too difficult for you or beyond your reach. It is not up in heaven, so that you have to ask, "Who will ascend into heaven to get it and proclaim it to us so we may obey it?" Nor is it beyond the sea, so that you have to ask, "Who will cross the sea to get it and proclaim it to us so that we may obey it?" No, the word is very near you; it is in your mouth and in your heart so you may obey it. —Deuteronomy 30:11-14

Jesus fully revealed this truth when He said:

"If you love me, you will obey what I command. And I will ask the Father, and he will give you another Counselor to be with you forever—the Spirit of truth. The world cannot accept him, because it neither sees him nor knows him. But you know him, for he lives with you and will be in you." —John 14:15-17

He is right there inside of you. All you have to do is open the door of your heart to reveal Him.

"Here I am! I stand at the door and knock. If anyone hears my voice and opens the door, I will come in and eat with him, and he with me."

—Revelations 3:20

Jesus is speaking to you even now. If only you will *hear His Voice* and *open the door* of your heart by *obeying* what He Commands then His Spirit will make Himself known to you. So are you listening? What is He Commanding you to do?

> *Jesus replied, "***If anyone loves me, he will obey my teaching.*** My Father will love him, and we will come to him and make our home with him. He who does not love me will not obey my teaching. These words you hear are not my own; they belong to the Father who sent me." —John 14:23-24*

By *obeying Christ's teachings* you demonstrate your *true love* for Him, and by this the Father and the Son *make their home* in you through the indwelling of the Holy Spirit. This is how *the Kingdom of God is in you*—literally. Here's where to begin: Simply pray each day, "Here I am Father, in Jesus' Name use me for your will." After that, do what He places upon your heart to do each and every day. When you do this—and do it consistently, I assure you the Spirit will make Himself known to you. He will expose every lie you have ever received into your heart and lead you to fulfill your own personal repentance. He will also use you to convict the world of its guilt:

> *"When he comes, he will convict the world of guilt in regard to sin and righteousness and judgment: in regard to sin, because men do not believe in me; in regard to righteousness, because I am going to the Father, where you can see me no longer; and in regard to judgment, because the prince of this world now stands condemned." —John 16:8-11*

Being *One* with the Father and the Son, the Spirit will burden you to *testify* His Truth and His Name to many. No longer will you ignore sin, but you will yearn for the salvation of the lost. Some of you will *testify* on a large scale and some in small, though equally important ways:

> *If the whole body were an eye, where would the sense of hearing be? If the whole body were an ear, where would the sense of smell be? But in fact God has arranged the parts in the body, every one of them, just as he wanted them to be.*
> *—1 Corinthians 12:17-18*

Wherever you are in the Body of Christ, every one of *the elect* from the ancient prophets to today's servants has been born to *testify* "Jesus Christ." That is why that angel told the apostle John, *"For the testimony of Jesus is the spirit of prophecy."* The Spirit is the *true love* your Heavenly Father expresses for you and through you. If He loved you as the world does then He would let you perish with your sin. However, because He does truly love you, He will indeed beckon you to come up and sup with Him, and at that moment you will begin to understand the real meaning of solid food:

"On that day you will realize that I am in my Father, and you are in me, and I am in you." —John 14:20

Nonetheless, take care that you do not dishonor the Spirit of Grace after you have received it. When you unite your body and soul with the Body of Christ, you become a part of the third and final Temple, which Christ raised to Life on the third day. Within this temple is the Throne of the Lord, the Ark of the Testimony. Look back throughout Israel's history and consider what happened to those who did not respect the Ark. When it was captured by the uncircumcised Philistines and taken into their god's temple, their idol was broken to pieces and the Philistines were plagued by tumors and rats. This is what happens to a people who come near unto God with idolatrous hearts. Moreover, when King David attempted to bring up the Ark to his city for the first time on a cart, the oxen pulling it stumbled and Uzzah reached out to steady the Ark with his hand, after which he instantly fell dead. This man represents those who come near unto God while persisting in sin, having treated with irreverence the blood of Christ's Covenant. Those who perished before the Ark revealed the reality of God's wrath, which burns against this sinful world. Without Christ's atonement, you will fall subject to the Law established through Moses:

The LORD said to Moses: "Tell your brother Aaron not to come whenever he chooses into the Most Holy Place behind the curtain in front of the atonement cover on the ark, or else he will die, because I appear in the cloud over the atonement cover." —Leviticus 16:2

Therefore, make every effort to graduate from milk to the solid food of the Holy Spirit so that you can resist Satan's temptations and remain clean in Christ before the Lord your God. This calls for perseverance in abstaining from any sin, even one promoted by your religious establishment, and in testifying "Jesus Christ" at every available opportunity. Demonstrate your *true love* through *obedience* to God's Word and Spirit and you will be able to come near unto God with confidence in Christ. Yet, if you are not burdened for the salvation of others, pray the Lord makes your heart like His Heart. My family did this, and the Spirit taught us the meaning of His *true love*. We demonstrate His love by bringing these difficult truths before you, because we desire that not one Christian, whether Catholic or Protestant, is lost to the deceitful ways of Satan, which will soon enslave the whole earth—though not the Spirit-filled Church.

26

The Mark

By the summer of 2011 the Lord brought our time in Arizona to a close by directing us back to Ohio, giving us just one week to pack up and get on the road. The only problem was we had next to no money! Based on fuel prices I had calculated we needed at least $480 for the trip, not including the cost of food and lodging, but we had only $16 and less than a quarter tank of gas! I don't know how many times Clara and I have looked at each other and said in our hearts, 'Again?' Just how many tight scrapes can one family of six endure? The answer is just as many as the Lord desires in order to refine and grow your faith to a measure pleasing to Him:

And without faith it is impossible to please God, because anyone who comes to him must believe that he exists and that he rewards those who earnestly seek him. —Hebrews 11:6

Though you believe your faith is strong and secure, the Lord knows better. So by His gracious love He drives those of us who truly seek Him to strive towards new and ever-reaching heights. You can be sure that Peter, Paul, the rest of the original apostles and all the prophets before them had not found their faith complete until Christ had welcomed them into the Kingdom of Heaven. So we too must persevere through every trial, seeking to know and learn the lessons the Lord is trying to teach us, and never being satisfied until that day we come to see God.

In this you greatly rejoice, though now for a little while you may have had to suffer grief in all kinds of trials. These have come so that your faith—of greater worth than gold, which perishes even though refined by fire—may be proved genuine and may result in praise, glory and honor when Jesus Christ is revealed. —1 Peter 1:6-7

If you walk with Christ in this manner then not only will your faith grow, but so will knowledge and wisdom in His Word. By this time in our journey, my family had already received so much, yet the Lord had so much more to show us, and the next revelation would be among the most disturbing of all.

But mark this: There will be terrible times in the last days. People will be lovers of themselves, lovers of money, boastful, proud, abusive, disobedient to their parents, ungrateful, unholy, without love, unforgiving, slanderous, without self-control, brutal, not lovers of the good, treacherous, rash, conceited, lovers of pleasure rather than lovers of God. —2 Timothy 3:1-4

As a servant of the Lord, sometimes it is the simplest of encounters that speaks the most volume. So it was with a man my family met at a park one day. When asked if he loved Jesus, he disdainfully replied, "I'm Christian, but I don't wear *it* on my sleeve." We have heard these same sorrowful words in nearly every state we have visited along the way, including from virtually every denomination of so-called *faith*. So, if they are not wearing *"Jesus"* on their sleeve, just whom are they wearing? You had better believe they are wearing something, because nobody wears nothing. Either they have Christ and His Holy Spirit *seal*, or they have *the mark of the beast:*

He also forced everyone, small and great, rich and poor, free and slave, to receive a mark on his right hand or on his forehead, so that no one could buy or sell unless he had the mark, which is the name of the beast or the number of his name. —Revelations 13:16-17

Such as the Lord revealed to my family, it is important for you and yours to understand that *the mark of the beast* is spiritual, just like real communion with the Lord cannot be achieved with your stomach, but must be sealed in your heart. Although some tattoo their hands and foreheads with all sorts of satanic markings, even they may be saved if they turn their hearts over to Christ. Remember, *the flesh counts for nothing.* Thus, the *forehead* represents what is on one's *mind* and the *hand* symbolizes *actions.* That *the mark of the beast* would be connected with the right hand in conjunction with buying or selling is significant, because this is the hand one shakes to symbolically consummate deals, including laws and international treaties.

As I was seeking the Lord's Face on this matter, He made the spiritual significance of *the mark* clear to me by directing me back to ancient Israel when, through Moses, He told them to bind *His Law* to their foreheads and their arms that they might not forget the requirements of their God:

> *Fix these words of mine in your hearts and minds; tie them as symbols on your hands and bind them on your foreheads. —Deuteronomy 11:18*

The ancient Jews took this literally by binding *tefillin* to their foreheads and arms, which some Jews still do today for their morning prayers before they go out into the world to engage the day's work. Tefillin, also called *phylacteries,* are two small black leather boxes with fastening straps that contain miniature hand-written copies of the four verses in the Torah where these instructions are given [Ex. 13:9, 16; Deut. 6:8, 11:18]. The Jews tie one box to their foreheads and another to their left arms, pointing it to their hearts, but they clearly misunderstand the spiritual truth the Lord is instructing them to obey. God's instruction was to *fix His Word in their hearts and minds,* and this can only be accomplished through Christ Jesus:

> *Now the glory of the God of Israel went up from above the cherubim, where it had been, and moved to the threshold of the temple. Then the LORD called to the man clothed in linen who had the writing kit at his side and said to him, "Go throughout the city of Jerusalem and **put a mark on the foreheads** of those who grieve and lament over all the detestable things that are done in it."*
>
> *—Ezekiel 9:3-4*

That *mark* revealed to Ezekiel is rendered in the Hebrew as a *Tav* [Taw], which in the ancient Hebrew script literally has the appearance of the cross. It is interesting to note that the Tav is also the last letter of the Hebrew alphabet, symbolizing the end. Thus, the event shown to Ezekiel by the Spirit was a foreshadowing of the seal of Christ, to be placed upon the foreheads of all the true servants of God before the great harvest of the earth:

> *Then I saw another angel coming up from the east, having the seal of the living God. He called out in a loud voice to the four angels who had been given power to harm the land and the sea: "Do not harm the land or the sea or the trees until we **put a seal on the foreheads** of the servants of our God."*
>
> *—Revelations 7:2-3*

What the Lord wants His people today to understand is that we must constantly have His Law on our *minds* and so be evident in the actions of our *hands,* which is possible only when the *seal* of the Holy Spirit of Jesus Christ has been written upon our *hearts.* This will be most reflected in our desire to testify His Great Name. However, those whose *minds* direct the actions of their *hands* to chase after the *deceitfulness of wealth* reveal that they bear *the mark of the beast* upon their *hearts.* In this you see how the enemy is always mimicking God, but for the opposite ends. Satan seeks to supplant *obedience* in the hearts of his followers with *rebellion,* leading any who will fall for his lies to deny or ignore Christ's sovereignty for the benefits of *mammon.* Among these liars are those who call themselves "Christians," yet recoil at the idea of publicly testifying their love for Christ. Actually, they are repulsed by anyone who does. Still, the most dangerous are those pretended shepherds who in any way justify another path to heaven apart from Christ.

The Lord prepared an incredible witness of this specific blasphemy when we had first arrived in Arizona. It began with a club-card checker we met at the entrance of a warehouse store in Scottsdale. When my eyes met his, we had an instant recognition in the Spirit. I said, "You're a believer in Jesus aren't you."

His face lit up and he replied joyfully, "I am!"

I embraced him as a brother and briefly shared my family's testimony. Gracefully, like a true brother, he paid no mind to any boss, colleague or patron who might find our discussion offensive. Instead, he offered his support. "You have got to come to our church," he said, referring to a megachurch he attended, which we have since called *Desert Church.* "We love hearing testimony from missionaries. Our pastor invites them in all the time." He gave me his pastor's contact information, we prayed, I wished him blessings in Christ, and we let him return to his job. I subsequently called his pastor on three separate occasions, but he never bothered to call me back. Having cast three lots, I commended it to the Lord.

Around the time I was attempting to engage *Desert Church,* a brother and sister in Christ from Ohio called my family with a timely message from the Spirit. They said, "Have you heard anything about a religious movement called *Chrislam?"*

"No," we told them. "What is it?"

"It's some sort of unholy mixing of Christianity and Islam," they replied. "They *take the cross out of the church sanctuary* and preach that Allah is the same as our God."

Removing the cross of Christ to appease Muslims sounded outlandish, but having already received the Lord's understanding concerning the real *mark of the beast*, we were not entirely surprised. So, we made a mental note of *Chrislam*, anticipating the Lord would make clear His witness in due time. This came during our very last day in North Phoenix, starting with a kitten named Poof, one of the cutest brown and gray tabbies we've ever seen. In spite of our difficult living conditions, my family picked up this kitten from that dairy farm in Ohio where the children were the first to discover her birth, a one-litter kitten. Because she appeared suddenly and unexpectedly, they said, "Let's name her *Poof!*" Wanting to reward the children for all their sacrifices, we adopted Poof and brought her along with us to Arizona. She was young, vibrant, mischievous, and very content with our children. However, when the Lord provided a temporary home for our family in North Phoenix, the owners adamantly insisted, "No cats inside!" For a couple of days Poof seemed to be adjusting to being a fulltime outdoor kitty, but on the third day she disappeared. We searched and searched, put up signs, checked shelters—everything, but could not find her. We were crushed. The hardest thing for me was to see the hurt on Clara's and my children's tearful faces. It just didn't seem fair that the Lord would bring this kitten into our lives, only to take her away. Nevertheless, in everything the Lord has His own purposes, including pets.

Sometime after Poof had vanished, Clara and the kids decided to go to the local library. On their way out our five-year-old Jazelle called out to a man walking by, "Excuse me, have you seen our gray tabby cat? Her name is Poof!"

"I'm sorry, I haven't, but I'll keep an eye out for her," said the man and he continued on.

"Um, excuse me," Jazelle stopped him again, "one more question. Do you love Jesus?" And this is why God loves the children!

By no coincidence this man, a brother in Christ, turned around and came back, saying to me later, "I felt the Lord's magnet pulling me over to your family."

Clara naturally engaged him and learned that he was very active in prison ministry and other fellowships outside the walls of the religious establishment. Before coming to Christ, he had been a pilot running drugs for the Mexican cartels. Yet, while serving time in prison, the Lord rescued him from that life and set his path straight. When Clara later shared this encounter with me, I tried unsuccessfully for two weeks to meet with him, but he just couldn't find time in his schedule. It turned out he and his wife were in the midst of a difficult bankruptcy with their small business, spurred on by the IRS, which refused to forgive their tax debt. All of this further spoke to the Lord's timing.

On the day before we were to leave for Ohio, in spite of having just $16 and less than a quarter tank of gas, the Spirit burdened me to reach out to this man one last time. We were so busy packing and cleaning I wanted to ignore it, but the Lord would not let me have peace until I reached out to him a third time. So, I contacted him and, sure enough, he invited me over to his house that afternoon to speak with him and his wife. While Clara and the kids stayed behind to finish preparing for our departure, I went to their house to share the Lord's message. Sitting in their living room, I explained that my family was leaving for Ohio the next morning, then I rapidly shared two year's worth of testimony concerning the Lord's instructions for His Church: Vote 'Christ The Lord,' the Truth Serum, the Sanctity of Human Life, the real *mark of the beast,* and our president's reelection and impending awakening. If they didn't have the Spirit, they would have thought I was nuts, but since they did, they received everything and gave praise to God.

When I concluded, I politely excused myself, explaining that I had to get back to help my family finish packing and cleaning. I did not share with them our need. As far as Clara and I were concerned, the Lord was going to deliver us. Even if we had to drive to a parking lot the next day and sit there and wait for the Lord's provision to materialize at our feet, that's what we were going to do. However, the woman asked me to wait a moment, and so I continued talking with her husband as she walked into another room. A moment later, she returned with two checks in hand. "These are for you," she said, asking me to whom she should make them out. Everything but the *'pay to'* was filled out. I was dumbfounded. I truly had not expected to receive anything from them. She explained, "Two weeks ago the Lord told us to stop giving money to our church, because it had fallen away. He said He would send us a man of God and that we were to tithe to him." Shaking her head, she admitted, "This morning the Lord told me that man was you, but I didn't believe Him."

"I did," her husband said with a grin.

With a smirk she continued, "Well, I was wrong."

I started laughing. For a whole week my family had remained faithful the Lord would provide—and He did, but not before stretching our faith! "You don't know this," I explained, "but we didn't have any means to cover the cost of our journey to Ohio."

"Oh, I hope it's enough," she said with genuine concern.

"It's enough," I quickly told her, not wanting to burden them, nor did I realize what I was saying. They had given about half of what we had calculated we needed for fuel alone.

As the woman made out the checks, I asked what had happened at their church. They explained that at the close of the service two weeks back their pastor had made some enigmatic statements about his admiration for Oprah Winfrey and Rick Warren, author of *The Purpose-Driven Life*. They said his comments seemed out of place and awkward. They really didn't understand the meaning at the time, but the Spirit in them did. When they went back to this church the following week, they quickly noticed that *the cross of Christ had been removed* from the podium inside their sanctuary, though the cross outside remained.

Astonished by the Lord's witness, I said, "It's Chrislam!"

They had never heard the term, but they had been firsthand witnesses of its rotten fruit, packaged under the universalist ruse of *unaccountable love, social justice, world peace, tolerance, human rights* and *all roads lead to heaven.* Taken together this is a modern-day Gnosticism, a bankrupt pursuit of knowledge. I asked them the name of their church and they revealed that it was that same *Desert Church* whose pastor hadn't returned my calls. Unbelievable! I was overwhelmed by the revelation the Lord had just given, together with all the pieces of the puzzle He had masterfully brought into alignment. It was *Chrislam* that had barred that pastor's heart from calling me back. What's most disturbing, however, is that this couple had truly believed their pastor was a Holy Spirit-inspired teacher. Yet, when he intentionally removed the cross from the sanctuary, the Spirit revealed that he was not. This couple has since left this synagogue of Satan and I wonder if our brother at the warehouse store has as well. I suspect many milk-drinkers have not.

After receiving the revelation about Chrislam, God led my family consecutively before two Muslim families to testify the truth about the cross and His Son, whom He had sent to die that we all might live. The first encounter occurred in a grocery store. Soon as we entered, the Spirit told me I would be testifying to a Muslim, but where? Just before we went to check out, a Muslim family, a man, his wife and their five children, walked into the store right in front of me. 'This is the one,' the Spirit said, and I waited for my opportunity. It didn't take long, because their youngest son ran over to our shopping cart, jumped on it and offered Justin a piece of candy. Praise you Jesus! The man came over apologetically to collect his son and I wasted no time engaging him. I began by complimenting him on his family, testifying that this nation did not value children as the blessed seed God gives, but continues to destroy them by this scourge called abortion. He agreed that this was wrong, demonstrating an appreciation for the truth. I asked him if he was with Christ, though I knew he was Muslim. He confirmed this, so I asked him if anyone had told him who Christ is. He said no one had, but offered that they believe Jesus was a prophet, born of a virgin, and was uniquely set apart by God to one-day return to gather the faithful. Still, Muslims do not believe that Jesus Christ is the Son of God, even though the Spirit of God plainly testifies He is:

As soon as Jesus was baptized, he went up out of the water. At that moment heaven was opened, and he saw the Spirit of God descending like a dove and lighting on him. And a voice from heaven said, ***"<u>This is my Son,</u> whom I love; with him I am well pleased."*** *—Matthew 3:16-17*

The disparity over Jesus being the Son of God represents the critical divide between Islam and Christianity, which Chrislam proponents are specifically trying to blur. They follow Satan's deception in the Koran, which repeatedly attempts to discredit Jesus' Sonship, seeking to cast Him merely as a prophet. The point of this is to convince lost sheep that Christ's Way is *optional,* which condemns them to hell, because the Son is the *only Way* to the Heavenly Father.

Jesus answered, "I am the way and the truth and the life. ***No one comes to the Father except through me."*** *—John 14:6*

Chrislam also targets the cross, because Satan in them knows it symbolizes the entire process of taking mankind from rebellion to restoration, and that any who remain in rebellion will suffer his fate. The Lord has repeatedly shown my family over the course of our journey that when our Savior *comes on the clouds of heaven,* it will be the sign of His Cross that leads the way:

"At that time the sign of the Son of Man will appear in the sky, and all the nations of the earth will mourn. They will see the Son of Man coming on the clouds of the sky, with power and great glory." —Matthew 24:30

By His symbol *all the nations of the earth will mourn,* for by then they will have all heard the Gospel, so none will be able to deny its meaning. Any who have not believed in *the Son who was slain* for their salvation will wallow in shame, realizing their rebellious reign has come to an end. Repentance will cease to have any value, for when the *mystery of God is fulfilled* faith will no longer be faith. Like Satan and his demons, which knew the Glory of God and yet despised Him, so shall the rebellious peoples of the earth recognize their King and dread His judgment. Therefore, acceptance of the cross is synonymous with accepting Christ's Sonship, and both are *required* for entrance into heaven:

*Therefore Jesus said again, "I tell you the truth, **I am the gate for the sheep**. All who ever came before me were thieves and robbers, but the sheep did not listen to them. —John 10:7-8*

As a proper servant of Christ, I told this man that Jesus is indeed the Son of God and that no true prophet has ever been born who has not testified about Him. I further told him that because Jesus Himself testified that He was God's Son, we must either hold that His testimony is true or dismiss him as a false prophet, because no true prophet of God would declare such a thing were it not true.

"But what about you?" he asked. "Who do you say I am?"

Simon Peter answered, "You are the Christ, the Son of the living God."

Jesus replied, "Blessed are you, Simon son of Jonah, for this was not revealed to you by man, but by my Father in heaven." —Matthew 16:15-17

I further testified, "I know Jesus is the living Son of God, because He has personally cared for my family's needs during all the days of our journey serving Him on the road without any worldly income."

It was my personal testimony that really pierced his heart, for he said, "That's commendable. I don't think I would have the faith to do that." By his convicted demeanor, I understood that this man truly desired to be obedient to God. He just didn't know who God is. Further demonstrating his heart for the truth, he asked, "What did Jesus say about himself and God?"

"But the world must learn that I love the Father and that I do exactly what my Father has commanded me. Come now; let us leave." —John 14:31

There is so much to say, but I asked the Spirit and told the man what I received, "Jesus taught His disciples to obey God. This is why He submitted Himself to the cross. Because God is so pure, no one with sin can come near unto Him and live. Yet, because He loves His children, He gave them another way to prove their obedience by submitting themselves to His Son. Is any man without sin?"

"No," he replied with a wrinkled brow.

"This is why you must honor the Son, because it is the only way you can demonstrate your obedience to the Father." Being an Arab emigrant, I also asked him if a king of the Middle East would accept any subject who did not honor his son. He agreed the king would not. In fact, that king will put that rebellious man into prison. Furthermore, the king invests all of his power and authority in his son. Thus, when the son speaks, he is speaking with the authority given him by his father. I concluded by saying, "God will never receive anyone who rejects His Son, because this would introduce rebellion into heaven. But a man who respects and honors the Son proves his obedience, even though he is a sinner."

After all this, he agreed to pray with me. In "Jesus' Name" I asked the Lord to make Himself known to the hearts of this man and his family, and I felt a powerful movement of the Spirit. The Islamic bonds were broken. As a further witness to how the Lord was calling this family, while Clara and I testified to the man and his wife in the middle of the market for nearly two hours our nine children sat together peacefully playing games until we were finished. Now that has to be the grace of Christ!

Some days later, my family met another Muslim family at a small amphitheater in an outdoor shopping mall. The moment we saw them, the Spirit told both Clara and me, 'Appointment.' Their son quickly joined our children at play and Austin went over to them to open the door for Christ, saying, "It's amazing how much energy Jesus bundles up into these little children, isn't it?" After making this very simple confession of Christ, he pointed to us, saying, "Those are my parents," and he proceeded to join the other children at play.

This couple got up from their seat and came over to Clara and me. We pleasantly exchanged introductions and immediately the man said, "You are Christian?"

"We are," I said and briefly shared our testimony.

"Tell me," he questioned, "does the Bible really say that Jesus is the Son of God?"

Indeed, this was an appointment! With joy I replied, "It does."

"Where?" he questioned.

"Everywhere," I told him, and this sparked another two-hour engagement. Incredibly, as he and his wife testified, they had several Arab-Christian friends who had mistakenly told them the Bible does not explicitly state that Jesus is the "Son of God."

> *For this reason the Jews tried all the harder to kill him; not only was he breaking the Sabbath, but he was even* ***calling God his own Father, making himself equal with God****. —John 5:18*

We went to a nearby bookstore, pulled a Bible off the shelf and I pointed out where Jesus is indeed revealed as the "Son of God." So great was this man's respect for the Word that he said a heartfelt prayer and kissed the Holy Christian Bible before reading it himself! How God must grieve that more "Christians" don't share his reverence. In "Jesus' Name" my family also prayed with this family before we parted, again breaking the bonds of Islam. True to the Word by which he was being called, this man even tithed to us, albeit just $3. He sincerely apologized that they did not have more cash on hand, but my family rejoiced, understanding the significance of the number—*Father, Son and Holy Spirit!*

Now imagine if my family had ignored our responsibility to testify the truth to these two families, dismissing them as *Muslims,* rather than viewing them as God's lost sheep and being concerned for their salvation. How will they get to heaven if those who know the Truth are too timid or complacent to share it? God does not see as man sees. Man looks at the exterior, but God sees the heart. Do not judge people based upon their present beliefs, for God knows all who will come to Him through Christ Jesus before the end. Thus, today's Muslim, falsely believing he can get to heaven through Mohammad or Allah, is tomorrow's servant of Christ. The same can be said of Buddhists, Hindus, Atheists, Jews, and "Christians" who love their religion, but have not a true love for Christ in their heart—especially those who purport any path to heaven aside from Christ.

The most disturbing reality about *the mark of the beast* is the source from which it spawns. It is not stemming from Islam, as some believe and are in the habit of teaching. Rather it is apostate "Christians," following after Judas Iscariot's betrayal, who are ushering it into being, and with it *the rebellion that causes desolation:*

> *Then I heard a holy one speaking, and another holy one said to him, "How long will it take for the vision to be fulfilled—the vision concerning the daily sacrifice,* ***the rebellion that causes desolation****, and the surrender of the sanctuary and of the host that will be trampled underfoot?" —Daniel 8:13*

This is the *great tribulation* that will fall upon the whole earth *for a time, times and half a time* [three and a half years] before Jesus comes to deliver His true and faithful Church from the grips of *a beast coming up out of the sea:*

> *The beast I saw resembled a leopard, but had feet like those of a bear and a mouth like that of a lion. The dragon gave the beast his power and his throne and great authority. —Revelations 13:2*

When you study out this vision described by the apostle John, and seek the Lord's Face for wisdom, you will learn that this *beast* is Satan's proxy on earth, an international coalition of nations, as well as a *stern-faced king,* the last antichrist, who will rise to power and lead the world in a rebellion against God and His Church:

> *"In the latter part of their reign, when rebels have become completely wicked, a stern-faced king, a master of intrigue, will arise." —Daniel 8:23*

As you search the Scriptures, remember that every matter of the Lord's Truth must be established by *two or three witnesses,* such as the Messiah was appointed to come not once, but twice—once for salvation and a second time for judgment. The history of nations and kings is no different. Therefore, Daniel was shown *a stern-faced king,* Antiochus IV Epiphanes, who would descend from Alexander The Great's parceled empire in the 2nd century BC, and would serve as a model for the last antichrist. Like Antiochus, who purported himself to be "Zeus Manifest" and set up an altar to himself in the Second Temple in Jerusalem, so the last antichrist will similarly blaspheme the Father and the Son by declaring himself to be "God Manifest," and by erecting man's altar in the Last Temple. Indeed, he will lead the world to believe that *man is created in his own image.*

There are all sorts of theories about *the beast* and the *last antichrist,* focusing primarily who or what they will be. Because the beast will exact his *authority over every tribe, people, language and nation,* many suspect the United Nations.

Of course, this presumes this institution supposedly devoted to *peace* will somehow avoid repeating the folly of the League of Nations, which failed to prevent WWII. Still others speculate the United States is the antichrist's seat of power, though *the beast* looks nothing like a bald eagle. Instead, they point to the *American Dollar's* present dominance over world markets, given that *no one could buy or sell unless he had the mark*. Yet, as we are already seeing, America's economic prowess is slipping. Her military superiority will diminish with it, since one cannot sustain itself without the other. Nonetheless, if you want to pinpoint who *the beast* is and discover the centre of his power and authority, just *follow the money,* because it will indeed lead you right to the *stern-faced king*. When he is revealed, you will also find that he has *a mouth like that of a lion,* which will speak boastfully against God Most High and Jesus Christ. This *lion* also represents the heraldic symbol of his throne.

Though the antichrist is a king, do not think of him as a despotic dictator, because he will present himself as a champion for *human rights,* and he will not be alone. Another beast will rise up after him to serve as his ecclesiastical authority, a *false prophet:*

> *Then I saw another beast, coming out of the earth. He had two horns like a lamb, but he spoke like a dragon.* ***He exercised all the authority of the first beast on his behalf, and made the earth and its inhabitants worship the first beast,*** *whose fatal wound had been healed. —Revelations 13:11-12*

The *two horns like a lamb* signifies one who comes posing as a servant of Christ, but his speaking *like a dragon* clearly exposes his true master is Satan. The purpose of this *false prophet* is to *anoint* the *stern-faced king,* thus establishing his *divine right* to rule the nations, and certifying *his mark* for international consumption. Within a carefully woven cloak of *benevolence* and *peace,* they will seek to maintain a pretense of *separation of church and state*, but in reality they will be united in heart, mind and action on behalf of the dragon whom they serve. Through the *deceitfulness of wealth,* the antichrist and the false prophet will yoke the strength of ten kingdoms, making an alliance of twelve. Yet, this is not the only way in which Satan will seek to imitate God's holy order:

> *Then the LORD said to Moses, "See, I have made you like God to Pharaoh, and your brother Aaron will be your prophet." —Exodus 7:1*

Just as God sent forth Moses and Aaron to deliver Israel from slavery, presenting Moses *"like God"* to Pharaoh and the Israelites, and Aaron as his *"prophet,"* so shall Satan send his messengers to deceive Israel in order to lead them *into slavery.* Sadly, many "Christians" will follow, primarily because the *benevolent king* and his *peace-preaching prophet*—themselves "Christians"—will tell the people exactly what they want to hear. They will justify mammon worship and promote the idea that *enlightened society* can and should define its own moral code, thus fostering the delusion that man is his own god. Much of the collective "Christian" religious establishment has already fallen for this lie, joining itself with the *Whore of Babylon.* With this *Prostitute* they commit adultery before an altar dedicated to themselves, which is drenched with the blood of the innocent and whose flames are fueled by money. This altar is called *human rights.*

> *I saw that the woman was drunk with the blood of the saints, the blood of those who bore* ***testimony to Jesus****. When I saw her, I was greatly astonished.*
> *—Revelations 17:6*

That *woman,* which the Bible also calls *The Mother of Prostitutes,* is not merely one religious establishment, but an ecumenical society of faith spanning virtually every religion under the sun, including nearly every denomination of Christianity. For this reason, the *faithful* Church of this age will be *astonished* when this *Prostitute* is fully exposed, because people will not want to believe their "Christian" religions could be capable of the abominations in which they partake. This is at the very heart of *the rebellion that causes desolation,* and the reason why *the beast* will be given great power and authority not just over the world, but also over the *unfaithful* Christian Church:

> *Then another sign appeared in heaven: an enormous* ***red dragon*** *with seven heads and ten horns and seven crowns on his heads.* ***His tail swept a third of the stars out of the sky and flung them to the earth.*** *The dragon stood in front of the woman who was about to give birth, so that he might devour her child the moment it was born. —Revelations 12:3-4*

That *red dragon* is Satan, but what are the stars? My family has received visions of these *stars* falling to the earth. It is an incredible sight. It fills you with a sense on inevitability, like there is nowhere to run or hide, nowhere to escape the fallout. All you can do is stand your ground in Christ and trust in His deliverance. But when disaster strikes whom will you follow? The meaning of the *Greek 'Christ'* is the same as the *Hebrew 'Messiah';* they are the biblical titles for *'God's Anointed,'* hence the important role the *false prophet* will play in deceiving the nations by *anointing* the antichrist. Therefore, you need to know that those *falling stars* represent both *fallen angels,* who followed in Satan's rebellion in heaven, and they are also *fallen saints,* who will follow after Satan's rebellion on earth, led by the *false Messiah*—the *last antichrist:*

> *Out of one of them came another horn, which started out small but grew in power to the south and to the east and toward the Beautiful Land.* ***It grew until it reached the host of the heavens, and it threw some of the starry host down to the earth and trampled on them.*** *It set itself up to be as great as the Prince of the host; it took away the daily sacrifice from him, and the place of his sanctuary was brought low.* ***Because of rebellion, the host of the saints and the daily sacrifice were give over to it.*** *It prospered in everything it did, and truth was thrown to the ground. —Daniel 8:9-12*

Have no misgivings about the tribulation at *end of the age,* for as Christ warned His followers, He will not come to *rapture* His faithful Church until *after the distress of those days:*

> *"Immediately after the distress of those days 'the sun will be darkened, and the moon will not give its light; the stars will fall from the sky, and the heavenly bodies will be shaken.'" —Matthew 24:29*

Again, *the stars will fall from the sky,* serving as a witness and a warning for servants of Christ to persevere through every struggle and to reject every deception. You can be sure no ecumenical religious council will institute *Christ's millennial reign* on earth, either. The King will establish His own Kingdom, putting every enemy beneath His Feet. As the Scriptures declare from the Law given to the prophet Moses to the Revelations given to the apostle John, and as my family has witnessed over the course of our journey: Because of *rebellion,* which is sin, the Christian Church will be handed over to *the beast* to be *trampled upon,* in order that our faith might be tested and proven genuine. Every wicked seed the enemy has planted in the Lord's harvest field will be expunged. The true and faithful Church in Christ must be refined and made spotless, for our Husband, Christ Jesus, will not come to join Himself with a harlot. No, the Church must be made pure, an unblemished Bride such as our Lord and Savior deserves. If the King were to come too early, hardly any would be spared His wrath. Likewise, if He were to come too late, hardly any would survive the awfulness of the tribulation:

"If the Lord had not cut short those days, no one would survive. But for the sake of the elect, whom he has chosen, he has shortened them." —Mark 13:20

Therefore, *Christ The Lord* will come precisely at the perfect time the Father has appointed. You will know that time is near when you see the *abomination that causes desolation* standing in the Holy Place, where he does not belong:

"So when you see standing in the holy place 'the abomination that causes desolation,' spoken of through the prophet Daniel—let the reader understand—then let those who are in Judea flee to the mountains." —Matthew 24:15-16

Those who are walking with the Spirit of Christ when this day comes will know when this event occurs, and we will know that the days of darkness are come. Then, as Christ has instructed us, we must flee to the places of refuge He will reveal to us at that time for an approximate period of three and a half years:

"From the time that the daily sacrifice is abolished and the abomination that causes desolation is set up, there will be 1,290 days. Blessed is the one who waits for and reaches the end of the 1,335 days." —Daniel 12:11-12

Those extra forty-five days between *1,290* and *1,335* are a warning to the Church to hold on, even though we may think our time of trial should have reached its fulfillment.

If these truths are in any way difficult to receive, consider how God separated His true servants from rebellion twice before in history: The fall of Judah to ancient Babylon represents God's first judgment meted out upon His chosen people. The second judgment came just four decades after Christ's crucifixion with the fall of Jerusalem to the Romans. In both instances, God handed over His people, His city and His Temple to be *trampled upon* by pagans, and God's chosen people were utterly destroyed—save a remnant of survivors, those whom the prophet Ezekiel witnessed were marked in Christ. This will be repeated again during the third and final judgment that is soon to befall the whole earth, only this time the Temple and God's Holy City are *the host of the saints,* the Body of Christ, who like the First Temple are filled with God's Holy Spirit. Again I ask you, if the Father would not take *"this cup"* from His only begotten Son, will He somehow spare the Church in Christ?

> *He was given power to make war against the saints* ***and to conquer them****. And he was given authority over every tribe, people, language and nation.*
>
> *—Revelations 13:7*

I tell you the truth, the same reality facing the Jews before Babylon battered down their walls is now facing the church in America and the world. This is why the apostle John reflected *Jeremiah 15* when he wrote:

> *He who has an ear, let him hear. If anyone is to go into captivity, into captivity he will go. If anyone is to be killed with the sword, with the sword he will be killed. This calls for patient endurance and faithfulness on the part of the saints.*
>
> *—Revelations 13:9-10*

Taking all these truths into consideration, let me warn you what is about to come, so that you may recognize the lies and separate yourself from the adulterous filth of *Babylon The Great,* that *Whore* which sits upon *the beast* and leads the world to betray Christ in exchange for worldly profit. Then, when you see that your religious establishment has fallen under the spell of the antichrist and his false prophet, my family prays you will put aside old religious loyalties and put on new wineskins. Let your heart embrace a newfound and unbridled devotion to Christ, and may you starve *the beast* of any aid or comfort. Do not cast your pearls to dogs and swine, because every penny you put in *the beast's* coffer will in turn be used to make war upon the host of the saints. This is why you must hearken to the Holy One of Israel when He says, *"Come out of her, my people,"* lest you too be stained by innocent bloodshed and join *the beast* in his inevitable fate:

> *Then I heard another voice from heaven say: "Come out of her, my people, so that you will not share in her sins, so that you will not receive any of her plagues; for her sins are piled up to heaven, and God has remembered her crimes." —Revelations 18:4-5*

In the years ahead, you will see two distinct movements of unity in faith emerge. On the surface, these movements may look similar, but within you will find that one bears the *seal of Christ,* originating with the Holy Spirit, while the other has *the mark of the beast,* soon to be championed by the coming antichrist.

The movement in Christ has been outlined within this book and is most perfectly expressed from cover to cover in the Holy Bible. It recognizes that God is not a denominated religion, but His followers are united in our Heavenly Father, Creator of all the heavens and the earth; and in His Word, revealed to us through His Son, the Messiah; and in His Spirit of Truth, by whom we must testify that Jesus Christ is the only Way, the Truth and the Life.

Alternatively, Satan's movement will be focused on consolidating the power of nations by controlling *money*, because through the doctrine of *economic prosperity* [deceitfulness of wealth] he will gain control over the hearts of many disparate peoples, nations and languages. Within these nations that flock to his banner, the powers and authorities will persecute those who insist that salvation can only be found in Jesus Christ, because we oppose *human rights* that violate God's Law.

> *Don't let anyone deceive you in any way, for that day will not come until the rebellion occurs and the* ***man of lawlessness*** *is revealed, the man doomed to destruction. —2 Thessalonians 2:3*

The *man of lawlessness* is the antichrist, who rejects God's Law for man's. In this way, he will lead the entire world in a rebellion against God, throwing *truth to the ground*. Even so, he will not come proclaiming, "I am the antichrist, come follow me into hell!" Instead, he will use the tactics exposed in this book to shower the nations and peoples with flatteries, celebrating their cultures and traditions. He himself will be a proclaimed "Christian," but he will deny Christ's *only Way* and will pay special honors to what God detests—all under the banner of *human rights.* These will be among the *blasphemies* the Bible says he will boldly speak:

> *The beast was given a mouth to utter proud words and blasphemies and to exercise his authority for forty-two months. He opened his mouth to blaspheme God, and to slander his name and his dwelling place and those who live in heaven. —Revelations 13:5-6*

Because Satan deals his schemes from both sides of the world deck of cards, he will simultaneously promote the universal cause of *world peace* while inspiring religious zealots to propagate violence, death and destruction. Such is how radical Islamists are being used today, so as to justify the violent suppression of Christ's servants who refuse to capitulate to the antichrist's homogenized one-world religion of *human rights* in days to come. This is what will make the tribulation so excruciating, because all of *'enlightened society,'* religious and secular, will brand the true Church as *'a threat to society.'* Just as the religious Jews hunted down Jesus Christ, and later His followers, handing them over to the Romans to be jailed, tortured and crucified, so shall it be for the true followers of Christ at the end of the age; only at that time it will be "Christians" hunting Christ's servants and handing them over to *Babylon The Great.* On the surface, *human rights* and *world peace* will be hailed as the primary issues at stake, but it is *money, power and greed* by which Satan will galvanize his support. Like the ancient Jewish Sanhedrin, in their hearts the universalist hierarchs don't want the King to come, lest they be dispossessed of their fiefdoms:

> *"But the tenants said to one another, 'This is the heir. Come, let's kill him, and the inheritance will be ours.' So they took him and killed him, and threw him out of the vineyard.*
>
> *"What then will the owner of the vineyard do? He will come and kill those tenants and give the vineyard to others." —Mark 12:7-9*

When the marriage between the world's political and religious authorities is consecrated on the altar of *human rights*, the *man of lawlessness* shall be revealed and he will lift himself up as mankind's savior *on a wing of the Temple.* He will be anointed by the *false prophet* and declared the instrument of God's favor, the Lion of Judah. United in a lie, the antichrist, his false prophet and the worldwide universal church of lawlessness over which they preside will openly wage war against the saints, replacing the Gospel of Christ with the Gnostic lies of *unaccountable love, social justice, world peace, tolerance, human rights* and *all roads lead to heaven.* They will take the world back to the tree of death. Every false faith will be accepted, the worship of idols, demons, all the starry hosts, and especially *Mother Nature,* so long as these abide by a core belief in *human rights.*

> *For the secret power of lawlessness is already at work; but the one who now holds it back will continue to do so till he is taken out of the way. And then the lawless one will be revealed, whom the Lord Jesus will overthrow with the breath of his mouth and destroy by the splendor of his coming.*
>
> *—2 Thessalonians 2:7-8*

If you watch closely the various political and religious establishments in America and across the world, you will see the *secret power of lawlessness* already at work in them today. Put aside official statements of doctrine and public policy and recognize who is endorsing and defending innocent bloodshed, Sodom and Gomorrah, and are denying the Sonship of Jesus Christ and His only *Way* to heaven.

Who is the liar? It is the man who denies that Jesus is the Christ. Such a man is the antichrist—he denies the Father and the Son. —1 John 2:22

During the latter part of our journey, the Spirit led me to the above passage and overwhelmed me with His Power. I asked the Lord, "Is it now, is this the age of the antichrist?"

The Spirit answered, 'Yes, it is now.'

Brothers and sisters, Chrislam is just one of many tactics by which Satan has already infiltrated the Christian Church to prepare a crooked path for his forthcoming antichrist. Jesus did not speak in parables when He said, *"No one comes to the Father except through me,"* yet the very institutions that are supposed to be defending this truth are trampling upon it! Their actions prove the focus of their minds and the mammon devotion that corrupts their hearts, but who has the courage to call out *the mark of the beast* where it lies?

"If anyone is ashamed of me and my words in this adulterous and sinful generation, the Son of Man will be ashamed of him when he comes in his Father's glory with the holy angels." —Mark 8:38

Do not place a paycheck, a customer, a constituent, bread, water, or anything in preference to your own flesh above your Savior. You must be willing to sacrifice all these things, even your own life to glorify His Name. But since this nation does not threaten your life for sharing the *only Way* to Life, what is inhibiting you? Is there anything in this world worth losing the *crown of life* over?

"Whoever finds his life will lose it, and whoever loses his life for my sake will find it." —Matthew 10:39

There is only *one Way* to obtaining immunity from to *the mark of the beast.* You must receive the gift of the *Holy Spirit seal* of the Son of God who died upon the cross so that you and the rest of this sinful world might live. It's free for the having, but you must open yourself to receive it. This is how you do it: Kneel and issue a heartfelt confession of your sins before Christ, believing

He is real and sees your repentance from His Father's throne in heaven. Then commit your life into His Hands, turning away from your sins, submitting yourself as His servant and devoting your heart to sharing the Light He gives you with any He sends your way. This you do by openly confessing the Name of Jesus Christ as mankind's sole Lord and Savior. Simply tell anyone who will listen about Christ's sacrifice for their sins, and be ready to share something Jesus has done for you that personally fortified your faith and belief in Him. If you haven't before, also seek a place to be baptized in water so that your Lord and Savior will see that your repentance and desire to serve Him is genuine. Whether you have come into Christ for the first time or re-committed your heart to His purpose for your life, you must begin to study His Word daily. Make your spiritual armor complete by constantly praying and holding fast to His teachings. Always trust in His provision, no matter how the persecutions of this world bruise and batter you, for if you do not fall away, the *seal* of your salvation in Christ will not fail you when the end has finally come.

> *"Be careful, or your hearts will be weighed down with dissipation, drunkenness and the anxieties of life, and that day will close on you unexpectedly like a trap. For it will come upon all those who live on the face of the whole earth. Be always on the watch, and pray that you may be able to escape all that is about to happen, and that you may be able to stand before the Son of Man."*
>
> —*Luke 21:34-36*

27

Fire Alarm

Ever heard of a 2004 Chevy Tahoe getting 30+ miles per gallon? Ours did! In the world those two checks we received in Arizona should have only covered about half the fuel cost for our trip back to Ohio, but by the Spirit that money alone got us all the way there, and with three-quarters of a tank of gas to spare! About the time we reached St. Louis I noticed we hadn't stopped for gas as often as I thought we should have. That's when I looked at our digital MPG readout and saw the miracle unfolding before us. I showed it to Clara and she could hardly believe it. Then, as we kept watching it, the MPG reading started to go down to its normal 16 to 17 level. "Don't look!" The Lord also provided shelter and food, as well as multiple opportunities to testify His Name and Truth along the way. After three days we arrived safely in Northwest Ohio. Praise be to Jesus, because not only can He add fuel to an empty tank, He can stretch it twice as long as it should last!

Following the Lord's instructions, we retrieved *The Whale* from the farm where we had left it and then sold it. It was a strange feeling, like saying goodbye to our home a second time, for it had kept the rain off our heads more than once when no one else was willing. Do you suppose Jonah felt the same way about his giant fish?

We revisited some harvest ground we had covered the year before then finally headed back to Texas at the end of August 2011. For nearly two and a half years we had been homeless on the road for Jesus. We were excited to get back home, though we had *no home* to return to. Moreover, we hardly recognized the place when we rolled back into Austin. The once lush Hill Country we recalled was now dry, withering and dead—physically and spiritually. It was shocking to see just how far the beautiful crystal-blue waters of Lake Travis had receded below the cracked and barren limestone slopes. As we soon learned, the whole State of Texas was gripped by its worst drought in history.

> *At noon Elijah began to taunt them. "Shout louder!" he said. "Surely he is a god! Perhaps he is deep in thought, or busy, or traveling. Maybe he is sleeping and must be awakened." So they shouted louder and slashed themselves with swords and spears, as was their custom, until their blood flowed. Midday passed, and they continued their frantic prophesying until the time for the evening sacrifice. But there was no response, no one answered, no one paid attention. —1 Kings 18:27-29*

The very first witness the Lord put forth upon our return to Texas was that a group of people had recently gathered in Round Rock to do a *"rain dance."* Just like the Israel of old had turned to Baal in the midst of a terrible drought, so were these Texans, and the result has thus far been the same. "Christians" likely participate in these and similar abominations "just for fun," but the Lord is not amused.

> *At the time of sacrifice, the prophet Elijah stepped forward and prayed: "O LORD, God of Abraham, Isaac and Israel, let it be known today that you are God in Israel and that I am your servant and have done all these things at your command. Answer me, O LORD, answer me, so these people will know that you, O LORD, are God, and that you are turning their hearts back again."*
>
> *—1 Kings 18:36-37*

Until this nation fulfills repentance, starting with making the Sanctity of Human Life its highest law, God will not restore the dew of heaven to the parched land. Consequently, the drought in Texas has been and will continue to be reflected across the nation. In addition to this, we have suffered tornados, hurricanes, earthquakes, birds falling from the sky, fish turning up dead in the rivers, plagues to man and beast, blighted crops, and the beginnings of a great and terrible famine. All of this has been appointed to demonstrate the Lord's authority. But how much must this nation suffer before the people's hearts turn back to Him? If we do, our merciful Father in heaven will heal

His people, together with our flocks and herds, and the land He has given us to tend.

> *Do any of the worthless idols of the nations bring rain? Do the skies themselves send down showers? No, it is you, O LORD our God. Therefore our hope is in you, for you are the one who does all this. —Jeremiah 14:22*

My family might have been back in Texas, but our journey was far from over, and the church in Austin was hardly more accommodating than it had been in other places. Consequently, we were once again relegated to hotel hopping. It was terribly frustrating, because by this time we desperately wanted to settle somewhere, but naturally the Lord knew what He was doing. In keeping us unsettled and constantly on the move, He brought us before many among His flock in need of testimony at the most auspicious moments in their lives. We reached the rich, the poor, the homeless, the hopeless, struggling brothers and sisters in Christ, lost sheep and rebellious goats recently humbled. It seemed like every time we stepped outside another appointment suddenly appeared before us. The Lord also had more revelation to deliver; such as He did on the night of August 31st at our hotel.

Just as we prepared for bed the hotel's fire alarm suddenly went off. Like most people, we waited to see if it was a false alarm, but it persisted. Then a hotel attendant banged on our door, yelling in that this was the real deal! Quickly, my family grabbed my laptop, containing this book—then in progress, and went out into the hall. There was a thin layer of smoke in the hall and even more in the stairwell, which really had us believing this was indeed the *real deal*, but it didn't smell burnt. After taking refuge in the hotel parking lot, Jazelle and Justin enjoyed watching the arrival of the fire engine and firemen, Rielle and Austin were amused at the business people reduced to pajamas and bathrobes, and Clara testified to a woman with a towel on her head whose son was an Austin firefighter. Meanwhile, I prayed for the Lord to reveal what this was all about. I knew He was witnessing something important to us. I could feel it in the Spirit. In almost every place we have visited, a fire or smoke alarm has gone off at the most conspicuous times for no discernable reason, but this was the first time we had actually been evacuated.

After the firefighters swept the building, they determined it was a false alarm. Evidently, someone had taken a fire extinguisher and shot one of the fire sensors, which had ejected fire retardant smoke. So we made our way back into the hotel and that's when I received the Lord's response. He simply said, 'Fire alarm,' and He planted in my heart an understanding of what was coming. Back in our room, I told Clara and the kids that fires would soon beset the Austin area. Four days later, on Sunday, September 4th, just after I had delivered the Lord's message to a Sunday School gathering at a local church, those fires broke out. I felt a stiff wind unexpectedly kick up and in the Spirit I instantly knew it was from the Lord. Then we heard sirens begin to wail in the distance. First it was one, then another, then it seemed the entire city was surrounded with sirens. We drove to a hill just across Lake Austin from Steiner Ranch and hiked up to its peak. From this vantage point we took in a stunning panoramic view of multiple wildfires. The fire of the Lord had surrounded the Capital of Texas, showering its people with billowing clouds of ash.

> *The LORD called you a thriving olive tree with fruit beautiful in form. But with the roar of a mighty storm he will set it on fire, and its branches will be broken.*
> *—Jeremiah 11:16*

From that hilltop, my family got out and prayed for the Lord to reveal to us the meaning of all this, aside from the obvious. Very quickly, He sent us two different men to whom we were to witness. The first man came up and looked at the fires with a wicked fascination. I could see the unclean spirit in him reveling at the devastation. When Clara asked him if he believed in Jesus, he snuffed derisively and said, "No." She asked him why not and he became belligerent, going into a stream of obscenities, paying no regard to our children's ears. I walked towards him in "Jesus Name" and thankfully he fled.

Shortly thereafter, another man approached us, very concerned for his home in the Steiner Ranch community. I asked him if he was a believer in Jesus and he said, "Well, I am now!" This fence-sitting believer—now humbled, joined hands with my family and we prayed the Lord would spare his home and draw this man into His service. In fact, the Lord spared a great many homes in Steiner Ranch that day. As for the rest of Austin and Central Texas, those wildfires could have caused much more damage, but within a week the Lord's Hand relented. The weather changed and the firefighters were permitted to get the upper hand.

These fires were the first of a series of witnesses the Lord began to impart to my family concerning how He intends to deal with this rebellious nation.

The next witness, specific to Texas, was delivered on our son Austin's birthday. For some reason he decided that he wanted to visit the Alamo. We had been there before, and truthfully there is little to do for a twelve-year-old boy, but this was what he wanted. So we agreed, not realizing that it was the Spirit moving him. When my family arrived we instantly felt a dark spiritual presence surrounding that old Spanish mission, though we hadn't noticed it during our last visit. The meaning behind this was made clear as we walked into the old chapel. I was shooting some video and a security guard snapped, "Shut off that camera!"

Calmly, I turned to him and asked, "Why?"

"Because this is a shrine," he replied shortly.

"A shrine?" I said, struck by the literal meaning. I turned off the camera and studied the young man's face.

"Yes, brave men died here," he insisted.

By the Spirit I understood the witness being given. Texas, like the rest of the nation, is so dedicated to defending the dead and their monuments, but they will not defend the Name of Jesus Christ or the blood of His innocent children. I was also reminded that Roe v. Wade originated in Texas. It made me consider just how much time, energy and money Texas expends each year to preserve the Alamo, but what effort has it made to turn back the grave evil it unleashed upon the whole nation through legalized abortion?

We subsequently left the Alamo with heavy hearts—especially Austin. The Lord had used our son's birthday to reveal to us that while Ohio represents the heart of the nation, Texas represents the nation's rebellious spirit. Some patriots out there might cheer at the sound of these words, but I'm not talking about defying an over-reaching federal government, I'm talking about rebellion against the King of kings. This was hard news for my family, because we had once been *'proud Texans.'* Nonetheless, in a spiritual sense Texas had ceased to be our home.

You adulterous people, don't you know that friendship with the world is hatred toward God? Anyone who chooses to be a friend of the world becomes an enemy of God. —James 4:4

Never become attached to any place on this earth, because in the end it will all pass away. However, true followers of Christ will share in His Glory. So while a good Christian-American citizen will lead his government to reflect Christ's teachings and defend his nation against the *enemy,* foreign and domestic, do not waste yourself on nationalistic pride. If applied today, would Texas pass the Truth Serum? Would any state in our nation? Love your nation for the sake of its people, and care for the land as the Lord Commands, but do not love this world. To do so is highly offensive to God.

While still in San Antonio, the Lord delivered another witness to my family right outside our hotel window. One day the Spirit drew my attention to a whirlwind dancing back and forth in a field across the parking lot. It's not uncommon to see these in Texas, but this one sustained itself in the same area for an unusually long period of time. The Spirit said to me, 'Dust storm,' and He planted in my heart an understanding that this nation would see another emanation of the 1930s Dust Bowl, which plagued the nation from the Great Plains to Washington, D.C. during the Great Depression. As it was then, so it shall be with this generation, for it will come at the worst possible time for man and his dominion, but at the best possible time for the Lord to remind His subjects of His dominion.

> *"The ground is cracked because there is no rain in the land; the farmers are dismayed and cover their heads. Even the doe in the field deserts her newborn fawn because there is no grass. Wild donkeys stand on the barren heights and pant like jackals; their eyesight fails for lack of pasture."*
>
> *Although our sins testify against us, O LORD, do something for the sake of your name. For our backsliding is great; we have sinned against you.*
>
> —*Jeremiah 14:4-7*

A short time after receiving this witness, on October 17, 2011 a massive "Dust Bowl" reminiscent dust storm a mile and a half high and 250 miles wide struck West Texas. These and other signs have only been warnings. The real firestorm is yet to come if the church in this nation will not fulfill repentance, beginning with the Sanctity of Human Life. If our nation continues to seek death by laying waste to the seed God gives us, then our land will be made a wasteland and we will be given death. My family has been shown witnesses of the coming of locusts, exploding rockets, revelry turned to horror, and the sounds of endless sirens. This nation has been coddled so long, at first Americans will see these disasters as entertainment; that is, until devastation and bloodshed falls upon their doorsteps. Great walls of flames and billows of smoke and dust will sweep across this nation, forcibly reducing it, from the *greatest to the least,* to sackcloth and ashes. The *day of disaster* now coming will be unlike anything in our national history. In that day, few will doubt that we have aroused the burning anger of the Lord our God on account of our rebellion.

The earth dries up and withers, the world languishes and withers, the exalted of the earth languish. The earth is defiled by its people; they have disobeyed the laws, violated the statutes and broken the everlasting covenant. Therefore a curse consumes the earth; its people must bear their guilt. Therefore earth's inhabitants are burned up, and very few are left. —Isaiah 24:4-6

Heading into our third holiday season on the road, the Lord finally relieved my family from hotels and other less desirable accommodations by planting us in a short-lease apartment—unit 111. In this relatively small one-bedroom space, the Lord would deliver unto us some of the most profound revelations yet. But first, He delivered my family another cat. I left the door to the porch open to let in some fresh air and in walked a long-legged orange tabby cat. He came right into the middle of the living room, looked around and meowed, as if to say, "Here I am y'all, the Lord has sent me to you—*feed me!"* The kids named him "Boots" for his white socks, and he has been with us ever since. Boots the cat has seen a lot!

After the holidays, the whole region fell under a severe "cedar fever" outbreak, resulting from a record-breaking explosion of cedar pollen in the Hill Country—and this despite millions of trees having been killed by extreme drought and fires. My family was not immune to it, though we didn't run for antihistamine drugs. Instead, we followed the Spirit to Isaiah:

"The bricks have fallen down, but we will rebuild with dressed stone; the fig trees have been felled, but we will replace them with cedars." —Isaiah 9:10

Such as it was after the September 11, 2001 terrorist attacks, and Hurricane Katrina in 2005, and the devastating tornadoes that hit Joplin, Missouri in 2011, Americans vow to *rebuild* better and stronger than before, and they turn to their *American spirits* for strength, but our nation has only drifted farther apart from the *Holy Spirit of God* and has been weakened all the more. As my family has already witnessed with the Texas wildfires, when disaster strikes many find it within their *humanitarian* hearts to feed, shelter and clothe those dispossessed of their livelihoods—at least for a time. However, few actually take stock of their idolatry, adultery, bloodshed and blasphemy and repent. The *cedar pollen outbreak* has spoken of our rebellion and our coming fate, but who is listening and obeying?

> *But the LORD has strengthened Rezin's foes against them and has spurred their enemies on. —Isaiah 9:11*

For some time I had known that the Lord meant for this Scripture to be understood concerning the 9/11 attacks, not so much to explain what had happened, but what was yet to come. *"Rezin's foes"* were the Philistines in the West, as well as the Assyrians and Babylonians in the East. Isaiah specifically warns of the coming of Assyria, knowing by the Spirit that this nation would bring about the total annihilation of the Northern Kingdom of Ephraim, and nearly spell destruction for Judah in the South:

> *"Therefore the Lord is about to bring against them the mighty floodwaters of the River—the king of Assyria with all his pomp. It will overflow all its channels, run over all its banks and sweep on into Judah, swirling over it, passing through it and reaching up to the neck. Its outspread wings will cover the breadth of your land, O Immanuel!" —Isaiah 8:7-8*

The ancient capital of Assyria, Nineveh, was located on the eastern bank of the Tigris River. In order to prepare us to receive more of this revelation, the Spirit gave me a profound dream in January 20, 2012. My family stood in a big city park at night, when suddenly a major event took us by surprise. It was like a storm, a massive clap of thunder and an earthquake all in one. Immediately, a large cat, like a panther or a leopard, ran by us on the road, coming up against a very tall, black wrought iron, spired fence at the end of the street. He stood up against it on his hind legs. On the opposite side of the fence, I saw what appeared to be a massive Bengal Tiger come forth from the darkness. Alongside it walked a man, like a handler, holding it by a leash. When the tiger saw the panther, it lunged at it in a rage, rising up against it on its side of the fence. It roared and writhed violently, growing to a towering height. At its fullness, it was twice the size of the panther and its head and shoulders rose above the fence spires. I understood that its rage was the source of its growth and strength. Also, as it grew, its yellow and brown coat became jet-black. I was awestruck by its ferocity and size. It was terrifying, and its fearsome roars echoed in my ears, like a locomotive or explosive concussions. I also witnessed great clumps of grayish-black foam falling from its massive jaws, which I understood to be like hydrochloric acid. It lurched at the lesser cat, but it was so enraged it couldn't coordinate its attack. If the panther was struck, I was sure it would be dashed to pieces, but it easily eluded the larger beast. This made the black beast even angrier. Its head continued to expand and contract with its roars, but it could grow no larger, so it remained contained behind the black-spired barrier. If this beast was loosed upon the world, I was sure it would crush everything in its path. In spite of this, the beast's handler stood by undaunted, neither afraid nor in control of it. The beast was a force of its own, to be unleashed at the proper time.

Clara awakened me from this dream, saying, "The Lord woke me up, telling me, 'The spirit is willing, but the flesh is weak. Stand and keep watch with me.'" It was between 3 and 4 AM. I got up to pray with her, still shaken by the image and sound of that beast's awesome rage. It reminded me of Daniel's vision:

> *"After that, in my vision at night I looked, and there before me was a fourth beast—terrifying and frightening and very powerful. It had large iron teeth; it crushed and devoured its victims and trampled underfoot whatever was left. It was different from all the former beasts, and it had ten horns." —Daniel 7:7*

Together, we prayed and kept watch till sunrise, during which time Clara shared with me that she had a dream of the prophet Daniel, appearing about eighteen or nineteen years old. He stood across a room and held out to her a silver cup filled with water on a silver platter. She interpreted it to mean that our family was to begin a fast. At the same time, I was led to Daniel 10:

> *On the twenty-fourth day of the first month, as I was standing on the bank of the great river, **the Tigris**, I looked up and there before me was a man dressed in linen, with a belt of the finest gold around his waist. His body was like chrysolite, his face like lightning, his eyes like flaming torches, his arms and legs like the gleam of burnished bronze, and his voice like the sound of a multitude.*
>
> *—Daniel 10:4-6*

Before this encounter, Daniel had fasted for 21 days, eating *no choice food,* letting *no meat or wine touch his lips,* and *using no lotions.* Having received our instructions, our family engaged a *Daniel fast* for the next three weeks. Over this period, the Lord woke us up each morning to *'Watch and pray'* with Him, repeatedly at 1:11, 2:22, 3:33 and 4:44 AM. We quickly took note that there is precisely 1 hour and 11 minutes separating each of these hours, and the Spirit led us to understand that these were the hours that Christ awakened His disciples in the Garden of Gethsemane, warning them to *"Watch and pray."* After the third time he found them sleeping, just before 5 AM, Judas arrived with the Temple guards to arrest Him:

Returning the third time, he said to them, "Are you still sleeping and resting? Enough! The hour has come. Look, the Son of Man is betrayed into the hands of sinners." —Mark 14:41

On the 21st day, such as the Lord delivered unto Daniel the revelation of the events leading to the very end, the Spirit gave my family an understanding of how Daniel 11 correlates to world events now unraveling before our eyes:

"Now then, I tell you the truth: Three more kings will appear in Persia, and then a fourth, who will be far richer than all the others. When he has gained power by his wealth, he will stir up everyone against the kingdom of Greece."
—Daniel 11:2

The angel Gabriel described to Daniel a series of conflicts that must take place before the end. These have already occurred in history, but again the Lord always provides *two or three witnesses*. Therefore, the events we shall see unfold before the end will begin with a modern day *Persian* uprising that stems from Iran and threatens the *sons of Greece,* which is Europe, and the United States. Like all wars, the catalyst for this conflict will be money and power, although Islamist authorities will use *religion* in order to galvanize the Middle East, *stirring up everyone against the kingdom of Greece*. Russia, China and India, in particular, will be among those that rouse themselves to war against the West. Their motivation will be connected to oil, because it is the lifeblood of their mammon-driven economies. Together, these nations represent the black beast in my dream. When Persia, armed for battle, crosses the Tigris River into the heart of Iraq, we will know that spired, black iron fence—the coalition of nations now holding it back—will have fallen. Nevertheless, the West will retaliate with swift and lethal precision, just like Alexander the Great. The Persian threat will dwarf the West, but its rage will make it uncoordinated, allowing the West to exploit its weaknesses and defeat it.

That panther, however, will grow into an even greater threat to the world, and especially to the Church in Christ. From it will emerge a *contemptible king of the North,* the final antichrist:

"His armed forces will rise up to desecrate the temple fortress and will abolish the daily sacrifice. Then they will set up the abomination that causes desolation." —Daniel 11:31

Satan's goal is not to rule the earth. Christ The Lord has already condemned him to his fate, which is why he is desperately trying to trick mankind into following after him. Therefore, do not be fooled into rooting for one side or another when the world falls again into war. Instead, look to your Father in heaven for guidance, take heart in your Savior when the world around you falls apart, and follow the path the Spirit lays before you. Then you and your loved ones will not be left behind.

28

The Eleventh Hour

In accordance with the Lord's perfect timing, the next day after being settled into our new shelter, apartment 111, my family sat down before the television that had been provided to us and happened upon the Veteran's Day ceremony at Arlington National Cemetery. It was 11 AM on 11/11/11. After President Obama laid the wreath at the Tomb of the Unknown Soldiers, the military choir began to sing the "The Battle Hymn of the Republic." At precisely 11:11 AM they sang, *"His truth is marching on."* This hymn, the popular anthem of the North during the Civil War, is all about Christ's final judgment upon the rebellious nations of the earth. At that moment, the Spirit said to me, 'This is the eleventh hour.'

"About the eleventh hour he went out and found still others standing around. He asked them, 'Why have you been standing here all day long doing nothing?'

"'Because no one has hired us,' they answered.

"He said to them, 'You also go and work in my vineyard.'" —Matthew 20:6-7

The *eleventh hour* is the last hour of the biblical workday, after which night falls and Christ comes to judge the nations. By now you should understand that the whole point of the Church's existence is to perform the work of the *Lord's vineyard* in anticipation of His Second Coming. Yet somehow the church is standing around the marketplace, *doing nothing!* At this late hour, Jesus is calling upon you, His Church, to rise up and finish the work of His harvest field, for His final hour draws near, but it shall not come until His Gospel has covered all the nations of the earth, including the United States of America! This is His Great Commission:

> *"Therefore go and make disciples of all nations, baptizing them in the name of the Father and of the Son and of the Holy Spirit, and teaching them to obey everything I have commanded you. And surely I am with you always, to the very end of the age." —Matthew 28:19-20*

Brothers and sisters, we know the end is truly near because of the almost total falling away of the Christian religious establishment. God will never let His Great Commission be fulfilled under false pretenses, for Christ Commanded: *"Teaching them to obey everything I have commanded you."* This means the Gospel shall be completed in obedience, not in some *false grace* rebellion. Consequently, the Spirit has made known to my family that His Commission shall be accomplished in this Church age, meaning your time to make straight paths for the Lord is short. The *harvest* is nearer than you think:

> *"Swing the sickle, for the harvest is ripe. Come, trample the grapes, for the winepress is full and the vats overflow—so great is their wickedness!" Multitudes, multitudes in the valley of decision! For the day of the LORD is near in the valley of decision. The sun and the moon will be darkened, and the stars no longer shine. —Joel 3:13-15*

My family has repeatedly been given visions and dreams of this event, so we know it is at our door. When night falls upon the whole earth, no work can be done. Then what will you have to show for your fruitfulness? Will you be harvested for judgment or redemption?

> *"As long as it is day, we must do the work of him who sent me. Night is coming when no one can work." —John 9:4*

Night is symbolic of Satan's dominion, which will begin when the *abomination that causes desolation* is setup in the Temple. This is why the Church, the Virgin Bride of Christ, called Israel, is depicted as coming down out of heaven, clothed in the sun, with the moon under her feet:

> *A great and wondrous sign appeared in heaven: a woman clothed with the sun, with the moon under her feet and a crown of twelve stars on her head.*
>
> *—Revelations 12:1*

The sun represents the light of God's tent being spread over His Church, just as the prophets of old spoke. The twelve stars above her head represent the crown of life, inherited through the twelve tribes of Israel and the Twelve Apostles, through whom the Gospel of the risen Christ was heard. The moon is symbolic of night, which will be put beneath the feet of the Church in Christ, as David once wrote:

> *The LORD says to my Lord: "Sit at my right hand until I make your enemies a footstool for your feet." —Psalm 110:1*

What the Lord wants His Church to understand about the *eleventh hour* is that this is no time to be building storehouses and hoarding up treasure on this earth. Disaster is coming! Do not follow after the pagans of Noah's age who went along with their daily business, not looking up until the flood was already upon them. Only those who follow the Lord like Noah and his family in this age will be spared the coming judgment, though not from a flood. The destruction now being kindled against this world is unquenchable fire, and since nothing you presently have or are working to acquire will survive, why persist in rebellion?

> *"Son of man, if a country sins against me by being unfaithful and I stretch out my hand against it to cut off its food supply and send famine upon it and kill its men and their animals, even if these three men—Noah, Daniel and Job—were in it, they could save only themselves by their righteousness, declares the Sovereign LORD." —Ezekiel 14:13-14*

While you toil for food that is spoiling, moth-ridden clothing and houses that are perpetually rusting and rotting, this world is coming swiftly to and end. Therefore, take care to work for things that do not decay and spoil, but are saved up for everlasting life, and this work is all about drawing lost souls into the Kingdom of Heaven.

> *Dear children, this is the last hour; and as you have heard that the antichrist is coming, even now many antichrists have come. This is how we know it is the last hour. They went out from us, but they did not really belong to us. For if they had belonged to us, they would have remained with us; but their going showed that none of them belonged to us. —1 John 2:18-19*

Over the course of my family's journey the Lord exposed a present-day emanation of *those who have gone out from us* to partake of the antichrist's universal *world peace* movement. It is known as the *"Spirit of Assisi,"* named after

Francis of Assisi who founded the Franciscan Order of Monks in Assisi, Italy. In 1986 this *"spirit"* was presented at the World Day of Prayer summit held at the Basilica of St. Francis in Assisi, hosted by Pope John Paul II. On October 27, 2011, Pope Benedict XVI commemorated the 25th anniversary of this event. On both occasions, *Catholics and Protestant Christians* united in prayer with Muslims, Jews, Buddhists, Hindus, Sikhs, Shintoists, Zoroastrians, Baha'ists, Atheists and Animists [Voodoo], each appealing to their respective gods to bring about *"world peace."* Think about what this means, for as priests, bishops, reverends and pastors are lifting up prayers in "Jesus' Name," others are praying to demons! What do they think God will do with a people who are supposed to be leading the lost to the truth in Christ, but instead are justifying Satan's lies?

> *"Do you think I came to bring peace on earth? No, I tell you, but division. From now on there will be five in one family divided against each other, three against two and two against three." —Luke 12:51-52*

As Christ Himself testifies, He is called the *Prince of Peace* not because He makes *peace* between man and this world, but because He makes *peace* between man and his Maker. The universalist world establishment rejects this, because their first love is *money,* meaning themselves. Religious hierarchs gather together with world leaders to endorse and spread the promise of *prosperity* by way of *world peace* to please their constituents, having no real intension of sharing their wealth with the poor and destitute. Even while they are congratulating themselves for promoting *peace,* shaking hands, smiling for cameras and patting each others backs, their generals gather secretly in another room, plotting war and plunder:

> *"Nation will rise against nation, and kingdom against kingdom. There will be famines and earthquakes in various places. All of these are the beginning of birth pains." —Matthew 24:7-8*

If the flock would only study the Lord's Word, they would reject the *world peace* lie, knowing God has firmly decreed that war will continue to the end:

> *"After sixty-two 'sevens,' the Anointed One will be cut off and will have nothing. The people of the ruler who will come will destroy the city and the sanctuary. The end will come like a flood:* ***War will continue until the end****, and desolations have been decreed." —Daniel 9:26*

Understand what I am saying, because I am not advocating war. Quite the opposite! But one who pursues a goal the Spirit has specifically declared as false is like that rich man whose land produced a bountiful crop. He ignored God's will and planned to store away his abundance for a future of *life at ease* that would never be:

> *"But God said to him, 'You fool! This very night your life will be demanded from you. Then who will get what you have prepared for yourself?'*
>
> *"This is how it will be with anyone who stores up things for himself but is not rich toward God." —Luke 12:20-21*

Terrible wars are coming on account of this world's rebellion against its Maker. We each have been born to give glory to God, but the world at large, consumed with *greed,* persists in a *world peace* lie, hoping to establish its own kingdom. Instead of sowing seeds for the Gospel, it stores them away and seeks to *take life easy.* In general, people share the heart of that man who asked Jesus to tell his brother *"to divide the inheritance"* with him. Think about it. This man got to see the Christ in the flesh and some vain pursuit for money was all he could think to ask for?

> *Jesus replied, "Man, who appointed me a judge or an arbiter between you?" Then he said to them, "Watch out! Be on your guard against all kinds of greed; a man's life does not consist in the abundance of his possessions."*
>
> *—Luke 12:14-15*

For those who reject Christ, there is no *peace,* only wrath, for they have no *arbiter* between themselves and God. Sadly, much of the church will not hear these words, even though wars continue to breakout across the world. Because their religious establishments will persist in *prosperity* through *world peace,* most of the flock will accept it. Truly, the rebellious sheep are all too eager to accept a man's version of the truth, so long as it sounds logical, beneficial to himself and the institution he serves, and has been certified by a religiously ordained authority. Isn't that ironic, how man sets up his own ordaining authority? Are they not honoring themselves?

> *"He who speaks on his own does so to gain honor for himself, but he who works for the honor of the one who sent him is a man of truth; there is nothing false about him. —John 7:18*

The international community says they are *"committed to world peace,"* but in reality they have declared war on God's Word, and at present America has joined them. From the greatest to the least, we follow after the example of ancient Israel, whom the Lord destroyed, hoping to dissuade future generations from their apostasy:

> *And he said to me, "Son of man, do you see what they are doing—the utterly detestable things the house of Israel is doing here, things that will drive me far from my sanctuary? But you will see things that are even more detestable."*
>
> *—Ezekiel 8:6*

Read all of what the Lord showed Ezekiel and you will discover just how late the hour is! Are we not that Israel today, standing before the shrines of our own idols and offering incense on the altars of our own delusions? God's Law is both eternal and unchangeable. Certainly, the Law of the Creator cannot be changed by one who is created. What man can alter the pattern of the seasons, turn back time or call all the stars of the universe by name? Man can neither change what God has declared is sin nor justify any path to heaven apart from Jesus Christ. When any Christian religious authority gathers with Muslims, Buddhists, Hindus, and the likes of Voodoo witchdoctors to pray to a generic *god* for peace, who do they believe is listening? Will God honor any prayer offered to idols and demons? Is he going to hearken to that prayer merely because a supposed "Christian" joined the group and so defame His Great Name by lending some credibility to false faiths? Unlike mankind, our Heavenly Father will never ever discredit or disown His Son!

Many will struggle to comprehend all of this, because the religion of *'To Each His Own'* has already become so pervasive amongst peoples all across the world. In their desire to remain loyal to their culture, heritage and religion, or to *"respect others,"* they are making Christ out to be *optional* for salvation, when in fact He is *essential.* These ideals have long been encouraged and celebrated in writings, music, various artistic reliefs, as well as in the laws of nations and states. Since people will not all agree on Christ, they replace God with a self-aggrandizing pursuit for one's self-potential and self-gratification—the *American Dream*. Their mantra is that, whether we agree, we all should just get along, respecting everyone and everything, and especially *Mother Nature*. As you are already witnessing, many will say, "We must learn to *coexist*." Yet, in reality, it is their love for themselves and money that unites them. So beneath the flowery exterior lays a rotting corpse that says,

"Forget about God, since we both love money, let's walk together to the bank!" Then they attempt to rob each other along the way.

> *"Beware of your friends; do not trust your brothers. For every brother is a deceiver, and every friend a slanderer. Friend deceives friend, and no one speaks the truth. They have taught their tongues to lie; they weary themselves with sinning. You live in the midst of deception; in their deceit they refuse to acknowledge me," declares the LORD. —Jeremiah 9:4-6*

Seeing that the fruit at Assisi was of Satan, the Spirit burdened me to dig deeper to its root. It's incredible what following the fruit can reveal! The first obvious signs of the *Spirit of Assisi* grip on this present generation is that he is the patron saint of animals and the environment, which evolved from certain legends about the man's relationship with nature. While it is not wrong to care for and appreciate God's creations, it is entirely wrong to worship them, which is what many people who devote their lives to saving animals and the environment do. Ask the next animal or environmental activist if they believe in the Sanctity of Human Life and you will see how lost the vast majority of them are. In addition to this, I discovered that Francis of Assisi was killed by a religious phenomenon called *stigmata*. This is where a person is mysteriously afflicted with the wounds Christ suffered during his chastisement and crucifixion; the nails punctures on the hands and feet, lashes on the back, the lance wound in the side, and the crown of thorns on His head. Francis was the first documented in history to receive this supposed *gift*. However, the real Spirit of Jesus spoke to me and unequivocally said, 'I don't torture my servants and I don't kill them.' This is also consistent with His Word. The torture and crucifixion of Christ was absolutely evil, and since the Lord is incapable of doing evil, stigmata cannot come from Him. Thus, the rotten fruit of Satan is fully exposed. Like the apparitions of the *Blessed Virgin,* the *Spirit of Assisi* is evil. No bad fruit comes from a good tree! Even so, you will find Francis of Assisi idols standing all over this country, not merely at Catholic churches and homes, but in the yards of people from all walks of faith. Some would argue this is a beautiful thing, but now you know the truth.

Therefore, beware of the *Spirit of Assisi,* because it not only leads shepherds to deny Christ in favor of *world peace*, it also causes sheep to engage in illegal and prescribed drug abuse, adultery, homosexuality, greed, envy, deceit, thievery, strife, slander, murder, depression and suicide. Through His appointed witnesses the Lord has revealed all of this to my family. San Francisco, California, for example, is named after Francis of Assisi. Moreover, if you have ears to hear the truth, let it be known that the *Spirit of Assisi* is the spirit of the *false prophet,* and yes, he will come from the Roman Catholic Church. This in no way makes every Catholic evil; neither does it justify Protestant religions. The Lord has shown my family that His people are scattered across nearly every religion on the face of this earth, though each individual must receive Christ before the end. Conversely, we have also been taught that virtually every world religion, including Protestant Christian denominations, will fall under the Catholic mantle before the end, and this will fall into the hands of the antichrist. This has already been demonstrated with the Catholic-led ecumenical conferences held in Assisi. Not everyone will formally join the *Roman Catholic Church,* but they will become members of a one-world universalist religion, united in *human rights.* In fact, '*Catholic*' literally means *'Universal.'*

So that my family would better understand how a whole host of religious establishments that are supposed to be defending His Word and Truth could so easily fall away, the Lord directed Clara and me to a peculiar witness in November 2011. We had just been gifted a painting of the cross, dated 3/11, which was a conspicuous number that had repeatedly—in various forms—grabbed our attention for more than a year. That same night, as we drove back to our apartment, discussing what, if anything, it might mean, the Lord immediately served up two consecutive witnesses to confirm that '311' was no coincidence. First, a city transit bus turned towards us, bearing the number '311.' A moment later, we passed a gas station whose advertised price was '$3.11.' We both recognized the Lord's Hand. I understood it had something to do with 'the eleventh hour,' but it would be several months before the Lord finally made His point clear by directing me to the following in His Word:

> *But Moses said to God, "Who am I, that I should go to Pharaoh and bring the Israelites out of Egypt?" —Exodus 3:11*

Through this, the Lord revealed to me the connection between my family's journey and Pharaoh's ploy to keep the Israelites from following Moses out from Egypt to worship their God on His Holy Mountain. You see, after Moses and Aaron had first appeared before him, Pharaoh ordered the slave drivers and foreman over the Israelites to take away their straw, saying:

"You are no longer to supply the people with straw for making bricks; let them go and gather their own straw. But require them to make the same number of bricks as before; don't reduce the quota. They are lazy; that is why they are crying out, 'Let us go and sacrifice to our God.' ***Make the work harder for the men so that they keep working and pay no attention to lies."*** *—Exodus 5:7-9*

Notice how Pharaoh specifically targets *"the men"* by increasing their labors, for Satan knows that a man who does not look up from the ground over which he toils will not hearken to the Voice of his God. Do you see how your straw has been taken away in this present economy? You have the same car payment, house payment, higher utility bills, gas bills, fuel and food costs, but fewer resources to keep your *life raft* afloat. At one time, this was me, and I also subscribed to the lie that *'God does for those who do for themselves,'* which kept me bound to the wages of this world, and of sin. Consider further how Pharaoh calls the truth Moses had spoken *"lies."* Satan is doing the very same thing today, both within and outside the walls of the establishment church. My family has been eyewitnesses. As we have called for repentance and urged America to turn from its wicked ways, we have been called *"liars."* Dare to expose their hypocrisy and the wolves quickly jump out of their sheepskins baring their teeth!

My family has encountered their ferocity many times. Once, we went before a ministerial association in Ohio to plead with them to accept God's call to repentance so that they may share it with their flocks. Their *"Bishop"* opposed the Lord's message, accusing me of coming forth with my own agenda. When I called him out on his lies, the other members viciously rebuked me in front of my wife and children, accusing me of not coming "in love," though it was *true love* that had brought me before them. Worse, they called the police to have us taken away. So brazen were their rebellious hearts, when I warned them what a true servant of Christ must do when rejected, their chairman defiantly replied, "Yeah, go shake the dust off!" Sadly, we did, hearing them laugh at us from their conference room. The officer arrived as we were leaving. He looked at my family with confusion, seeing we were no threat. In fact, our family was huddled together by our Tahoe in prayer, grieving for the flocks being overseen by those wolves in shepherd's clothing.

On another occasion, we went before an ecumenical group of churches in Northern Indiana, again pleading for them to accept God's call to repentance. Together, a *Jezebel* and her pastor, whom she had on the end of her leash, rebuked the Lord's message and had my family ejected from their sanctuary. All I had asked was that they join me in a prayer of repentance and beseech the Lord's Hand to awaken our president. As my family was leaving peacefully, one of the deacon-bouncers slapped me in the cheek while I held Justin, then just a toddler, asleep in my arms!

"You have a spirit of witchcraft and sorcery and disorder in you!" this man grated.

"And what spirit was in you that you would unrighteously strike your brother?" I asked in return.

Denying he had struck me, he and another deacon-bouncer proceeded to try to goad me into a fight. Overcoming their antics and abuse with a peace only the Spirit can give, I left that church with my family intact. Again, thanks be to Jesus, because He rescued us from these "Christian" wolves!

Moses suffered these same hostilities from the very people to which he was sent to deliver. They hated him, because when Moses put forth the Lord's demands to Pharaoh, he reciprocated by increasing Israel's afflictions:

> *And they said, "May the LORD look upon you and judge you! You have made us a stench to Pharaoh and his officials and have put a sword in their hand to kill us." —Exodus 5:21*

God's plan for me and my family had indeed been set from the very beginning. Remember that the initial message with which we had been sent forth was to warn the church in America that our nation has become just like the rebellious Israel of old—*the first nation founded under God.* While the ancient Israelites were slaves to Pharaoh, We The Church have been enslaved by a false ideology called the *American Dream.* Ironically, I had even been compelled to expound on the *American Dream* in that book I wrote for Joe The Plumber, subtitled *"Fighting for the American Dream,"* and now we understood why it wasn't permitted to succeed. Glory be to Jesus for setting my family free from the bondage of this world! In doing so, the Lord made us firsthand witnesses to testify the truth that the American Dream has passed, and will not be revived for sake of all His Church. The Lord shall reward His people by His Hand alone.

Just as Israel was handed over to slavery by God's own Hand when He brought them into the land of Egypt during the famine of Joseph's era, so too has the church in America been handed over to the unmerciful whip of *capitalism,* the American Dream engine, which is all about growing *capital* [money]. Suffering from famine, Israel came from a foreign land into Egypt for food and prosperity. So did the church in America come from foreign lands suffering from famine and persecution, seeking food and prosperity. In the beginning, Israel flourished in Egypt. So did the church in America. There were twelve tribes of Israel that went into Egypt, counting a thirteenth when you consider Jacob's adoption of both of Joseph's sons, Manasseh and Ephraim. Thus, it was thirteen tribes that would later enter into the Promised Land of Canaan. This was later reflected in the Twelve Apostles, with Christ, the High Priest, serving as the thirteenth. Likewise, the United States of America began with thirteen colonies. I am not saying that the United States is Egypt, nor has it replaced Israel. I am saying that the promised riches of the American Dream is a direct reflection of the wealth of Egypt and the church in America has been cast in the mold of Ephraim. Moreover, just as ancient Egypt used her wealth to lord her authority over the other nations, so too has the American Dream. However, no manmade dynasty lasts forever. Eventually Egypt's prosperity was sapped by the Assyrians, conquered by the Babylonians and Persians, and finally usurped by the Greeks and Romans. So shall be the fate of the American Dream. Look on the back of the One-Dollar Bill, what do you see?

"Will they not return to Egypt and will not Assyria rule over them because they refuse to repent?" —Hosea 11:5

The reason why that pyramid is there is that it symbolizes how God's chosen people have gone back to Egypt, just as God declared through His servants the prophets. This applies both to the United States and our sister nation of Israel, whose borders are sustained by our present economic and military world authority. Yet consider how modern-day Assyria, which is the Middle East, rules over us by virtue of her oil. Many may not wish to see it this way, but in truth we bow down before them, for without their oil, we have nothing to fuel our economy. Would we ever tolerate the vitriol and bloodshed that spews out from the Middle East against Israel and America were it not for our dependency upon their oil? Of course not, but we have indeed gone back to Egypt. Still, the day is soon coming when that pyramid image will be supplanted by the image of *Babylon The Great,* the throne of the coming antichrist, through which he will control what the world can buy and sell.

But as for you, the L*ORD took you and brought you out of the iron-smelting furnace, out of Egypt, to be the people of His inheritance, as you now are.*
—Deuteronomy 4:20

The Lord used Egyptian slavery as an *iron-smelting furnace* for the purpose of tempering and purifying His people Israel before they were to receive their allotted inheritance. This was brought about to symbolize the painful process through which God separates His children from the world and gathers us unto Himself.

When the sun had set and darkness had fallen, a smoking firepot with a blazing torch appeared and passed between the pieces. —Genesis 15:17

This vision shown to Abraham was a sign of the covenant the Lord was making with him and the process by which He would come to purge his descendents of worldly devotion, which is totally invested in sins of the flesh. The *firepot* was the *iron-smelting furnace,* wherein Israel would be refined and carried through the blood of the divided heifer, goat and ram, being led by the *blazing torch*, which was the Holy Spirit. This played out when the *pillar of fire and cloud* led Israel through the Red Sea to their freedom from Egypt. Notice that Israel was not carried on olive branches, but in a *smoking firepot!* Remember that in Christ you too are a bona fide descendent of Abraham, one of those stars in heaven the Lord pointed out to our ancient patriarch, saying, *"if indeed you can count them."* Therefore, Abraham's vision was not for ancient Israel alone, but for all of Abraham's offspring that would be reborn through Jesus Christ.

Such is why today the Lord is causing the American Dream to falter and shall not let it recover, lest His people escape refinement and perish in a *Dream* façade. The *Dream* promises wealth, prosperity and longevity to many, but delivers it to a scant few. Even then, the elite are plagued with diseases no measure of money can cure. If Upper Manhattan and Beverly Hills can't afford it, who can? One glance in the Thesaurus and you will see that the American Dream could easily be called the *American Fantasy*, or *Delusion*, or *Stupor*. Perhaps *Nightmare* is the best description, because an unbridled pursuit for prosperity in the world separates you from Christ's grace. No matter what you call it, a sleeping Church wastes itself on dreams.

There was no food, however, in the whole region because the famine was severe; both Egypt and Canaan wasted away because of the famine. —Genesis 47:13

Just as the ancient peoples sold their wealth, then their livestock, and finally themselves and their land to Pharaoh in return for grain, so shall it be in the days to come when the antichrist requires one to receive his mark before he or she receives their allotted provision. He will feed you, proving his benevolence to the world, but not before he imprisons your soul. Incredibly, his false prophet will make biblical arguments to justify it. In fact, it already has a name—*social justice.* You can see how easily these things can happen, because those who are enslaved by the American Dream have already exhausted themselves in debt—to cars, homes, credit cards, tuition, and healthcare. Consequently, a vast proportion of America is now feeding from the enemy's welfare in the form of food stamps, healthcare benefits, social security, worker's comp, disability and other subsidies. It's no wonder why so many American's are depressed; their chattel souls are constantly feeding into a system that has no love to offer in return. The only hope is in Christ Jesus, and He knows how to provide for your needs, both physically and spiritually. To this my family can personally testify!

> *Abraham took the wood for the burnt offering and placed it on his son Isaac, and he himself carried the fire and the knife. As the two of them went on together, Isaac spoke up and said to his father Abraham, "Father?"*
>
> *"Yes, my son?" Abraham replied.*
>
> *"The fire and wood are here," Isaac said, "but where is the lamb for the burnt offering?"*
>
> *Abraham answered, "God himself will provide the lamb for the burnt offering, my son." And the two of them went on together. —Genesis 22:6-8*

God indeed provided a ram, a male lamb that represented the Messiah to come who has spared Isaac and all of his descendants, including you and me:

> *So Abraham called that place* ***The LORD Will Provide****. And to this day it is said, "On the mountain of the LORD it will be provided." —Genesis 22:14*

Combine this witness with Abraham's former vision of a *smoking firepot with a blazing torch* and you realize that he was shown both of the Covenants through which God would claim His descendents. Both required refinement, fire, wood and the blood of sacrifice, but the *Lord provided* the most perfect Way through the redeeming blood of His Son, Jesus Christ. Nonetheless, just as Jesus was made to carry His own wooden cross and was bound to His fate by the Father, Isaac was also made to carry the wood for the offering of himself, and his father bound him for the sacrifice, placing him on the altar. This was put forth that you might take Christ as His own Word, when He says:

"If anyone comes to me and does not hate his father and mother, his wife and children, his brothers and sisters—yes, even his own life—he cannot be my disciple. And anyone who does not carry his cross and follow me cannot be my disciple." —Luke 14:26-27

We who persevere through the trials of the *smoking firepot* and the *cross* we take up in Jesus' Name will be delivered, from the altar and the grave, for we have a perfect Covenant on whom we can rely. My family can testify that beyond worldly reason, the Lord also provides food, clothing, shelter, and will heal those who place their trust in Him. But who is willing to choose that narrow road? So many, for the sake of their flesh, would rather make the most of this short life, persevere in a paycheck and submit to Pharaoh. They do not understand the eternity to come. Like the ancient Israelites before them, they have made peace with their bondage and their *jailer*. If anyone comes unto them like Moses and Aaron, witnessing God's favor and deliverance, they will beat them away for disrupting the status quo of the American Dream they seek. They do not realize the plagues that are about to befall Egypt, which will ultimately deliver them to freedom, if only they will place their trust in God.

For I do not want you to be ignorant of the fact, brothers, that our forefathers were all under the cloud and that they all passed through the sea. They were all baptized into Moses in the cloud and in the sea. They all ate the same spiritual food and drank the same spiritual drink; for they drank from the spiritual rock that accompanied them, and that rock was Christ. Nevertheless, God was not pleased with most of them; their bodies were scattered over the desert.

—1 Corinthians 10:1-5

Just as the apostle Paul attempted to warn the Church in his day, so I am warning you now. The Israel that came out of Egypt symbolized the Christian church that was to come.

"When Israel was a child, I loved him, and out of Egypt I called my son."

—Hosea 11:1

They saw the wonders performed by God through Moses and Aaron, yet even as they were delivered from the ten plagues of Egypt, and were miraculously watered and fed in the wilderness, they tested God *ten times* and suffered His wrath.

"But the more I called Israel, the further they went from me." —Hosea 11:2

In the end, not one Israelite twenty years or older who was delivered from Egypt was permitted to enter the Promised Land, save Caleb and Joshua. They alone brought back a favorable report after spying out the land of Canaan. The other ten princes of Israel and all the mature among their tribes perished in the wilderness!

Though you already know all this, I want to remind you that the Lord delivered his people out of Egypt, but later destroyed those who did not believe.

—Jude 1:5

I tell you the truth, just two of every twelve supposed "Christians" you know have the heart of Joshua and Caleb, who alone put their trust in God. The other ten will suffer the fate of that generation of Israel in the desert, unless they repent of their wicked ways and turn back to the Lord with faith and belief.

*It takes **eleven days** to go from Horeb to Kadesh Barnea by the Mount Seir road. —Deuteronomy 1:2*

Horeb is where God consecrated all Israel to His First Covenant. Kadesh, an eleven-day journey from there, was the ancient gateway into the land of Canaan. When Israel finally arrived at the border of their Promised Land this was their eleventh hour. Albeit, the Canaanites weren't just going to role over and let Israel have their kingdom. Israel was going to have to fight for it, by faith, for it was the Lord their God who had promised their inheritance. This should mean to you that while you have been in the wilderness of affliction, and your longing for the Promised Land has never been greater, you must hold on to what you have gained in Christ. Don't let go when the final hour is upon you and you stand at the very gates of Paradise. Just one hour longer and you will be delivered!

*In the fortieth year, on the first day of the **eleventh month**, Moses proclaimed to the Israelites all that the LORD had commanded him concerning them.*

—Deuteronomy 1:3

Israel began their tribulation as slaves in Egypt. By the grace of God they were delivered out from bondage and through the sea, though their deliverance through blood and water was not without birth pains. The Egyptians, on the other hand, were crushed, representing the fate to be shared by all who reject the covering of the blood of the Lamb. Likewise, those who turn away from following Jesus Christ will also be turned away from the heavenly mansions He has promised. They will not be permitted to enter. Just as the Israelites were defeated by their enemies while trying to enter Canaan after God had rebuked them for their lack of faith, so shall it be for rebellious Christians whose repentance comes too late. God does not stand with rebels, so they cannot stand before their enemies. Knowing this, what will you do in this final hour before nightfall? Will you sustain your faith when every "Christian" around you is grumbling, moaning, complaining, and crafting a golden calf? Learn to walk straight while the light remains, for if you do not, when darkness comes you will surely stumble.

> *Jesus answered, "Are there not twelve hours of daylight? A man who walks by day will not stumble, for he sees by this world's light. It is when he walks by night that he stumbles, for he has no light." —John 11:9-10*

On 11/11/11 at 11:11 AM the Spirit said, 'This is the eleventh hour.' Shortly thereafter, I watched as the color guard came forward and the one bearing the Star-Spangled Banner suddenly stumbled and fell upon the colors he bore—at the last step! 9/11/2012 marked the eleventh anniversary of the 2001 attacks, leaving just 111 days in the year. The 2012 presidential contest marks the eleventh season of televised debates. Hear O Israel: The hour is late, the harvest is ripe, our nation is stumbling, and any who fail to repent before this hour is through shall be *crushed:*

> *"He who falls on this stone will be broken to pieces, but he on whom it falls will be crushed." —Matthew 21:44*

29

The Storm

On Friday, June 29, 2012, like an arrow shot from the bow of God Almighty a massive *derecho storm* cut through the heart of Ohio with hurricane-force winds, tearing a path of destruction all the way to Washington D.C. No one had seen anything like it before.

In speaking of his angels he says, "He makes his angels winds, his servants flames of fire." —Hebrews 1:7

After months of nonstop testifying, witnessing and receiving revelation in Texas, the Lord sent my family back to Ohio in time to witness that storm, and to teach us a difficult lesson about His will. Our first assignment was to tend to a sister in Christ dying of cancer. We hoped the Lord might be sending us to Ohio to heal this woman, but instead He spoke, 'Resurrection.'

By this time my family had seen the Spirit of Jesus heal multiple people through us, including our daughter Rielle, who once suffered from a severe allergic reaction and went into anaphylactic shock. She had never suffered from any allergies before, but this was an attack from Satan. As Rielle's airway began to fail and she became faint, Clara and I were about to take her to the emergency room when the Lord spoke to me, saying, 'If you take her there, she will die.' At that moment, the Spirit convicted me to believe in His Healing Hand and call it into action. We had seen it before, but this was our daughter, our firstborn, and this was life and death! So Clara and I cried out to the Lord, laying hands on our thirteen-year-old. Incredibly, within five minutes she was well! First, her dizziness and nausea went away, then she could breathe again and finally the swelling and blotchiness around her face and arms receded. Praise be to Jesus, He healed her!

When we arrived in central Ohio and went to the home of this sister suffering from cancer, she and her husband remained hopeful for a last minute miracle. As a nurse, she knew her odds of survival going the chemotherapy route were slim, so she had made the brave decision to walk out her deadly disease in faith. The last six months had been the worst. Our hearts went out to her, standing beside her bed, looking upon her emaciated form and pain-stricken countenance. She was happy to see us, but she was suffering terribly.

It was a strange feeling not really knowing what to pray for, except that the *Lord's will be done.* We did pray for pain relief, and thanks be to Jesus, He responded immediately. Nothing hospice had been offering her had been working. If you don't know anything about hospice, their role is basically to facilitate death by numbing your body with drugs until your heart gives out. However, our sister was cleaving to life. She had actually been abstaining from pain meds, knowing they would only speed her demise. Alternatively, when Jesus relieved her pain, it afforded her the ability to get some real rest for the first time in months. Her condition then slightly improved, but she was not healed.

While my family was away up in northern Ohio, her pain returned with a vengeance and she opted for relief through morphine. This in turn weakened her body beyond what it could sustain and she was gone in a day.

In obedience to God's instruction, Clara and I gathered with her husband and four others at a funeral home in Springfield the next day, June 29th, to pray for our sister's awakening. We did not do this for our sister's sake, because servants of Christ do not die. The flesh may perish, but the spirit is set free in Paradise. We went forth for the glory of God's Name. As we lifted up our prayers and petitions before the Lord, the Spirit moved me to pray for 'a national repentance.' I then asked a brother in Christ to blow the shofar he had brought. Immediately, we heard a howling wind erupt outside, together with a deep, rolling thunder. We all praised God Most High and Jesus Christ, anticipating her awakening at any moment. Yet, despite every sign we had been given, she did not awaken.

Clara and I were numb as we made the two-hour drive back north to where we were staying, but disappointment soon paled in the face of the devastation left in the wake of that *derecho*. Emergency crews sprinkled every town and city we passed through, power lines were down everywhere, and numerous hundred-year-old trees littered the roads in jungle-like heaps. Some trees were snapped in half like toothpicks and others were uprooted, causing the asphalt and concrete pavement over their root systems to breach and thrust upwards like an earthquake had struck the area. That's how powerful those *derecho* winds were. In farm country, many storehouses had been crushed by the winds and others had been completely blown apart, yet a barn with the words: 'Where you going without Jesus?' painted on its roof remained standing. Strangely, in every place we visited along the way the homes were largely unscathed. It was like a precision knife had swept through the land—the Lord issuing His warning to any with eyes to see.

Altogether, 22 people died across 7 states stuck by this storm, many crushed by falling trees. The tree debris was incredible, but it was the widespread power outages that affected the majority of people, including in the nation's Capitol. The Spirit said to my family, 'See, I have removed them from power.'

It was especially revealing to watch how Ohioans dealt with this disaster. Like the wildfires in Texas, many people banded together in a charitable spirit. For instance, just before the storm my family had gone grocery shopping and the Spirit told me not to buy any eggs or meat. So I told Clara, "No eggs or meat."

Giving me a funny look, she questioned, "What do you mean, 'No eggs or meat'?"

"Somebody has a cow in the freezer," I told her.

She chuckled, "I know *that.* What does that have to do with us?"

"Just trust me, put them back," I replied.

"O-kay..." She said, looking to the kids, and together they raised their brows in suspense.

Immediately after the storm, having no power to keep their food from spoiling, a local restaurant gave a whole case of *eggs* and boxes of shrimp, chicken, pork and *beef* to the place where we were staying. At the same time, another man delivered packages of hamburger patties, breakfast sausage and lunch meats. Someone else dropped off cases of bottled water "for the children." We didn't ask for these things. They just arrived at the door, and at a time when we very much needed it. The power was only out a week, but that food fed this missionary family for two months, serving as yet another witness of how ably the Lord provides for those who place their trust in Him, even in the midst of great disaster.

Nonetheless, as we listened for signs of repentance amongst various circles of people discussing the storm and its effects, hardly anyone acknowledged God's witness and warning. Then, when roads were cleared and power was restored, it seemed most everyone went back to *life as usual.* Did that storm order itself? Absolutely not, but Americans continue to believe in science, and so they ignore God's call to repentance, even when they have had their power taken away just in time for Independence Day. When the Lord sends a storm that tramples storehouses and fells trees by the thousands from one state to the next, He is warning His people what He will do to them if they do not turn from their wicked ways.

> *"All the trees of the field will know that I the LORD bring down the tall tree and make the low tree grow tall. I dry up the green tree and make the dry tree flourish. I the LORD have spoken. I will do it." —Ezekiel 17:24*

The trees snapped like toothpicks are those who will be humbled and laid low. They will not perish, but like Nebuchadnezzar their pride will be broken. The trees that were uprooted are those who will be slain. Nothing of them will be left. Their dominion over the lesser trees will be vanquished, and my children can testify that saplings were spared beneath the giants the angels had toppled. Remember the *fruitless tree* witness the Lord gave my family in Florida? *The ax is already at the roots!*

> *These men are blemishes at your love feasts, eating without the slightest qualm—shepherds who feed only themselves. They are clouds without rain, blown along by the wind; autumn trees, without fruit and uprooted—twice dead. —Jude 1:12*

In the aftermath of the storm, Clara and I sought the Lord's Face concerning our perceived failure in calling our sister to rise. Believers who have been convicted in spirit to call for a miracle in "Jesus' Name" and have been similarly disgraced by the outcome understand these sentiments. Yet it is not always due to insufficient faith or a misinterpretation of God's will. Nearly all the ancient prophets were called to engage in strange and unorthodox behavior, shaming themselves in man's sight, but in the end God's Name and His Word were glorified. Therefore, in all things led by the Spirit, it is important for the servant of Christ to humbly walk in strict obedience, knowing that God will honor His Name in His way, and in His time. Our sole responsibility is to learn the lessons He is teaching us, and to apply them to the path ahead.

When we went to call our sister to rise, Clara and I understood by the Spirit and the Lord's Word that our deceased sister was a witness for the present condition of the church in America:

> *"Remember, therefore, what you have received and heard; obey it, and repent. But if you do not wake up, I will come like a thief, and you will not know at what time I will come to you." —Revelations 3:3*

My family can testify that our sister was a Spirit-filled believer in Jesus Christ, so we fully expect that she won her crown in heaven. However, when she did not rise, the Lord was speaking to the stubbornness of the church in America, which is selfishly refusing to *wake up* and *obey* God's will and Word. Consequently, this is what the Lord spoke to me about the witness I had hoped her resurrection would serve to the Church:

> *"He said to him, 'If they do not listen to Moses and the Prophets, they will not be convinced even if someone rises from the dead.'" —Luke 16:31*

Therefore, if the church in America will not hearken to the Gospel of the risen Christ, a woman who rises from the dead will in no wise convince it to repent. The Spirit also reminded me of how Jesus had performed many miracles in the region of Capernaum, yet they did not repent:

> *"Woe to you, Korazin! Woe to you, Bethsaida! For if the miracles that were performed in you had been performed in Tyre and Sidon, they would have repented long ago, sitting in sackcloth and ashes." —Luke 10:13*

I thought we had been called to Ohio to raise a woman from the dead, and in doing so, to spark a resurrection of the dead and sleeping church in America. Instead, we were being called to learn and put forth yet another witness of God's will. And what is His will?

> *"For my Father's will is that everyone who looks to the Son and believes in him shall have eternal life, and I will raise him up at the last day." —John 6:40*

My family can testify that if our sister had risen from the dead, great shouts of praise would have been lifted up to God, and word of this miraculous event would have spread far and wide. However, what incentive would there have been for the Church to turn from innocent bloodshed, Sodom and

Gomorrah, and appeasing our national denial of Jesus Christ? Would people not say, "Look, God is with us! Why change anything?" And how many "Christians" living like pagans would fall into the hands of Satan as a result of their unrepentant sin? The Church is looking for a *revival,* a sweeping movement of the Holy Spirit that takes the hearts of this nation by storm. Well, the Lord sent us a storm all right, just not the one we were expecting. God doesn't want His people falling over then getting up an hour later and going back to pagan life as usual. He wants His people who are called by His Name to truly awaken to embrace a heartfelt repentance so that we will not be lost when the final day of disaster falls upon the world. Yes, there will be miracles, healings and resurrections, but it is a wicked and adulterous generation that asks for a sign before it will turn from its evil ways:

> *"A wicked and adulterous generation looks for a miraculous sign, but none will be given it except the sign of Jonah." Jesus then left them and went away.*
>
> *—Matthew 16:4*

Simply put, this life isn't it. Only the Life to come in Christ Jesus matters. This life has been provided as a proving grounds to temper and purify souls for heaven, but few are passing the test. People in this country are so concerned about the life of their flesh, they are forgetting about the Life of their soul, and the souls of their neighbors. What good are the riches you store up for yourself on this earth if you fail to repent and lose the riches of heaven? "Christians" want to be healed and to live long peaceful, prosperous lives, but they do not want to live moral lives pleasing to their Savior. Here's the proof: The Church is still pursuing money first! The Lord has witnessed this reality to my family in nearly every appointment we have kept in His Name. In God's sight this inexcusable! His Kingdom alone is worthy of being our first priority. Until people start planning for a future beyond the grave, restoration will remain out of reach. In a sense, most "Christians" really don't believe in the resurrection of the dead, otherwise they would shudder at their sinful rebellion.

> *Endure hardship as discipline; God is treating you as sons. For what son is not disciplined by his father? If you are not disciplined (and everyone undergoes discipline), then you are illegitimate children and not true sons. —Hebrews 12:7-8*

Our nation is being disciplined because the Lord loves us. This is the truth, and more punishment is coming, not because we are faithful, but because we have let rebellion seep into our national way of life. Incredibly, rebellion has become so pervasive in our society the Church has erroneously stamped it with God's approval. If the Lord did not love us, He would simply destroy us with the breath of His Mouth. Yet, because He does love us with a true and everlasting love, He will teach us to distinguish good from evil behavior by force. Then, after the heart of this nation has turned from it wickedness, He will outstretch His Hand and heal us in every way.

No discipline seems pleasant at the time, but painful. Later on, however, it produces a harvest of righteousness and peace for those who have been trained by it.

—Hebrews 12:11

Therefore, when you find yourself and the ones you love suffering from all kinds of afflictions, take a long honest look within yourself and purge anything the Bible calls sin. Even if you feel your are already walking along the Lord's path, you know He is just and righteous in all of His dealings, so you know you are being tempered for something good. It goes against human nature to walk in the midst of a fire, but I tell you that if you do not shrink from righteousness for the sake of your flesh, you will be gratified when the Lord's purification process has been fulfilled. Don't use a measuring stick in the world to gauge whether you are being wise, but turn to God's Word and His Holy Spirit. Where there is little-to-no gain in the world, there is great and everlasting gain in heaven. Your Heavenly Father will never lead you to ruin. Somewhere down the line you will be delivered, you will be restored and you will realize a *better resurrection* in Christ:

Women received their dead, raised to life again. Others were tortured and refused to be released, so that they might gain a better resurrection.

—Hebrews 11:35

Our sister's cancer was torturous, and she was not released from its grip until the point of death. Even so, I promise you that no one who suffers the same and receives their prize in heaven is in any way disappointed. If you live your whole life on this earth, suffering from afflictions, having rarely if ever partaken of this world's delicacies, but you obtain a resurrection in Christ, have you missed out on anything? It would be good for the whole Church to understand that the riches of this earth can add nothing to heaven. One who lives a rich, full life on this earth and somehow passes through the eye of a needle to get to heaven doesn't say upon his arrival, "Wow, what a great deal. I got to live two rich lives!" Instead, the riches and brightness of heaven bleach out any memory of this brief life of affliction so that the slave and the king equally rejoice together. In other words, heaven is so surpassingly great, even the best this world has to offer will seem like a prison sentence by comparison.

"See, I have refined you, though not as silver; I have tested you in the furnace of affliction." —Isaiah 48:10

The liars in shepherd's clothing will scornfully reject these words, but if they knew the horrifying fate awaiting them, they would repent at once. Do not seek peace on this earth, and so be disappointed, but seek peace with your Father in heaven, so that when your flesh perishes you are not disappointed in your resurrection.

If anyone's name was not found written in the book of life, he was thrown into the lake of fire. —Revelations 20:15

The church in America may have been chosen, but this does not mean it won't be required to persevere through challenges, and some of these will be excruciating. When these trials fall upon your doorstep, don't give up. Instead, remember Job and follow his example, because the Lord rewards those who weather the storm and still give glory to His Name:

At this, Job got up and tore his robe and shaved his head. Then he fell to the ground in worship and said: "Naked I came from my mother's womb, and naked I will depart. The LORD gave and the LORD has taken away; may the name of the LORD be praised." —Job 1:20-21

For many months the Lord repeatedly led me to Job so that I would learn the purpose for which He established Job's testimony. As you may recall, Job was a righteous man, blameless in God's sight, but He permitted Satan to afflict Job in the worst possible ways. He lost his children, his servants, possessions, and his own body was painfully afflicted from head to toe. Yet, in spite of all the trouble the Lord allowed Satan to bring upon Job, he remained steadfast in honoring the Name of the Lord. I asked the Lord, "Why O Lord did you let Satan do all those things to a righteous man?" I know that many Christians these days, themselves suffering from various afflictions, are asking the Lord this very question. We have been taught that Jesus took up all our infirmities and vanquished them upon the cross, so why are we still suffering, and some to the point of death?

In response to my question, the Lord first told me, 'Job was untested,' and it disturbed me deeply. My family had purposely purged ourselves of any devotion to this world, and yet we too found ourselves suffering from many afflictions. Why? When I was ready to receive it, the Lord led me again to His Word:

"My ears had heard of you but now my eyes have seen you." —Job 42:5

Then the Spirit said, 'Before his trial, Job did not truly know me, but afterwards, he did. Likewise, before your trials, you did not truly know me, and now you do.' And what did Job say when he realized how foolish he had been to question the motives of the Almighty?

"Therefore, I despise myself and repent in dust and ashes." —Job 42:6

Indeed, who is man that he should question His Maker in anything? Let us simply trust in the Lord's righteousness and faithfully endure any trial and test He sends our way. I do not put this forth to you as a *righteous man,* but as a sinner who has been taught to embrace righteousness, especially when I did not want to. That is the measure of the Lord's true grace, which He forces upon those whom He loves. So when Satan seeks to tempt you in any way to *"curse God to His Face,"* let your response be as Job's, *"May the Name of the Lord be praised."* Then, even if your flesh should perish, your soul will bask in your Savior's eternal Light.

"Do not be afraid of what you are about to suffer. I tell you, the Devil will put some of you in prison to test you, and you will suffer persecution for ten days. Be faithful, even to the point of death, and I will give you the crown of life."

—Revelations 2:10

When you decide to walk straight before the Lord, divesting yourself of worldly devotions, the world will mock and scoff at you. As it was with Job, some you deemed *'friends'* will see your sufferings and will falsely accuse you. Some will call you, "Fool!" for trusting in the Lord, and others will say, "You sinned, and so are being punished!" Do not think your church will hesitate to heap insults upon you the way Bildad the Shuhite piled them upon Job:

"Does God pervert justice? Does the Almighty pervert what is right? When your children sinned against him, he gave them over to the penalty of their sin. But if you will look to God and plead with the Almighty, if you are pure and upright,

even now he will rouse himself on your behalf and restore you to your rightful place." —Job 8:3-6

Read the scathing remarks of all of Job's so-called *'friends'* and you will see that they sound righteous, logical and wise, but the Lord's anger burned against them, because they spoke without understanding and accused without knowledge:

After the LORD had said these things to Job, he said to Eliphaz the Temanite, "I am angry with you and your two friends, because you have not spoken of me what is right, as my servant Job has." —Job 42:7

Above all, remember how Jesus, our Savior, was treated. He predicted His death from the very beginning of His Gospel journey:

Jesus said to them, "Surely you will quote this proverb to me: 'Physician, heal yourself! Do here in your hometown what we have heard that you did in Capernaum.'" —Luke 4:23

Three years later, while Jesus suffered upon the cross, the Jews fulfilled His prophecy:

The people stood watching, and the rulers even sneered at him. They said, "He saved others; let him save himself if he is the Christ of God, the Chosen One."
—Luke 23:35

Now how could Jesus, the Son of God, who performed all those miracles, including raising the dead, not deliver Himself? In answer to this question, two months after our sister's passing, Clara opened her Bible on her nightstand, discovering this highlighted passage:

Going a little farther, he fell with his face to the ground and prayed, "My Father, if it is possible, may this cup be taken from me. ***Yet not as I will, but as you will.*** *" —Matthew 26:39*

Jesus submitted Himself to torture and death because it was His Father's will. He knew that He had to die to provide us all with a better resurrection. Therefore, when you, a Spirit-filled believer, find yourself in the midst of a great and terrible storm, and are suffering painful afflictions, finding no relief in spite of unceasing prayers and petitions, simply accept God's will and trust in His deliverance. He knows what He is doing, and He will surely come to your aid at His appointed time. Whether by poverty or wealth, sickness or health, life or resurrection to everlasting Life, the Lord your God will testify to His glory, and He will deliver you to shore:

> *A strong wind was blowing and the waters grew rough. When they had rowed three or three and a half miles, they saw Jesus approaching the boat, walking on the water; and they were terrified. But he said to them, "It is I; don't be afraid."* ***Then they were willing to take him into the boat, and immediately the boat reached the shore where they were heading.*** *—John 6:18-21*

The *rough waters* symbolize the peoples, nations and languages that tempt, deceive, afflict, and rage against Christ's Church, desperately trying to cause us to fall for fear of drowning. Nonetheless, Jesus *walks upon the waters,* placing ever enemy beneath the feet of the faithful Church that stands firm in Him—even when it seems impossible in the world. The *three or three and a half miles* represents the *three and a half year* tribulation that will fall upon the whole earth; it is also the length of the journey every believer must endure in the storm. The disciples being *willing to take him into their boat* is the Church accepting its trials, understanding God has appointed them. Therefore, we must rebuke fear in "Jesus Name" and persevere through every personal struggle in faith and obedience, no matter how far away the shore may seem, or impossible to reach. Hang in there, brothers and sisters! Submit yourselves to God's will, because the *boat reaching the shore where they were heading* is the Lord's deliverance, which will come to all who hold firm to the very end.

> *"But when he saw the wind, he was afraid and, beginning to sink, cried out, "Lord, save me!"*
>
> *Immediately Jesus reached out his hand and caught him. "You of little faith," he said, "why did you doubt?" —Matthew 14:30-31*

On October 31, 2012 another storm, *Sandy,* humbled the Northeastern United States, felling trees, flooding cities, and usurping man's power just in time for the elections. For the first time since the *Blizzard of 1888,* God's force of nature rendered Wall Street still, yet this nation continues to accredit *Mother Nature,* ignoring God's authority. As my family was positioned to witness, *Sandy* tracked inland to Northeastern Ohio, ravaging the only area that had escaped the former *derecho.* Likewise, when the full cup of the Lord's wrath has been poured out upon this nation, no place and no one—except those like Job—will escape. How long O Israel before you awaken and humble yourselves in obedience before your King?

30

On Eagles' Wings

Leading up to the conclusion of the 2012 elections, the Lord brought my family to stay at an old farmhouse in Clarke County, Ohio—the heart of the heart of the nation. While there, campaign buses and jets repeatedly made stops in and around the area, making news headlines as the candidates vied for the all-important *bellwether state.* Such as it had been revealed to my family, no presidential contender ever stepped forward to take a definitive stand for leading the nation back to God Most High and Jesus Christ by making the Sanctity of Human Life their highest priority. Since Life is God's highest priority, why isn't it ours? So rather than engage a fruitless political frenzy as we had in 2008, we stood aside to let man exhaust his plans and earnestly sought the Lord's Face to piece together all the revelations He had given us concerning the bigger and infinitely better plans He has made for our nation. Man has had his chance, now let us turn ourselves wholeheartedly over God's plan.

If America did not matter to God, why restore it? Understand that anyone who operates under the auspices of a contract, or covenant, though no formal agreement has been established, is still bound by the understood terms and conditions. In the event of a dispute between the two parties, a judge makes his ruling based upon the inferred provisions under which both parties agreed to operate. By this principle, though our country may not have executed a written legal instrument declaring it a "Christian Nation," we nonetheless shall be bound by the terms and conditions of God's Word, because we reside on the King's land and draw our sustenance from it. Moreover, the vast majority of our "Christian" citizenry has entered into a spiritual covenant with God Most High and Jesus Christ. Consequently, the Judge shall hold our nation to a higher standard of obedience. There may be nations more vile and wicked that ours, but they were not chosen to be a *light to the nations* as we were. To whom much is given, much is expected. That is why our judgment will be swift and harsh if we fail to repent. Whether by restoration or judgment, the Lord our God will make an example of us, just as He did with the Israel of old:

> *However, if you do not obey the LORD your God and do not carefully follow all his commands and decrees I am giving you today, all these curses will come upon you and overtake you: You will be cursed in the city and cursed in the country. Your basket and your kneading trough will be cursed. The fruit of your womb will be cursed, and the crops of your land, and the calves of your herds and the lambs of your flocks. You will be cursed when you come in and cursed when you go out. —Deuteronomy 28:15-19*

Even so, you can be sure our Savior will not simply throw away the single largest *Christian Nation* on the face of the earth. At the very least, where there is found the most concentrated population of "Christians" there is also the largest *remnant* of true servants of Christ. The Lord will lay claim to us, though the hour is late:

> *"Now learn this lesson from the fig tree: As soon as its twigs get tender and its leaves come out, you know that summer is near. Even so, when you see these things happening, you know that it is near, right at the door."*
>
> *—Mark 13:28-29*

No man knoweth the day or the hour when the Lord will come, but we know we are in the season of the end. The leaves have turned green and the fruit is ripened for the harvest. This is why it is critically important that you discover and embrace not only your identity in Christ, but also the identity of your nation before the day of disaster strikes. I want you to understand something that is critical for both our national restoration, and yours personally: Nations are merely a collection of individual people. Therefore, the restoration of the United States must begin with you. You cannot remain neutral, deeming yourself a citizen of heaven alone, because God has fixed your flesh upon this nation's soil. Like it or not, people are bound by their nation's fate, including the Church. Were you able to ask the faithful remnant of ancient Israel that lived through their nation's division and subsequent civil wars, or the eventual subjugations by the Assyrians and Babylonians, they would tell you that their nation's rebellion dramatically altered their individual lives. Moreover, they would encourage you to do whatever you could to compel your nation to return to God, through Christ Jesus, because His is the only Hand that can save. When the cup of the Lord's wrath is poured out, to whom will you turn for aid and comfort? In Christ alone will you find succor.

These truths have been made evident to my family at various waypoints along the course of our journey, but the Lord made clear His plan for our nation and the ultimate purpose for our mission in the spring of 2011. He said, 'You are preparing the *wings of the eagle.*'

> *"You yourselves have seen what I did to Egypt, and how I carried you on eagles' wings and brought you to myself." —Exodus 19:4*

Since the fate of our nation is dependent upon individuals like you, taking action to fulfill God's will, it becomes important to understand the purpose for which God set this New World apart from the Old. Otherwise, how will you know whether you are dedicating your time, energy and wealth to something the Lord deems profitable for His purposes? Such considerations prove the wisdom of the wise, and *eagles' wings* is the key the Lord has provided to lead us to that wisdom. The Founders may have thought they were selecting the *Bald Eagle* for our national seal, but in reality it was the Lord's Hand moving them to fulfill His will, and in doing so, to reveal our biblical identity. *Eagles' wings* are a biblical expression of the Lord's anointing on a people or nation, a symbol of His favor, which He demonstrated to Israel by carrying His people out from Egyptian bondage to a place prepared for them in the wilderness.

> *Like an eagle that stirs up its nest and hovers over its young, that spreads its wings to catch them and carries them on its pinions. The LORD alone led him; no foreign god was with him. —Deuteronomy 32:11-12*

It was no *nameless god* that had carried Israel to freedom, and they certainly did not carry themselves, but the *Living Rock* that is Christ Jesus delivered them to freedom. It was Christ's Spirit that led them to the Holy Mountain of God to worship, and it was His Word that sustained their flesh and souls in every way. Without Christ, Israel would have had no *eagles' wings* to fly to safety. This also can be said of the United States, for what good is an eagle whose wings cannot bear it in flight? On the farm, such birds are called "chickens." Thus, this nation, which calls upon "God" for blessings, but rejects the Son, will be grounded and appointed for slaughter! It will surely not escape the Father's wrath, unless the American people humble themselves before the Son and have their *eagles' wings* restored.

God's plan for the restoration of the United States is not about a nation made in man's image, and it's certainly not about preserving our Constitution. It's about a nation called Israel, which is more than a place on a map, it is His Church, a Body that consists of *all* His sheep—including Judah:

> *"Son of man, take a stick of wood and write on it, 'Belonging to Judah and the Israelites associated with him.' Then take another stick of wood and write on it, 'Ephraim's stick, belonging to Joseph and all the house of Israel associated with him.' Join them together into one stick so that they will become one in your hand." —Ezekiel 37:16-17*

This is the ultimate purpose for which God formed our nation in the cast of Ephraim. What this means is that the United States is a modern-day emanation of the Northern Kingdom of Israel, while the State of Israel is representative of the Kingdom of Judah. There are all kinds of theories out there about the lost tribes of Israel, so don't confuse this with some argument concerning bloodlines of men. Christ's precious blood is all that matters anymore. Therefore, America has not supplanted Israel; we are a part of Israel, God's chosen Church in Christ. Accordingly, God has fixed a spiritual bond between the United States and Israel that cannot be severed. We are *'Joseph and all the house of Israel associated with him,'* a house appointed as a chief witness to reunite the scattered children of God across the globe within the Gospel of Jesus Christ. Yet, the primary object of our witness at this late hour ought to be the Jews in Israel, who are *'Judah and the Israelites associated with him.'*

The United States and Israel are sister nations, formed by Providence and destined to be reunited in God's Hand. The Lord displayed the kinship of our two nations for the whole world to witness on May 14, 1948. It was the United States that led the way in formally recognizing the rebirth of the Nation of Israel. Since then, our brothers in Judah have been relying upon our *eagles' wings* for political and military support. You can be sure the rest of the world does not love them. The Nazis only escalated the Jewish pogroms much of Europe and Russia had already been practicing. The British and Arabs certainly weren't in favor of the reestablishment of the Jewish homeland. Nevertheless, the primary role for our *eagles' wings* remains unfulfilled:

> *"I will make them one nation in the land, on the mountains of Israel. There will be* ***one king*** *over all of them and they will never again be two nations or be divided into two kingdoms." —Ezekiel 37:22*

That *One King* is Jesus Christ, and We The Church of the United States have a divinely appointed duty to lead our brother Judah back to the Messiah who led us all out of Egypt. Think about it, why do we defend the Jews when the rest of the world hates them? What resource can we claim in Israel that better suits our national interests than oil? It is not our humanitarian spirit that is guiding us along this path, but the Holy Spirit of God. Nonetheless, the church in America must reconcile the matter of support for Israel in our hearts, because deadly deceptions of Satan are coming. In all things, the enemy seeks to trick Christians into committing apostasy against our Savior, so be on guard! For instance, what will you as a servant of Christ do when it is proposed that a Third Temple be built in Jerusalem? Will you send your gold and silver to the commission appointed to the construction project? Will you rejoice when the Temple is completed and Jewish rabbis reinstitute the Sanhedrin and the daily offerings of lambs and other sacrifices of blood?

> *"My dwelling place will be with them; I will be their God, and they will be my people. Then the nations will know that I the LORD make Israel holy, when my sanctuary is among them forever." —Ezekiel 37:27-28*

That *sanctuary,* or Temple, is not manmade. The *New Jerusalem* has been made by God's Hands and comes down from heaven. The apostle John reflects Ezekiel when he shares this revelation:

> *Then I saw a new heaven and a new earth, for the first heaven and the first earth had passed away, and there was no longer any sea. I saw the Holy City, the new Jerusalem, coming down out of heaven from God, prepared as a bride beautifully dressed for her husband. And I heard a loud voice from the throne saying, "Now the dwelling of God is with men, and he will live with them. They will be his people, and God himself will be with them and be their God.*
>
> *—Revelations 21:1-3*

This is a profound mystery, a vision of what heaven on earth will be like. So far as our human minds can grasp it, the Third Temple is the Body of Christ, *a bride beautifully dressed for her husband,* meaning the Church. Jesus fully explained this spiritual relationship when He spoke with that Samaritan woman at the well:

"I have no husband," she replied.

Jesus said to her, "You are right when you say you have no husband. The fact is, ***you have had five husbands, and the man you now have is not your husband.*** *What you have just said is quite true." —John 4:17-18*

Those five husbands symbolize the five kingdoms the Assyrians had resettled in Northern Israel [Samaria] after exiling Ephraim and his ten tribes. They also represent five pagan religions, which the Samaritans had syncretized with Judaism, much like the United States has melded various pagan heritages and traditions with Christianity. The woman referred to Jacob as *"our father,"* though she had not descended from Israel. In reality she was a Gentile, expressing the Mosaic heritage passed down to her through the generations, but with one important distinction:

"Sir," the woman said, "I can see that you are a prophet. Our fathers worshipped on this mountain, but you Jews claim that the place where we must worship is in Jerusalem." —John 4:19-20

She was referring to Mount Gerizim, from which Moses had once instructed the ancient Israelites to proclaim blessings for obedience to God's Word. Still, the Jews held no substitute for the Temple in Jerusalem. Little did she know that she was posing this question to the Son of God, the literal authority on the Word. Therefore, consider deeply the Lord's response:

Jesus declared, "Believe me, woman, a time is coming when you will worship the Father neither on this mountain nor in Jerusalem. You Samaritans worship what you do not know; we worship what we do know, for salvation is from the Jews." —John 4:21-22

Indeed, when Christ returns in His Father's glory, no church building, synagogue or temple, whether in Jerusalem or on any mountain will suffice. The mountains will flee from His presence, so how much more a structure built by man! The world ecumenical church establishment will certainly encourage the building of a Jewish Third Temple, and will hail it as a remarkable achievement in their pursuit for world peace, but they and everyone who joins them will be committing a grave offense against God.

> *"Yet a time is coming and has now come when the true worshipers will worship the Father in spirit and truth, for they are the kind of worshipers the Father seeks. God is spirit, and his worshipers must worship in spirit and in truth."*
>
> *—John 4:23-24*

Jesus Christ was the last sacrifice of blood God the Father would ever accept. Any sacrifice put forth after Christ's precious blood is a denial of the Son of God and a blasphemy against the Father. Yes, we must love and protect our brethren in Israel, but we must first love God *in spirit and in truth* by teaching the Jews the true identity of their *Messiah:*

> *The woman said, "I know that Messiah" (called Christ) "is coming. When he comes, he will explain everything to us."*
>
> *Then Jesus declared, "I who speak to you am he." —John 4:25-26*

Understanding the entire witness God has put forth, Jesus told that Samaritan woman, *"the man you now have is not your husband,"* because He was her true Husband. Like the Jews in Israel today, as well as a great many "Christians" in America, she had been taught about God, but she didn't really know Him. However, when she realized who Jesus was, she went and testified to her village. This is what the Church is supposed to be doing today, teaching both lost Jews and Gentiles the identity of the Messiah and the role He serves for us in heaven before the Father:

> *Now there have been many of those priests, since death prevented them from continuing in office; but because Jesus lives forever, he has a permanent priesthood. Therefore he is able to save completely those who come to God through him, because he always lives to intercede for them. —Hebrews 7:23-25*

Jesus Christ is the only path to salvation and the only intercessor for the forgiveness of sins. Without Him no sin has been taken away, in which case the sinner remains in God's judgment, no matter how much livestock you slaughter. Consequently, Jews still worshipping the temporal Jerusalem need to accept Christ in order to have an inheritance in the New Jerusalem along with the rest of the Church. Will they somehow be given a special pass to heaven by another route? No! Anyone who persists in rebellion against the Son of God, regardless of ancestry, will be stripped of his birthrights before

Christ. This is why our witness is so critical to God's plan. How can we let our Jewish brethren not know who their true Husband is?

"Return, faithless people," declares the LORD, "for I am your husband. I will choose you—one from a town and two from a clan—and bring you to Zion."
—Jeremiah 3:14

To God, history is little more than a reflection of light—*that light which He called into being*. God's sight is so infinite, He stands on the outermost reaches of the universe and beholds the whole of human history in the blink of an eye. God is that big! Everything from the beginning to the very end is held in the palm of His Mighty Hand. As such, He has always known those among His children who would stand with Him and those who would rebel. So when He set the foundations of the earth, He also created a perfect plan for sifting out rebels from servants, establishing the test for the crown of life exclusively through His Son. This plan has shaped the whole of human history. Man has shaped nothing.

Taking God's historical framework into account, our nation's biblical identity really took shape when Joshua and Caleb set themselves apart, by faith, from the other ten spies sent out to Canaan, which shrunk from fear of the Canaanites' superior stature and their fortified cities.

"Because they have not followed me wholeheartedly, not one of the men twenty years old or more who came up out of Egypt will see the land I promised on oath to Abraham, Isaac and Jacob—not one except Caleb son of Jephunneh the Kenizzite and Joshua son of Nun, for they followed the LORD wholeheartedly."
—Numbers 32:11-12

Caleb of Judah and Joshua of Ephraim represent two chief *witnesses,* whom the Lord would later appoint to rule over the other ten tribes of Israel at the proper time. These men of God also established the chief houses through which Christ's Gospel would be declared to the whole world, a commission that is nearing fulfillment in this present age. Furthermore, the nature of their relationship, through shared faith, will come to fruition when the Church is called to take a united stand against the antichrist.

And Ahijah took hold of the new cloak he was wearing and tore it into twelve pieces. Then he said to Jeroboam, "Take ten pieces for yourself, for this is what the LORD, the God of Israel, says: 'See, I am going to tear the kingdom out of Solomon's hand and give you ten tribes. But for the sake of my servant David and the city of Jerusalem, which I have chosen out of all the tribes of Israel, he will have one tribe.'" —1 Kings 11:30-32

When Solomon led Israel into idolatry in his later years, the Lord punished him by tearing ten tribes away from his son, Rehoboam, giving them to his official, Jeroboam the Ephraimite. These formed the Northern Kingdom of Israel, also called Ephraim. The Lord did not strip the whole kingdom away from David's line in order to preserve his throne over Judah. As for Jeroboam, son of Nebat, and all the kings of Ephraim after him, every one of them was evil, leading Israel into pagan idolatry and all the detestable ways of the other nations. Eventually they exhausted God's longsuffering grace, forming an alliance with Aram and planning to replace Ahaz, a son of David's line, on Judah's throne with *the son of Tabeel:*

"Aram, Ephraim and Remaliah's son have plotted your ruin, saying, 'Let us invade Judah; let us tear it apart and divide amongst ourselves, and make the son of Tabeel king over it.'" Yet this is what the Sovereign LORD says: "It will not take place, it will not happen." —Isaiah 7:5-7

In anticipation of man's vain attempt to usurp David's throne, God raised up the Assyrians. He sent them like a sweeping flood through Ephraim, dispossessing his ten tribes of their inheritance and scattering them among the nations. They have been lost to history ever since, though they have never been lost to God:

"For I will give the command, and I will shake the house of Israel among all the nations as grain is shaken in a sieve, and not a pebble will reach the ground."—Amos 9:9

The judgment that fell upon Ephraim was twofold: It served to punish Northern Israel for her adulteries and it put forth a witness to Judah of what would happen to her if she did not turn from her wickedness. Judah, however, did not heed the warning. As the Lord permitted, she was severely weakened by multiple successive enemies penetrating all of her borders, then handed over to Nebuchadnezzar and the Babylonians. Even though Jerusalem and the Temple were completely destroyed, and the Jews were banished from their homeland, unlike their Israelite brethren in the North the Jews sustained their identity throughout the ages. Again, this was in accordance with the Lord's design, because He had promised David an *everlasting kingdom* through one of his descendents:

"When your days are over and you rest with your fathers, I will raise up your offspring to succeed you, who will come from your own body, and I will establish his kingdom. He is the one who will build a house for my Name, and I will establish the throne of his kingdom forever. ***I will be his father, and he will be my son.*** *When he does wrong, I will punish him with the rod of men, with the floggings inflicted by men. But my love will never be taken away from him, as I took it way from Saul, whom I removed from before you. Your house and your kingdom will endure forever before me; your throne will be established forever."*
—2 Samuel 7:12-16

That *Son* is Jesus Christ, He is the One who built the Father's House, and His is the only Kingdom that has been eternally established. Is there a king among men from the line of David sitting on Jerusalem's throne today? Was not the Christ the One who suffered *the floggings inflicted by men* for the wrongdoings of all Israel? Remember that We The Church are Christ's Body. So, though *no wrong* was ever found in Christ, He came and took upon Himself, His Body, the punishments for our sins.

Of the increase of his government and peace there will be no end. He will reign on David's throne and over his kingdom, establishing and upholding it with justice and righteousness from that time on and forever. The zeal of the LORD Almighty will accomplish this. —Isaiah 9:7

Nonetheless, as the Gospel declares, the Jewish nation did not recognize their Creator when He came unto them. So they plotted His death; such as it was appointed for the Messiah to die for those whom He loved:

And not only for that nation but also for the scattered children of God, to bring them together and make them one. So from that day on they plotted to take his life.

Therefore Jesus no longer moved about publicly among the Jews. Instead he withdrew to a region near the desert, to a village called Ephraim, where he stayed with his disciples. —John 11:52-54

Jesus knew the Jewish nation would ultimately reject Him, crucify Him and suffer all the things that were to befall them in generations to come. So when Jesus withdrew to *Ephraim,* He was leaving us a clue about where He would establish the foundations of His Church. It was the Gentile nations among which *Ephraim* and *the house of Israel associated with him* had been scattered that first embraced the Gospel. Ephraim, therefore, symbolizes the scattering of Israel across the face of the earth, such as a farmer scatters seed; only this Farmer was God. Moses foresaw this eventuality as a consequence of Israel's disobedience, but also as a measure of God's overcoming grace:

When the Most High gave the nations their inheritance, when he divided all mankind, he set up boundaries for the peoples according to the number of the sons of Israel. —Deuteronomy 32:8

The Lord also expressed his plans to Ezekiel:

"You are to distribute this land among yourselves according to the tribes of Israel. You are to allot it as an inheritance for yourselves and for the aliens who have settled among you and who have children. You are to consider them as native-born Israelites; along with you they are to be allotted an inheritance among the tribes of Israel. In whatever tribe the alien settles, there you are to give him his inheritance," declares the Sovereign LORD. —Ezekiel 47:21-23

The meaning of all this can be summed up as thus: Every race of man was planted by the Lord, sprinkled with Ephraim and watered with Judah, so that from every nation, language and people fruit would spring forth for the glory of His Name. As God told Abraham:

"I will surely bless you and make your descendents as numerous as the stars in the sky and as the sand on the seashore. Your descendents shall take possession of the cities of their enemies, and through your offspring all nations on earth will be blessed, because you have obeyed me." —Genesis 22:17-28

Abraham's *offspring* is Israel, but the One that brought them all to life with *living water* is Jesus Christ. Indeed, God did not send His Son for the Jews alone, but they were the *first* to receive the Gospel:

"So the last will be first, and the first will be last." —Matthew 20:16

The Jewish nation was the first to receive the testimony of everlasting life in Christ, but it will be the last to accept Him. Ephraim and the Gentile nations, over which he was scattered, were the last to receive the Gospel, yet were the first to accept Jesus as the Son of God. This was appointed, for the Lord knew that those who were least among His children, being the most steeped in sin and divided from His grace, would be the most grateful in return for His pardon through Christ. Out of this gratefulness would spring forth much fruitfulness, a fervent desire to spread the testimony of the Gospel, thereby drawing many more sons and daughters into the Kingdom of Heaven. This is why Jesus declared:

> *"Therefore I tell you that the kingdom of God will be taken away from you and given to a people who will produce its fruit." —Matthew 21:43*

Over the ages the Gentile nations would become as stiff-necked and hard-hearted as the Israelites before them. For this reason, the Lord set aside a New World, in which He established a Christian Nation. He then placed a magnet on this land to gather His children from Europe and every other nation under the sun to which He had scattered Israel—sprinkled with Ephraim, watered by Christ. Every nation maintains a remnant in Christ, but the United States has grown the largest Christian populace on the face of the earth, as well as the second largest Jewish populace next to Israel, and that only by a slim margin. These are not accidents. The Almighty appointed all of it, including our nation's fruitfulness for the Gospel. Yet our *eagles' wings* remain unfulfilled. We have forgotten how to use *envy* to God's advantage.

> *"The workers who were hired about the eleventh hour came and each received a denarius. So when those came who were hired first, they expected to receive more. But each one of them also received a denarius. When they received it, they began to grumble against the landowner." —Matthew 20:9-11*

The Gentiles are those hired in the eleventh hour while the Jews were those hired in the first, and both are paid the same wage, *a denarius,* which in spiritual terms is the crown of life in Christ. Despite the Jews' grumbling, the Owner of the vineyard didn't send them away without pay, He only said:

> *"Don't I have the right to do what I want with my own money? Or are you* ***envious*** *because I am generous?" —Matthew 20:15*

If you have ears to hear, Christ's parable referred to the Word He had formerly spoken to Moses:

> *They made me jealous by what is no god and angered me with their worthless idols. I will make them* ***envious*** *by those who are not a people; I will make them angry by a nation that has no understanding. —Deuteronomy 32:21*

'Those who are not a people' meant a people yet to emerge with a national identity, or perhaps a nation *"too shattered to be a people":*

"For the head of Aram is Damascus, and the head of Damascus is only Rezin. Within sixty-five years ***Ephraim will be too shattered to be a people.****"*

—Isaiah 7:8

In other words, though *"too shattered to be a people,"* Ephraim's seed would eventually give birth to a new nation, *'A nation that has no understanding,'* at least until it would receive the Gospel, brought to them by Jewish apostles. This in turn stirred up a great deal of *envy* amongst the Jewish Nation, because former pagan Gentiles were claiming their birthright through *their Messiah.* Imagine you're a Jewish priest amidst the first century Christian Church. You have been versed in the Laws of Moses, the Writings and the Prophets all your life. Then you meet a Roman Gentile, a soldier no less, who proclaims to you the Truth about the Jewish Messiah and the Kingdom of Heaven! In a way, it might seem to you like the Gentiles have hijacked your inheritance, even though it was never man's to distribute. Nonetheless, it is good for the lost to stew in *envy* lest they have no incentive to come to the Truth, and be saved by it. The apostle Paul, a Jewish Pharisee himself, understood all of this, for as he wrote the Roman Church concerning his Jewish brethren:

Again I ask: Did they stumble so as to fall beyond recovery? Not at all! Rather, because of their transgression, salvation has come to the Gentiles to make Israel ***envious.*** *—Romans 11:11*

Paul labored intensely to convince the Jews that Jesus was the Christ, but his testimony was largely rejected. So he served Christ, and the Jews, as an apostle to the Gentiles, those in whom the lost tribes of Ephraim were harbored; and always in the hope that one day, the Lord's inspired *envy* would lure the Jews into repentance and acceptance of their Messiah, Jesus Christ.

I do not want you to be ignorant of this mystery; brothers, so that you may not be conceited: Israel has experienced a hardening in part until the full number of the Gentiles has come in. And so all Israel will be saved, as it is written: "The deliverer will come from Zion; he will turn godlessness away from Jacob. And this is my covenant with them when I take away their sins."

—Romans 11:25-27

Brothers and sisters, I want you to know that the Jews are already being called in, which means *the number of the Gentiles* is nearly fulfilled. To demonstrate this reality to my family, the Lord gave me a profound dream near the time we completed this book. I found myself coming up a road over a hill at twilight and discovered a large courtyard teaming with tens of thousands of people below. From above, I could see the people filled the courtyard with the exception of the southeastern corner. In this exposed section I saw the pointed edges of the Star of David imprinted on the paving stones. Suddenly, I was transported by the Spirit to that corner and found myself standing with others on the edge of the crowd. At that moment, the Light of the Holy Spirit within me lifted up from my chest, and I saw the same happening to all who were in the courtyard. These Lights, thousands of them, went straight up to heaven. Then, with a flash, the Light of the Spirit came back down upon us, magnified a hundred times what went up. We were all overwhelmed with the Spirit's Power and we lifted up our voices to God with great shouts of praise. It was an incredible feeling, and I knew that we were being given an even greater anointing of the Spirit for the calling in of the last of the Jewish remnant.

Like ancient Ephraim before us, We The Church have been set apart to serve as an example to our Jewish brethren, but that example must be *in Christ.* I assure you our nation will suffer God's judgment if we do not fulfill His calling. If He must, the Lord will raise up a testimony against us, displaying clearly to all the nations, and especially to Judah, what happens to a people who forsake His Son. Whether by the call of this book and my family's testimony, or by some other trumpet, the Lord will make the consequence of our rebellion clear to the world. There's a reason why *Ephraim* is not listed by name among the tribes of Israel redeemed in Revelations 7. Let us not perish in his error:

> *When Ephraim spoke, men trembled; he was exalted in Israel. But he became guilty of Baal worship and died. —Hosea 13:1*

Compare our history with Ephraim's. Have we once honored the Name of the Lord as we should? Are we not overrun with idolatry, committing adultery with the pagan ways of the other nations? Let this serve as an urgent warning for the church in America: If God would not spare Ephraim from His righteous judgment then He will surely not spare the United States. Some might argue that today we have the grace of Christ. This might have been true, except that our nation has rejected Christ.

But those who hope in the LORD will renew their strength. They will soar on wings like eagles; they will run and not grow weary, they will walk and not be faint. —Isaiah 40:31

My family was sent forth to prepare the *'wings of the eagle,'* but how will you be set apart among the Lord's anointed, those on whom His favor will shine, if you do not submit yourself as a servant of Christ in faith and obedience? Open your eyes and ears to the evil that surrounds you and stop ignoring it! You were born to be a witness for Jesus Christ. So why not start now, before that last hour of daylight expires and you have nothing to show for your fruitfulness?

"Then the man who had received the one talent came. 'Master,' he said, 'I knew that you are a hard man, harvesting where you have not sown and gathering where you have not scattered seed. So I was afraid and went out and hid your talent in the ground. See, here is what belongs to you.'"

—Matthew 25:24-25

Every servant has been given some measure of *talent,* and is expected to do something with it. A "Christian" in title alone is like one who buries his *talent* in the ground, meaning his head! Your head is supposed to be Jesus Christ, but how will you be fruitful if you hide your Light under a bowl? To succumb to any fear of ridicule, scorn, or even physical abuse for sharing your love for your Savior is to love yourself more. This may be natural in the world, but it is unnatural and unrighteous in heaven. Don't risk being found *worthless* in God's judgment, for the price is more than you can bear:

"'Take the talent from him and give it to the one who has the ten talents. For everyone who has will be given more, and he will have an abundance. Whoever does not have, even what he has will be taken from him. And throw that worthless servant outside, into the darkness, where there will be weeping and gnashing of teeth.'" —Matthew 25:28-30

Remember that Nineveh's repentance began *from the greatest to the least,* meaning everyone from government officials to the business community and the workers in the field—each of them taking God's judgment seriously. Are you? Is your family or your church? If the church in America will rise up and lead the way for the nation to fulfill repentance then we will no longer be Ephraim, but will become Joseph, on whom the Lord's favor was poured out full-strength. God willing, we will be restored to a place we have never been, a city upon a hill that has never shined so bright, a place where we raise a great beacon to the nations that says, "In God we trust and in Christ Jesus we stand."

This is where you personally can and should begin:

> *Hear, O Israel: The LORD our God, the LORD is one. Love the LORD your God with all your heart and with all your soul and with all your strength. These commandments that I give you today are to be upon your hearts. Impress them on your children. Talk about them when you sit at home and when you walk along the road, when you lie down and when you get up. Tie them as symbols on your hands and bind them on your foreheads. Write them on the doorframes of your houses and on your gates. —Deuteronomy 6:4-9*

Christ referred to this Word, which He had given to Moses, when questioned by one of the teachers of the law about the most important of God's Commandments. It is the definitive path to restoration, a simple, to the point instruction about how you can serve the Lord your God. To it, Christ added, *"Love your neighbor as yourself,"* and later clarified His standard for true love, saying, *"Love each other as I have loved you."* If you really want to see our nation's *eagles' wings* restored then personally take these Commands from your Savior *upon your heart,* bear His Gospel and His Teachings and *impress them on your children, talk about them when you sit at home and when you walk along the road,* reflect on them in His Spirit and Word *when you lie down and when you get up*, and let the Spirit of Christ take hold of your whole life so that He may direct all your actions. If enough of the church in America will follow this example, perhaps the Lord will turn aside from His fierce wrath. Then, from the *doorframes* of our houses to the *gates* of our cities, even to the threshold of the White House, will the blessings of the Lord abound:

> *"Then your light will break forth like the dawn, and your healing will quickly appear; then your righteousness will go before you, and the glory of the LORD will be your rear guard." —Isaiah 58:8*

POSTSCRIPT

The Life

On the 311th day of the year, the United States of America reelected President Barack Obama, just as the Lord had revealed to my family in February 2010 while sitting in the driveway of the house of the fruitless tree. Like the predominant church in America, he remains asleep. Not until the Church truly begins to repent will our president awaken. As it stands, We The Church are still worshipping ourselves and money. Imagine how much wealth and wasteful toil could have been saved if the Church had simply submitted to God's will and repented. On Election Day morning, our family sat together and read the local paper, discovering that city officials in Springfield had searched far and wide for a Christmas tree for their annual downtown display. After considering 22 candidates, they finally settled upon a 40-foot, 39-year-old fruitless spruce tree. The woman who owned it had grown up with the tree, which had stood beside her grandparents' house. She became its owner when she bought the house four years ago. In other words, after four years the fruitless 39-year-old tree was cut down, a task that took "less than three minutes." On Sunday January 20, 2013, our reelected president will be officially inaugurated for his second term. On January 21, 2013 a public ceremony will be held in conjunction with Martin Luther King, Jr. Day, in memory of the Civil Rights, *or human rights,* champion. On January 22nd Roe v. Wade will have been the highest law of the land for 40 years. As you can see, *sword, famine and plague* are already at our nation's door.

In accordance with the Lord's instructions, on Election Day Clara and I faithfully cast our votes for '*Christ The Lord,*' simply writing in His Name on our ballots. We pray those who received our testimony and those to whom it was subsequently spread did the same. Any who did shined as witnesses in heaven. As we left the polling place, I noticed a pair of Confederate flag decorated cubes hanging from the rearview mirror of the car parked next to us. This is just one of many witness by which the Lord has spoken to me of our nation's forthcoming division, manifesting itself in 'civil unrest.' The aftereffects of Hurricane's Katrina and Sandy demonstrate how easily *civilized society* can descend into chaos.

> *"Let both grow together until the harvest. At that time I will tell the harvesters: First collect the weeds and tie them in bundles to be burned; then gather the wheat and bring it into my barn." —Matthew 13:30*

Brothers and sisters, the harvest season is upon us. As my family concluded this book at that farmhouse in the heart of the heart of the nation, the Lord brought unto us multiple conspicuous witnesses of sickles, circling carrion birds, and eagles—all pointing to His eminent judgment. In obedience to God's will, my family has sacrificed everything normal and natural by human standards in order to put forth this book of testimony to urge you to repent, and to bolster your faith for the unavoidable challenges that are soon to come. Because we refused to corrupt ourselves by making *money* a priority, at various stages of our journey we were deprived of showers, bathrooms, wash sinks, the conveniences of a kitchen; a stove, an oven, a dishwasher, a refrigerator; and Clara somehow made due without her washer and dryer. We slept many nights without bed, blanket or mattress, in the Tahoe, in a storage unit, in the homes and on the floors of perfect strangers, in *The Whale* without air-conditioning in the blazing heat of summer and in the freezing cold of winter. We blew tires, lost a wheel, ran out of money for gas, money for groceries, money for toiletries, money to replace worn-out clothes, money for car parts and maintenance, money for healthcare, and money for our own private space. In addition to all of these relatively simple comforts we Americans take for granted, we also repeatedly endured abuse by "Christian" wolves, twice suffered arrest and were nearly killed in *Casketville.* Altogether, we were put on a three and a half year fast, but we still anointed our heads with oil, cleaned up well, made ourselves presentable in the joy of the Lord, and saw to the work He appointed us day by day.

As a result of our perseverance in the face of many trials, the Lord Jesus Christ delivered my family just as He saw to the needs of His ancient servants in the Bible. In His perfect timing, the Spirit of God moved specific people He chose to supply our every need along the way. Once, a minivan drove up to an event where I had delivered the Lord's message and a woman inside handed some money to one of the organizers, saying, "This is for the pastor," referring to me. She hadn't participated in the event in any way and couldn't have known anything about me. I certainly wasn't dressed in any special *pastor's clothing.* Even so, she provided *exactly* the amount of gas money my family needed to get to our next destination. We never met her. This sort of unexpected and miraculous occurrence has been my paycheck from the Lord for three and a half years, so that my family, as well as you and yours would know that He provides. Indeed, we were fed, clothed, sheltered and set free from every obstacle, infirmity and enemy, though not before we had been refined. We asked the Lord to set our hearts on His path of righteousness, and He taught us the meaning of *seeking first His Kingdom:*

> *"So do not worry, saying, 'What shall we eat?' or 'What shall we drink?' or 'What shall we wear?' For the pagans run after all these things, and your heavenly Father knows that you need them. But seek first his kingdom and his righteousness, and all these things will be given to you as well."*
>
> *—Matthew 6:31-33*

Many of our struggles were painful and grueling at the time, but today we rejoice in the Lord that He has given us the opportunity to testify His miraculous provision and deliverance. We therefore encourage you and the rest of the church in America to put aside selfish plans and petty worldly schemes and get to our Father's business! But know this, for those who refuse to repent and serve the Lord as He Commands, the trials my family endured by choice will fall upon the rest of the obstinate Church by force. Warnings have been set forth, but the real hammer stroke is yet to come. When disaster strikes this nation, many will run to the hand of the government, but what will they do when that hand has nothing left to give?

My family's journey of faith all began with a simple decision to be obedient to God's Word, beginning with taking one Sabbath Day a week to read the Holy Bible as a family. In seeking His Word we discovered the Way of Christ and we were convicted to follow it. Since then, the Lord has been graceful with all our stumblings along the way. We have fretted when we weren't supposed to, tried to plan when we were to listen, remained silent when we were to speak and started running when we were supposed to remain still, but we never quit. Only the unblemished Lamb has been perfect. Therefore, when you stumble, and you will, do not lose heart and do not give up. No matter what happens in the process of your refinement, don't fall out of the race, because the Lord is capable of carrying you through the finish line so that you will not fail to receive your prize.

If ever you become discouraged on your mission for Christ, or begin to doubt the impact a choice few believers can have upon an entire society or nation, remember the witnesses who came before us. In Christ, Moses defied Pharaoh in Egypt, leading an entire nation of slaves to freedom across an inhospitable wilderness; Gideon and three hundred warriors defeated 135,000 Midianites; a shepherd boy named David slew Goliath and led Israel to subdue her enemies on every front; and just Twelve Apostles armed only with the Sword of the Gospel conquered the indomitable Roman Empire. Follow these examples, place your faith and trust in the Lord God Almighty, and one way or another He will surely lead you to victory as well.

And if you should ever find yourself, or others, questioning if the Lord could ever forgive this nation for its vast chasm of sin, consider how God demonstrated His limitless capacity for grace through King Manasseh. As the Bible states, Manasseh did great evil in the sight of the Lord, leading Judah to worship all sorts of idols, practiced witchcraft and sorcery, built altars to worship all the starry hosts in the Lord's Temple, and *shed so much innocent blood that he filled Jerusalem from end to end.* So evil and depraved was this king that he even sacrificed his own sons in the fire to false gods.

> *The LORD said through his servants the prophets: "Manasseh king of Judah has committed these detestable sins. He has done more evil than the Amorites who preceded him and has led Judah into sin with his idols. Therefore this is what the LORD, the God of Israel, says: I am going to bring such disaster on Jerusalem and Judah that the ears of everyone who hears of it will tingle."*
>
> *—2 Kings 21:10-12*

In keeping with the words of His prophets, the Lord sent the Assyrians against Judah and they took King Manasseh prisoner. With a hook in his nose and bound with bronze shackles, he was taken to Babylon where he was imprisoned. There, as one can imagine the conditions of an ancient Babylonian jail cell, Manasseh was humbled before the Lord.

In his distress he sought the favor of the LORD his God and humbled himself greatly before the God of his fathers. And when he prayed to him, the LORD was moved by his entreaty and listened to his plea; so he brought him back to Jerusalem and to his kingdom. Then Manasseh knew that the LORD is God.
—2 Chronicles 33:12-13

Having his heart pierced, Manasseh repented and went from being the worst king in Israel's history to leading his nation in a restoration. He removed idolatry from the city of Jerusalem and told the people to worship only the Lord their God. For the remnant in Judah that had faithfully served the Lord during all the days of Manasseh's reign of terror, what an incredible blessing this was.

When my family began our homeless walk with Christ, our children were ten, nine, three and two, and Justin was still in diapers. Our daughter Rielle is now fourteen, Austin is thirteen, Jazelle is seven and Justin is now six, and has been potty trained for some time now—thanks be to God! As a family, what a difference three and a half years can make. Even so, our journey has not concluded. No servant of Christ rests until he or she is called heavenward. Our present mission for America will not be settled until the Almighty has decided upon restoration or judgment. We pray this book will help bring about the former, inspiring you to become a dedicated servant of Christ by taking up His banner in whatever capacity He has enabled you. You have been born to bring glory to the only Name in which salvation is found—Christ Jesus. There is nothing more important in your life and for your Life than to share your testimony of Christ with those whom the Lord sends you way. People who don't know Christ have no Life in them.

Again Jesus said, "Simon son of John, do you truly love me?"

He answered, "Yes, Lord, you know that I love you."

Jesus said, "Take care of my sheep." —John 21:16

If you want to demonstrate your true love to your Savior then love His lost sheep by telling them the truth about the only path to salvation. It's simple to do. Wherever you go and whatever you do in the course of your daily affairs, look to engage people in simple conversation, such as about the weather, current events, gas prices, shopping bargains, entertainment, fashion trends—anything to break the ice. Then, as quickly as possible, find a way to introduce your love for Jesus Christ, asking whomever you are speaking with if they share your love. If they do then embrace them as a brother or sister and share something recent the Lord has done for you or revealed to you by His Word or Spirit. How exhilarated you will feel in your heart to have met another sibling in the Kingdom of Heaven! However, if that person does not share your love, simply ask them, "Has anyone told you about Jesus?" You will be surprised at how effective this simple, honest question can be in opening doors. Tell that person about Christ's sacrifice for their salvation, and share with them anything Jesus has personally done for you. If the Lord places something on your heart to say, then say it, trusting the Spirit in you knows the perfect words that are needed. Should that person attempt to engage you in a debate don't lose your patience and don't disengage. Stand firm in your faith in Christ and speak whatever the Spirit gives you. Don't try to win an argument with your mind. Let the Lord speak the Truth by His Word and Spirit. As my whole family can testify, speaking the Truth is enough, and the Spirit will lay upon your heart when you should disengage and let any planted seeds perform their work. If anyone you meet should abruptly close the door, let them go. If you can, tell them briefly the Gospel in whatever words the Spirit gives you at the time. Here's an example: "I pray you find it within yourself to open your heart to Jesus, because He loves you so much He died on the cross so that you might live." Even with a seed so small as this, God can do wonders. No matter if you are received, rejected or ignored, become a consistent testifier and witness for Jesus Christ and you will be found walking fruitfully repentant before your Savior in heaven. This is how you can fulfill your God-appointed role in turning your nation, one soul at a time, away from *death and destruction* and into *life and prosperity:*

> *See, I set before you today life and prosperity, death and destruction. For I command you today to love the LORD you God, to walk in his ways, and to keep his commands, decrees and laws; then you will live and increase, and the LORD your God will bless you in the land you are entering to possess.*
>
> *—Deuteronomy 30:15-16*

During His travels, Jesus healed the blind, deaf, lame, lepers, those near death, and resurrected the dead. In all these witnesses Jesus was testifying who He is and the spiritual truths that exist beyond the flesh—blindness, deafness, immobility, numbness, callousness of heart—all leading us to spiritual death. Believe in all these miracles, but especially believe in the resurrection of the dead, because this is Christ's ultimate promise to His Church, proving that He is the resurrection and *The Life.*

> *Jesus said to her, "I am the resurrection and the life. He who believes in me will live, even though he dies; and whoever lives and believes in me will never die. Do you believe this?" —John 11:25-26*

Now all has been heard; here is the conclusion of the matter:

Fear God and keep his commandments, for this is the whole [duty] of man. For God will bring every deed into judgment, including every hidden thing, whether it is good or evil. —Ecclesiastes 12:13-14

NOW THAT YOU'VE MET OUR FAMILY AND HEARD OUR TESTIMONY...

Circulate this book!

Brothers and sisters, in the Name of Christ Jesus, get this book into the hands of everyone you can. In doing so, you will be fulfilling a major part of your duty in Christ, which is to testify His Word and His Truth. If the Lord Jesus has inspired you to support to our ministry in order to better enable us to bring more testimony like this before you and the rest of Christ's Church, please go to www.pearlgate.org to make your tax deductible donations. Your tithe to us will be used 100% for Christ's Kingdom, because we are all about our Father's business.

May the Lord Jesus bless you and your family abundantly...